THE IDEOLOGY OF IDEOLOGIES

How countries strengthened their economies,
reasons for successes and failures, and the
inevitability of Trump's rebellion

ERNST ZAHRAVA

Rondelet Press Publishing
a division of Silversmith Press
Houston, Texas

ISBN 978-1-967386-14-7 (Softcover Book)
ISBN 978-1-967386-15-4 (eBook)

CONTENTS

PREFACE

This book will delve into how major countries have strengthened their economies, exploring the causes behind their successes and failures. Understanding the patterns revealed in
these processes can benefit anyone interested in strengthening
their own country's economy and improving its standard of living. At its core, this book is scientific work presented in simple,
accessible language, aiming to impartially examine events as
well as draw unbiased conclusions. Such work is best kept free
from ideological influences. Yet, the timing of its publication is
unique, as it coincides with the rise of another ideological wave.

Today, a wave of conservatism is replacing earlier Marxist
and liberal waves. Ideologies are shaped by the interests and
perspectives of specific groups, but ultimately, they are a matter of belief. Each ideology, over its lifespan, develops logical
and convincing arguments, supported by numerous examples.
Thus, choosing an ideology is less about discerning "right"
from "wrong" and more about adopting a particular perspective.
This choice often stems from chance, family traditions, or an
alignment with personal interests. Nevertheless, an ideological
wave can sweep almost everyone into its powerful current—
even those whose interests may not fully align with it. This is
the true nature of a wave: it carries everything in its path.

At the time of writing this book, we are witnessing a rising tide of conservatism. This wave gains strength even as the liberal wave remains robust. In such times, it becomes particularly challenging to avoid ideological influence—even in a book like this. At the very least, it becomes impossible to omit mention of ideology. Ideological belief can drive individuals, parties, and even entire nations to act against their objective interests in pursuit of ideological justice or to fulfill their aims through an ideological lens. However, this ideological self-interest may diverge significantly from objective interests. To avoid endorsing any particular ideology, this book defines each ideology, exploring its foundation, perspectives, and core priorities. This approach allows for a more detached view, reducing the risk of ideological influence.

Freed from ideological influence, this book examines the experiences of economic growth across various countries and periods, identifying common patterns behind such growth.

These patterns can serve as a rough guide both for countries aiming to raise their economic level and for highly developed nations concerned about potential decline in a shifting global landscape. This roadmap can only be approximate, as each country—while following similar steps to its predecessors—has always introduced its own unique characteristics.

Mechanical, uncreative copying will not yield the desired results. Rather than addressing the "eternal" ideological debates—like market vs state intervention, democracy vs authoritarianism, monopoly vs small private enterprises, state vs private ownership—the book finds a suitable role for each of them. In essence, all are valid, depending on a country's stage of economic development, its place in the global economic hierarchy, and the ambition of its national goals. More importantly, the book highlights the predictable challenges faced by countries whose governments strive for decisive economic transformation. In these cases, the "elite" resist change with unwavering resolve, and this book explores the reasons behind this resistance.

The book is recommended for specialists in economic development, political economy, and anyone interested in exploring the necessity and practicality of democracy and authoritarianism, state and private ownership, and other ideological issues.

AUTHOR'S NOTE

In this paper, the word "enterprise" is used synonymously with words such as firm, company, corporation, farm, etc., i.e., referring to any entity capable of generating income.

The words "corporation" and "workshop" are also used synonymously in a social context.

Society is viewed from the perspective of its three defining components: the state, the economy, and the population.

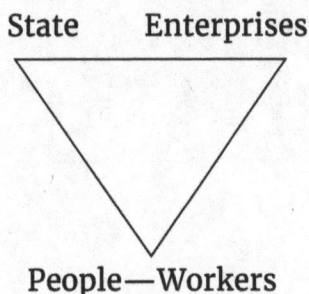

State   Enterprises

People—Workers

For the state, the population is the people, citizens, taxpayers, etc. The economy deals with subsets of the population—the workers.

PART I

THE POLITICAL ECONOMY OF REBELLION

THE WORLD BEFORE THE EMERGENCE OF GLOBAL ECONOMIC PYRAMIDS

EUROPE BORROWED CIVILIZATION
FROM THE EAST

The first civilizations emerged in Africa and Asia, yet Europe managed to outpace these regions in economic development. How did this occur? Unlike the countries of the world's earliest civilizations, European first civilizations operated as democracies and were soften mall entities—political systems that encompassed a city and its surrounding areas. Thus, in Europe, everything began with democracy, which may have contributed to its success. Let's explore further.

Search for patterns

Egypt had a significant need for wood, metals, and precious stones for its mega-projects of building temples, pyramids, and irrigation systems. Although Egypt had its own navy, well-established Phoenician trading settlements on the coasts of modern Lebanon and Israel, had superior and more numerous merchant ships, experienced sailors, and convenient, well-equipped ports. The presence of such ports deterred the Egyptians from developing their own. After all, it was much easier to utilize Phoenician ships and their maritime expertise—whether by force or through payment—rather than to invest in or cultivate their own resources. Conversely, Egypt's demand for goods drove the further development of Phoenician shipping. *This pattern of specialization is one we will encounter repeatedly in the future: when an economy or country possesses complex knowledge or skills, it often proves more efficient for others to leverage those services instead of acquiring them independently. In some cases, this pattern can even be detrimental.*

Over time, Greek cities along the coast began to specialize in trade and shipping. Borrowing, often viewed as a primary driver of development for nations, became a crucial aspect of progress. Today, we might call this "stealing," but at that time people were unaware of the rules established by the WTO. *This theme of borrowing or stealing will be a recurring motif throughout the book.*

Why did the Greeks adopt seafaring from the Phoenicians, while the Egyptians did not? The Egyptians highly valued their primary specialization—the ability to sustain their entire population through irrigated agriculture—viewing seafaring as a relatively unimportant auxiliary endeavor. In contrast, the Greeks, lacking a defined specialization at that time, were more open to adopting the maritime skills of the Phoenicians.

Orders from abroad provided the Phoenicians with the opportunity to build an extensive network of colonies and trade between them and the metropolises. Similarly, Greek cities formed a network of colonies and connections between them throughout the Mediterranean. The Greek metropolises (the polities that founded the colonies) primarily exported products to the newly established colonies that their former compatriots (now colonists) were accustomed to. These exports included jewels and jewelry, pottery, metalwork, wine, oil, fabrics and clothing. Seafarers who travelled to distant uncivilized regions sent back (at least in the early stages) primarily simple products such as timber, metals, and agricultural products—mainly grain, but also dried fish and skins[1]. The products of the metropolises were generally more expensive as they required more skills and knowledge in manufacturing, thus, they had more value-added. Skilled masters and knowledgeable craftsmen hardly ever travelled overseas, thus, the metropolises remained monopolies in the manufacturing field of these kinds of goods for their colonies. This allowed them to rise to the peak of the economic hierarchy which was facilitated by their trade ties with the colonies. *The formation of such economic hierarchies will later become a deciding factor in shaping the development or economic outcome of some nations over others.*

POLITICAL EVOLUTION OF POLIS
(IS THE POWER OF THE MONARCH SACRED?
AND WHAT ABOUT DEMOCRACY?)

Polis. The cradle of democracy

The polis was not a real state, if by state we mean a power that has the ability to enforce its decision, even in spite of the resistance of the citizens. That is, the polis had no coercive apparatus. Administrative positions in the poleis were unpaid, which meant that neither an average peasant nor a craftsman could hold these roles for an entire year without external income. Consequently, only the wealthy could afford to take on such responsibilities. Additionally, those elected to higher administrative positions were required to cover public expenses from their own funds, including the construction of public buildings, celebrations, and the maintenance of warships.[2]

This context explains why Solon's laws divided Athenians into four categories based on the income generated from their plots. Only individuals in the first three categories could hold administrative positions, with only the top class eligible for the most important roles. The fourth class was limited to voting and speaking at meetings. Since members of this class could not compensate for any potential harm they might cause to the polis during their time in office, their election was deemed unjustifiable.

Thus, *the poleis lacked coercive apparatus. Does this mean that they had no "framework", or hierarchy that organized their lives? This is where patronage networks came into play.*

Patronage (Patron-client relationship)

The owners of successful enterprises had the opportunity to provide material assistance to poorer citizens. It was their act of solidarity. Poorer citizens could not return the favor, so they tried to repay their benefactors in other ways. For example, during elections (or in "anti-elections.") In Athens, there was a custom called ostracism. At a special meeting, each citizen would write on special shards—the name of someone whom they believed should be expelled from the city. The individual whose name appeared most times was forced into exile. Modern analyses of many of these fortunately preserved shards have revealed that the inscriptions on many of them were written by several people and apparently distributed among the crowd[3]). The wealthier a citizen (patron) was, the more people (clients) they could patronize, the greater their support, and the greater their social influence. As this social influence grew, the patron could assist their clients not only financially but in social matters, such as securing a good job, obtaining a lucrative business contract, or being nominated for a prestigious position. This attracted not only poor compatriots to the patron but also wealthier individuals who needed a "quick start." The loyalty between the patron and the clients was strengthened by a cycle of mutual services. Failure to fulfill traditional duties was equally shameful for both patron and client and damaged prestige (and thus influence).

Such a pyramid could be multi-storied, as clients might have their own clients, and a patron could have his own patron. The number of clients alone determined the overall prestige of the patron in the polis and must have been a significant factor in elections or in choosing a partner for political or business ventures. Clients were naturally inclined to vote for their patron (as the patron's success directly benefited them) and this also worked to influence others as these social pyramids clearly became centres of social power.

These pyramids were greatly strengthened by non-citizens living in the city. Such "outsiders" (metics) could reside in the polis for generations without evergaining citizenship (except those who earned it through some truly exceptional service or act). Lacking the right to speak at general assemblies or to make decisions on matters that concerned them, as well as not being able to defend themselves in court, metics were often compelled to become clients.[4] Considering that their numbers were always significant and comparable to the number of citizens, it becomes clear just how much social power each patronage pyramid could wield.

That is, we can come to the following conclusion: it was the presence of large enterprises owned by the patron that enabled strong patronage hierarchies to thrive. These hierarchies, operating within a democracy and in the absence of a coercive apparatus, introduced internal, externally invisible structuring into the seemingly formless, fluid body of the polis, thereby reinforcing it. In other words, a thriving (what we would now call "successful") enterprises created the conditions for significant social and economic influence. The entire set of large enterprises built social hierarchies, which, in turn, formed the organizational framework of society.

In other words, in the absence of coercion used by the state to organize society, society can be structured by socioeconomic influence. The ability to wield such social and economic influence arises from the property-based stratification of society. This observation clearly highlights the fact that the economic hierarchies can, and under certain conditions, become direct competitors to state administrative hierarchies.

The struggle of tyrants and oligarchy for the favor of the people

A tyrant, in the original Greek sense, is someone who came to power illegally. Tyrants came to power on a wave of popular discontent. They maintained their "illegal" power with the support of the people. As is often the case with historical events from that time, we have limited factual evidence for drawing firm conclusions. Nevertheless, what we do know allows us to assert that, in many instances, "under the Tyrants, land allotments were made to many of the poorer citizens, who were thus enabled to become full members of society."[5] The text 'The Constitution of the Athenians', most likely written by Aristotle, describes the reign of the Athenian tyrant Pisistratus, who came to power almost immediately after Solon. The author portrays this rule as moderate and beneficial to ordinary peasants. Pisistratus introduced mobile courts to bring justice to the countryside and provided loans to impoverished farmers.

Overall, the economy flourished under Pisistratus: Athenian pottery dominated competitors throughout the Mediterranean and coins were introduced into circulation. Magnificent public buildings and temples were built (providing employment for the poor) and festivals were also established.[6]

When the aristocratic party attempted to seize power by force and overthrow Pisistratus, "it was not supported by the common people and was driven off"[7]. In the historical accounts we have of tyrants, we frequently see a similar pattern. We know that Aristodemus in the Greek Sicilian colony of Cumae "declared general equality among citizens, redistributed land and canceled debts."[8] Similarly, according to tradition, the ancient Roman king Servius Tullius implemented comparable reforms in Rome. And there are many such examples.

If a tyrant is not known for his reforms, he is known for his efforts to strengthen the polis (otherwise he would have no justification for abolishing democracy). For example, Gelon, after seizing power in Syracuse, united the Sicilian Greeks in the fight against the Carthaginians, emerged victorious, and transformed Syracuse into the strongest and most economically prosperous polis in Sicily[9]. The philosopher Archytas, being the tyrant of Tarentum (in the south of the Apennine Peninsula), focused on crafts and trade, and under his leadership, Tarentum reached its greatest prosperity.[10]

Thus, each tyrant established a three-tiered pyramid, with himself at the peak of the pyramid, and the citizens at the base. The elite was in between. It continued to occupy positions at the peaks of its patron-client pyramids, each of which relied on a part of the population and thus shared the same base as the tyrant Such a pyramid could exist quite stably, because the bottom supported the peak as a means of control and influence over the elite, allowing the bottom to exert pressure on the elite. The peak, on the other hand, needed the bottom in its confrontation with the elite, which did not want to have anyone above it.

In other words, it seems that tyrants were a positive phenomenon for the people. But history was written not by the demos (the people), but by the elite (the owners of large enterprises), who sooner or later took power into their own hands again. That is why the word "tyrant" today carries such negative connotations. After all, these periods were "tyranny" for the owners of large enterprises.

Afterall, the murderers of Pisistratus' son and successor, the lovers Harmodius and Aristogeiton, were revered as the greatest national heroes. Their names were included in the oath to protect the democratic system.[11] Poets composed poems and created statues in honor of the tyrants. This is also a pattern in history.

Nevertheless, from the scant ancient data, we can conclude that most (if not all) poleis went through a period of tyranny (Athens and Rome, among others). Moreover, it can be generalized from this data that democracy could not have been established if poleis had not gone through tyranny. "The historical importance... [of tyranny] is that the rule of the tyrants provided existing institutions and offices with a legitimized and ultimately monopoly of power... It enabled them to function backed by a structural exercise of power and thus to become permanently accepted, as a consequence of which they remained functioning as a 'state' after the tyrant had disappeared."[12] In other words, tyrants created a structure (governing bodies, rules for their functioning, general laws, etc.) and maintained it for some time. The people became accustomed to viewing this structure as a convenient and expedient organization of life. After the tyrants left, the structure took on a life of its own and continued to function. And this structure was the state.

The heyday of Greek democracy

From the above, it becomes clear that democracy was possible thanks to property inequality as it led to the formation of socio-economic hierarchies that structured society in the absence of state coercion. However, an interesting pattern that we will observe many more times is that each society had the opportunity to be more democratic the higher it rose in the hierarchy of other societies.

The Persian invasion united most Greeks, especially after the Persian defeat in a decisive naval battle. The Persians retreated from mainland Greece, but the Greek poleis of Asia Minor and the islands remained under their control. As the struggle shifted to the islands and Asia Minor's "overseas" poleis, the main burden of the war was on the navy. Consequently, all the poleis of the alliance allocated contingents of ships to the common fleet. The Athenian fleet was the largest, so Athens led the alliance. Each liberated polis naturally joined this union and its ships were incorporated into the alliance fleet. However, some poleis were too weak to maintain even one warship, so they simply contributed funds. The money from several such weak poleis could provide one ship, which was built and manned by the Athenians because they had shipyards and a large work-force. This arrangement was fair in this alliance: the weaker poleis paid money, while the Athenians lost their lives, built, repaired, and equipped the ships. One might assume everyone was happy with this equitable alliance.

But one day, the islands of Naxos and Thasos decided that there was no longer a threat and that they should leave the alliance and save money. However, the Athenian battle fleet soon appeared off their shores to convince them that the Persian threat still existed and that they should not leave the alliance. The Naxians and Thasians had no way to defend themselves, because their entire fighting fleet consisted of the same ships, they had paid the Athenians to build and man, and which now came to persuade them to remain in the alliance. Therefore, they were not able to insist on their withdrawal from the alliance and agreed to continue to make contributions to the struggle against the enslavers.[13] But who was the enslaver anymore?

It is this unexpected outcome of this union that gave rise to the name of empire. (Although it may be more accurate to say that this union was actually a state centered in Athens, because this entity had a tool for enforcing decisions—a navy). Since the Athenians owned the navy, they could use it to attack and punish uncooperative allies, most of whom were located on the islands. And at the same time, they were protected from these allies by the same fleet.

The main thing was that since other poleis gave Athens money for the construction, manning, and maintenance of warships, it was Athenian workers in the shipyards who received wages, as well as those who harvested wood, made ropes, resin, sails, and so on. The navy was manned by the Athenian poor, who until then had taken minimal part in the war effort because they could not afford to pay for military equipment. Now, when the navy became the main military force of Athens, the status of the poor, as well as the perception of their fellow citizens, rose sharply. In addition, Athens could use "the surplus from the league treasury for an ambitious building program... This also provided jobs for the poor."[14] Thus, both the standard of living and the social standing of the Athenian poor increased.

It is therefore hardly surprising that this time of economic and political prosperity coincided with the flowering of Athenian democracy. During this period, Athens had the funds to compensate citizens for most positions. Moreover, as democracy flourished further, there was also money to compensate citizens to attend the assembly. The assembly met forty times per year,

12

with at least six thousand citizens attending each meeting. Paid positions, along with the selection by lot, provided the poorer citizens with a real chance to serve as officials for a year. At the same time, the burden on the wealthy, who had previously supported the fleet with their contributions, decreased significantly during the "imperial" period. The incomes of the owners of trade and olive enterprises increased significantly. Thus, the contradictions between the layers of citizens were minimized, allowing such a community to thrive in a democracy without resorting to coercion.

The loss of its position at the peak of the political hierarchy of the polis was also accompanied by the decline of Athenian democracy. Clearly, the need to limit democracy began to be felt in society as Athens' difficulties grew. The opposition matured gradually, and after the defeat of the Athenian expedition to Sicily, led to an open coup and the transfer of power to the oligarchic Council of Four Hundred in 411 B.C. This council did not last long and was replaced by the broader (but still oligarchic) Council of Five Thousand. Subsequently, different regimes succeeded each other, but the extent of Athenian democracy decreased in proportion to Athens' loss as a leading political and economic power. Eventually, power returned to the aristocratic assembly, the Areopagus, which had ruled before democracy was established.

Thus, Athenian democracy became the model of democracy as we know it when inequality between citizens diminished. This seems to contradict the previous conclusion that democracy was possible due to property inequality. However, this was only an initial observation. The inequality remained; now, it had just shifted outward—Athens reached the political peak of the hierarchy of poleis. As long as Athens was an ordinary polis, its democracy was like that of all other poleis—plutocratic, as the Greeks themselves would say, or oligarchic, as we are

13

more accustomed to saying now. In the Athenian Empire, it became evident that the absence or weakening of state coercion and the influence of socio-economic hierarchies in society could be compensated for by transferring them outward. The society of Athens had a collective coercive apparatus in the form of a military fleet and an advantage in economic specialization.

The rise of despotisms

Using the disunity of the Greek poleis, Macedonia conquered Greece and established a monarch, Alexander the Great. Alexander died early in life, but the countries of the Hellenistic world that emerged from his conquests were almost entirely ruled by despots. Such a system was alien to the Greeks, but it was natural for the conquered Eastern peoples and, to some extent, for the Macedonians. Therefore, "the Greeks had no choice but to accommodate themselves to it. This happened with surprising speed despite their long-standing antipathy to a strong executive and their tendency to characterize the subjects of kings as slaves."[15] Moreover, nothing prevented the deification of kings, just like the Eastern despots. "[T]he rule of the kings was absolute and unrestrained . . . The people were simply the subjects of the king, and life and death lay in his hands."[16] The main detail of the state—the bureaucracy—was also adopted from the Eastern states.

The transition was so easy, apparently because of the empowerment—since the rejection of democracy promised the active part of the Greeks an improvement in living standards, this segment accepted this change: "Paradoxically, the breaking of the narrow citizenship-power connection provided new opportunities... Practically speaking...until the kings took political power into their own hands, great restrictions limited the opportunities open to Greeks and non-Greeks alike."[17] The polis was based on amateurism. Since all positions were held for a year and most people were rarely "in power" more than once, administrative professionalism was not adequately developed. However, the kings, as professional managersand commanders needed a professional bureaucracy to govern, which they had learned and appreciated in the East. This approach extended to other areas of life: ". . . professional actors, musicians, and athletes replaced the amateurs of the past and made their rounds from city to city. Physicians, technicians, engineers, generals, and scholars were in great demand and moved as the opportunities presented themselves."[18]

In the best Eastern traditions, states became patrons of culture and science. The Ptolemies of the "new" Egypt were particularly distinguished in this regard, founding (and supporting), in modern terms, a research center, the "Museum." Libraries were opened by kings in many cities of the Hellenistic world.

Artists, scientists, and engineers travelled not only from city to city but also from country to country. The entire wider Hellenistic world, not being a single state, worked as a single generator of new things. Bion of Borysthenes from the Dnipro River (then Borysthenes) introduced a new kind of sharp denunciation that became a characteristic feature of the philosophical school of cynics. Menippus of Gadara in modern Syria introduced new forms of satire that are still named after him. Epicurus, from the island of Samos, developed the philosophy that bears his name and also elaborated on the doctrine of Democritus' atoms. Archimedes, from the remote island of Sicily, invented various mechanical devices, discovered the law of the volume of displaced water, and calculated the number pi. All corners of this new world contributed to the general chorus of universal development.

Not surprisingly, this was the time of the greatest discoveries and inventions. The scientific achievements of this era were not surpassed until two millennia later. Aristarchus of Samos claimed that all the planets, including the Earth, revolve around the Sun and the Earth also rotates on its axis. Euclid of Alexandria, Egypt, described the geometric theorems that are still taught in schools today. Hipparchus of Nicaea developed the principles of trigonometry and discovered the phenomenon of precession (i.e., the equinoxes are ahead of time—each year the equinoxes occur earlier than in previous years). Ctesibius of Alexandria invented a two-cylinder piston fire pump and a water clock. Eratosthenes of Cyrene, Africa, measured the size of the Earth, indicating that the circumference of the meridian is close to 40 thousand kilometers.

These are just a handful of inventions, discoveries, and innovations of the time. And as a natural result of all this, "The quality of housing, clothing, and furniture all improved."[19] And "There was more money in circulation and less social repression."[20]

"One figure suffices to indicate the enormous economic expansion during the Hellenistic age. The customs revenue of Rhodes in about 170 BCE was five times that of Athens in 400, with almost certainly the identical rate of 2 percent. It would be hard to demonstrate more clearly that the Hellenistic world operated in a completely different dimension."[21] This example illustrates that the flourishing of economies in the Hellenistic world was due to the flourishing of trade. Trade thrived under conditions of specialization of policies, in which they exchanged what they lacked from each other for goods in which they specialized. Thus, the source of the greater success of the polis enterprises than before was the fact that these enterprises were now part of a vast Hellenistic world. This world consisted of despotic states whose bureaucratic apparatus was almost at the level of a planned economy. For example, Hellenist agriculture was often "subject to the most detailed bureaucratic planning, at every level: what seeds were sown where, what dues were paid by the lessees, and when every step in the procedure, from the rental of royal storehouse equipment to the assessment of harvest returns, was subject to scrutiny by a swarm of local or government officials."[22]

It is interesting that the Eastern despotisms, on whose ruins the Hellenistic world emerged, did not experience such economic prosperity. Neither did the Greek poleis before. What drove this prosperity was the combination of the private economic initiative of the poleis with the strong state bureaucratic organization of the eastern despotisms.

Different hierarchies

We can see that the polis functioned as a kind of "giving" hierarchical pyramid—having substantial income from his enterprise, the patron could distribute part of that income to those in need, to which they could respond with services. Services could mean some economic or social benefits that the patron could also distribute to those in need. Thus, the pyramid was a circulation of economic and social services that began with a flow from the peak to the bottom.

At the same time, the countries of Africa and Asia and the Hellenistic countries that emerged in their place were hierarchical pyramids with a circularity that started from the bottom up. Subjects paid taxes to the king, who was able to send some of the funds back down to his people, who distributed some of the money to their own people, and so on. Eventually, the benefits could be returned to the subjects in the form of protection from enemy attacks or help in times of need. It was, so to speak, a "taking" hierarchical pyramid.

17

The first type of hierarchical pyramidcan be called an economic pyramid, as they relied on the income of the patron's enterprises, and this income was used to start the cycle of services.

The second type is a political pyramid, based on state revenues obtained through the coercive apparatus (army, police, etc.). which began the cycle in this hierarchical pyramid

Rome

Legends have preserved memories that in the beginning, Rome was led by kings, whose power existed alongside the assembly of family elders (the Senate). It is quite easy to see in these kings a resemblance to Greek tyrants, especially since legends (the only source of information about them) claim that one of them, Servius Tullius, redistributed land between the poor and the rich[23].

Trying to establish themselves in their struggle against the tribal nobility, the tsars "strengthened their property status by expanding their landholdings . . . "[24] Owning their own land obviously allowed the tsars to lease it to the poor (proletarians), entering into a patron-client relationship with them and thus increasing their influence in society.

This new and interesting detail of the Roman polis came to remain in the history of mankind. Political (state) power, in its struggle with economic power, entered the "territory of the enemy" and tried to rely on economic power—in this case, on land ownership. The same land ownership that brought socioeconomic influence to the elite. And we will continue to observe this pattern.

Ultimately, as in the Greek poleis, the tribal elite ousted the kings and established the republic. "The anti-royal movement was led by the tribal nobility, but in the ancient tradition, which reflected the aspirations and estimates of this nobility, the abolition of royal power and the establishment of the Republic were portrayed as a democratic national cause."[25]

The patron-client system, which existed among the Greeks, gained its zenith in Rome. Society became intricately woven with these relationships, creating a network where individuals were hereditary clients of others, bound by obligations to their patrons from birth. Patrons, in turn, owed duties to their clients. " The visible crowd of clients around an aristocrat, or the invisible but well-known web of his connections, increased the influence in which he was held and also gave him the power to coerce or intimidate"[26].

Although the Romans, like the Greeks, constructed a vast Roman world, they organized it differently. The Roman state (embodied by the Senate oligarchy) chose not to adopt the bureaucratic structures of the conquered Hellenistic kingdoms;[27] instead, they delegated this function to private enterprises. "Private—actually only semi-private—companies... were allowed to bid for the job of collecting taxes in the provinces. The company that won would then send out its agents . . . to make the collections, which had to cover expenses as well as provide a worthwhile profit."[28] A profit for both Rome and the company.

So, whereas earlier, the state, personified by the kings, sought to establish itself through control of economic resources like land, during the period of the republic, economic power encroached upon state functions, privatizing these responsibilities.

Roman democracy

This transition raises important questions. It appears to contradict our earlier conclusion regarding Greece, where transferring political coercion and social influence abroad enhanced democracy at home. This indicates that our conclusion may have been too broad and requires refinement.

As in Greece, Roman democracy was fundamentally rooted in property stratification, allowing the wealthy to govern while being elected by the poor. From its inception, Roman democracy exhibited oligarchic characteristics, with senators and consuls elected solely from prominent families. Likewise, judges were predominantly drawn from the upper echelons of society[29], making patronage hierarchies crucial in elections.

The extensive conquests of various nations resulted in a shift in the sources of wealth for the Roman elite. Their income increasingly stemmed from overseas—through the capture of slaves, the spoils of war, and the taxation of provinces. One of the governors, on trial for extortion, explained to the court that, "a governor had to acquire three fortunes when in the province—one to pay off the debts incurred in running for public office in the first place, one to bribe the jurors if he was unlucky enough to be brought to trial, and one to live on for the rest of his days."[30] Initially, the Roman Republic was founded on principles akin to those of Athens, emphasizing devotion to the common good of the polis, often at personal expense. However, over time, public service became a profitable endeavor rather than a financial burden. The economic power of patrons derived not from their domestic enterprises but from the coercive capabilities of the Roman state. Consequently, the socio-economic influence of the elite was fueled by their vast revenues from conquered territories, enabling them to benefit from shared state resources while investing in their private enterprises. In the end, however, all this income was invested in improving and expanding the enterprises of the elite by buying up the plots of the poor. The distribution of state income was temporary, but the private enterprise has always belonged to them.

The grassroots populace, however, generally remained

satisfied, as citizens were exempt from paying taxes and had access to bureaucratic social assistance to those who lost their income. The substantial profits generated during this period allowed for the maintenance of significantly larger patronage networks than in earlier times. This made it possible to grow the mass of "professional" clients—the lumpen. According to some information, in 50-40 B.C. the number of lumpen in Rome reached 300,000,[31] despite the fact that the entire population of Rome was about 1 million and the entire population of the Apennines about 7 million.

However, the capacity to support disproportionately larger number of clients through the privatized portion of public revenues, alongside the vast voracious crowds of lumpen, ultimately brought democracy to a standstill. "By 53 B.C., the Roman constitution was in its death throes. The atmosphere of violence and paranoia attested to in Cicero's letters was all-pervasive. Rioting instigated by rival gangs of "clients" prevented consular elections from being held"[32]. Armed groups of different parties terrorized the population. "The political anarchy in Rome prompted even the Senate oligarchy to seek a strong government. Cicero, the leader of the supporters of the Senate Republic [!], in his work 'De re publica' published in 51 BC, expressed the idea of the need for a statesman who would be a good ruler of the state in difficult times."[33]

Thus, the difference between Athens and Rome can be summarized as follows. *The Athenian "empire" was primarily economic and functioned as a giving hierarchy, while the Roman Empire was fundamentally political and functioned as a taking hierarchy.* Athens' political rise stemmed from its status as the most economically developed polis, which enabled it to possess the strongest navy. This fleet allowed Athens to assist in liberating other Greek poleis, demonstrating how economic leadership paved the way for political dominance. The political leadership, in turn, yielded economic benefits that further solidified that leadership, creating a cyclical relationship between the two.

In contrast, Rome's ascent was primarily driven by political factors, which were a combination of luck and strategic maneuvering. Rome emerged victorious in the competition among neighboring poleis, establishing itself as the sole winner. After defeating rivals, the Romans seized their lands and settled them with colonists. The availability of ample land fueled the growth of Roman enterprises and accelerated population increases, aligning with the Malthusian growth model. Roman citizens were exempt from paying taxes, as these were collected from the conquered territories. This situation led to the expansion of Roman agriculture—albeit extensively—an increase in the Roman population, and greater population satisfaction with the existing order, and a desire to maintain it.

Over the decades, the Romans extended citizenship to conquered peoples, integrating them into their efforts to conquer additional territories. This cycle repeated itself multiple times. Political leadership continued to yield economic benefits, which reinforced political authority, perpetuating the cycle once more. Thus, unlike the Greeks, the Romans did not need to specialize in trade with their overseas colonies and shipbuilding at the beginning of the process.

All this had consequences for democracy. The position at the peak of the economic pyramid allowed for further strengthening of the Athenian enterprises, and the benefits derived by different Athenians from this growth did not conflict with one another. Together, all Athenian enterprises—both oligarchic and otherwise—produced goods that bolstered Athens' economic leadership. The prosperity of these enterprises provided jobs to the poor and fostered a sense of respect and dignity among citizens. United in their common interests, all citizens demonstrated solidarity, which in turn gave rise to a robust democracy.

In contrast, over time, the Roman oligarchy increasingly derived its income not from its enterprises but rather from military plunder, the capture of slaves, and the collection of taxes in conquered territories. For this oligarchy, the pressing question became who would claim the lion's share of the profits from the Roman polis. This struggle among various oligarchic groups paralyzed the Senate, which had previously been effective in performing the functions of state governance. Meanwhile, the poor found themselves benefiting from the services provided to competing oligarchic groups. In other words, they did not gain from the coordinated efforts of a unified polis that would generate consistent income for them; instead, their benefits arose from the internal conflicts within the polis that created a demand for their services.

Thus, during its zenith in the hierarchy of poleis, Athenian democracy was both unquestioned and stable. In contrast, Roman democracy declined under similar circumstances.

This observation highlights the different nature of the economic pyramids that each polis represented. In Athens, the cycle of the giving polis began with the concern of each oligarch and Athenian householder for their own enterprise. The power and significance of their enterprises ensured Athenian economic dominance, which in turn secured political power, creating a feedback loop that benefitted each Athenian's enterprise and initiated a new cycle.

In contrast, the Roman cycle needed to start with the political dominance of the polis, which would enable the economic ascent of Rome and its individual enterprise. This cycle was expected to commence with the interests of the polis, whose satisfaction would lead to the fulfillment of individual enterprises. However, the interests of these enterprises were expressed through the individual owners, while the collective interest of the polis lacked a clear representation or personification. Ideally, this representation should have been the state, but it did not exist.

The fall of democracy

The abstract issue of the lack of representation of the public interest was hardly recognized in Rome. However, there was another pressing concern that could not be overlooked.

The Athenian polis was small enough to provide a better life and control over the governance of the polis to every citizen once he reached the top of the economic hierarchy of many poleis. The entire community was invested in the public interest. In contrast, the Roman polis expanded into a vast territory, rending such an arrangement impractical. As Rome grew, the need to grant citizenship to an increasing number of people became essential for maintaining order among non-citizens and for conquering new territories. This large population could not be effectively represented in a polis democracy, as it was impractical for all citizens to gather in an assembly and vote. Consequently, something was needed to represent the interests of all citizens throughout the empire, not just those residing in Rome.

The mechanism of realization of such representation was the emergence of the "first among equals" among the citizens of the polis, known as the princeps or emperor. He was unaccountable to citizens from Rome as well as to citizens from other cities within the empire. In this sense, all citizens were considered equal and their interests were equally and fairly represented through the will of the emperor. The emperor had an army at his disposal which allowed him to exert control over the Senate, on the one hand, and disregard the people's assembly, on the other. This independence meant that he was not beholden to the private interests of either the owners of large or small enterprises. Consequently, nothing impeded him from serving as the personification of the public interest for the entire country.

State property

The power of the princeps was fundamentally rooted in his command of a professional army, which provided him with an apparatus of coercion. However, his authority could not rely solely on violence; he also needed to establish credibility and respect within society, which economic power could facilitate. State property emerged within the empire, designated as the personal property of the reigning emperor. After Augustus captured Egypt, the entirety of that territory was declared the emperor's possession.

The governance of the country operated through the personal patronage pyramid of the princeps. In this pyramid, bureaucratic roles were filled by the prince's slaves and clients. As in any patronage system, the princeps compensated their efforts using his own resources. Thus, the more wealth he possessed, the stronger the "state" became—allowing him to reward a greater number of clients. This expanded patronage network enhanced the prestige of belonging to such a powerful social hierarchy, making individuals less inclined to accept bribes.

Imperial possessions were established in every province, with a significant concentration in the eastern provinces and Africa—regions where the royal estates of the Hellenistic kingdoms had traditionally flourished. "The imperial property in each province consisted of huge latifundia—saltes, which were not subject to the authority of neighboring cities and were administered by a special procuratorial official . . . "[34] The imperial assets also included nearly all the mines within the empire, as well as palaces and other holdings.

The presence of Roman legions stationed in border provinces, alongside the extensive imperial estates in nearly every region, positioned the emperor as the most respected figure throughout the empire. He served as the unifying force that held the Roman Empire together. Consequently, the emperor was the wealthiest individual in the empire; however, this wealth stemmed largely from his role as emperor. His personal wealth was comparatively modest and accounted for separately. Thus, it was the state, rather than the emperor, that emerged as the richest owner in the land—marking a significant transition from the earlier polis system.

Interest

Interestingly, after the fall of the Republic, the Senate made attempts to restore it for nearly a century, yet all these efforts received little support from either the populace or the military. Why was this the case? Perhaps it was the prevailing interests of the state that were asserting themselves.

During the Republic, the politics of the polis and its military campaigns were predominantly managed by the owners of large estates. Commanders, chief administrators of cities, and governors inconquered provinces were all part of the elite, temporarily stepping away from their estates to serve in office. Their positions were always intended to be temporary, and their enterprises remained their primary concern. Even while in office, they often felt a sense of obligation toward their enterprises, which influenced their decision-making and priorities.

For the emperor, the state interest of Rome was inherently linked to his own interests. The successes of the state translated into his personal successes, while its failures reflected on him as well. Unlike the governors and tax collectors in the provinces, who might engage in corruption, the emperor had a vested interest in maintaining order and prosperity within his realm. His power and authority could not be undermined by bribery; he had no incentive to accept a bribe that would compromise the economy or stability of the state. In essence, the emperor personified the state interest in its purest form, becoming the focal point through which the ideal state interest was realized.

Both the Greeks and Romans, the founders of democracy, ultimately abandoned this system voluntarily. Lacking ideologies to follow blindly, they navigated their political landscape by feeling their way through, seeking firmer and more reliable ground. Dictatorship and democracy were merely adaptive strategies employed in response to varying circumstances, chosen based on the needs of the moment.

ECONOMIC EVOLUTION OF POLIS
(MONOPOLY AND INNOVATION)

The Athenian Empire

An Athenian legend recounts one of the earliest instances of government intervention in the economy. In the 5th century BCE, Solon, Athens' chief reformer, enacted a ban on the export of agricultural products, with the sole exception of olive oil. This policy aimed to maintain a steady food supply for the polis, but at the same time it encouraged the local cultivation of olive trees around Athens.

Growing olive trees is a very complex and time-consuming endeavor. "Olive production differs from the production of annual crops, such as wheat, in that olive trees bear fruit only after a large, difficult-to-monitor investment of time and effort. High yields require years of labor from workers skilled in grafting, irrigating, pruning, and suckering."[35] In other words, olives require significant labor investment and, therefore, offer higher added value compared to crops like grain.

Whether it was due to Solon's directive or a natural shift, olive cultivation gradually replaced other crops in Athens. The ability to sell olives outside the polis allowed Athens to use the profits to purchase bread and other essential goods. The decisive factor was that the labor invested in olive cultivation made it possible to exchange more other products for these olives than it would have been possible to obtain by producing those products locally

That is, if the Athenians had grown grain, they would have been able to produce less bread than they could exchange for the olives they grew instead of grain.

However, reliance on olive cultivation had limitations. Olives were not a staple food, so households still focused on growing "daily bread" to sustain themselves and provide food for the entire polis (including artisans and other non-farming residents). Additionally, reliance on imported essentials carried risk, as the supply lines could be disrupted in times of war.

The Athenian economy transformed significantly with the rise of its "empire." Allied states contributed funds, which Athens used for its own needs. Even when these funds were directed toward their intended purpose—building new ships, equipping them, and paying sailors—the money largely stayed within Athens. Shipbuilders and sailors spent their earnings locally, stimulating the city's economy. Additionally, the demand for ship construction and maintenance boosted Athenian industry, attracting skilled artisans and expanding production. Furthermore, Athens' large fleet allowed it to control sea routes and ensure the safety of maritime trade. <u>This specialization lifted Athens' economy to new heights</u>, making it a powerful economic and naval centre in the Greek world.

This situation had important economic ripple effects. With its powerful fleet, Athens could now safely import essential goods like bread and slaves from regions such as the northern Black Sea, Egypt, and Sicily. Additionally, although the League members' contributions "were usually in the form of coin, however, every area within the alliance was also required to provide a certain amount of grain each year."[36] It seems that neighboring Euboea, for example, paid its entire contribution in bread[37]. This steady inflow of essential resources gave Athens the security to devote more land to olive cultivation, reducing reliance on other staple crops. Moreover, the need for allied states to supply Athens with grain limited their own capacity to cultivate olives, leaving Athenian producers with a virtual monopoly in olive oil production. This setup allowed Athens to benefit economically from its dominant role in the league, creating a self-sustaining cycle of agricultural and economic advantage within the region.

<u>In this way, Athens' position at the peak of the political and economic hierarchy enabled it to monopolize more profitable sectors, like olive cultivation and shipbuilding, while leaving less profitable activities, such as grain production, to its allies</u>. This strategic focus allowed Athens to concentrate labor and resources on high-value goods, boosting the city's wealth and securing a comparative advantage over its allies. This economic structure not only reinforced Athens' political dominance within the alliance but also created a cycle where Athens' economic and military (i.e. political) power sustained and expanded each other.

The loss of Athens' dominant political position following defeats in the Peloponnesian War had significant repercussions. No longer at the top of the political pyramid, Athens could no longer leverage its alliances for economic gain, forcing it to prioritize basic sustenance. This shift necessitated state intervention in the bread trade to ensure food security for its citizens. New administrative roles emerged to oversee trade relations, reflecting how the market became a matter of public concern. "Numerous court speeches show that the market had moved very much into the legal sphere, becoming the business of the city and the courts."[38]

The formation of the Athenian "Empire" introduced a new economic hierarchy that fostered specialization among the once-similar economies of the Greek poleis. Under this system, poleis did not specialize based on natural resources or local climate but rather on their place within the empire's economic pyramid. The peak of this hierarchy took on production requiring advanced skill and knowledge— such as olive oil and shipbuilding—goods that embodied high added value. Meanwhile, other poleis were relegated to producing less complex goods, like staple grains, which had lower economic returns. This structured specialization reflected and reinforced the empire's political hierarchy, concentrating wealth and technical expertise in Athens.

This economic hierarchy emerged somewhat naturally over time. However, if Solon had not introduced his innovative olive export law, Athens' political dominance alone would not have automatically placed it at the economic peak. *The Athenians were no more skilled or resourceful than other Greeks, but it was this strategic state intervention that positioned Athens uniquely. Because of this, when we study ancient Greece, we learn about it through the lens of Athens rather than any other polis.* Solon's policy created an economic foundation that not only supported Athenian political power but also defined its long-lasting economic leadership, setting Athens apart in history.

Interaction with a more powerful economical pyramid causes a crisis

The Macedonian unification of Greece and the conquest of Persia altered the trajectory and essence of Greek colonial expansion. Previously, Greek colonization was hindered by the risk of the unknown associated with relocating—establishing a life in foreign lands among unfamiliar people posed substantial risks. However, with the state's protection in newly conquered territories, these risks diminished considerably. The Greeks began to emigrate in masse to the former Persian lands, founding new Greek cities there. *This demonstrates an intriguing dynamic: the state's influence helped reduce risks for private enterprises and individual settlers, facilitating greater economic and cultural expansion.*

The cities established or expanded along the Mediterranean coast (notably Alexandria of Egypt and Antioch) significantly enhanced the economic functions of the Greek polis. Firstly, these cities evolved from serving merely the limited territory of individual poles to becoming crucial craft centres for expansive regions, thereby offering unprecedented opportunities for economic growth and prosperity. Secondly, they transformed into monopolistic gateways for foreign maritime trade, effectively controlling the flow of goods and commerce within their vast territories. Together, these two features elevated these new centres of craft and trade to heights previously unattainable for the traditional Greek poleis marking a significant shift in the economic landscape of the ancient world.

The most intriguing development during this period was the migration of capital and people from the once-dominant

31

poleis to these new centres of economic opportunity. Craftsmen, scientists, and traders flocked to places like Alexandria and Antioch, attracted by the promise of greater profits and stability. This mass exodus marked the beginning of a prolonged and desperate crisis in the older centres of the Greek economy. "...Athenian farmers abandoned land, leaving much of the surrounding countryside vacant, especially the islopes... that had successfully supported olive production. Much of the land that continued to be cultivated coalesced into large blocks under the control of single individuals. Monoculture, with a focus on cereals, replaced the diverse mixture of cereals, olives, and vines."[39] As the Greek poleis transitioned into the periphery of larger economic pyramids established by foreign powers, their agricultural systems shifted focus from export-oriented production to subsistence farming. It is interesting to note that the success of some may lead to the loss of success of others. Many workers, disinclined to migrate to distant lands, sought opportunities in the countryside as urban labor demands dwindled. In this pursuit, they often attached themselves to larger agricultural enterprises, either as local artisans or by renting plots of land from large enterprise to create their own "subenterprises" Consequently, these enterprises began to resemble economic hierarchies, with larger enterprises encompassing numerous smaller enterprises. "in Hellenistic and Roman times, either cultivated lands coalesce into larger blocks or enormous numbers of scattered farms come under the ownership of one man."[40] These emerging hierarchical agricultural enterprises set the stage for the feudal systems that would later dominate the landscape of rural economies in the centuries to come.

The defining economy

The development of the enterprises of the Athenian economy, which were engaged in trade, shipbuilding, and olive cultivation—was instrumental in its economic ascent and subsequent dominance over other Greek poleis. The unique political landscape of the time, characterized by the need to confront a common and formidable enemy, allowed Athens to leverage its economic superiority to rise to the peak of the political hierarchy among Greek city-states. This elevated position enabled key sectors of the Athenian economy to flourish, which in turn played a crucial role in solidifying Athens' supremacy within the broader economic system of the Greek world. Rather than merely defining Athens' specialization in this system, these industries were pivotal in facilitating its rise and consolidation at the pinnacle of a pyramidal structure of economic relations among the poleis. Consequently, it was these specific sectors that not only catalyzed Athens' economic growth but also positioned it to dominate the economic landscape of ancient Greece.

These industries, although crucial, comprised only a fraction of the overall economy. Prior to its rise to the peak of the economic pyramid the workforce engaged in these sectors was not significant. However, as Athens ascended to this peak, the scale and impact of these industries expanded dramatically, integrating them into a larger economic framework of the Athenian Empire. With the collapse of the Athenian Empire, these enterprises could no longer sustain their previous levels of output and began to decline. Despite their historical significance, the industries reverted to pre-imperial scales as competition from other emerging poles intensified. These new centers of trade, shipbuilding, and olive cultivation began to eclipse Athens, drawing away skilled labor and entrepreneurs. Many Athenian workers migrated to these more prosperous cities in search of better opportunities, leaving behind a diminished economy. The remaining Athenians who stayed in the polis were often forced into different activities, which not only failed to restore Athens to its former glory but also struggled to maintain the economic stability it had achieved. Over time, Athens experienced a gradual yet undeniable decline, both politically and economically. *This phenomenon suggests that the defining economy tends to concentrate on the peak of economic pyramids, further entrenching the disparities between the top and the periphery of the socio-economic landscape.*

Rome—The cause of the great crisis of the third century

In its infancy, Rome existed as a remote periphery of the ancient world. However, through centuries of brutal political violence, Rome managed to incorporate a vast expense of the Hellenistic world into its territory. This incorporation created a unified economic space that combine Rome's own economy with that of the Hellenistic regions and beyond. The Hellenistic enterprises had longstanding traditions in crafts and agriculture, producing goods of higher quality than those made by relatively crude Roman enterprises. Nevertheless, the Roman state granted greater rights and protections to its local enterprises. By leveraging these privileges, Roman enterprises gradually displaced the traders from the former Hellenistic regions, allowing them to dominate trade within the empire. The wealth generated from trade, along with the spoils of military conquests and the labor of countless enslaved people, began to concentrate in Rome. This accumulation of wealth transformed Rome into the richest city in the empire, making it the most desirable market for goods. As the central hub for the empire's commodity flows, Rome attracted craftsmen and artisans from across its territories. This influx of talent and labor led to a significant rise in artisanal production and construction within the city. Over time, the quality and sophistication of Roman products improved, matching that of the Hellenistic east of the empire. *Much like the Athenian Empire, the successes gained either through political or economic means attracted economic growth,* solidifying Rome's position as a powerhouse of trade and craftsmanship within the ancient world.

Moreover, the state of Rome played a crucial role in importing grain from Egypt and other conquered provinces, alongside other essential products. This arrangement allowed central Italy to specialize in the production of more refined goods that demanded a higher level of enterprise, such as wines, olives, and oils. These industries evolved into large-scale villas* that relied heavily on exporting their products and using the proceeds to import necessary goods for daily life. However, for the Hellenistic East to accept these Roman exports, additional economic coercion was necessary. A notable example of this is the edict of Domitian in 92AD, which prohibited the planting of new vineyards in the provinces and mandated the destruction of half of the existing ones.[41] This policy effectively stifled the potential for local industries to develop and thrive.

As a result, the state of Rome exported essential life-sustaining products from the East, which required less specialized knowledge and skill to produce, thus yielding lower added value. On the other hand, the state directly forbade the East to develop its enterprises in the same sectors of the defining economy. In this way the Roman state established a division of labor within the empire, favoring the economic interests of the West over those of the East. Additionally, the unequal treatment

* large specialized Roman farms

of citizens in Italy compared to those in the provinces further entrenched this economic disparity. State policies that favored Italian citizens over their provincial counterparts exacerbated the already significant economic divide, solidifying the West's more profitable position within the Roman Empire and limiting the potential for growth and innovation in the East. This strategic manipulation of economic relationships ensured that Rome maintained its dominance and that the benefits of imperial wealth flowed primarily in one direction—toward the West.

That is why when Emperor Caracalla granted equal citizenship to all residents in 212CE, a profound and protracted crisis unfolded in the western regions. The essence of this crisis lay in the East's refusal to purchase goods from the West, leading to a significant decline in the West's ability to export raw materials and agricultural products from the East. As a result, the Western provinces were compelled to shift from more specialized and cultivated agricultural sectors, such as olive and vine cultivation, to simpler crops. Simultaneously, urban crafts that had flourished under the previous economic conditions—bolstered by a higher standard of living in Rome and the prestige associated with residence there—began to decline, as work in Rome no longer attracted artisans from other parts of the empire[42]. This decline was inevitable once the West and East became part of a single economic space. Without the benefit of state intervention, these structural issues began to surface, underscoring the vulnerability of the western economy. It became increasingly clear that the West had relied heavily on trade and resources from the eastern provinces, ultimately leading to its economic downturn.

At the same time, the total area under cultivation declined, and average yields fell. Trade diminished to the point that it effectively reverted to barter. Taxes failed to generate sufficient revenue for the treasury, forcing emperors to reduce the precious metal content in coins, further harming trade. Salaries to the army and officials were paid in kind, and even taxes were collected in the same manner.[43]

Thus, within the framework of a "free market," the Western Roman Empire became economically subjugated by the Eastern Empire. The crisis of the 3rd century in the Western Empire was a direct consequence of this economic subjugation.

Historians rather tentatively date the end of this crisis to the beginning of Diocletian's reforms. Since the crisis in the Western Roman Empire persisted until its complete collapse, many historians interpret the end of the crisis as the stabilization of the imperial governance and the cessation of civil wars. However, this arbitrary definition of the crisis's end can be articulated more coherently: the crisis concluded when the state acknowledged the superiority of the imperial East over the West. In 286 CE Emperor Diocletian established his capital in Nicomedia, a city on the shores of the Sea of Marmara and placed his co-ruler in Mediolanum (Milan). Constantine followed suit by moving the capital of the empire to Byzantium (later Constantinople). Not surprisingly, it was around this time that the "endless" crisis in Greece finally ended. From a governance perspective, it was much easier to rule the declining West from the East of the empire than vice versa.

Rome's free-market presence in a single economic space with the developed economies of the former Hellenistic countries ultimately undermined its economy. Even though previously, when the state implemented appropriate measures and intervened in the economy, the Roman polis was able to rise above the eastern economies.

This modest observation is an ironclad economic law—a single economic space always subordinates a weaker economy to a stronger one. While government (state) intervention can enable a weaker economy to swim against the tide and rise, leaving it to free market forces will inevitably push the weaker economy back down the economic hierarchy.

It was the rise to the peak of the political hierarchy that allowed Rome to develop industries distanced from everyday needs, such as food and clothing. These industries were defining to Rome's prosperity. However, after losing this position, Rome also lost its defining economic enterprises and gradually became an ordinary city within the empire.

The reason for the failure was that Rome did not introduce decisive innovations that would have ensured its monopoly. Almost all the production technologies it had were actually adopted from the East, rather than developed independently.

Rural dominance over the city

The decline of trade in the West led to the downfall of market-oriented enterprises, such as slave villas, which were replaced by larger subsistence farms.[44] Former owners of medium and small market-oriented enterprises began to lose profits and going bankrupt. In their desperation, they turned to the owners of latifundia* for rescue; these larger landowners paid off debts and helped them recover as users of latifundiasub-enterprises (users of small plots on the territory of latifundia). As trade continued to decline, cities also faced a downturn. Townspeople lost their jobs and migrated to the countryside in search of substance. Craftsmen sometimes found employment within latifundia, which further exasperated the decline of trade and led to an even greater deterioration of urban life. This mirrored the earlier process seen in Greece, where the poleis diminished while large latifundia expanded.

* **latifundium**—large agricultural estate that used a large number of peasant or slave labourers.

This economic transformation brought about significant social changes. Cities had previously served as centres for tax collection from both the urban residents and surrounding peasants. However, it became increasingly difficult for the curiales (political officials) to collect taxes due to population shifts towards latifundia, while tax amounts (until the new census) remained unchanged. As a result, the curiales were forced to cover tax shortfalls from their own funds. Consequently, many curiales began to evade their responsibilities, abandoning positions that had once been respected and desirable. When caught, they were often returned to their roles.[45] The polis could also no longer effectively manage military recruitment, leading to the gradual transfer of these responsibilities to latifundia owners.[46] This situation further strengthened the latifundists marking *the emergence of a new economic power: large private enterprises. This new power steadily gained social influence, forcing the state to seek support from latifundia owners amid its collapsing hierarchy and loss of authority.*

State property

As the power of the oligarchs grew alongside the expansion of latifundia, the emperor's control over even larger enterprises positioned him as the strongest oligarch in the empire—a factor that was to strengthen the state. In the early days of the empire, emperors-princeps still reaped significant profits from wars of conquest. Instead, defensive wars drained both the state treasury and the personal wealth of the emperors-dominus (late Roman emperors). At this stage, the emperor's personal enterprises assumed a particularly vital role—the dominus was responsible for maintaining the army and bureaucracy while also providing assistance to troubled cities and districts.[47] Consequently, the emperor's economic distribution pyramid was expected to be the most powerful and generous in the empire. If the emperor was the richest of the rich, possessing the largest enterprises and the greatest resources to reward his supporters, he was seen as the first among the first.

The emperor's private enterprises contributed to the unity of the country. However, since the emperor embodied the state, his private property was effectively state property. *Thus, state ownership became a unifying factor within the country.*

The West

The owners of latifundia became very influential figures within their districts, able to sway state representatives to reduce both taxes and the number of recruitment quota for their enterprises. However, tax collectors and military representatives often redirected their efforts to "make up" for these shortfalls by targeting other free peasants and townspeople. Viewing the latifundists as a protective force against bureaucratic abuses, many free peasants opted to align themselves with these magnates, becoming their clients and further bolstering the latifundists' socioeconomic influence. As the power of large landowners grew, and emperors had no choice but to accommodate these competing pyramids of power. Perhaps for the first time in human history, socio-political power and economic power—the authority of the state and the power of large economies—clashed. The emperor retained the ability to dismiss any official and execute any oligarch, provided he had the army's support. However, the army required pay, supplies, and recruits. To secure these, the Western emperor had to appease the large landowners by granting them tax exemptions, appointing them to higher positions, allowing them to profit from their roles at the expense of public funds.

Moreover, in the Western Roman Empire, emperors sought

to buy the loyalty of prominent oligarchs by distributing imperial property. This practice diminished state assets while simultaneously increasing the private wealth of the oligarchs. *As a result, the authority of the emperor waned, while that of the oligarchs grew.*

In its powerlessness, the state resorted to a disastrous measure: to circumvent the magnates, Western emperors began to recruit barbarians in masse into regular troops—thus avoiding the need to gather recruits in latifundia. Eventually, entire tribes were enlisted; they were allowed into the empire and given land on the condition that they would protect the borders. This strategy effectively circumvented the need to collect sufficient taxes to sustain the army. As a result, "finally, the Roman army in the west consisted of practically nothing but barbarian hordes under nominal allegiance to the Roman emperor."[48]

The Western Roman state lost its struggle against private enterprises and eventually ceased to exist.

The East

The decline of the West also affected the East, but the latter did not experience the same level of decline. Skilled craftsmen from the East no longer needed to seek opportunities in the West and chose to remain at home. In fact, some of the largest cities in the East even experienced growth, while cities in the West were in decline.[49] The difference can be attributed to the distribution of land ownership. In the West "[m]ere handfuls of great families owned most of the land of Italy and Gaul"[50] whereas in the East, particularly in Egypt "[i]t is hard to tell what percentage of the land was state land, but one-third is a good guess"[51]. This allowed the emperors in the eastern part of the empire to collect sufficient funds from their lands. Additionally, the absence of such large private landholdings, as seen in the West, made it relatively easier to gather recruits and taxes from small landowners. Consequently, the economy in the eastern part of the empire proved to be more robust, leading to stronger imperial power. "Ultimately, then, the emperors succeeded in creating a true state bureaucracy and maintaining the allegiance of the educated and well-to-do classes in one half of the Empire but not in the other. In the west, the emperors failed, and the upper classes went their own private way."[52] *State enterprises played a crucial role in helping the eastern part of the empire endure.*

The interaction of economies (whether they are individual enterprises or aggregates of enterprises such as countries) creates a hierarchical structure. The peak of the political hierarchy can also simultaneously become the peak of the economic hierarchy, but only if it secures a monopoly over certain production. To maintain this peak position over time, the monopolistic focus must continually evolve, as the economies of the less dominant countries strive to adopt the most profitable production methods found at the top. Consequently, sustaining a peak status necessitates the ongoing renewal or complete replacement of production methods, which inherently requires the introduction of innovations. Without economic innovations, political domination cannot ensure economic supremacy. These two different forms of dominance—political, exercised by states, and economic, exercised by enterprises—may not even coincide geographically within the same nation. Nonetheless, a state can facilitate its enterprises' ascendance to the peak of the economic hierarchy through intervention. This means actively influencing the economy to foster growth and adaptation.

THE RISE OF WESTERN EUROPE OVER EASTERN EUROPE

All of the examples of economic pyramids discussed so far were temporary, unsustainable, and local. However, a tectonic shift eventually occurred—beginning with the rise of Western Europe, which ultimately led to the formation of a global economic hierarchy. This rise was primarily an intra-European affair—with Western Europe advancing at the expense of Eastern Europe.

Medieval cities of Western Europe

After the collapse of the Western Roman Empire, the cities of Western Europe were fundamentally different from those in other parts of the world. Typically, cities elsewhere housed the owners of large surrounding enterprises, as well as members of the local state administration, creating a dual structure of control. These elites managed the countryside and participated in city affairs, often prioritizing the interests of agricultural enterprises. For instance, " . . . in the conquered and newly created cities of the caliphate, the bulk of the conquerors settled in cities. The city became the center of feudal domination... thanks to this, mass urban crafts continued to be preserved . . . In Muslim society, the feudal lord's dominance over the city... was expressed in the fact that he and the traders associated with him were the main suppliers of agricultural products to the city market . . . "[53] In contrast, the collapse of the Western Roman Empire left a different legacy in Western Europe: the patrons of the most powerful agricultural enterprises resided in rural areas, tied to their lands. This separation allowed the industrial and commercial elite of cities to independently address city affairs, favoring craft and trade enterprises.

Adam Smith observed the following of medieval cities noting that "the inhabitants of a town, when gathered in one place, can easily combine. The most insignificant trades carried on in town have accordingly... been incorporated, and even where they have never been incorporated, yet the corporation spirit, ... the aversion to communicate the secret of their trade, generally prevail in them, and often teaches them, by voluntary associations and agreements, to prevent that free competition which they cannot prohibit by bylaws... The inhabitants of the country, [in contrast,] dispersed in distant places cannot easily combine. They have not only never been incorporated, but the corporation spirit has never prevailed among them."[54] This allowed the townspeople to " . . . raise prices without fear that they would not be able to sell their goods because of free competition . . . " Consequently, urban residents established a monopoly position in trade with surrounding agricultural enterprises, leading to an unequal exchange between the countryside and the city. This dynamic resulted in the formation of economic pyramids, with the city at the peak and the surrounding agricultural enterprises at the base. As a result, the exchange process facilitated the accumulation of wealth—and, thus, socioeconomic power—in cities. <u>From the outset, the rise of crafts and later industry occurred at the expense of agriculture.</u>

But cities did not become wealthy solely due to the products they produced. Agricultural enterprises brought their goods to the city not only to exchange them for urban products, but also because they often specialized according to their geographic location. In certain valleys, specific crops thrived while others struggled; higher in the mountains, it was more profitable to graze cattle than to cultivate crops. Additionally, the distance from the city influenced if perishable products, such as milk, could be delivered to the city market, as opposed to more durable items like grain and carrots. This specialization necessitated exchanges between enterprises, which took place within the city market. As a result, cities grew richer by becoming monopoly centers of transit trade, facilitating the movement of goods between different regions.

Cities thus formed mini-economic empires, uniting their

dependent areas into a cohesive economic pyramid through trade. By expanding their trade networks and production capabilities, these cities expanded their mini empires. However, the increasing complexity of delivering goods over greater distances, coupled with competition from local cities in more remote regions, eventually led to a halt in the expansion of these economic mini empires. In contrast, cities located on the seacoast found themselves in exceptional circumstances. Their trade could extend into overseas markets, allowing for potentially limitless expansion. The mini empires of these coastal cities were formed by economic control, and it did not matter that different parts of the "territory" could belong to various states. This dynamic enabled them to thrive even amid political fragmentation, solidifying their status as vital centres of commerce.

The formation of urban economic empires stemmed from their monopoly position in trade with the countryside. As cities began to compete with one another, the outcome of their economic struggles often favored the city that produced superior goods—those enriched with innovations. Typically, the losing city would cease producing its less competitive products and instead begin distributing the products of the victorious city. This shift allowed the winning city to extend its monopoly over the economically controlled territory of the losing city, further solidifying its dominance in the regional economic landscape.

Rus—an example of Eastern Europe
"Rus was essentially founded as a by-product of slave raiding by the Vikings passing from Scandinavia to Byzantium in the 9th century."[55] Perhaps this is an exaggeration. But it is clear that the unifying factor of Kyivan Rus was its involvement in trade along the renowned route "from the Varangians to the Greeks." (or, in other words the route from Vikings to Byzantine). Following the conquest of the surrounding Slavic

tribes by the first Kyivan princes, these tribes largely continued their traditional ways of to life, resulting in a lack of economic integration among the diverse territories. What effectively bound these territories into a single entity were the "poliudie." The Byzantine emperor Constantine Porphyrogenitus noted that a Knyaz (prince) and squad of his warriors (druzhina*)would embark on these winter journeys, traveling among the various tribes to collect tribute. Chronicle accounts, such as the murder of Knyaz Ihor by the Drevlians during such a pilgrimage, highlight that the tribute often took the form of goods like black marten fur and salves—typically one from each household. After gathering these tributes over the winter, the Knyaz would send them to Byzantium for sale in the spring.

Kyivan Rus did not focus on producing goods to economically dominate other lands; rather, it capitalized on "what the land gave" and traded items that were marketable elsewhere. Among these commodities were slaves. Before the Viking period, historical records indicate that the Eastern Slavs came under the control of the Khazars or, at minimum, faced constant raids by them. "Khazaria . . . was a traditional supplier of Slavic slaves to the Mediterranean market."[56] In general, 'bony Slavs became a favorite commodity. Jewish merchants and Vikings acted as intermediaries and carriers, especially through the Crimea... and later on the Baltic Sea and in Central Europe... The associative connection between the Slavs and the slave trade was so strong that the words "Slav' and 'slave' were widely perceived as synonymous. The Arabic name for a eunuch, the word sacaliba, is also allegedly derived from 'Slav.'[57]

With the rise of Kyivan Rus, the Kyivan Knyaz primarily benefitted from trade, and this consolidation of power

* Druzhina, in early Rus, a prince's retinue, which helped him to administer his principality and constituted the area's military force.

strengthened the state itself, enabling the Kyivan Rus to establish a firm foundation. The Kyivan princes repeatedly led military campaigns to Tsargrad (Constantinople) and according to legend, even nailed their shield to its gates as a sign of victory. The Kyivan Knyaz Sviatoslav famously defeated Khazaria, eliminating a longstanding rival. Under the rule of Yaroslav the Wise in the mid-11th century, Kyivan Rus expanded significantly westward, crossing the Carpathian Mountains, and became the largest state in Europe. His father, Volodymyr also expanded Rus by conquering the Slavic and Finno-Ugric tribes northeast of Kyiv.

Participating in the bustling trade between the north and south of Europe, Kyivan Rus flourished and earned the title "country of cities" due to the economic prosperity of its urban centres. Chronicles record about 240 cities and towns, with around 90 being likely significant. The population of Kyiv alone was 35-40 thousand (a size London would reach only a century later)[58]. However, while the economy of Kyivan Rus was based on foreign trade and boasted many large cities, it did not resemble Western Europe. In Rus, as in Eastern societies, cities housed large landowners, the boyars, along with their retinues, who drove the vigorous trade and economic activity." Many boyars lived in cities, renting out their land to peasants, for which they took a portion of their produce and sold it on the market. It was their urban orientation, interest in commerce, and mobility that distinguished the boyars of Kyivan Rus from Western European feudal lords."[59] Unlike the cities of Western Europe, the cities of Rus did not produce handicrafts for export or establish their mini empires. Instead, the boyars, much like after the poliudie, collected a significant share of their estates' output to sell to foreign markets. Indoing so, they competed with a substantial merchant class that has developed in the Rus cities, as well as, for a time, with traders-Varangians." As follows from Russo-Greek negotiations and place-name data, lively trade with the participation of Scandinavian merchants developed ... on the Volkhov-Lovat-Dnipro route, where the objects of exchange were rather Rus goods—tribute received from the population in the form of furs, honey, and wax. It was this trade that was described by Constantine VII Porphyrogenitus."[60] In addition, leather, tin, and, among other things, slaves were sent to Byzantium. Carpets, silver and leather goods, pearls, etc. were sent back. Thus, the structure of trade reveals that the economy of Rus was characteristic of the base of foreign economic pyramids—exchanging raw materials for manufactured goods.

With the decline of Byzantium and the rise in nomadic attacks on southern Rus, trade diminished, weakening the state that depended on it. As a result, Rus fragmented into smaller principalities. "Now the squads were small, because there was nothing to support a large one, and the squad, with the settling of the princes, also settled in the ground. From the packs of warrior merchants, they turned into landlords, because trade, in general, was falling into decline due to the loss of steppe and midday roads, and the economic ruin provided many unfree or semi-free, serf hands with whom one could run a large household. The squad mixed with the local nobility, and together with it became the highest layer of local citizenship."[61] The state was weakening, and as a result, elements of democracy were becoming stronger. Cities had a tradition of public assemblies, or veches, which decided critical matters such as war declarations, the highest judicial rulings, trade issues, and relations with other lands. Control of the veche often rested with the boyars and merchants due to their socioeconomic influence, creating a power struggle between the state and large enterprises, i.e.

between the *Knyaz* and these influential groups. Although the *Knyaz (prince)* had a personal guard and could impose his will by force, many matters required popular support or financial resources. The balance of power between the *Knyaz* and the *veche* depended on the determination of each *Knyaz* and his ability to handle conflicts without force.

Novgorod's role in Baltic trade greatly enriched its merchants and landlords (boyars), ultimately allowing the city to expel its *Knyaz* in 1136 and establish a republican government. The *veche* continued to invite princes, but they served primarily as military leaders and judges, with limited power. This trade-based wealth allowed Novgorod's elite to create a "free city" much like those in the Hanseatic League. However, Novgorod was distinct in its economic function: it did not produce export goods but traded raw materials like furs, wax, and honey for Hanseatic products requiring advanced production techniques, such as fabrics, metals, and alum. Novgorod thus embodied a dependent economy, exchanging raw resources for the finished goods of technologically advanced cities, reinforcing the monopoly of its trading partners rather than building its own economic independence.

Drang nach Osten

The influence and pressure of Western Europe on Eastern Europe began even before the growth of urban centers. "Charlemagne did not give the Slavs peace... In 789, he conquered the Bodricians and Serbs east of the Elbe. In 805-806, he forced the Bohemian Czechs to pay tribute, as well as the Carinthian Slavs on the Sava and Drava rivers. Out of respect for the great conqueror, the Slavs formed their word 'king' based on his name."[62] The rise of cities in Europe intensified the push eastward, particularly through the Crusades, which sought to reclaim Jerusalem and other holy sites. One of the main results of these campaigns was the fall of the Byzantine Empire, paving the way for increased Western European influence in the region. Simultaneously, other crusades extended Western European impact along northern seas. Organized by the Catholic Church under the pretense of converting pagans to the true faith, these efforts had profound implications for the Western European economy." Slavery itself continued to exist in every Christian country throughout the Middle Ages and the church did not attempt to abolish it. Indeed, it did not free its own slaves. For generations, the German clergy was implicated in the export of Slavic people by Jewish merchants to Moslem countries."[63] That is why, "The word slave, a variant of Slav, gradually came into use from about the eighth century because of the number of captives from Slavic tribes."[64]

However, the economic impact of the Crusades was far more significant than their political consequences: Western agriculture, which had been more advanced since the Roman Empire, began to shift eastward." Sometimes the pagans fled; sometimes they submitted, oftentimes ending up little better than slaves. But . . . sometimes they organized and stood their ground. As Frankish and Germanic farmers moved east . . . some villagers in Bohemia, Poland, Hungary, and even distant Rus copied their techniques . . . to farm their own lands more intensively. Their chiefs, turning Christian, persuaded or forced them to become tax-paying subjects and fight the colonists. . . ."[65] However, economic advantages dictated this shift, leading Slavic states to invite German settlers, who brought with them enhanced agricultural productivity and, consequently, greater profitability.

However, the most significant consequence was the integration of Eastern European lands into the economic pyramid established by the Hanseatic League. The Crusaders constructed fortresses in the conquered lands, which served not only as bases for further conquest into Eastern Europe but, more importantly, as key trading posts. They founded new cities or built their fortresses near existing settlements, including Toruń and Elbląg (both now in Poland), Riga (now Latvia) Tallinn and Tartu (now Estonia), and Königsberg (now Kaliningrad in Russia). These cities mainly functioned as centers for the distribution of goods from Hanseatic cities in the territories under their economic control, rather than producing their own goods for export.

The very success of one eliminates opportunities for others[66]

The so-called "free cities" of the Hanseatic League originated as urban mini empires, engaging in trade with an expanding network of farms (agricultural enterprises) and growing wealthier through this exchange. Their primary product for distant markets was coarse woolen cloth. However, their trading success enabled them to enhance their production capabilities, leading to the creation of finer woolen fabrics and the development of new industries such as linen, silk, knightly armor, and metal engraving. Over time, though, their role in trade became increasingly intermediary. In the West, cities in the Rhine, Scheldt, and Meuse deltas (mostly in the territories of the modern Netherlands and Belgium) and eventually England began to flourish. Therefore, the Hanseatic intermediary trade, as the Encyclopedia Britannica writes, ". . . ran from the economically advanced and populous west-with its large markets for raw materials, its large production of manufactured goods, and its contacts with the products of the Mediterranean and Asia the "colonial" lands of eastern Europe, which could supply food surpluses and raw materials for industry. Grain, timber and pitch, tar, potash and charcoal, wax and honey, and hemp and flax were all drawn from the huge hinterland to the south and east of the Baltic (modern-day Russia and Poland) and shipped to the industrial west (Flanders and England), which in turn sent cloth and other manufactured goods eastward to the Slavs. That east-west carrying traffic, with the economic leverage that the merchants secured in the countries that needed their goods, was the mainstay of Hanseatic power."[67] Though referring to the "industrial West" and the "colonial lands of Eastern Europe" may reflect a perspective shaped by later historical developments, it is important to acknowledge that Hanseatic trade initiated a long process. This process ultimately contributed to the eventual realization of the described today.

The Hanseatic cities drew the eastern coast—comprising the territories of Sweden, Poland, the knightly orders of the modern Baltic states and northern Kyivan Rus—into the foundation of their economic pyramids. The cities of these territories were weak and unableto resist the influence of Hanseatic and later Flemish cities. Just as states established fortified towns, and garrisons, in conquered territories, the Hanseatic and Flemish cities turned these local towns into outposts of their trade in the hinterlands. For instance, Danzig served as an outpost for economic control over Poland, Riga over the Baltic States, and Novgorod over northern Kyivan Rus (future Russia).

The Hanseatic League actively soughtto establish a free trade policy long before the emergence of liberalism. It aimed to secure duty-free trade privileges for itself across various regions. However, the Hanseatic League was unwilling to extend similar privileges to merchants from other countries within its cities. When diplomatic efforts failed, the Hanseatic League resorted to military means to achieve its goals, as demonstrated during the nine-year war against Denmark and Norway from 1361-1370.

Just as cities inevitably conquered and subjugated surrounding villages, so too did the Western cities of Europe eventually conquer the East. As the East became increasingly reliant on Western goods, its need to produce them locally diminished. Instead, the East focused on producing items that the West sought in exchange for their goods. Therefore, while agricultural hunting, and mining enterprises flourished in the east, craftsmen's enterprises declined. In the West, a growing segment of the population moved to cities as fewer farms were required due to the influx of agricultural products from the East. Conversely, the demand for Western handicraft goods in the East created a greater need for artisanal production in the West, leading to an increased necessity for a larger part of the population to engage in handicraft industries. This process not only opened opportunities for the West but also restricted them from the East.

The West was on the verge of rising, though its potential remained unseen by many." The slight edge of the fifteenth century became the great disparity of the seventeenth and the monumental difference of the nineteenth"[68].

Where Europe's East was superior to its West

After the collapse of the Western Roman Empire, the city of Venice became part of the Eastern Roman Empire, known today as Byzantium. When the Frankish kingdom began to strengthen in the West at the end of the eighth century—aspiring to revive the legacy of the Western Roman Empire—Venice capitalized on the conflict between these two powers, skillfully negotiating for various concessions and privileges. Venetian "Ships transported... [to Constantinople] the products of the countries that were contiguous to it on the east and the west: wheat and wine from Italy, wood from Dalmatia, salt from the lagoons, and, in spite the prohibitions of the Pope and the Emperor himself, slaves which she easily secured among the Slavic peoples of the shores of the Adriatic."[69] Thanks to this, her fleet grew and strengthened, becoming both a significant economic and military factor. In the struggle between the Eastern and New Western empires, Venice changed hands several times but continued to trade with both sides. Eventually, after 812, "[w]hile formally dependent on the Eastern Empire and having a treaty-based relationship with the Western Empire, Venice achieved ... almost complete independence in internal governance and began to acquire great importance as the sole intermediary in trade affairs between . . . East and West."[70] Another rule: if you don't choose a side, both sides will choose you.

Eventually, Venice's advantageous position allowed it to seize a significant opportunity. In the twelfth century, as the Byzantine Empire grappled with a series of uprisings and military invasions, it turned to Venice for assistance from its fleet. In return, Venice was granted complete tax exemption on its trade. However, recognizing the risks of becoming overly dependent, Byzantium extended similar privileges to the Genoese and Pisans as a countermeasure.[71] This decision immediately benefitted Italian merchants, as their cheaper products from Northern Italy began to displace local consumer goods.[72] Nevertheless, Byzantine production of high-quality goods remained robust, and Italian trade positively influenced it through increased purchases. Moreover, this period marked a time of considerable strength for the Byzantine state.

However, gradually, things began to shift during the 13th and 14th centuries, as large private agricultural enterprises in Byzantium gained power, overpowering local authorities and crafts. Feudal enterprises, some stretching for tens of kilometers, spread across Byzantium[73]. The expansion of these large self-sufficient enterprises led to a decline in trade and the outflow of crafts from urban centres to the countryside. This was the path the West had travelled before, with the Western Roman Empire and later feudal states. Now it was time for the East. Though the East resisted for a time, it ultimately lost this internal economic "civil war."

The decline of Byzantine cities also led to the loss of crafts that could not adapt to agricultural enterprises, such as the production of high-quality clothing, luxury goods, paper, or even soap. Italian merchants began importing these goods into Byzantium,[74] a process that further strengthened the crafts sector of Northern Italy. In turn, this strengthened its cities themselves, leading to a shift where the agricultural outskirts began focusing on cultivating industrial crops instead of food. This created a demand for food, primarily grain, which could be conveniently supplied by the expanding agricultural economy of Byzantium. After all, Byzantium needed to export resources in exchange for Italian manufactured products. "In the first half of the fourteenth century, Italian merchants gradually monopolized not only Byzantium's foreign trade but, to a large extent, the internal wholesale food trade as well. Even control over the supply of Constantinople passed into the hands of the Genoese. Their search for sources of raw materials led them to participate in its development and exploitation and thus to take an active part in the Byzantine economy. At the same time, the import of Italian finished goods to Byzantium, including con-sumer goods such as fabrics, metal products, glass, and weap-ons, is growing. Italian imports began to have a detrimental effect on Byzantium's handicraft production... The feudal lords' "ties" with Italian merchants increasingly narrowed the scope of Byzantine merchants' activities as intermediaries... They were increasingly being pushed out even from domestic trade. Its impoverishment began. Accordingly, the state's revenues were reduced. Trade duties were minimized due to the privileges granted to the Genoese and Venetians."[75] As the Byzantine weakened, it increasingly lost the capacity to influence its economic landscape. Large Byzantine agricultural enterprises began buying up warehouses, shops, and even craft workshops. The owners of these large agricultural enterprises engaged in direct trade with the Italians, finding state control as much of an obstacle as Italians did. Byzantine artisanal and commercial enterprises increasingly became "junior partners" to the Italians, as collaboration with them became more profitable and reliable. By the end of the fourteenth century, this alignment had left the Byzantine economy in a state of profound decline. 'Even in the production of luxury goods, Byzantine craftsmanship degraded and primitivized, finally losing its competitiveness with Italian craftsmanship.'[76]

The consequence of all these shifts was the fall of Byzantium. "The power of the weakening Byzantine Empire and the growing Ottoman state were already incomparable in the fourteenth century. But the main reasons for the death of Byzantium were still the decline of cities, craft production, and trade . . ."[77]

This is a classic example of how a previously self-sufficient economy becomes part of another's economic pyramid. Italian cities' enterprises exported goods with higher added value, primarily handicrafts, to Byzantium while importing raw materials and food and providing transportation services. This dynamic strengthened Byzantine enterprises that supplied the Italians, particularly agriculture, which began to exert significant socio-economic influence, eclipsing that of the Byzantine state. Over time, these agricultural enterprises seized power at the regional level. Meanwhile, those sectors weakened by this process, such as local craft and trade, shifted toward distributing goods from foreign enterprises and offering services to them—effectively, they voluntarily became subcontractors to their former competitors.

It's essential to note a significant distinction here: while Rome was unable to secure the East as the base of its economic pyramid, Venice and Genoa succeeded. This difference lies in their timing and approach. During Rome's reign, the eastern territories were flourishing, shaped by the prosperous Hellenistic kingdoms. Rome's conquest united these regions into a single Eastern Roman economic zone, with growing cities and vibrant trade. The economic might of this region eventually grew beyond Rome's control, especially once trade restrictions were lifted, rendering it difficult for Rome to maintain dominance. In contrast, the era of Venice and Genoa's rise coincided with the East's fragmentation. Byzantium was weakened by invasions from Arabs, Slavs, Turks, and Vikings, leading to a decline in Eastern cities and disruptions in trade routes. This decline in urban centers shifted power to agricultural enterprises, which then started challenging state control. Simultaneously, the shortage of handicraft goods created opportunities for Italian city enterprises to step in and supply these products, initiating a self-sustaining cycle that ultimately brought the East into their economic pyramid.

By achieving political independence from both Byzantium and the Frankish Empire, Venice and Genoa strategically preserved economic ties with each. This choice was driven purely by profitability rather than foresight into the consequences. Had they aligned exclusively with either Byzantium or the Frankish Empire, their economic ascent might have been stunted. In fact, this neutrality was crucial; it fostered the conditions for their economic expansion, laying the groundwork for the future formation of international economic hierarchies.

WHY WESTERN EUROPE AND NOT CHINA?

The question of why Europe advanced ahead of other regions, such as China, has puzzled researchers for centuries. A commonly suggested answer is that China's highly centralized state was too powerful. However, everything that has been discussed here so far actually demonstrates exactly how the strength of the state failed China. Let's examine the root cause closely.

3. Western Europe's rise can be attributed to unique conditions that distinguished it from other regions. Namely, a key factor was that owners of large agricultural enterprises were typically not based in cities. This separation allowed craft, commercial, and later financial enterprises to organize powerful communes. Consequently, these urban centers functioned as cohesive economic entities, forming a "conglomerate enterprise" referred to as a "city." The growth and strengthening of cities enabled monarchs to leverage the socio-economic power of urban centres in their struggles against feudal lords. Thus, dynamic facilitated the decline of oligarchic democracies—often characterized by the chaos of feudal rivalries—and supported the establishment of a centralized state. Thus, strong nation-states emerged in Western Europe. Equally significant was the ability of these Western European cities to forge direct connections with the agricultural enterprises of Eastern Europe. This relationship allowed them to exert influence over the development of Eastern economies, effectively integrating them into the burgeoning economic networks of the West.

2. But why are there such unique conditions in Europe? Why did the same conditions not develop, say, in China?

This phenomenon can be explained by the fact that the Chinese state firmly held socio-economic power in its hands (like almost all other ancient states). Throughout its history, China underwent several cycles where agriculture flourished, leading to the establishment of significant socio-economic influence (SEI) by large agricultural enterprises. However, after these periods of growth, the Chinese state intervened to dismantle these large enterprises, reverting the agricultural landscape back to smaller family-operated farms. In contrast, the Western Roman Empire experienced a different trajectory. As agricultural enterprises expanded and accumulated substantial SEI, the state struggled to maintain effective governance. This expansion not only diminished the central authority but also contributed to the decline of urban centres. Large landowners, later feudal lords, retreated to their vast estates, further weakening the urban enterprises and eroding the interconnectedness that had once supported thriving cities.

1. But why was the Chinese state (and others) able to assert its power and control the excessive influence of private enterprises, while the Western Roman state was not? This is because Rome conquered a significantly more economically developed East and by providing it economic freedom, it triggered the decline of Western Roman cities and the rise of substantial agrarian enterprises.

THE FIRST MINI PEAKS OF THE WESTERN EUROPEAN ECONOMIC PYRAMID

Southern peak

The process of Byzantium's economic strangulation through imports paralleled the rise of Northern Italian exporters. As the once-mighty Byzantine Empire decline, the cities of Northern Italy leveraged the empire's weakening state to extract valuable resources, allowing them to expand their trade networks ad solidify their dominance across the Mediterranean. This dominance was characterized by their control over the flow of goods; Northern Italian cities became oligopolistic trade cetres, ensuring that goods from other regions would first pass through their markets before being redistributed elsewhere. Northern Italian cities also facilitated trade in a manner that did not require goods to physically enter Italy. They employed their own ships to create armed convoys, which transported goods under the protection of their military strength. This system allowed them to maintain control over trade routes and access to various markets while financing transactions through loans. As a result, Northern Italy emerged as a pivotal player in Mediterranean commerce, effectively reshaping trade dynamics in the region while exacerbating Byzantium's economic decline.[78]

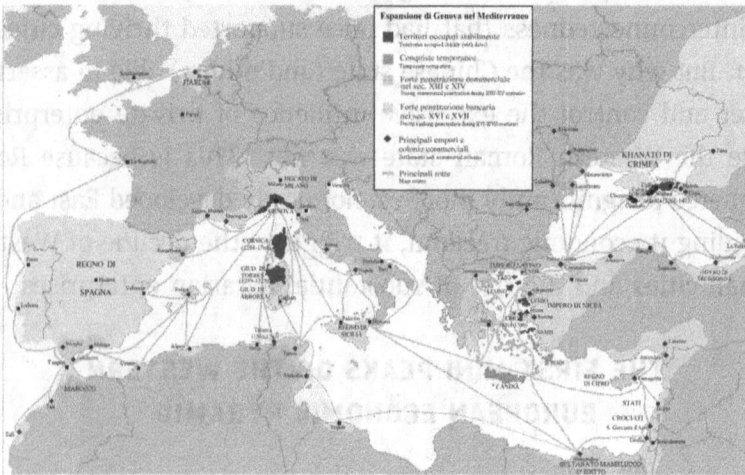

Repubblica_di_Genova. Source: By Kayac1971 – Codex Parisinus latinus (1395) in Ph. Lauer, Catalogue des manuscrits latins, pp.95–6, CC BY-SA 3.0, httpscommons.wikimedia.orgwindex.phpcurid=12865417 63

As a result, Northern Italy emerged not merely as a centre within the trade network but as the peak of an economic pyramid, with its connections to other cities forming the sides. The flow of profits from nearly all Mediterranean trade converged on this region, reinforcing its monopolistic position. Northern Italy's dominance was further solidified by its ability to control trade routes and influence the distribution of goods throughout Europe.

The strategic advantage of being at the center of trade in one of the richest regions of Europe attracted merchants from various other areas. Regions lacking sufficient finance and goods sought to align themselves with Northern Italy, investing their resources and efforts to ascend to the base of this economic pyramid. This phenomenon, while seemingly counterintuitive, exemplifies a fundamental economic principle: regions will often willingly subordinate themselves to a dominant center in pursuit of greater access to wealth and trade opportunities. As such, Northern Italy became a magnet for commerce, drawing in traders who were eager to benefit from its lucrative market and extensive trade connections.

For instance, merchants from distant continental Germany, where it was difficult for Italian galleys to reach, often made the journey to Italy themselves, despite not being favored there. In Venice, these merchants were relegated to ghettos, where they were obliged to conduct their business under strict regulations.[79] They were obliged to bring their goods to designated quarters and stay in rooms provided by the city. Their activities were closely monitored, with rules designed to prevent them from engaging in transactions outside of this controlled environment. This tactic was implemented to ensure that merchants' goods would not bypass Venice in favor of direct exchanges between different cities. By restricting access to information about pricing and buyers, the Venetian authorities aimed to maintain their position as the central hub of trade in the region. Why would merchants want to navigate the complexities of reaching distant markets, incurring substantial initial costs and effort, when they could sell their products conveniently in Venice? Similarly, the search for various goods across numerous locations—requiring local knowledge, relationships, and logistical arrangements—was rendered unnecessary by Venice's consolidation of trade. Everything was conveniently centralized, allowing merchants to focus on transactions within the Venetian system rather than branching out into the wider, more uncertain world of trade. This ensured that Venice remained a vital economic center, benefiting from the traffic of goods and the fees associated with facilitating these exchanges.

Since the enterprises of other countries voluntarily positioned themselves in a subordinate role at the base of the Venetian economic pyramid, this system, once established, became increasingly self-sustaining. Venice's deliberate efforts to maintain this hierarchical structure only further solidified its stability.

As a result, the agricultural enterprises of Northern Italy could shift their focus toward more lucrative activities—such as industrial production, trade, grape and olive growing "leaving the less profitable tasks to others."[80] This specialization was crucial; without a sufficient supply of essential goods, Italy would have struggled to concentrate on these economically defining products.

The strength of the economic pyramids established by the Northern Italian cities lay not only in their own achievements, knowledge, capital, and influence on other cities and even countries but also in the fact that other independent economies voluntarily invested their resources and efforts to become part of this economic hierarchy. By choosing to operate within this framework, these countries contributed to the growth and prosperity of Northern Italy, thereby reinforcing the very system that sustained their own subordination.

The betrayal of enterprises

The success of the Northern Italian cities was achieved through the efforts of private households. Private enterprises worked for their enrichment, and the whole city grew wealthier with them. Let's examine how the harmonious alignment of interests between private enterprises and interests of cities transformed into a contradiction.

The Genoese had long established factories on the Iberian Peninsula, and their importance grew significantly after they established maritime connections with Flanders and England in the 13th century. These factories became crucial intermediate bases for the long voyages to the north. The Genoese sold the imported goods in bulk to local dealers, who became dependent on these supplies and found little incentive to seek out alternative sources from other Italian producers. Having secured dominance in wholesale trade, the Genoese began to infiltrate the retail market, even though states typically reserved retail trade for domestic traders.[81] In this context, states aimed to supports local economies by assigning retail trade to local enterprises. However, rather than taking initiative to organize trade independently, many local enterprises opted to sell their signage to the Genoese. This arrangement allowed the Genoese to further penetrate and conquer the local market, effectively sidelining the very businesses that were supposed to represent local interests. This phenomenon reflects a broader pattern of economic dependence, where local enterprises, instead of competing and innovating, surrendered their autonomy to foreign traders in exchange for immediate gains. While this may not be seen as outright betrayal in the traditional sense, it illustrates how local entities inadvertently facilitated the expansion of foreign dominance in their markets, ultimately undermining their own economic power. But this is not the betrayal we are talking about here.

The Turkish conquests stripped the remnants of Byzantium from the Italians and blocked the Silk Road in the 1340's, creating a significant disruption in trade routes that had previously been vital to the Italian city-states. As Iberian states embarked on their quest for new trade routes to India, the Genoese saw an opportunity to leverage their extensive experience in navigation and the resources they had accumulated from the dying Byzantium. "Could the Portuguese and the Merchant-King of Lisbon have financed unaided the long and expensive East Indies shipping route—a far more demanding one than the route ... between the Spanish West Indies and Seville?"[82] It is well-documented that Genoese financing was not the least important in the exploration and subsequent discovery of the West Indies. However, the Genoese contribution extended beyond mere financial support. Their expertise facilitated the establishment of sugar plantations, which migrated from the Mediterranean to southern Portugal and Spain, eventually reaching the Atlantic islands of Madeira, Cape Verde, and the Canaries.

Meanwhile, Italy itself was experiencing a period of decline. Historically, the Italian mini-empires had imported grain from their overseas colonies, such as those in Crimea, which allowed local agricultural enterprises to focus on producing crops needed for urban industries. This dynamic enabled a significant portion of the population to migrate to cities for work. However, with the loss of these colonies, Italy faced a bread famine that shifted agricultural priorities towards grain production. As a result, some enterprises andurban residents began returning to the countryside, leading to a notable deindustrialization of Northern Italy. The capital that had been accumulated over centuries was not reinvested into improving conditions in Italian cities; instead, merchants and bankers sought opportunities elsewhere. This shift marked a significant turning point, as the once-flourishing Italian economies began to lose their competitive edge in a rapidly changing global landscape.

The time of other players was approaching; the era of state initiative was beginning to overshadow private initiative. States had the determination to confront the uncertainties of risk. This resolve enabled them to explore the New World and venture into Africa. They were supported by the knowledge, experience, and funds of the free cities' enterprises, which sought greater opportunities than their cities could provide. The cities had no mechanisms to prevent this transition, as they were governed by the councils of these very enterprises that were extracting their capital. Consequently, capital fled the cities, resulting in the decline of their economic empires.

The economic pyramid expanded because the activities of the enterprises of other independent countries bolstered its ascent. However, it started to wane when the initiatives of the enterprises at the peak began to foster the rise of alternative economic pyramids.

Northern peak

Almost simultaneously, Flanders was rising in the northern seas. During Roman times, there was a military clothing factory here, but in later years, production focused primarily on woolen clothing made from wool imported from England. The success and the wealth generated by this industry attracted additional craftsmen and traders. The importation of grain from both England and the Baltic (at that time from northern Germany) also played a crucial role during this period.

England was the first to fall into base of burgeoning economic pyramid of Flanders. It began supplying wool for Flanders' textile manufacturing and wheat for its population in exchange for Flanders' cloth and other goods that arrived via sea and river routes. However. Flanders' fate was ultimately shaped by the German expansion to the east, which brought the vast Slavic lands in the east into the realm of Western civilization. The Hanseatic League, which soon supplanted the Vikings in trade, economically linked these lands to Flanders—specifically Poland, Novgorod, and the newly emerging Scandinavian countries.

THE FORMATION OF THE GLOBAL ECONOMIC PYRAMID

**The dooming force of economic circumstances—
The North Center and the East.**

For centuries, the West's trade with the East along the "southern route" (involving India, China, etc.) proved unprofitable. As early as the Roman Empire, vast quantities of gold flowed eastward in exchange for spices, silk, and brocade, depleting Western mines over time. This situation continued into the Middle Ages, during which the Venetians could maintain their trade with the Levant only through the inflow of precious metals from southern Germany, whose mines were gradually being exhausted.

The West's trade with the East on the "northern route" was similarly unprofitable. Traders frequently exchanged Western handicrafts, sugar, and spices for mast trunks, tar, resin, wax collected from wild bees, and so on. However, Western Europe required Eastern goods far more than the reverse, creating a deficit that had to be covered by precious metals. Europe also needed these metals for producing currency for internal exchanges, crafting jewelry, and purchasing spices from India. The production of these metals within Europe was limited, which in turn constrained the development of Western industries. The goods sourced from the Eastern Baltic states were primarily used for production rather than consumption. With the exception of furs, these materials were essential for shipbuilding and other timber construction projects, including houses, bridges, and mills. Additionally, wax played a role in foundry work, such as in the casting of cannons.

The arrival of the Spanish galleons laden with precious metals following the discovery of America dramatically changed the economic landscape, as trade restrictions were lifted. The

West could now purchase as many goods from the East as it required, freeing Western crafts from previous constraints. Consequently, the outskirts of Dutch cities began to cultivate industrial crops such as flax, hemp, rapeseed, hops, tobacco, and plants for making paint: rubia and woad.[83] In this environment, the flourishing of the craft sector also necessitated the importation of food products from Eastern Europe. Trade surged, with the Dutch almost monopolizing these exchanges.

The other side of this process was the persistent backwardness of Eastern Europe. Which relied on the West for all necessary handicraft goods. Consequently, private enterprises in the East focused solely on increasing the production of fur, wood, and grain. This division of labor led to distinct specializations, which have since defined the rise of Western Europe and the stagnation of Eastern Europe. "By 1560, the Dutch had succeeded in attracting 70% of the heavy Baltic trade... it was precisely the redistribution of Baltic grain that led to the successful penetration of the south by Dutch shipping."[84] The economic conquest of the Baltic was the foundation of the future global Dutch economic pyramid.

As we can see, the trade deficit itself is not the decisive factor. The East experienced a surplus for many centuries, but its specialization failed to yield significant economic benefits. Profits were merely consumed rather than reinvested. Meanwhile, the West, despite facing a trade deficit, confidently accepted dominance over the East, primarily due to its specialization in decisive commodities.

The dooming force of economic circumstances— The North Center and Portugal

Upon reaching the Indian Ocean and controlling much of the local trade, the Portuguese rose to the peak of the regional economic pyramid. However, there was no established political hierarchy there, as the Portuguese did not conquer coastal territory. Instead, they typically rented small areas for their trading posts. With superior ships and practical immunity to local pirate attacks, the Portuguese built secure transit warehouses in fortified factories*, which garnered trust among trading rivals. This safety factor granted them an edge—local merchants increasingly preferred Portuguese vessels for transporting goods. Consequently, Portugal's primary export became transportation services. By 1506, income from Asian trade surpassed half of the income from Portugal's domestic economy. As they eventually began cultivating high-value crops on Eastern islands, the Portuguese centralized profits from South Asian and East African trade in Lisbon, setting the stage for a new world economic hub.

The Portuguese had initially ventured out to discover a direct route to pepper and spice sources in Asia, aiming to bypass Northern Italy, and soon these spices began to reach Europe. If the Portuguese had chosen Lisbon for unloading spices, it might have become Europe's new centre.[85] For this to happen, they would have needed adequate warehouses, expanded markets, money changers, and banks—all elements likely to migrate to Lisbon from other regions. Wealth, ships, and merchants would have been drawn to the city, opening offices, building courts, and establishing connections. All of this would have occurred, given time. However, the Portuguese, in possession of significant spice volumes, were unwilling to wait. And what after all to do with surplus goods that couldn't be sold immediately?

Thus, the Portuguese, loaded with spices and other goods from the Indian Ocean, preferred to go to the already established economic center. They could not choose a southern center, because Northern Italy itself traded spices obtained from

* trading posts

Arab merchants in the Levant, so the northern center was the best choice. That's where the Portuguese ships were headed, as they needed to sell their goods as quickly as possible. After all, equipping each ship for the journey to the Indian Ocean cost a lot of money; and the ship would return only six months later, and it was necessary to immediately cover all the debts incurred. In addition, rivals Venetians gave their spices on credit to retailers, waiting up to a year and a half for repayment[86]. To compete with them, the Portuguese had to do the same. How much more attractive it must have seemed to them to offload the headache of distributing goods to the Dutch, who were ready to pay for all their goods at once! The Portuguese state accepted this path, deepening its dependency with each journey and complicating any escape from it.

This development laid another cornerstone for the northern economic centre's rise above Southern Europe's. Unlike Venice, which imported spices from Arab middlemen, the Portuguese sourced directly from producers or even cultivated spices them-selves, giving the northern centre a trade advantage—also enriched by Baltic furs and shipbuilding materials. At the same time, Northern Italy's labor costs elevated since Roman times, exceeded those of the northern centre, thereby strengthened the latter's competitive edge in production.

Moreover, Spanish gold and silver (and later Brazilian gold from Portugal) enabled the Portuguese to access the internal trade of Asian coastal countries, boosting their profits and increasing their exports from Asia. This flow brought even more goods into Amsterdam, furthering its prominence. Portugal continued to contribute humbly to the growth of others.

The Portuguese believed their goods were paramount, yet it was the services provided by the Dutch trading center that proved essential. These services became the primary commodity, and played a decisive role in driving the formation of what soon evolved into a global economic pyramid.

The dooming force of economic circumstances—
The North Center and Spain

The vast expanse of the Americas now demanded resources far beyond what Spain alone could supply. The colonies urgently needed, especially in the first period, clothing, weapons, and even food (wheat and rye). Ships were essential to deliver these goods, and their construction required high-quality ship timber, resins, and cables, all sourced from the Baltic east. Gold and silver from America now flowed eastward in exchange for these materials, and the volume of this exchange grew significantly due to both increased demands and opportunities. In addition, the colonies required linen and woolen fabrics and various handicrafts, which Antwerp warehouses supplied by importing them from Germany, England, France, and the Seventeen Provinces (Netherlands) themselves.

Thus, most of Spain's fleet was committed to transporting these essential goods to Americas and returning with precious metals, while other ships were needed for security. It was therefore logical for the Spanish king to entrust the Baltic trade route to Dutch ships. In 1544, Charles V even bought the right of passage through the Sound Strait from Denmark for the Dutch. With this right and Spanish silver on board, the Dutch were no longer hindered by the Hanseatic control that previously dominated this trade. Eventually, Dutch ships began serving routes between Spain itself and the Netherlands, transporting essential goods to Spain and returning with wool, salt, wine, alum, oil, sugar from island plantations, dyes from America, and, naturally, precious metals.

The Dutch Revolution left the Netherlands outside the

empire—or, rather, left the empire outside the Netherlands. Yet Spain still had to send its wool to the Netherlands for processing, relying on Dutch ships for transport.

Spain may have viewed itself as the ruler of the Netherlands, but economic forces compelled it to labor obediently in support of the growing Dutch global economic empire.

Formation of the peak of the global economic pyramid

The Dutch economic hierarchy could not have evolved into a global economic pyramid without incorporating other economic hierarchies. It was able to emerge by embedding these hierarchies as sub-pyramids or by positioning itself at their peaks, which became its foundations. The Spanish colonial economy, while officially under Spanish control, operated almost entirely in service of the Dutch. The Dutch economic pyramid also assimilated the remnants of the Hanseatic League's economic hierarchy, centred on cities like Danzig (now Gdansk), Riga, Revel (now Tallinn), and Novgorod, each itself a peak in its own economic hierarchy. For example, Danzig included the entire Polish-Lithuanian Commonwealth in its economic pyramid, and Veliky Novgorod controlled the expansive Novgorod lands. The Dutch pyramid also encompassed trading network across the Indian Ocean, previously under Portuguese control, with coastal cities in India and other regions economically linked to vast, resource-rich areas of the Asian mainland, etc. All these intermediary cities prospered by trading Dutch industrial goods, which were more valuable, for the cheaper raw materials from the towns and villages at the base of their pyramids. Conveniently, the Dutch supplied these goods, sparing the intermediaries from needing to produce them. Such a position in the intermediate level of the economic hierarchy was very convenient and appreciated by the intermediaries.

Everything found in each of the sub-pyramids was also available in Amsterdam. Those offering loans, knowledge of seafaring, trade expertise, military protection for goods in transit, and many other services flocked to this central hub. There was no need for conquest or coercion; instead, the economic pyramids of other cities sought to become sub-pyramids of Amsterdam. The transit trade that had always existed in cities was elevated to new heights. The production of the United Provinces (as the Netherlands came to be known) constituted a small portion of the goods moved and exchanged within the Dutch economic world; the majority consisted of transit goods. Consequently, the efforts of other countries' enterprises, rather than competing, bolstered Dutch economic dominance and further enriched the United Provinces.

As enterprises flocked to the Dutch economic pyramid, becoming part of this vast network of trade relations, none could challenge the dominance of those in the United Provinces. The Dutch controlled the connections between each sub-pyramid, with their warehouses serving as the primary hubs for goods that changed hands. This central position gave them complete statistics on the flow of goods, allowing them to understand where items originated, where they were headed, and how to maximize their benefits from these transactions. Crucially, Dutch enterprises, backed by their wealth, consistently had funds available for prepayment—they would often pay a year in advance to produce goods or the cultivation of necessary products. Producers appreciated these loans, as they enabled them to acquire essential raw materials and more. In this arrangement, everyone benefited, but most of all, it was the Dutch who thrived.

The monopolisation of even the most insignificant link in the production chain raises the enterprises of this link to the top of the pyramid, into which this chain turns.

For example, the owners of production enterprises in German countries or Switzerland believed that creating high-value products was paramount. They assumed that by selling these goods, they would always have enough revenue to pay for the services of those who deliver them raw materials and buy their products. However, it was the Dutch who held a dominant position in this scenario, as they not only supplied raw materials for production but also bought from them their final products. And their auxiliary function suddenly became the main and most profitable. Similarly, agricultural producers in Eastern Europe and Latin America thought that their role in producing food was of utmost importance, something essential for survival. Yet, the sheer number of producers meant that they could not leverage their position effectively against the Dutch, who operated on a different scale and with greater market influence. Producers in regions around the Indian Ocean also believed they were the linchpins of the spice trade, an industry that enjoyed global demand. They tended to outsource transportation and marketing, viewing these tasks as secondary. However, the Dutch, having pushed the Portuguese out of the Indian Ocean, had monopolized these crucial links. This monopolization of the exchange of goods and services ultimately allowed Amsterdam to ascend to the peak of the global economic pyramid, establishing it as the world's center for trade and commerce. By controlling the flow and exchange of goods, the Dutch positioned themselves as indispensable players in the global economy, transforming their auxiliary roles into the most lucrative and influential positions within the network of international trade.

Formation of the foot of the global economic pyramid

In the sixteenth century, a significant economic transformation was underway in Europe. As free wage labor in agriculture and land leases began to replace the traditional peasant tribute system in Western Europe, serfdom took root in Eastern Europe and Latin America[87]. However, the nature and severity of serfdom in Eastern Europe proved to be much harsher compared to the "true" feudalism observed in the West.

In Western Europe, feudalism was characterized by subsistence agriculture, where lords extracted a portion of the agricultural output to support themselves and fulfill their roles in local governance, law enforcement, and military defense. The lord's claims on the peasants' production were largely defined by the need to maintain livelihood of those peasants during lean years, resulting in a relatively balanced relationship between lords and serfs. The reason for this was that the global economic system did not yet exist.

In contrast, Eastern European lords began to adopt more aggressive capitalist practices by the sixteenth century, and they did so because the emergence of a world economic system opened the possibility for them to sell their products on the world market[88]. This shift transformed the peasant's relationship with the land; rather than merely working a plot of land under the lord's jurisdiction, peasants effectively became the property of the landlord, bound to work the land and produce surplus for the market. Consequently, the spread of serfdom in Eastern Europe largely originated from the points of contact between the East and the West, especially through Baltic ports. The demand for grain and other agricultural products fostered conditions that led to the legislation and social structures necessary for the establishment of serfdom. This expansion can be tracked through its historical progression: serfdom first took root in Prussia and the Polish-Lithuanian Commonwealth during the fifteenth century, later spreading to Hungary and Austria in the sixteenth century, and finally reaching its full expression in the seventeenth century across East Germany, the Czech Republic, and Muscovy.

At the same time, "monopolistic tendencies of the Dutch fleet gradually led to the ruin of the fleets of the Baltic towns, including that of Gdansk, Poland's chief port."[89] Thus, the cycle was intensifying, and breaking it became increasingly difficult: the more crafts and then industry developed in the West, the more they degraded in the East. Consequently, Eastern Europe increasingly specialized in the export of agricultural products and raw materials.

Similar processes took place in the American colonies of Spain and Portugal. There, state encomiendas were established, where natives worked for a salary—this arrangement was achieved through agreements with natives leaders. However, if the natives refused to work voluntarily, the use of state-sanctioned force was permitted.[90]

Over time, the encomiums fell under the control of their managers, who became their masters in practice, if not officially. These private owners transformed the encomiendas into forms resembling Eastern European serfdom, as they produced not for the needs of the local market, or even Spain, but for the demands of the Western European economy.

As Western Europe ascended, Eastern Europe declined, and these two processes were interlinked—they conditioned and reinforced each other. Simultaneously, this dynamic laid the groundwork for the continued backwardness of Latin America and the countries of the Indian Ocean.

THE FIRST REBELLIONS

**The dooming force of economic circumstances
and rebellion against them**

King Charles I inherited a diverse array of unrelated European territories from his parents and grandparents. Among the primary components of this political super-pyramid were the Spanish kingdoms, the Netherlands, the Kingdom of Naples, Sicily, Austria, most of the lands in the Balkans, etc. Thus, for the king, Spain was merely one part of his vast possessions, and he approached the situation with an eye toward maximizing the benefits of his entire political and economic influence across this expansive pyramid.

In his view, Spain's vast grazing lands, coupled with the Netherlands' limited uncultivated land but robust production of woolen products, made it practical for Spanish enterprises to send their collected wool to the Netherlands. This arrangement aligned well with the interests of large agricultural enterprises, which enjoyed guaranteed profits from wool exports. However, this unimpeded import of Dutch goods into Spain stifled the growth of local production. Yet, the king had this production base in his other territory, the Netherlands.

But now, with the loss of the Netherlands, Spain, like a skittish mare, was trying to throw off its rider—that is, Dutch control over trade. Trade bans were announced, and Dutch ships were confiscated, yet the rider remained firmly in place. All bans were either rescinded or enforced only for show. Portuguese traders even sold their names to the Dutch for signage, benefitting from the arrangement. Most importantly, Spain and its colonies continued to need the same materials as before. Spain feared that the Netherlands would begin importing from other countries goods, which had previously been supplied by Spain, potentially leaving it without export opportunities and supplying Spain's enemies. Proud Spain, fully aware of its prestige as the largest empire in the world, found itself obliged to export its wool for processing to its adversaries—the Dutch. Moreover, it had to do this on the Dutch ships and pay them the privilege, knowing that this money financed the anti-Spanish struggle in the Netherlands. <u>Spain seemingly failed to notice its descent into economic servitude.</u>

Economic revolt often goes unnoticed. However, it becomes evident when contrasting different behaviors.

In earlier times, England faced a situation where its enterprises increasingly focused on exporting wool to the Netherlands. However, King Edward III (reigning from 1327 to 1377) sought to change this dynamic. At the outset of the Hundred Years' War, he took advantage of the position of the Count of Flanders, a vassal of the French king, and banned the export of wool to Flanders in 1336. Since England already supplied wool to Flemish cities, they were already on England's side, but Edward's actions further incited an uprising in Flanders and led to its defection to England. This desperate act prompted the resumption of wool imports from England to Flanders, but at much higher prices, and came with the stipulation that the Flemish would provide loans for the war to the English king.[91] Flemish towns issued loans at exorbitant interest rates, but the king was not inclined to repay them. By inflating wool prices and failing to repay loans, Edward strangled Flemish production while simultaneously encouraging Flemish craftsmen to migrate to England. As a result, by the end of the fourteenth century, Flemish production had collapsed.

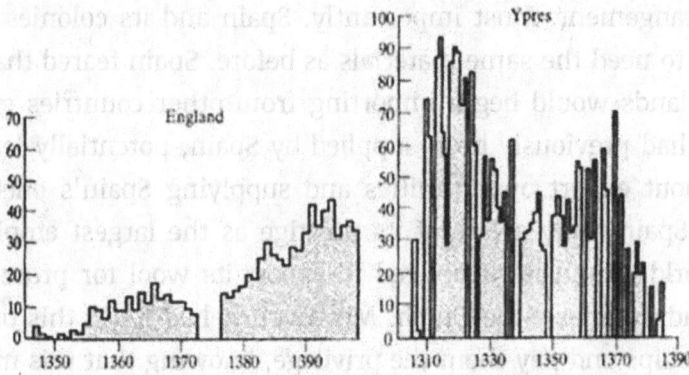

2.2 Trends in the Cloth Trade: Shipments from England and Production at Ypres (thousands of cloths)

Source: Giovanni Arrighi, " The Long Twentieth Century.
Money, Power and the Origins of our Times";
Verso, London, New York, 2010, pg. 101

By settling Flemish craftsmen in Worsted and North Walsham, England initiated its own weaving production using English wool. Later, under Henry VII (reigning from 1485 to 1509), this policy was further solidified with the introduction of bans on the export of raw wool and even finished fabric, allowing only finished clothing to be exported. In other words, government intervention in the economy promoted the production of final products and prevented England from becoming merely a source of raw materials for others. Additionally, Henry VII encouraged traders to export their goods independently, thereby reducing England's reliance on Hanseatic and Italian intermediaries. This approach allowed the state to 1) artificially close the economy into an internal cycle and 2) stimulate the development of crafts. As a result, England soon became a major, and ultimately the largest, supplier of woolen cloth and clothing, paving the way to becoming the first industrialized country in the world[92].

Thus, both England and Spain were wool suppliers to produce woolen goods in the Netherlands. However, the key difference lay in the approaches of their respective states. The English state actively intervened in the economy through state prohibitions and incentives, successfully pulling the country out of the bottom of the emerging Dutch economic pyramid. In contrast, the Spanish state not only failed to this process but, in fact, facilitated the integration of the Spanish economy into a "common economic space" with far more developed economy of the Netherlands. This disparity in state intervention and economic strategy ultimately determined the different fates of England and Spain*

The dooming force of economic circumstances and a lucky break

The French northern cities flourished similarly to those in Flanders, which facilitated a transition from serfdom to lease in this region in the 12th and 13th centuries. This region became a harmonious peak of the economic pyramid, receiving grain and other food products from England and other countries. At that time, France was significantly ahead of England in economic development. However, in the mid- 14th century, French lords began to make attempts to revert to serfdom. This shift may seem like an unexpected setback if one overlooks the fact that Flanders had been occupied by France in 1305, which integrated

---

* as noted, the Spanish state, after the Dutch Revolution, tried to remedy the situation, but very hesitantly and inconsistently, because then it became incomparably more difficult to achieve economic independence

French agricultural enterprises into a common economic space with the cities of Flanders. This integration inevitably transformed the economy of northern France into a raw material appendage of Flanders.

Conversely, this was a time of prosperity and wealth for Flanders. Its more developed economy coexisted with the less developed French economy, leading to significant growth in production. For example, data from the city of Ypres indicate that production volumes increased two or even three times. The profits from trade at this time were so substantial that Flanders could afford to erect statues of the Mother of God and the Child in ivory.[93]

At the end of the 15th century, France lost Flanders, prompting Louis XI to take action to protect the domestic market and promote domestic producers (protectionism). This shift marked a turning point—crafts and industry began to rise again in France, and serfdom began to recede. Yet, it was too late. Having been integrated into a single economic space with a more developed economy, France, which had once been ahead of England, began to lag in economic development.

The presence of a weak economy alongside a strong one has historically benefited the stronger economy, regardless of which holds the political center. The political and economic pyramids do not always align, which can be considered a fundamental law of political economy. Nevertheless, state actions can alter this dynamic, as seen in ancient Rome and more recently France. This, too, can be regarded as a law of political economy.

DEPLOYMENT OF THE FIRST REBELLION

With the emergence of economic peaks, countries had a choice and had to choose

Since about the sixteenth century, countries have had to choose: either to give their agricultural enterprises an easy opportunity to get rich by satisfying foreign demand for agricultural products and to buy craft products with the profits received; or to try to establish craft and manufacturing production at home, ignoring such an attractive foreign demand for agricultural goods and such an easy opportunity to make a profit by satisfying it. Many did not even recognize this choice and followed the prevailing trend, while only a few saw the option clearly—and even fewer had the resolve to defy the current. This environment paved the way for The choice shaped each country's position in the economic pyramid, determining whether they would rise to the peak of the hierarchy or remain at its base. Ultimately, this decision unknowingly set the standard of living for entire nations.

The British became a great nation because of the choice they made at the time

In the fourteenth and fifteenth centuries, English enterprises were quite happy with the opportunities offered by the rise of Dutch cities. These cities needed wool and English enterprises were happy to be able to provide it. This situation gave rise to the famous enclosures: lords with a business mindset began to take away the land common to the whole community from the peasants (enclosing it) and start grazing sheep on it. "In England, the movement for enclosure began in the 12th century and proceeded rapidly in the period 1450–1640, when the goal was mainly to increase the amount of full-time pasturage available to manorial lords"[94]. If the lords did not have such business acumen, then the most enterprising peasants began to do it, with the same result. In other words, the process was quite similar to the processes that took place in Eastern Europe and should have had the same result—serfdom and centuries of economic lag. This did not happen because the English state intervened and challenged this fate.

The will of fate was the will of the free market, and English kings since the 15th century have been diligently defying it. During the War of the Roses (1455-1485), Edward IV, based on a difficult conflict, received permission from Parliament for the lifetime right to collect customs duties (and thus made it possible for the state to influence foreign trade). At the same time, he pursued a policy of state encouragement of trade and industry. He also banned the export of the most valuable varieties of wool. In this way, he forcibly stimulated the development of cloth production. Since the country was embedded in the foundations of the Hanseatic and Venetian economic pyramids, the essence of which was to control the trade of all with all, he made efforts to ensure that only English merchants exported English cloth to the Netherlands and Italy.

To be able to effectively influence the economic processes in the country, the state had to become the strongest pyramid of socio-economic influence. To do this, the next king, Henry VII, Edward's rival, who eventually established himself on the throne, "razed to the ground the castles of rebellious magnates, decisively suppressed several rebellions of the nobility . . . The confiscated lands and estates of the rebels significantly replenished the royal treasury and were partially distributed to supporters of Henry VII"[95]. He thus strengthened state ownership in England. He established a new, "Tudor Nobility," consisting of representatives of the small or middle nobility—those who had helped him win the war. Having taken over the enterprises from the magnates, this 'new gentry' turned to commodity production on their new estates, raised sheep, traded profitably in wool and other products of their enterprises, and began to successfully use hired labor to cultivate the land, rapidly increasing their income.

Most importantly, Henry continued the protectionist policy

of his rival: he banned the export of not only wool but also raw cloth (encouraging manufacturers to complete the production cycle in England rather than send semi-finished products abroad). The so-called Navigation Acts made by Henry and his son encouraged English merchants to transport goods themselves, rather than outsource the export of goods to foreigners.

During the reign of Elizabeth I, the state actively encouraged the development of the mining and metallurgical industries by establishing joint-stock companies on the state's initiative and with state participation. The state provided special subsidies for shipbuilding. Patents and licenses for breaking through workshop traditions were actively granted in the areas of "new technologies"—in the production of glass, paper, cotton fabrics, etc. The policy aimed at promoting the export of finished goods was deepened—the transportation of some goods was generally allowed only on English ships with most of the crews made up of English sailors. In this way, government measures were driving out the now Dutch competitors of English companies. Finally, the state itself was actively investing in merchant transactions.

The state's protectionist policy led to the fact that from the beginning of the sixteenth century, it was no longer raw materials such as grain and wool that were exported from England, but rather the finished product, cloth. In the middle of the sixteenth century, cloth exports accounted for 81.6% of all English exports[96].

It is important to note that the state of England at that time was able to make its own independent choice The implementation of such a policy naturally encountered resistance from both the economic pinnacle of the world and domestic economies that had already managed to "fit in" with the schemes introduced by the Dutch. For example, in 1614, James I banned the export of undyed clothing from England. He was outraged by the fact that the Dutch dyed English clothes and then charged 47% of the sale price. He wanted English manufacturers to dye their clothes and keep all the profit. However, the Dutch responded by banning the import of dyed clothing. Then England responded by banning the export of wool (the raw material for Dutch clothing). Three years later, English exports fell by a third and the government had to repeal the laws in 1617.[97] Of course, it was the dissatisfaction of domestic enterprises that had to lead to such a result. The same fate befell the Navigation Act, adopted in 1651, which prohibited foreign ships from bringing to England products not produced in their countries. Of course, it was adopted specifically against the Dutch, who went up the rivers that passed through their territory and exported products from Germany and Switzerland. But already in 1667, England agreed to consider these countries to be the "hinterland" of the Netherlands. These examples were the result of the fact that England did not yet have the capabilities of its own to replace Dutch services and Dutch ships carrying essential goods from around the world, and their credit, which was so popular with English merchants. Nevertheless, the struggle of the English state was not entirely in vain: the Dutch were forced to refuse to import goods that did not originate in Dutch ports to England.

To be able to pursue its policy despite economic resistance, the state had to be strong and independent. In parallel with the events described above, the conquest of Ireland took place, which lasted for the entire sixteenth century. During this period, the state constantly conquered Irish lands, which were later distributed as a reward to the nobility, which maintained the position of the state as the most influential pyramid of socio-economic influence. In the middle of the sixteenth century, during the state-sponsored Reformation (1536-1540), enormous wealth was confiscated (in favor of the state), primarily the lands of the church and all monastic orders. Most of this land was also gradually distributed to the nobility, but the rest was leased by the state. It was during this period that the absolutist monarchy began to take shape in England. And the strengthening of state ownership played an important role in this. The state used its primacy in the distribution of society's efforts to lead its country to the peak of the global economic pyramid (at least, as a start, to pull it out of the bottom of the Dutch pyramid).

The choice made by England at that time was a choice of rebellion—a rebellion against fate, a rebellion against the role that the free market attributed to it.

The second stage of rebellion

At the first stage of the rebellion, England formed an independent national economy, i.e. an economy where English households exchanged goods and services with each other and did not need foreign services and goods. But many other countries were also behind walls that separated them from Holland, whether they were walls of protectionism (as in France) or walls of distance, as in Asia. Their subsequent experience showed that isolation from the world's leading economic pyramid by itself only leads to economic lagging behind. Former advanced zones of the Earth's civilization: China, India, and the Ottoman Empire were pushed back into the past by the rapid economic development of Europe, into a lag, both economic and military. This eventually led them to the foundation of the Western European political and economic pyramid.

The rise of cities came at the expense of the countryside.

After the economies of the Dutch cities had risen above the surrounding rural areas, the further rise of the Dutch cities to the peak of the world economy was at the expense of the economies of other countries (both rural and urban). England did not have its economic pyramid, and its enterprises had no one to rise at the expense of after the rise of domestic enterprises had largely exhausted itself in the 16th century.

Most importantly, this path was unable to raise English cities to the level of Dutch cities, which relied on the global economic pyramid. Unable to compete with it, English enterprises began to form their own, separate, isolated economic pyramid, with trade within it taking place between English enterprises in the metropolis and English enterprises in the colonies. The English did not have to fight with others for these newly formed "countries" and did not have to push the Dutch out of them. It was their garden, and they ruled it. And it became their "world," which they turned into their economic pyramid, with Britain at the peak. Of course, it was still a small 'world'. But it was theirs. In which no one else was allowed. In it, Britain could increase the strength and size of its economic pyramid to challenge the Dutch pyramid. But not just to challenge, but to be ready and able to intercept the connections of the decaying previous economic center. Or, in other words, to move the peak of the existing economic pyramid of the world to London.

The Amsterdam peak of the pyramid was, first, a giant transshipment base, a massive warehouse where incoming goods were unloaded and from where goods destined for all parts of the world already involved in the globalized world were loaded. And next to it, a new, similar peak of the (even smaller) pyramid was already being built, where goods came and went from the colonies and to the colonies. But this was not enough. London began to resemble Amsterdam at the peak only when

England began to re-export colonial goods, taking them all over Europe. Because re-export was the essence of the Dutch economic pyramid. But at the initial stage, the more powerful capabilities of the Dutch enterprises needed not to wrest their colonies from the English hands. For this purpose, special laws were subsequently issued (for example, the Navigation Acts of the 1660s), which prohibited the colonies from purchasing goods from other countries and selling their products to non-English traders (although reality corrected this trade into a triangular trade, which still included third countries as the third corner).

Sure, at first, the sparsely populated and economically weak colonies could hardly really affect the economic growth of the much larger England. But what was important was that, first, the path was paved, and it has been expanding ever since. And secondly, the fact that exports were growing steadily (to begin within the port cities) was important. Exports, which were constantly growing, were an incentive to improve production. The English economy had a good outlook, assessed risk as low, and could invest more boldly in production and, in particular, in improving technological processes. And, even more importantly, only in such conditions could the famous Smithian specialization of workers in the workplace emerge—in conditions of almost guaranteed sales and encouragement to improve (otherwise, craftsmen would be afraid of losing their versatility).

So, this spontaneous tactic was to create more non-craft enterprises outside of England, which could be used to grow the craft and trade enterprises of the metropolis. In the end, this is another way of saying that the tactic was to create as many enterprises as possible at the base of the separated British economic pyramid to make the enterprises at the peak rise faster and larger.

The second stage of the revolt was a private initiative

The aforementioned "tactic" was not a well-thought-out plan. English households began to show interest in the colonization of North America in the early seventeenth century. They invested money in starting a business in the New World and transporting people there. In many cases, people paid for their transportation. At first, English enterprises hoped to find gold in the lands not yet occupied by the Spanish, but when they did not find it, they almost immediately switched to other goods that were "lying on the surface." At first, it was high-quality wood (especially suitable for shipbuilding), a little later tobacco, and even later sugar, fur, rum, cotton, indigo, and iron. These goods yielded such high profits that they fully paid for all the money invested. Moreover, these profits attracted new enterprises and new colonists (workers for these enterprises).

So the colonization was carried out on the initiative and at the expense of private enterprises. But we need to take into account two things. First, this could only happen after the state created the conditions in which these enterprises became independent of the current world leader and were able to grow successfully. Second, this could only happen after the Spanish and Portuguese state-owned economies were able to overcome the risk of the unknown—that is, uncertainty. Uncertainty carries too much risk, and private economies are usually unable to take such a risk, especially when it requires the capital of not just one desperate entrepreneur, but a large number of pooled capitals. Thus, we see that private initiative came into play only after a sufficiently long and targeted government action.

Third stage of rebellion

When the English independent economic pyramid was built in parallel with the global economic pyramid of the United

Provinces, the economic struggle between them began to regularly turn into a political one, exploding into wars. And these wars were waged on behalf of their economies by their states. The three major Anglo-Dutch wars decided the case in favor of the United Kingdom (Britain).

But so far, the wars of other states against the United Provinces have always ended in disaster for these states. The power of the United Provinces lay not only in the fact that they were able to buy the services of numerous mercenaries and to convert countries to ally with them by making lucrative business offers. The power of the United Provinces also lay in the fact that none of the countries wanted the United Provinces to fall to others.

However, the United Kingdom was able to defeat the United Provinces and push them off the peak of the global economic pyramid. The reason for this was that the United Kingdom was already able to offer itself as a substitute for the Dutch peak. Even before the victory in the wars, the United Kingdom was confidently transforming its separate independent economic pyramid into another global pyramid.

The United Provinces: Economic treason

The formation of the Dutch economic pyramid could not have been successful if Spanish enterprises, in agreement with their state, had stopped trading with the United Provinces. But they benefited from this trade and continued it. This economic betrayal of the interests of their country helped Dutch enterprises survive the hardships of the struggle for independence from Spain and the later period of initial growth.

But the collapse of the Dutch pyramid itself might not have happened (or would have happened much later) if it had not been for the betrayal of their own enterprises. When the Dutch enterprisers saw that English enterprises were making as good a profit as their own, they began to invest some of their capital in English enterprises. And the more and more painfully the English fleet continued to defeat the Dutch naval power and seize control of the sea routes, the more and more Dutch capital flowed into English enterprises. Dutch capital "changed horses".

Once upon a time, when Greek poleis were in decline, their enterprises fled to the more successful poleis of the Hellenistic states. Others fled to the surrounding villages. When the Roman poleis declined, there was nowhere to flee to, and the enterprisers (i.e., master craftsmen) could only move to the surrounding villages with their enterprises or simply become employees of proto-feudal enterprises. Now, at a time when banks and corporations already existed, enterprises did not have to run away with their owners and workers to foreign lands. They simply had to transfer their capital to enterprises in foreign lands. Treason against one's country was becoming easier and more invisible. That is why it began earlier when Dutch rule was still undisputed, and its decline was not guaranteed. Even then, "Dutch merchants, annoyed by the V.O.C. and jealous of its privileges, should have launched, or supported with their capital, rival Indies companies—in England, Denmark, Sweden, France... they should have invested money in French privateering out of Dunkirk, which was occasionally directed against ships belonging to their compatriots."[98] The Dutch sold weapons to their enemies, with which these enemies attacked them. And "[d]uring the War of the Spanish Succession, payments to the French troops fighting in Italy were made [from France] through Amsterdam, to the infuriation of the English who were allied to the Dutch against France."[99]

From the point of view of the Dutch economy, they were

90

simply fighting for their place in the sun. From the point of view of private success, it did not matter whether they invested in transactions within the Dutch pyramid scheme the English pyramid scheme, or even some other scheme. But, from the point of view of the confrontation of economic pyramids, their capital going into the English pyramid strengthened the opponent and weakened their country's pyramid. But enterprises do not know patriotism, they are looking for an opportunity and it is not rational to miss it. If Bolivar can't stand two, then the saddle must be one*.

Thus, the rise of Britain consisted of three steps. It is noteworthy that while the first two steps were the result of the efforts of the British themselves (the state and the economies), the third step was already assisted by the enterprises of other countries and even the enterprises of the peak. This assistance would not have happened if not for the success of the first two steps.

The United Provinces: A betrayal of the future
By investing in the enterprises of competing countries, Dutch enterprises were betraying their country in a direct, obvious way. But there was another kind of betrayal. The United Provinces had risen on trade-connecting producers with each other in the exchange of their goods. Their own production was weak. And the Dutch enterprises did not invest in its development. They had high wages at the peak of the world. It was more expedient to establish the necessary new enterprises where wages were lower and where it was easier to get to by waterways. Such a favorite "place" was the villages along the Rhine and Meuse, where Dutch merchants delivered the necessary raw materials

* A quote from O'Henry's "The Roads We Take." Gives an image of a cynical approach to business

(and money in advance for future products) and then brought the finished goods down to the warehouses in Amsterdam. This system helped maintain the position of the United Provinces at the peak of the global economic pyramid. But in this way, Dutch enterprises sowed the seeds of the future rise in the German states, Switzerland, and partly France. Later, when Dutch trade dominance ended, the United Provinces were left in the lurch–Dutch enterprises helped boost production in other countries, but not in their own. It was to their advantage.

In addition, Dutch enterprises profited from the direct sale of technologies.[100] Everywhere in Europe, from the west to the east, you could find villages of Dutch people working on the organization of protective dams or drainage works, or weaving, or building ships for someone, or doing other useful things in which the Dutch were ahead. Although the money paid for wisdom further strengthened the economic power of the United Provinces, the distance between Holland and its competitors in terms of technology and culture was inexorably shrinking. An exquisite network of trade relations, and a huge pyramid of financial domination, grew and, to a certain extent, continued to be based on technical advancement and a superior culture of production. And this base was steadily eroded by the efforts of Dutch companies.

The Dutch enterprises retained the defining economy of their time, i.e. trade. But by giving away production, they were giving away the future-defining economy, just as the Portuguese once did when they gave away their trade to the Dutch. Such a betrayal was not obvious and was made unwittingly, but even today, when this kind of betrayal of the future is already obvious, many countries give away their industry in exchange for transitory advantages.

Eastern Europe

In the Rzeczpospolita, as in Hungary, the state did not see the need to oppose the trade of its enterprises with those of the economic peak. After all, Eastern European trade was very profitable at the time. These states believed that the enrichment of private enterprises in this trade was the enrichment of the country. But the enterprises, which were getting stronger, were losing their temper. "The rise of a Polish wheat-exporting economy meant, as we have seen, the rise of large domains with coerced cash-crop labor. It meant also the rise of the political strength of the nobility, whose economic interest in removing obstacles to trade matched that of Western European merchants. Their combined efforts maintained Poland as an open economy."[101]

Thus, the economies of Eastern European countries grew successfully. But this growth had three main consequences: 1. These countries increasingly fell behind Western Europe in economic development. 2. The importation of handicraft goods from Western Europe was killing the development of Eastern European cities. The cities, which initially also participated in the parliaments of these countries, eventually lost this right. This development was inevitable because, in this economy, domestic cities were declining. Their influence was also declining. Agriculture ruled unchallenged and serfdom became the norm. 3. Such a powerful development of private economies in the conditions of free trade led to the fact that a powerful oligarchy took over the power in the parliaments (Sejm, Diet). "In anticipation of John Locke, the noble estate "proclaimed their right to defend the welfare of the kingdom even against the king should he seek to act in opposition to the common interest".[102] The Polish-Lithuanian Commonwealth and Hungary, along with England, are the first harbingers of modern democracy. They were the first countries where house-holds constitutionally forced the state to listen to them. This meant that the states of these countries, which had previously chosen not to intervene in the course of events, were now unable to intervene even if they wanted to.

The involvement of Eastern European economies at the foot of the Western European economic pyramid enriched them and increased their socioeconomic influence. This led to the democratization of these countries. And this, in turn, led to the inability of the state to speak the lag. Moreover, this led to a lack of understanding that the situation needs to change.

The United Kingdom: The revolt of the enterprises and the coming of democracy

England's economic pyramid, which it was gradually building, was beginning to bear fruit in the form of foreign capital that was drawn to England as a place for reliable capital investment. And most importantly, the main rival, the United Provinces, was finally pushed off the peak. In this situation, entrepreneurs (both industrial, commercial, and agricultural owners) gradually increased sales of their products, especially abroad, and were interested in strengthening existing trends. Now that most enterprises were working for English exports and were no longer interested in working for Dutch imports, the interests of different types of enterprises were no longer opposed. Moreover, as agrarian owners invested their earned capital in trade and industry, and industrial owners bought agricultural enterprises to acquire a noble title, the distinction between them became blurred. In addition, as English enterprises grew stronger and dominated the world, their need for protection from their state or its assistance decreased. Therefore, the need for an arbitrator and protector, in the state, decreased. Therefore, it is not surprising that in the middle of the seventeenth century in England there was a revolt of enterprises—the English Civil War or revolution.

The point of such an economic revolt was to remove the independent state from governing the country. Initially, this was a complete radical removal of the independent state in the form of the execution of the king (in 1649). But perhaps because the dictatorship of Cromwell that followed was much harsher than the rule of the executed king, it was decided to return royal power over time. But now only as the executor of the will of the enterprises—large enterprises sent their representatives to parliament and they decided among themselves all the issues of governing the country, and the king led the executive branch—the government. With the rise of England (already the United Kingdom) to the peak of the global economic pyramid, the influence of an independent state on the economy was finally over—the king was left with purely ceremonial functions.

The situation at the peak of the world's economic pinnacle was ideal, and state intervention could no longer improve the situation, but could only spoil the ideal.

The United Kingdom would never have become a global economic leader without a strong state that was able to lead the economy against the fate of being at the bottom of someone else's economic pyramid. However, after reaching the peak, the state became unnecessary and even dangerous. The ideal was achieved, and the state's initiative could have ruined everything. The Moor had done his duty, the Moor can go.

United Kingdom: Borrowing (theft)

The new Navigation Acts required that foreign ships entering Britain carry only their domestic goods. That is, they were not to re-export, which the United Kingdom wanted to keep for itself. Concerning its colonies, the United Kingdom strengthened the Navigation Acts by prohibiting them from trading directly with other countries, let alone transporting their goods on foreign ships. All colonial trade had to go through Britain (even when the colonies traded with each other). So, everything was done to ensure that goods flowed to Britain, on British ships, stored in British warehouses, insured by British insurance companies, and that loans for the purchase of goods or ship repairs were taken out from British banks. And each of these elements brought its separate profit. British colonies and factories in the key straits and ports of the world provided services to ships and traders from other countries and made a solid profit for this. The result of all this was that by the end of the 17th century, re-exports began to reach one-third of all British exports.[103]

Trade statistics of the time clearly show that the big jump in exports of British products in the mid-18th century coincided with a decline in re-exports[104]. The United Kingdom was the center of trade in its economic world and knew which goods went where in what quantities and for what price. Therefore, its enterprises knew what goods in what quantities made sense to produce and where to ship them. British private enterprises knew that the enterprises at the bottom of the global economic pyramid did not. This knowledge provided British entrepreneurs with the ability to properly assess risk.

Increased exports provided an opportunity for economies of scale to manifest themselves. Products made from the same patterns and reproduced in many thousands of copies greatly reduced production costs. Thanks to these economies of scale, British products became cheaper and, as a result, conquered foreign markets even more widely.

A valley must steal from the peak to get to the peak, which is what King Edward III of England did when he moved Flemish masters to

England. The rise of the Greats has always begun with theft. But the mountain no longer needs to steal from the valley, because the valley itself brings its knowledge to it—that's how traders from the valley countries brought knowledge about where things are produced and sold to England along with their goods. However, was England not committing theft when it used this knowledge without paying for it?

The two most important conclusions that should stay with us from this chapter are the following. First. The British economic recovery went through three stages: I. The separation of its market from the existing world market, which allowed the emergence of domestic industry; II. Formation of a self-dependent market (its economic pyramid), which allowed the development of the most important industries of the time; III. Use of the strengthened economies of the crucial industries to capture the global economic pyramid, i.e. to displace the previous leader. Second. The formation of the global pyramid contributed to the establishment of democracy in the world. At the peak were established the enterprises (or better to say enterprises) of the crucial economy, which had a common interest in strengthening exports, as well as enterprises that imported agricultural and mining products for the needs of export industries and the population. Their combined economic power, based on their dominance in the world, gave them the ability to withstand state power. The result was the establishment of either a republic or a tame monarchy (i.e., a constitutional monarchy). In the valley, the agricultural and mining industries, as well as the service industries that the exporting enterprises of the mountain had in this country, were strengthened. Their common interest in preserving this situation, as well as their economic power as the largest enterprises in the country, gave them the ability to resist state power and contributed to democratization. This democratization also helped to consolidate these enterprises and their countries at the bottom of the global economic pyramid.

So, British domination of the world was the result of British rebellion against the fate of being at the bottom of someone else's economic pyramid. But having risen to the peak of its economic pyramid, Britain itself faced the rebellions of the countries it placed at the bottom.

CONTINENTAL SYSTEM

Of course, the French Revolution had many causes. But from a political economy point of view, it began as a revolt against France's slide into a subordinate role to the United Kingdom, against being embedded in its economic pyramid. Eventually, it became a struggle for France's leading position in the European economic world. The specific trigger, to a large extent, was the signing of the 1786 Free Trade Agreement with the United Kingdom. The connection was not direct and probably not realized by most people—the agreement was canceled only in the fourth year of the revolution. But the point is that the influx of British goods undermined French industry, especially in the north, and caused unemployment, economic crisis, and unrest. All this eventually led to the revolutionary explosion. The United Kingdom's assistance to the French counterrevolution led to the decrees of 1793 and 1796 aimed at combating British goods.

It was a common practice for the United Kingdom to constantly resort to blockades of European ports during conflicts. Taking advantage of its best navy in the world, the United Kingdom brought its enemies to their knees with almost impunity through naval blockades. And the more the United Kingdom itself accustomed European countries to overseas goods and raw materials and its industrial products, the more intolerable such blockades became. So, according to established practice, the United Kingdom established a blockade of French ports.

But France, after Napoleon's victories over most of Europe,

was not inclined to make concessions. Napoleon, I realized that the power of the United Kingdom rested on its position at the peak of the pyramid of the European economic world, i.e., it was based on ties with the "subordinate" countries that lay "below" in the body of the pyramid. He could not cut off the United Kingdom's ties with the colonies (although he made such plans) and he could cut off its ties with Europe. For this purpose, the Continental Blockade was declared, which prohibited the import of British goods or imposed huge duties on them. The more the coast fell under the influence of Napoleon I, the more comprehensive the Continental Blockade became.

Damage

Given the absolute superiority of the British navy, it is quite obvious that entire industries associated with colonial trade and the servicing of the needs of merchant marines, especially ship construction and equipment, perished. These industries were concentrated in ports serving overseas trade and in areas adjacent to them, especially along the rivers that flowed to these ports. Bordeaux, for example, had 40 refineries before the Revolution and 8 in 1809. The city of Tonnay, to the east, had 700 rope-making enterprises (needed to rig ships) in 1783, 200 in 1801, and none in 1811. Production of linen fabrics across Western Europe decreased by two-thirds[105].

All of these ports, and the industrialized land economies tied to them, were not able to resume their full functioning after the overthrow of Napoleon. But this was a consequence of the complete domination of British maritime trade after his overthrow, as well as the separation of the Latin American colonies from their metropolitan areas and the complete takeover of their trade with Europe by the United Kingdom.

Benefits

But further inland, other trends prevailed. In these areas, which had previously consumed British products, the elimination of the British embargo created two of the most important incentives for production: demand and guaranteed high prices. This allowed local enterprises to establish production. For example, cotton production was already gaining strength in France, Switzerland, Saxony, etc. during the 18th century, but it was mostly manual. Private initiatives, for whatever reason, did not spread spinning devices (jennies). However, starting in 1796 (with the outbreak of the revolutionary wars), mechanization began to move across Europe from France to the interior of the continent—to Bohemia (Czech Republic) and the center of the Austrian Empire. Mechanization was driven by a wheel turned by harnessed mules, a river, or a waterfall. With the official introduction of the Continental Blockade, obtaining British yarn became almost impossible, and from that time on there was a boom in the introduction of spinning and weaving machines. In France, yarn production roughly doubled from 1806 to 1808 and doubled again by 1810[106]. A strong impetus for mechanized weaving was given in Alsace and Saxony (where the number of mule-driven spinning looms increased from 13,000 in 1806 to 256,000 in 1813). Even on the left bank of the Rhine, where mechanization was practically unknown before 1806, mechanization grew from a few mechanical machines to one and a half million during the years of the blockade. It was only with the introduction of high tariffs that French enterprises began to invest in expanding steel production. The enthusiasm of entrepreneurs grew so much that the state even began to try to avoid the dispersal of available capital and encouraged the formation of larger enterprises by granting concessions for the development of ores and coal to only a limited number of enterprises[107] (the prototype of the later cultivation of national champions).

Further east

During the blockade, the economy of the riverside territories flourished. Even though the enterprises suffered greatly from the disappearance of necessary raw materials and semi-finished products, one-fifth of the population was involved in industrial (primarily textile) enterprises. The concentration of production also reached a significant level. Of the 1200-1300 enterprises that employed 125,000 people, the largest 46 employed 17,000.[108] Steam-driven spinning machines, which had long been used in the United Kingdom, were first introduced in Aachen, in present-day North Rhine-Westphalia, in 1812.[109] In neighboring Krefeld, the textile mills of the von Der Lehn family alone employed 3,000 workers.[110] The entire region experienced rapid expansion in metallurgy and textile production.

The most remote sector of the continental blockade

In the Russian Empire, the blockade lasted the shortest time and was implemented with the least persistence. The Russian Empire was "joined" to the continental blockade in 1807 as a result of the defeats at Austerlitz and Friedland. By that time, the Russian Empire had already become quite involved in European trade—from one-third to one-half of all ships calling at St. Petersburg were British[111]. In general, "it can be assumed that in the early 19th century, Russian-English trade accounted for about 25-30% of the turnover of Russian foreign trade (in terms of value)."[112]

Of the goods exported from St. Petersburg, 77% of lard, 80% of bristles, 91% of flax, 42% of wheat, plus other goods in smaller proportions, went to the United Kingdom. All of these were products of the large serfdom enterprises of the Russian aristocracy, which had their estates closer to the capital. This aristocracy's dissatisfaction with the blockade was combined with wounded national pride that the blockade was imposed by the will of the victor. In addition, along with agricultural enterprises, commercial enterprises also suffered. It is therefore not surprising that it was St. Petersburg merchants who had the largest number of complaints about the disastrous consequences of the break with the United Kingdom,[113] which was certainly true.

At the same time, as expected, faint positive trends in Russian industry began to emerge. The number of cotton weaving mills increased from 199 in 1804 to 423 in 1814, even though cotton itself was imported from overseas. It seems that the absence of imported clothing encouraged domestic weaving mills that could work on expensive "neutral" or simply smuggled cotton. When the blockade was lifted, these factories began to strengthen and flourish. No wonder "the main years of growth in the number of these factories were in 1812–1814 when there was no longer any continental blockade."[114] But keep in mind that in 1812–1814, cotton imports were hampered by the American–British War (cotton was primarily imported from the United States). In addition, this leap did not occur before the Continental Blockade, when there was the same free access to cotton from abroad.

The same can be seen in other industries for which data is available. For example, the production of sugar, which was largely imported from abroad, did not change its from 1801 to 1805, but by 1809 it jumped fivefold[115].

The brief absence of good quality and cheap goods from British competitors allowed local entrepreneurs to enter the business. The absence of goods created a high price for them and thus gave them a chance to create new imperfect enterprises with high production costs. Once established, they had to grow, reduce their costs, and improve their quality. The subsequent lifting of the blockade, on the one hand, restored competition from better quality British goods, and on the other hand, resumed the import of colonial raw materials, which gave Russian enterprises a chance to improve their quality.

If we look at the immediate consequences of the continental blockade, it is possible that the losses in trade, customs duties, and difficulties with raw materials at enterprises exceeded the timid sprouts that the industry had produced during the blockade. But from a long-term perspective, the opportunity to develop our industry should look more important. Moreover, the positive consequences (not for the entire economy, but specifically for the industry) were already visible at the time and were reflected in the statements and notes of people of the time. For example, one of these notes prepared in the first half of 1810 notes that trade with England hindered the development of many branches of domestic industry. Producers of various types of material "who have barely begun to appear have been suppressed by English needlework. They had difficulty recovering after the cessation of . . . trade. The calico and printed factories had the same fate."[116]

The Continental Blockade and the United Kingdom

The conclusions for the United Kingdom are quite the opposite—the blockade slowed down the development of the United Kingdom's industry. England experienced two crises in 1808 and 1811. Export revenues for the first quarter of 1808 fell by about a quarter compared to the previous year, and in the second quarter by almost a third.[117] Its export industries were in decline. In Lancashire, riots broke out because of the high cost of food. The ratio of the price of grain (which the United Kingdom imported) to the price of textiles (which it exported) increased on average (domestically) by 41% per year between 1807 and 1814, while in France the ratio of the price of textiles (which it imported) to grain (which it exported) increased on average by 20% per year during the same period.[118] That is, while the introduction of its industry mitigated the effects of the blockade in the valley of the economic pyramid, at the peak, it was difficult to expand the capacity of agriculture.

Nevertheless, the Continental Blockade failed to speak the countries of the continent from falling behind the United Kingdom. While the latter's textile production grew by about four times (based on the amount of cotton processed in factories), France's grew by only three times. This suggests that although development in the United Kingdom slowed down, it continued to be faster than on the continent.[119]

It seems that the peak has a greater margin of safety than the valley. However, this is the secret of its dominance and the severity of the rebellion against it.

Therefore

Napoleon sought to replace British economic domination with French domination. However French industry was not as developed as British industry and was not able to completely replace it and subjugate the economies of other countries. And this gave other European countries a chance to raise their industries.

Perhaps the main consequence of the Continental Blockade was that even after the end of the Napoleonic Wars, customs walls continued to stand in the way of free trade. Their initial removal allowed the arrival of better-quality British goods, which, together with the depreciation of raw materials accumulated on the continent, which had been acquired at exorbitant blockade prices, dealt a crushing blow to the continental industry. This led to the restoration of the customs barrier, but in peacetime, without excesses of wartime caused by the desire to strangle the enemy. It is clear that if the Continental Blockade had been established simply as a factor of economic influence, the positive consequences for the continent would have been much greater because the number of duties could have been adjusted according to needs so that it would have been easier to import raw materials and export industrial products. But since only the war made this experiment possible, it was not perfect. It should be remembered that at the beginning of the 19th century, continental Europe was already threatened with becoming a raw material appendage of the United Kingdom, something similar to what India was turned into.[120]

During the blockade, local industry managed to strengthen. This was especially true of those countries that had been under French rule for the longest time, i.e. France itself, Italy, and the westernmost German states. Industrial enterprises even began to develop in the interior of the United Provinces (Netherlands), whose global economic pyramid was finally destroyed at that time.[121]

After the blockade was lifted, the continent's enterprises gained access to colonial raw materials and were able to improve their quality and reduce their costs. They were under the British press, but they already existed and could fight for existence!

At the same time, the needs of cotton and woolen enterprises gave impetus to the development of machine-building enterprises in cities such as Paris and Mulhouse (France), Liege and Verviers (now Belgium), Essen and Chemnitz (now Germany), and Zurich (Switzerland). They were weak and imperfect compared to the British, but it was a start. The impact of the blockade on the chemical industry, which began to develop due to the lack of colonial raw materials, which were tried to replace with surrogates, should not be forgotten. After the blockade ended, this industry declined, but flourished again later, especially in Germany.[122]

From the point of view of liberal theory, the efforts of continental countries to develop their industrial economies were an irrational waste of resources. It would have been more rational to invest resources in the development of those industries that were needed in the existing market, i.e., the production of raw materials and foodstuffs that the United Kingdom needed. This is true, but the rebellious continental countries (and especially France) did not want to be at the bottom of someone else's economic pyramid.

THE BETRAYAL OF BRITISH ENTERPRISES

British enterprises (British private initiative) flourished under the protection of and with the help of the state intervention in the economy. The instrument of this intervention was primarily the Navigation Acts. In addition, there were bans on the export of certain raw materials, such as wool. This was done to keep the price of wool low in the country and to support a higher price for it abroad. Thus, domestic exports of finished goods had better competitive conditions. On the contrary, the Indian printed calico was banned from importation to promote the establishment of new British enterprises that would produce such products themselves. Almost all goods that were allowed to be imported were subject to significant duties.

Private initiatives have always sought ways to enrich themselves by circumventing government restrictions. Businesses often evaded these laws and smuggling bypassed duties. However, the strength of the state and the island location of the country, which made it easier to control exports and imports, allowed it to implement its decisions and bring the country to the peak.

After England's economy rose to the peak, its state was weakened by economic rebellion, and the betrayal of the enterprises took on a completely different character. An example of such betrayal, in the absence of state control, is the purchase of Louisiana by the United States. Napoleon I put it up for sale because he needed money to organize the landings in the United Kingdom. The acquisition of Louisiana, a huge French territory that stood in the way of the US expansion to the west, was more than desirable for the United States. But they did not have the money for it. And then the British Barings Bank came to the rescue. This bank, together with the bank of the French-occupied United Provinces, sent gold across the Strait to France as soon as it received securities from the United States. This money was used to continue the war with the United Kingdom. But in the long run, it turned out to be more important that France was replaced by the United States as the United Kingdom's main rival in the struggle for the peak of the world economy. And the purchase of Louisiana with British money was a decisive event in the American rise.

But besides this, albeit a significant and isolated betrayal, there were myriads of smaller betrayals that together tirelessly eroded British world domination. In the national interest, the state prohibited the export of the latest technologies, such as looms. It was also forbidden for qualified personnel to emigrate from the country[123]. But a powerful stream of both flowed unrestrainedly to where profits could be made. British enterprises grew the power of future rivals of the British Empire. After all, the horizon of enterprises is tomorrow's income, and the horizon of workers is today's salary. The state's horizon is a distant national perspective, but whether it can implement its plans depends on its independence and power at the peak of the pyramid of socio-economic influence in the country. The oligarchic state of the United Kingdom was no longer such a state.

Enterprises at the bottom of the economic hierarchy benefit from interacting with the peak by satisfying its demand and buying up its sales. Despite this, the state of England managed to impose its national policy on its enterprises and lead the country upward. Other states failed to do so and remained in the bottom. To stay on peak, it is profitable for enterprises to maintain the exclusivity of their technologies. But it is even more profitable for them to export these technologies because it brings profit faster and easier. Only the independence and power of the state can tip the scales in favor of preserving technology. However, the state at the peak is no longer strong and independent of its enterprises. This was once the case with Britain, and it is now the case with the United States.

IDEOLOGY AT THE SERVICE OF THE PERPETUAL MOTION MACHINE

"Perpetual motion machine"

At the end of the 18th century, the already established industry of the United Kingdom no longer needed the protection of the state, under whose cover it had been able to develop for so long in greenhouse-like conditions, protected from more powerful European continental exports (primarily Dutch and French). Now these enterprises were rushing into battle in foreign lands. They no longer needed government subsidies and were hampered by government barriers to imports. This onslaught of industrial enterprises was like hot steam in a metal boiler, tearing through its walls and pulling out the rivets. Under this pressure, the state was forced to open the dampers to let the steam out. And lo and behold, the state created a steam engine for the national economy. The United Kingdom began to buy more foreign raw materials, which enabled it to produce more industrial products and gave other countries more money to buy these products. This gave the British the opportunity and the need to buy more of these raw materials. The flywheel began to spin incessantly. The economy was becoming completely complementary, as Adam Smith wrote about. In this system, everyone was needed and important to each other. The United Kingdom could live less and less without imported raw materials, and other countries could live less and less without British industrial products.

Britain as an ideological leader
Naturally, it was at this time that the idea of a free market became so popular in the kingdom. More than that, the massive decline in production that took place in Britain during the continental blockade clearly showed that the United Kingdom, at the peak of the European economic pyramid, was very much dependent on Europe's openness to trade with it. Watching a hostile empire rally the forces and actions of an entire continent to fight it, Britain naturally came to realize that the ability of any peak of socio-economic influence to maintain its influence over a large territory was both a political and economic threat to it. In this regard, Britain could not but appreciate the new ideas that originated on its territory—economic liberalism.

The United Kingdom's assistance in the struggle for independence in Latin American countries was perhaps the first such conscious support for liberalism. The United Kingdom rightly expected that having freed themselves from Spain, Latin American countries would become completely and indivisibly economically dependent on it. Moreover, in the eyes of Latin Americans (as well as the liberal community in Europe), the United Kingdom became a defender of the freedom of people and democracy. And now, in addition to the owners of large enterprises, who have always been in opposition to their states because of these states' obstacles to free trade with Britain, regiments of rebellious intellectuals were growing behind the rebel states. While the rebel states were rebelling against the world power of the United Kingdom, the liberal rebels were rebelling against the rebellion of their states.

The rebel intellectuals saw the example of liberal freedoms in the United Kingdom and wanted them for their countries. In the struggle for this, they were ready to accept help from the peak—from Britain. They wanted the best-they wanted constitutions and freedoms for their economically weak countries that existed among the leaders of the world. Their states, which were building walls around the countries to become the leaders of the world (and thus to bring the arrival of constitutions and freedoms that existed among the leaders of the world), were becoming enemies and despots for freedom-loving citizens.

Once upon a time, a set of circumstances brought Athens to the economic peak of the world of Greek poleis. As a result of this fact, Athens saw the rise of enterprises that were part of the decisive economy of the time. A millennium later, Britain discovered that cause and effect can be reversed—if you develop the modern decisive economy, you can reach the peak of the world and stay there. This same accidental rise to the economic peak brought Athens the flowering of democracy. Similar processes took place in Britain. In this situation, Britain discovered that an ideology that seems to be one thing from within the country can be quite different when viewed from the outside. And this ideology can be used as a tool of influence. Since then, the propaganda of liberalism (both economic and political) has become a weapon in the hands of the country of the peak.

USA—FORMATION AND ACCELERATION

The first step to the peak

Having freed themselves from the United Kingdom, the colonies of North America formed their own common state, but the one they wanted—a state that did not interfere in their affairs. Among other things, such a state had to "not drink blood from the enterprises"—that is, not collect taxes. Therefore, to exist, the federal state resorted to the method used by medieval monarchs who were unable to collect taxes from their feudal lords. This method was to collect duties at the borders. And each colony was already collecting duties on its borders with each other.

Thus, one of the first decisions of the newly formed United States Congress was the introduction of duties on July 4, 1789. The Customs Administration was the first administration introduced by George Washington (even before the Treasury). Although the main purpose was to generate funds necessary for the existence of the state, the second purpose was to protect local production against cheaper products from the United Kingdom and other European countries (for example, although the average percentage of duties collected on imports was 8.5%, the duty on carriages was 15%). In addition, goods imported on American ships were given a 10% discount.[124] In the 1790s, Alexander Hamilton, urged Americans to protect industry from foreign competition to allow it to grow stronger.[125] These measures did indeed provide opportunities for American production, especially in glass and ceramics, to grow. Before having a chance to fully develop, local enterprises began pressuring the government to strengthen their protection.

A very convenient opportunity for the United States arose during the Napoleonic Wars in Europe. The two sides declared blockades against each other, and both suffered from a shortage of their usual imports. The United States tried its best to compensate both sides for this shortage as a neutral party. This brought considerable profits (contributed to the initial accumulation of capital). But later, because the warring parties began to persecute American ships for helping the other side, the United States declared an embargo on them. At this time, and especially during the blockade of the American coast by the British fleet during the War of 1812, the United States itself found itself under a blockade. Prices for, say, textiles (which were imported into the United States) increased relative to cotton (which the United States exported) by 51.4% compared to the pre-war period and by 110.2% compared to the post-war period[126] or by 200% according to another work by the same author.[127] The absence of British goods created a need, and the increase in their prices was an opportunity, to establish domestic production. Along with textile factories, glassworks, distilleries, and breweries began to take off. If in 1790 there were approximately 2000 spinning enterprises, in 1809 there were already 8000, which to some extent may be due to the opportunity to "help" continental Europe, which was under the pressure of the blockade. But their number began to grow explosively with the outbreak of the armed conflict between the United States and the United Kingdom—in 1812 their number had already reached 93,000, and in 1817 it was 333,000. "Thus, the take-off of the American cotton textile industry coincided exactly with the virtual elimination of imports from Britain."[128] Finally, when the Napoleonic Wars ended and the blockades were lifted, better and cheaper British goods began to threaten American enterprises that had barely begun again to stand on their own. Once again, northern industries put pressure on the state to protect them, and they received it in the form of new duties in 1816.

Another consequence of the Napoleonic Wars was that

they left behind a lasting effect—the acquisition of Louisiana from France. From that moment on, the American federal state became the owner of huge land reserves, and this turned it into the most powerful pyramid of socio-economic influence in the country. Therefore, it is not surprising that in the following years, the central (federal) government was strengthened at the expense of the local (state) governments.[129]

In this way, the Americans repeated the first step of England on its way to the economic peak of the world: they put obstacles in the way of foreign goods and foreign trade. Now it was time for the second step. Products from the United Kingdom were skillful because they were the result of a long process of improvement during the Industrial Revolution that had already begun there. They were cheap because they were produced with advanced machinery. But even more importantly, they were produced under conditions of economies of scale—each industrial enterprise had a huge number of consumers of its products, which reduced the cost of each unit of production. This economy of scale in the United Kingdom was achieved through the acquisition of colonies and semi-colonies—independent countries that depended on industrial products from the United Kingdom.

The Americans had to set up everything from scratch, they had no experience, and they did not have as much free capital as the United Kingdom. And most importantly, they did not have colonies. Economic walls don't create industrial enterprises. They are needed to protect the still weak but existing economies. But left behind this wall, in the vast majority of cases, they will remain rickets, existing on artificial state drips that keep these semi-viable entities alive. Only training, going outside the walls, and engaging in the struggle there, ultimately produces heroes and champions. But taking these rickets outside the walls and hoping that they will train to fight giants is a way of killing them.

These enterprises need to be brought outside the walls, but to fight rivals weaker than themselves. That's what colonies are for. There are no rivals at all or they are too weak. There, domestic rickets become self-confident giants.

The first part of the second step: The United States had no colonies. But the North had the South.

Since gaining independence, the United States has enjoyed the dominance of trade with the Spanish and especially Portuguese colonies, established by the United Kingdom. Napoleon's invasion of Spain and Portugal brought confusion to the Latin American colonies, which already then began, quite legitimately, to refuse to obey the new authorities in their metropolitan areas appointed by Napoleon[130]. When the secession took place, it was the United States (along with the United Kingdom) that won and "took over" the "liberated" peoples. In other words, they gained additional markets. But this trade was too weak.

Intra-American trade, it turned out, held greater promise. Using the invention of the cotton gin, the southern United States was able to turn its cotton plantations into large-scale capitalist production that exploited economies of scale. However, being an agricultural, this production needed industrial products to function. And the American North offered the South such goods. However, the South bought better goods in the United Kingdom, where it sold most of its products. The economic wall, which the American state initially built to raise funds to finance the activities of its state apparatus, simultaneously made foreign products more expensive, so that the products of the North became more attractive. This made Americans realize that duties could be an instrument of economic influence, a tool for building a national market. The fact that in the first few years after the blockade was lifted in 1814, imports jumped more than tenfold was an incentive to act. Wool, cotton, and chemical manufacturers began to put pressure on the government, and in 1816 new duties were introduced.[131] The purpose of the increase in customs duties in 1816 (up to 20%) was not only to ensure the existence of the state (and to raise prices for better quality British products) but also a conscious attempt to provide the state with sufficient funds to provide loans to enterprises.[132] In 1824, again at the request of Northern enterprises, duties were again increased and the list of goods covered by them was also expanded.

Cartoon "The Crisis of Nullification"—The North is getting fat at the expense of the South.
Source: Library of Congress, Washington, DC.

And the more the state's measures helped American enterprises grow and become stronger, the more voices in the North demanded even more protection. But the more irritation grew in the South, where enterprises had to buy lower-quality northern manufactured goods at a higher price. In addition, since British enterprises could now sell less on the American market, they were inclined to buy less American products, which were mostly the products of southern plantations. A new increase in tariffs in 1828 caused the first serious crisis in relations between the South and the North.[133] It was followed by others.

From a political point of view, the plantations of the South could live without the industrial enterprises of the North, simply by exchanging their products for those of Europe. The northern industry could not live without the South. Therefore, the South's desire to secede was predictable. So was the North's desire to prevent it.

In an attempt to prevent secession, the United States government offered the South various concessions and constitutional amendments that protected slavery in the South. However, no compromise was offered on the amount of duties. After the Southern deputies left Congress, nothing prevented the North from passing new duty increases (especially since the additional money was now needed for the conflict with the Southern states). Several successive increases in 1864 brought the average duty to 47 percent[134].

This policy of the American state was met with hostility from the peak of the global economic pyramid, the United Kingdom. This is not surprising. The peak goal was to complicate the development of industry in other countries and to actively engage in "free trade" with the extractive and agricultural enterprises of other countries. Therefore, it is natural that the democratic United Kingdom sympathized with the slave-owning South in the conflict. The United Kingdom, which had achieved its leading position in the world economy not by any means due to free-market policies, considered it necessary to point out to the United States its deviation from the principles of free trade. "The British nation was then on a wave of excitement with enthusiasm for free trade ... and was inclined to regard protective tariffs as fundamentally and inherently immoral, not much better than theft or murder ... 'We don't like slavery,' said Palmerston* .... 'but we want cotton, and don't like your Morrill tariff.'"[135]

The American response to British dissatisfaction was, "What right does a foreign country have to question our actions?"[136] This was the response of a future leader. The United States understood that those who agree to be built into the base of the economic pyramid kill their chances of ever being at the peak.

At the end of the Civil War, the walls of the customs convenient for the industry were not abolished and remained at the level set for "wartime needs."[137]

*Other countries in the world could challenge the leader only after their strong, authoritarian state turned away from agrarian enterprises and deliberately sided with industrial enterprises. If the state continued to stand on the side of agrarian enterprises, then the rise of the country became possible only after the industrial enterprises revolutionarily seized the state and subordinated its power to the goals of their development (bourgeois revolutions in Marxist terminology). In the United States, the opposite event occurred: agrarian enterprises, which were steadily losing their influence on the state, challenged it. Their loss in the Civil War eliminated the danger of the country being drawn into the British system—the power of the southern plantations was broken, and their trade with the peak became unprofitable**. The breakdown of the power of the non-decisive economy opened the way for the rise of the decisive economy.*

* Prime Minister of the United Kingdom

** apparently, due to the abolition of slavery, the cost of American cotton ceased to be attractive to the British, who switched to Indian cotton

The second part of the second step:
A new horse—internal immigration

Since slaves were freed during the war, southern enterprises had to pay their workers after the war and could no longer be as profitable as before. But the main thing was that during the war, the United Kingdom switched to Indian cotton and when the Southern enterprises returned to the market, cotton prices fell dramatically. Therefore, although the South now had to dutifully consume northern products, it ceased to exist as a rich and crowded market.

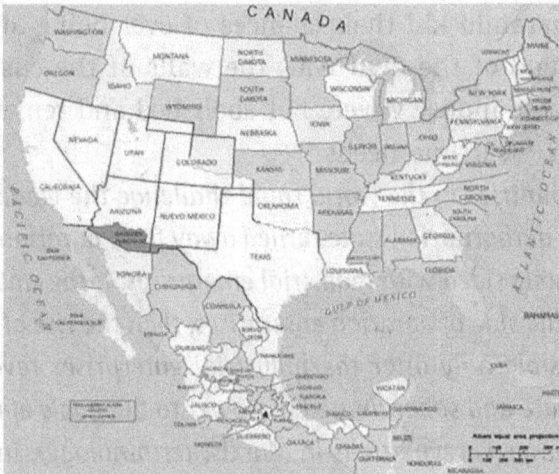

White marks the territories that Mexico was forced
to give up under the Treaty of Guadalupe Hidalgo.
Source: Public Domain U.S. Government

Limiting the market opportunities could have hurt the development of American industry. But the United States set about creating a new market. The French Louisiana that the United States had acquired was inhabited by Indians, who bought virtually nothing from American industrial enterprises.

Therefore, it was necessary to populate it with other residents who would need industrial products. And the American state began to do so. On the one hand, in 1830, the Indian Removal Act was passed, according to which Indian tribes living east of the Mississippi River were relocated to the west. Later, the pushing of the Indians further west resulted in a series of "Indian wars" that resulted in their settlement in "reservations". On the other hand, the border was moving southward. First, it was Florida. Then it was Texas. And then there was the whole of northern Mexico.

All this activity brought the desired result—a stream of immigrants poured into the "liberated" lands. Between 1820 and 1870, more than seven and a half million immigrants moved to the United States from Western Europe, more than doubling the country's population![138] And the part of the immigrants who went to the West to establish farms provided work for the part that joined the industrial enterprises of the eastern cities as labor.

In addition, these new territories were also an expanded source of raw materials that American firms did not have to import from abroad and compete with foreign enterprises for their purchases.

The lands taken from Mexico and the Indians became internal colonies of the United States in the economic sense. Subsequently, they opened the potential for American enterprises to exploit economies of scale and grow at a rapid pace. Anyone who tries to criticize the United States for the "injustice", for the "blood", for the "violence" of those years must understand that if it were not for them, the United States would never have become the peak of the world economy. And then they would not have become the owners of the Statue of Liberty, which shines a torch of hope and example to the whole world.

Just as in the lives of private people, those who try to be more honest and kinder tend to remain on the lowest rungs of the hierarchy.

In general, in the 19th century, the American economy developed in a continuous cycle: the state seized new land, the flow of settlers paid money for land and created the need for transportation, and the state could invest the money received from the sale of land (as well as from duties) in the development of roads, railroads, etc., thus financing industry. Then it was the time for a new cycle.

American immigration

The fact that immigrants from Western Europe settled in the uninhabited territories of the United States was very important for the development of American industry.

France, for example, was conquering new, already populated territories at an accelerated pace. However, it was not easy to turn them into a wide market because the people who lived in these African and Asian territories stuck to their traditional products and were very slow to adapt to French goods. The departure of the French to the colonies certainly created demand but at a very slow pace. Or, for example, Russia had vast territories that had long been inhabited by Europeans (both in Europe and Asia). And these people needed goods similar to those produced by the industry of the time. But the villages that had already existed before the Industrial Revolution were already producing such goods themselves. The industrial goods of that time, such as fabrics and clothing, metal products (nails, buckets, horseshoes), etc., were already produced by local artisans, blacksmiths, or even just in the household. Industrial goods imported from distant cities had to compete and only gradually, displacing traditional goods, reach the production scale necessary for the economy of scale to come into play.

In the United States, the market grew by leaps and bounds. On the one hand, immigrants were already accustomed to industrial goods and needed them. On the other hand, local traditional handicraft production had not yet developed in the newly formed villages and farms. From the very beginning, industrial goods from the northeast of the United States took its place. The number of these settlements grew continuously, creating a continuous demand for industrial products. While from 1820 to 1911, the population in Western Europe roughly doubled, and in the Russian Empire almost tripled, in the United States it increased almost tenfold[139]. As a result, American industry could produce and sell the same product in huge quantities. This opened the door to large economies of scale in production.

Over time, this allowed the productivity of American workers to overtake that of British workers, even in the face of a technological lag the United Kingdom. "Demand factors played a role here, as American consumers were more willing than their British counterparts to accept standardized products"[140]. After all, not only did British goods have to compete with local products in the colonies, but even the British colonists themselves needed goods with local characteristics in Canada, Australia, etc., and the population in Britain itself was very class-different and even more so in need of different goods.[141]

In the case of the United States, the formation of the national market went hand in hand with "colonization"
The presence of an ever-expanding market was a decisive but not sufficient factor for the establishment of the United States industry. Without being tied into a single system of communication routes, American towns, and farms remained isolated

enterprises that conducted almost subsistence farming without forming a national market. In addition, the lack of transportation routes made it difficult to explore the western lands.

The most important initiative in the early 19th century was the construction of the National Road. The federal government financed the construction of the road through the Appalachian Mountains, which was done by private companies. After the road was extended into the western territories and completed in 1838, the federal government transferred the road to the states.

The roads themselves were not able to meet the needs of industrial enterprises and farms that were moving further inland. The construction of canals began almost simultaneously with the construction of roads. Private attempts to build a canal that would connect the Great Lakes with the Potomac River were made as early as 1792. Through this canal, goods and people could travel from the Great Lakes to New York City. But private funding was not enough. However, with the help of the state of New York, the canal was built in 1817, and it became the largest state-owned company in the state.

This canal was followed by others—Pennsylvania built its own, Ohio built its large canals, and other states built their smaller, but much-needed water transportation arteries for the development of private enterprises.

But the largest state contribution to the formation of the national market, as well as to the American Industrial Revolution, was the construction of railroads. The first steam engines, the locomotives themselves, and even the rails were imported to the United States from the United Kingdom. As soon as railroads showed that they could reduce the cost of transportation by 60-70 percent,[142] states began to redirect money planned for the construction of canals to the construction of railroads. Local governments (especially in places where the railroad had to pass through) also contributed to the financing of projects. Railroads grew rapidly and required more and more locomotives and other equipment. And the state, while facilitating their construction, on the one hand, did not ease the obstacles to the import of foreign equipment on the other. The result was that soon (in 1830) the first American steam locomotive was manufactured in New York. Moreover, with subsidies from the state, railroads could pay a higher price for domestic locomotives, etc., whose producers were just starting to produce and had higher costs. In a free market, the beginnings of such steel-rolling enterprises, or enterprises producing steam engines and the like, were simply doomed. Their products were both more expensive and of lower quality, and they were supplied intermittently. With the protection of the customs wall and financial assistance from the state, domestic production improved, increased its quality, and reduced its cost.

Already during the Civil War, the North passed a law in 1862 that anyone could take a plot of land in the new western lands for free (i.e., subsidized by the state). In the same year, a law was signed authorizing the construction of the first American railroad—from ocean to ocean—the first transcontinental road. Its construction was completed in 1869. This strengthened the wave of immigrants after the end of the Civil War even more. From 1880 to 1914, more than 22 million people arrived in the United States.[143]

The states and the unwitting betrayal of British enterprises

British enterprises needed cotton and invested in American plantations. "British capital ... remained critical... to the growth of the cotton trade from the early 19th century on."[144]

This was rational behavior. British direct investment went where it was most beneficial for the United Kingdom—to perpetuate the US dependence on British manufactured goods and consolidate them as the agricultural brick at the base of the British pyramid of political and economic influence. However, British enterprises lent money not only to American enterprises but also to state governments. The latter used the borrowed money to finance "transportation projects turnpikes and canals in the 1820s and 1830s, and increasingly railroads from the 1830s."[145] The improved transportation system, on the one hand, facilitated the settlement of new territories, on the other hand, tied the country's regions into one national market, and helped to develop American industrial enterprises. Thus, unlike private enterprises, state governments took on debt to finance the country's future.

However, state governments went further. In the early stages, even with state financial assistance, some projects discouraged private initiative by requiring massive investments and the need to organize large-scale construction. This primarily concerns the construction of large canals. In such cases, state enterprises were used. "Up until the end of the 1830s, the U.S. deployment of SOEs [state-owned enterprises] was similar to that of many other Western countries. The only significant difference was the reliance in America on state governments rather than federal authority to achieve the goal of accelerating economic growth . . . "[146]

The money of British enterprises thus confidently raised the future undertaker of their dominion. But only that part of the investment that went to the states.

**The deliberate betrayal of British enterprises
and the decline of US state enterprises**

Over time, the importance of American cotton for British industrial production declined dramatically as the United Kingdom
found another source in India. Therefore, although "in the
new wave beginning in the late 1840s, state government debt
remained important, foreign capital went increasingly to private
railroad corporations"[147]. Now British capital found a source of
reliable profit in the rapidly developing industrial enterprises
of the North and began to favor them over the agricultural
enterprises of the South. Since the initiative of industrial enterprises could now rely on another source for implementation,
the importance of state-owned enterprises and state capital
decreased accordingly.

Instead, American companies backed by British capital,
having gained momentum in the domestic market, soon entered
the international market. The total exports of the United States
grew from 590 million dollars in 1877 to 1371 million dollars in
1900 (excluding the export of precious metals).[148] Agricultural
products were still the main export item, but gasoline, and then
technical products, began to move to the forefront. And profits
from foreign trade were constantly increasing. The industrial
production of the United States, which was increasingly concentrated in centralized pyramids of corporations, grew rapidly.
As firms grew, so did the overall economy of the United States.
By 1890, industrial output in the United States was the largest
in the world. By 1900, the United States was already producing
half of the world's industrial output.[149]

Other British enterprises, as well as those of other European
countries that were bleeding their own economies, were quick
to join the success of American enterprises stimulated by
British companies. "The capital increase was partly the result of

immigrants who left Europe and created a shortage of available labor to support new investment projects in their home countries. Once internal stability returned after the war, investing in American railroads seemed more promising than spending capital at home in the dull European trade environment at the time."[150] At the same time, since the American state (since Hamilton) imposed huge taxes on the export of capital abroad, foreign investments tended to stay in the United States.

It is not too much of an exaggeration to say that the United States invited both producers and consumers from abroad. What was American was the initiative—both of private businesses and of the American government (primarily state governments).

The rise of the United States went through the same stages as that of Britain, although the implementation of the stages themselves was different. The United States also built its national market, independent of the world leader, and then set about building and expanding their own, separate from the leader, economic pyramid. It still had a third stage to go—the struggle for the global pyramid.

THE TRAP OF THE PEAK

The British state made considerable efforts to break the country out of its dependence on foreign production and trade, and later to make it a world leader. When the peak of European economic leadership was practically reached, the state was removed from governance. Since then, under the sensitive guidance of an oligarchic parliament, Britain had sailed at the mercy of capricious economic waves. Now it had to relax and just go with the flow. The current will not take you to the rock, because the current flows around the rock and carries the boat that trusted it (if it is light enough, of course, and for this, it is necessary to get rid of the ballast of public spending). But when the circumstances changed and the current was heading in a disastrous direction, there was no longer a firm hand of the state on the rudder to steer the boat in a different direction.

For the United Kingdom to export more of its goods, it had to buy more of the goods of others. This allowed other countries to receive pounds sterling to buy British goods. And following the signals of the free market, British companies invested part of their profits in expanding their production, and the other part in expanding the production of goods needed by the United Kingdom in other countries. Thus, the flow of British capital to other countries increased.

This system worked perfectly well for the glory and benefit of the United Kingdom until the states of some other countries began to interfere with the free market processes.

For example, the US government created its own separate market surrounded by customs walls, where they constantly invited new buyers of industrial products (and agricultural producers) for permanent residence. This had two consequences.

Firstly, British companies saw this situation as a source of quite attractive profits in which they wanted to invest. Thus, in this case, British enterprises contributed their capital to the rise of not complementary enterprises in other countries, not subcontractors for their work, but their own future competitors. But looking decades ahead is the privilege of states. The horizon of enterprises is years. Who cares about the distant future? And in it, at the beginning of the twentieth century, about half of British assets were already abroad and about 10% of national income was generated by interest from foreign investments[151]. Of course, only a part of them was invested in foreign industry, but undoubtedly this is a significant part of the capital that was diverted from the development of British industry to the rise of foreign countries.

A side effect of this first consequence was the following.

British capital, in particular, invested in the development of technologies, primarily machine tools, which made it possible to pattern the production of a wide series of identical, mutually compatible parts. It was these technologies that further fueled the rapid rise of American industry and later formed the basis of its cheap and numerous exports. But despite this, "British firms could not simply adopt the American machinery, which was very wasteful of resources but had to compete based on skilled labor. Subsequently, technical progress was more rapid with machine-intensive technology as American manufacturers developed the ideal of interchangeable mass production"[152].

The reason was that, as noted, the American market was homogeneous and growing rapidly, which allowed for the organization of production around the principle of economies of scale. The British market, on the other hand, was mosaic, "artisanal," and the British were very interested in the efficiency of production and machine tools in particular. They used other equipment for their smaller production runs. This ultimately allowed US production to surpass that of the United Kingdom.

A byproduct of this spin-off was that "the American mass production system required strong managerial control of the production process, requiring in turn a well-trained managerial class. By contrast, the British craft production system delegated control over the production process to the shop floor, thus requiring no such managerial elite.... it is... understandable because of the strategy of craft production pursued rationally by British firms faced with conditions less suited to mass production"[153]. However, the growth of the managerial class in the United States provided an opportunity for virtually unlimited growth for American companies, which were lined up in economic pyramids consisting of main branches, auxiliary branches, jointly owned subordinate companies, etc. This did not happen in the United Kingdom. Therefore, "[t]he slow development of a professional managerial class in Britain is regarded... as a major failure."[154]

Secondly, the leading position of the United Kingdom in certain industries provided enterprises with the best opportunities to seek profit. Investments in these industries promised quick and reliable profits, as opposed to investments in new industries and new inventions, where future profits were unknown and uncertain.[155] This, for example, can be seen in the decline of British patents registered in the United States.[156] Thus, the British position at the peak "naturally" directed the economic process in a certain direction, which was already well-trodden. At the same time, American companies, with British investments, invested in innovations in new industries and raised their profitability to a level that was interesting to an even wider range of British investors. In this way, British capital raised new industries in other countries (not just the United States).

Finally, we should mention the British version of the Dutch Disease. At the same time, exports of British services (transportation, bank loans, insurance of transactions, knowledge of where there is demand for what and where there is supply of what, lawyers, storage of goods, etc.) were growing, which gave British businesses huge profits[157]. It was in these industries that British businesses, like other countries, eventually formed large corporations.

Thus, the United Kingdom's total exports grew. However other countries could not increase their exports to the United Kingdom to pay for British manufactured goods plus services. They had to buy either one or the other. As British exports of services grew, it was no surprise that exports of manufactured goods fell. The industry needed fewer people and services needed more. British engineers were retrained as office clerks in the service sector[158]. Later, the process went so far that imports of industrial products to the United Kingdom surpassed its exports.

When England was at the bottom of foreign economic hierarchies, its state acted against the will of English enterprises and forced them to change their behavior. The state of the United Kingdom, now at the peak of the global economic hierarchy, was too weak to influence businesses and therefore no longer in a position to correct the situation. It was now a mere servant of its enterprises. As it once was with the Dutch state.

DEMOCRACY AS A PRODUCT OF COMPETING INTERESTS

In the second half of the eighteenth century, the British near monopoly on trade in the world made any British monopoly enterprise no longer a protection against risk, but a protection of guaranteed profits for the owners. But this very British monopoly on trade and the associated reduction of entrepreneurial risks allowed a large number of new small enterprises to enter the arena, which could do what only huge monopolists could do before. And the monopolies of the old giants stood in their way. In 1793, the East India Company was deprived of its monopoly rights to India's trade with East Asia. Later, the trading part of the company was taken away altogether, only the administrative part was left, and it now performed purely administrative functions as a private owner of the country of India. The East India Company is just an example—it was a period when the arrival of a new generation of enterprises (made possible by the activities of monopolies) led to general resentment of monopolies and their abolition. The abolition of monopolies weakened the oligarchy and gave democracy a chance.

However, the destruction of monopolies knocked out the support for the socio-economic influence of their owners. It was this socio-economic influence that made the state hierarchy manageable and stable through the patronage filling of public positions. Therefore, the state hierarchy required some other support for its stability and controllability.

A step in this direction occurred during the Crimean War (wars are a natural catalyst for efforts to strengthen the state). This step was the Northcote-Trevelyan Report, which was prepared in 1853 and published in February 1854. The report called for the recruitment of civil servants through examinations conducted by an independent board and for promotions based on performance. Interestingly, the report also called for hiring civil servants for the state apparatus as a whole, rather than for a specific department. Thus, the authors of the report envisioned the future state apparatus as a caste of civil servants. That is civil servants who, upon entering the service, could hold positions in any unit of the state apparatus and felt that they belonged to this apparatus as a whole, from which their loyalty to the interests of the state apparatus pyramid should have sprouted.

The recommendations were half-heartedly implemented in 1870, but the clause on the commission's acceptance of exams was even strengthened—the commission was created but placed under the control of the main ministry at the time, the Ministry of Finance.[159] In other words, the bureaucracy selected and hired people for itself. Imposing people from the outside in the form of patronage from the oligarchy or groups of politicians in parliament was becoming more difficult. The state apparatus was gaining some autonomy and began to work for itself. But its interest was inextricably linked to the country's interest. The future of the state apparatus is unthinkable without the future of its country. Businesses can flee abroad. The state cannot flee abroad.

Previously, large oligarchic enterprises were able to organize the main economic activity of the country around them. Their elimination gave rise to a great variety of interests based on the interests of various smaller enterprises (from different industries, different localities, belonging to different clans, etc.). In the absence of the decisive influence of large enterprises, these interests needed an arbiter of their disputes. And the introduction of a professional bureaucracy provided such an arbiter. At the same time, the very process of reconciling the numerous interests of different enterprises was nothing short of democracy.

And the conditions for democracy were provided by the conditions of the world's peak economy. First of all, the diversity of interests of many different enterprises (agricultural, industrial, service, and trade) can exist only in the conditions of the peak economy. But an even more important factor is the lack of opportunity for foreign, economically weaker enterprises in the valley to have a decisive influence on the enterprises and the state of the peak. And the same applies to economically weak valley states. Thus, the peak becomes truly independent of external influences, which is the second decisive factor in the emergence of true democracy.

INDEPENDENCE OF THE US STATE

The real American Revolution
In the United States after separation, unlike in the United Kingdom, the centers of the pyramids of socioeconomic influence of the old elite, i.e. large agricultural holdings, were relatively weak. They were not numerous and scattered within the territories of the first colonies on the Atlantic coast. Instead, the development of the western territories led to their settlement by new waves of immigration. Newcomers-farmers lived on their small enterprises, relied only on their strength, and did not depend on the enterprises of the old elite. Therefore, unlike the United Kingdom (UK), the pyramids of the socioeconomic influence of the oligarchs were not able to serve as

an organizing framework for society. In addition, small and medium-sized enterprises in the US and the UK were very different. In the UK, many of them were involved in the decisive economy—in the industries of the first industrial revolution, trade, and foreign services (global transportation, loans, transportation insurance, etc.). In the United States, the former basis of the British economic pyramid, such enterprises were mainly involved in agriculture and local services (stagecoach transportation or installation of gas streetlights, etc.). Finally, there was no strong state pyramid of socioeconomic influence.

Fate has given Europeans the opportunity for a large-scale experiment to realize the liberal ideal of a society of social equality—in other words, an experiment to organize a society without the pyramids of the socioeconomic influence. This experiment has shown that if the hierarchical pyramids of the socioeconomic influence are not imposed from above (by the state or oligarchy), they grow from below—the elements of the valley themselves, as it was in ancient Greece and Rome, organize themselves into hierarchies that begin to grow.[160] This process in the United States is called Jacksonian democracy.

The growth of small enterprises in a sea of similarly small enterprises is slow due to their small needs and high competition. Only orders for public needs provided a chance to expand the scale of production or services, with no competition after the order was received. That is why, with a little extra capital, enterprise owners promised to build roads, organize stagecoach transportation, pave city streets, install gas lights, etc. The respected person who headed such a business was often the organizer of a movement to support himself and the future services of his company. In this way, a pyramid of socioeconomic influence was formed to come to power. The opposite option was to organize opposition to such "powerful" interests by local standards. Active, often charismatic individuals organized an "anti-" movement around themselves and won elections on the wave of that movement. And the efforts of supporters had to be rewarded. 'In America . . . clientelism was a way for ambitious but non-elite politicians to become wealthy and increase their social status while delivering concrete benefits to their supporters.'[161] But in the end, these charismatic personalities (or their significant supporters), while in power, contributed to the formation of their enterprises, which could help them in the next election. Therefore, it can be argued that <u>this system was reduced to a confrontation between different groups of small businesses (but at the same time, the ability to use government orders and even the monopoly status granted by the government provided a convenient opportunity for the enterprises to grow). Patronage pyramids became the only available structure that organized society at the local level.</u>

But the whole country of the United States needed an organization. Therefore, over time, numerous local groups merged and absorbed each other, resulting in the formation of only two "centers of gravity"—the Democratic Party and the Whig Party, later the Democratic and Republican Parties. It was they who played the role of patronage pyramids that organized the societies of the states and the entire United States. "The legislative programs of the "regencies" and juntos that effectively ran state politics . . . characteristically focused on prosaic legislation that awarded bank charters or monopoly rights to construct transportation projects to favored insiders. That American parties would be pragmatic vote-getting coalitions, rather than organizations devoted to high political principles."[162] In other words, American mass parties originated as patron-client pyramids.

While in other countries, which tried to "catch up and overtake" the world leader, the state deliberately promoted the growth of domestic enterprises in the decisive economy, in the United States, such enterprises tried to grow on their own, and used the state to do so, which they subjugated to their influence. Why did the state have to intervene in economic processes in other countries? Because the natural course of events led to the fact that domestic enterprises purchased products of decisive sectors of the economy abroad, and therefore, primarily import-oriented enterprises grew, as did those that exported products of non-decisive domestic sectors. To reverse this situation, to break the resistance of these enterprises, which had already acquired a large socioeconomic influence, government intervention was needed. Moreover, the state initiated the emergence and supported the growth of the enterprises in decisive industries. In the United States, the state was weak and took little initiative. Instead, businesses grew on their own and tried to use the state for this purpose.

The spoil successfully runs the country

When Andrew Jackson came to power in 1829, he expressed the following thought: "The duties of all public offices are, or at least pretend to be, so plain and simple that men of intelligence may readily qualify themselves for their performance"[163]. (Lenin later picked up on this idea and spoke of "every housewife"). Jackson was constantly changing officials because "no man has any natural right to hold public office more than any other." In addition to such ideological justice, this policy provided opportunities to reward more supporters. But so did his Democratic Party rivals when they came to power. Each change in the ruling party not only led to a change in the top state leadership (ministers, etc.) but also went down the state hierarchy, rewarding people in the local and central government according to their contribution to the victory. Just as an example, President Zachary Taylor in 1849, in his first year in office, replaced 30% of all government officials.[164]

The system was called the "spoils system." This system made the United States government pyramid more manageable and cohesive. Filling government positions with party members or supporters ensured that the government pyramid did not resist the decisions of the president or the party. Party appointees worked with enthusiasm, trying to fulfill their election promises to extend their term in the state apparatus. In other words, the party hierarchy became stronger and more coherent, and the state hierarchy consistently implemented the party's plans. It is not without reason that the period of this system was the time of the country's greatest expansion and the time of the acceleration of American industrialization.

This "type of government was appropriate to the agrarian society the United States had been in the first half of the century. But by the final two decades of the nineteenth century, the nature of the American economy had changed enormously."[165]

The growth of enterprises has raised the stakes

Around the 1860s, large enterprises became so powerful and their appetites so great that the problem became evident. The emergence of large corporations gave rise to lobbying, which often boiled down to simple bribery of deputies. "In the early 1880s, the United States constituted the kind of small-government society that . . . modern libertarians hope it will someday become again. The federal government took in less than 2 percent of GDP in taxes . . . Presidents were weak and real power lay with Congress and the courts. [though this inevitably entailed another side that no one dreams of] Private interests were vigorous and expanding, and indeed succeeded in capturing a great deal of Congress through payoffs and patronage."[166]

Like cures like

The free development of the market (which was the flip side of a weak state) led to the emergence of monster enterprises that, having achieved a monopoly position in the economy, prevented other enterprises from entering the market and growing, on the one hand, and gained great influence on the state, on the other hand. This meant that the free market gave birth to such offspring that devoured their father —huge monopoly enterprises killed the free market that gave birth to them.* At the same time, the free society of free individuals gave rise to offspring that devoured their mother-the same large enterprises, along with the parties, actually abolished the society of free individuals. It was replaced by a society of hierarchical parties and corporations. *Parties were official patronage pyramids.*

The free market in the railroad space led to the inevitable: fierce competition on profitable lines resulted in parallel railroad tracks (for example, 20 such tracks were laid between St. Louis and Atlanta).[167] That is, resources were wasted and all companies remained underutilized and suffered losses. At the same time, in low-profit areas, the companies that laid the railroads often could not cover the cost of operation. Most importantly, having suffered losses in the competition on parallel railways by lowering ticket prices, the railroad companies eventually entered into agreements with each other and formed so-called trusts to jointly maintain prices acceptable to them.

But "reasonable prices" tended to rise rapidly. The result was that railroad users suffered, and this led to a change in the mood of American society. Numerous passengers (i.e., the people) and enterprises that transported goods by rail began to demand government influence on the railroads. However, the railroads became powerful enough to defend their interests before the state. On the one hand, they could easily bribe

---

* However, even before that, small and medium-sized farms were subjugating the local levels of the state, which shows that a free market can exist only in the complete absence of the state, which even libertarians do not dream of.

officials and parliamentarians, but on the other hand, their operation was critical to the entire U.S. economy, and so they quite officially demanded all sorts of concessions for themselves.

But the railroads were just one example of private enterprises that grew, become strong, and began to defend their interests. The result was a great influence of corporations on government decision-making at all levels of government—city, state, and federal.

Previously, the American ideal of individualism saw its main enemy in the hierarchical pyramid of the state. Now this ideal has met a new, unexpected enemy: the hierarchical power of large enterprises. "The Day of Unity has come to stay. Individualism is gone, never to return," said John Rockefeller, one of the founders of one of the largest business pyramids. He was the richest man in the United States and "had only disdain for those who still thought of the economy as depending on individualism and competition. Organization and consolidation was the future."[168]

Someone, somehow, had to save a free and liberal society. And this could only be done with the help of the state. Of course, society and market influenced by the state could not be "free." However, the owners of smaller enterprises who wanted to grow their companies and ambitious public figures who wanted to draw public attention to certain problems were not interested in these insoluble contradictions of liberalism. Their practical goal was to have a sufficiently strong state that was able to enforce fair "rules of the game." <u>It had to be an independent state, independent of the influence of large businesses.</u>

Giving and taking pyramids
A leading pyramid always has the resources to be a giving pyramid, at least in part. Those who challenge it usually do not have such resources and have to compensate with brute force. Giving pyramids start with

large profits of advanced enterprises. Taking pyramids start with the leader's promise to benefit everyone.

The struggle for the liberation of the state pyramid was waged at all levels (federal, state, city, and county). It was different everywhere and united different classes and strata of the population. The main thing is that patronage pyramids usually rely on the power of large enterprises—their profits and their ability to provide work and orders to a large number of people and enterprises. **Those who fight against such pyramids of socio-economic influence (and are unable to rely on their own enterprises) have to build their strategy on capturing the state hierarchy and weakening the pyramids of socio-economic influence with the help of the state pyramid. Moreover, since the enterprises can attract financial resources in their favor, those who oppose them are often forced to resort to violence as a "cheap substitute" for the lack of financial resources.** Such rebel groups were built as public associations involving parties, trade unions, and small enterprise owners. For example, in Wisconsin, powerful railroad and logging companies controlled the state pyramid. An alliance of farmers, bureaucrats, university graduates, and labor unions brought a new governor, Robert La Follette, to power. However, the finances of the mentioned companies were used to form a powerful opposition right inside La Follette's party and to get the right candidates into the party leadership. In response, violence was used—university graduates terrorized and intimidated this party's opposition at the Republican Party convention.[169]

On the contrary, when the state pyramid was captured by the groups described above, the owners of the enterprises could already "fight for democracy" by trying to bring the state hierarchy back under their influence. For example, the power in Chicago at the end of the nineteenth century was seized by the sub-pyramid of socio-economic influence of the Republican Party, headed by William Lorimer. The necessary votes in elections were usually bought with gifts ranging from portions of food or coal to pensions and licenses. Realizing the weakness of the pyramids of socio-economic influence that were not based on enterprises, Lorimer formed several companies that performed various contract work for the city, as a result of which Lorimer himself made a considerable fortune. However, the basis of his party pyramid was immigrants and the local working class. The struggle for an independent state in Chicago (i.e., against Lorimer's patronage pyramid) united local intellectuals and enterprise owners. "Ironically, while this group spoke in the name of democracy, it represented the upper crust of Chicago society, an overwhelmingly Protestant group that looked down on the way that Lorimer was empowering the city's new Catholic and Jewish immigrants."[170]

At the federal level, there were various attempts to reform the system, but they were hampered by the traditional US distrust of the federal state. The situation was set in motion by the assassination of President James Garfield, who was killed in 1881 by a client who believed that he had not received the position he deserved for his support.

The state gets professional workers—the bureaucracy.
To create an independent state pyramid, it was necessary, first of all, to make it professional and stable. It had to know how to do its job. But it was up to the winning party to decide what to do. To create a solid-state pyramid, the principle of filling government positions based on ability, which had already been tested in other countries, was applied. To achieve this goal, a bipartisan Civil Service Commission was established (the Pendleton Act of 1883). This commission established the rules for evaluating new candidates for the civil service (for which examinations were introduced) and which positions could be

filled with the arrival of a new party, and which could not. The top positions remained (and remain) up for grabs.

Then, in the early 20th century, civil servants' unions were introduced, which made the state apparatus even more cohesive and immune to political and private influences from outside. By joining the American Federation of Labor, an association of American trade unions, civil servants exerted organized pressure on Congress to expand and strengthen bureaucratic autonomy and to remove it from the influence of patronage and politicization. Thus, in the American system, the state acquired its voice.

The state receives state-owned enterprises (SOEs)

The "spoils system" state was most openly exploited by private interests at the city and county levels. It was here that businesses obtained orders for public projects, from which they grew rich. It was a time of rapid growth of cities and towns, and their needs for public services were constantly growing, bringing more and more profits to those who managed to find the "right" connections and take the "right" positions. It was the spread of popular dissatisfaction with this fact that led to the fact that "by 1900, forty-one of the fifty largest cities in the United States had public waterworks, and by 1910, 70 percent of cities with populations over 30,000 had shifted from private to municipal water services... Municipal SOEs were employed in transportation, production of antitoxins and vaccines, the generation and distribution of electricity, gas distribution, and healthcare."[171] State governments also had their hospitals, and water, gas, and electricity companies. But they often went further. They could have their own steamship companies, insurance companies, banks, and centralized elevators. California acquired packing houses that received fish from fishermen, as well as repair yards for those same fishermen. California was also the first state in the United States to have a fully state-owned port. Many cities and states opened their own telephone companies and even owned public transportation.[172] <u>State-owned enterprises knocked the ground out from under the feet of local patrons of client pyramids, making it harder to use the state as spoil. When the state gained a foothold in state-owned enterprises, it became less dependent on private interests</u>.

But the colossal size that the companies of the United States began to reach, their power, and their influence on economic and social processes, made them a serious threat to the independence of the not-yet strengthened state pyramid at the federal level. The future President Woodrow Wilson, relying on one of the founding fathers of the United States—Alexander Hamilton, began to campaign at this time "arguing that a strong centralized government was necessary for a whole host of purposes, from regulating railroads and telegraphs to controlling large corporations."[173]

Now the state could shape society

Thus, in the confrontation between the state and large enterprises, popular support shifted in favor of the former. With this support, the state was able to go on the offensive.

First of all, the state resorted to the traditional way of asserting its dominant position in society—to assert itself as the main landowner of the country. Next, the issue was raised that millions of acres of private land were held for speculative purposes, while other millions of acres were obtained through dubious means or were owned by logging companies or railroads that had not fulfilled their obligations under which they had received the land. In 1885-1888, under President Cleveland, agents of the Land Office were dispatched throughout the western states for a year to collect the necessary data. As a result, more than 81 million acres (33 million hectares) were returned to the state.[174]

In parallel, another "land process" was developing. In 1889, the U.S. Forest Service took over all the forests in the United States that had not yet been privatized. At that time, logging companies were cutting down forests uncontrollably and no one cared. In the eastern United States, forests had already virtually disappeared, and the same fate awaited other forests. No one could or wanted to protect the forests, because the immigrants themselves uprooted them to an even greater extent to establish agricultural enterprises on the vacated territory. In such a situation, only the state could stand in the way of natural market processes. "The restoration of these lands and their return to productive use was one of the great achievements of government intervention."[175]

However, the state's possession of the largest reserves of land was sufficient for its social influence in the agrarian society that was the United States until the last third of the 19th century. But starting in the 1870s, the state faced a different challenge, from industrial enterprises. In this new confrontation, the state could maintain its authority in the same way— by having its industrial enterprises. And individual states did indeed begin to acquire state enterprises, just as European governments did. However, since each state was distrustful of the strengthening of the federal government, the federal government did not have many opportunities to acquire its industrial enterprises. Therefore, the federal state, unable to strengthen itself, invented another way—the way of weakening its rivals. The idea was simple: break up corporations that had grown dangerously large (and therefore influential) into several smaller parts.

To this end, in 1890, the Sherman Anti-Trust Act was passed almost unanimously. It was this law that later became the most powerful weapon of the state in the fight against corporations whose power became dangerous for the state. It was used, for example, to destroy Rockefeller's Standard Oil, which was broken up into thirty-four small companies.

In addition, the state strengthened its supervisory functions. As an example, in 1887, the first regulatory body in the country's history, the Interstate Commerce Commission, was established to oversee railroads. In 1903, the commission was granted the right to set prices, and in 1906 even the right to force enterprises to comply with these prices. Finally, in 1910, it was established that it was not the commission that had to prove the correctness of the prices it set, but the enterprises had to justify the need to increase their prices.[176]

It is also worth mentioning that when during the First World War the American railroads were unable to meet the needs of military transportation in the given time, volume, and prices, the American state nationalized the entire railroad system, without stopping at all to considering ideological taboos. However, the roads were returned to private ownership in 1920.

How did the US manage to grow without authoritarianism?

In the United States, the strengthening of the state was the result of the assertive growth of enterprises, which was hampered by the monopoly of those enterprises that grew first. Monopolization, like a cooled crust on the surface of lava, slowed down and even stopped the process of economic growth.

The American state did not acquire authoritarian forms, as happened in other countries that successfully raised their economies. The reason was that the country was not involved in the foundation of foreign economic pyramids. This meant that the country did not have large enterprises with a large socio-economic impact, which worked either to export of goods of the non-decisive economy or to import goods of the decisive economy. The powerful enterprises that used to export agricultural products were "broken" as a result of the victory of the North over the South. This large, but one-time, violence decisively removed an obstacle to the development of the key economy. In such circumstances, authoritarianism, was possible, but not definitely necessary for further economic growth. Why? After the defeat of the South, the US government found itself under the undivided socio-economic influence of industrial enterprises, and the state maintained high tariffs to please American industry, which was still gaining strength. As a result, not only did the industrial enterprises not have competition from the products of the peak (the United Kingdom), but on the contrary, the capital of the peak helped these enterprises to develop (precisely because of the presence of this very customs wall).

Thus, in the United States, there was no conflict of interest between the interests of the enterprises interested in keeping the country at the bottom of the economic hierarchy and the interests of the enterprises that needed the country to rise in this hierarchy. In the United States, there was a conflict between two forms of these second enterprises. The first form was the concentration of resources in a small number of enterprises. This gave these enterprises 1. the ability to plan their production (because no competition could take away some consumers), 2. the ability to win through economies of scale (having almost the entire US market in their hands), 3. funds for scientific and engineering research (which were accumulated, firstly, because of the ability to maintain monopoly high prices, and secondly, because there was no need to maintain reserve funds in case of market loss due to competition). The second form was to increase the optimization of such enterprises as a result of competition from numerous small and medium-sized enterprises. The first form provided the means for improvement and development, but took away the need for them, while the second form provided the need for improvement and development but took away the means. The further development of the United States went in such a way that both forms of industrial enterprises remained. A spin-off effect was the preservation of democracy in the United States.

Because of the Anti-Trust Act, large enterprises had to grow abroad (which will be discussed later). Those parts of them that remained in the United States did not have a dangerous level of socio-economic influence—neither on other enterprises nor on the state. These parts, together with the small and medium-sized enterprises whose growth they had previously hindered, formed crowds of enterprises in every industry. The main thing was that **a large number of enterprises were formed in a large number of industries. In this way, they neutralized each other's socio-economic influence**. And it was this fact that made democracy possible. No one industry could have a decisive influence on the state, let alone any of the enterprises; neither on the state, nor on the people, nor on other enterprises.

As long as the enterprises hoped that by bringing the state under their influence they could improve their business, they were satisfied with a weak state. But since this hope has become weak, they have become more interested in the state as an arbiter of disputes with others (enterprises and own employees).

Again, this was made possible by 1. the violent destruction of large enterprises of the non-decisive economy (civil war); 2. the creation of conditions that encouraged the enterprises of the peak of the world economy to invest their capital in the enterprises of the decisive economy of the US. The latter was a consequence of, first, the rapid increase in population and territory; second, the fact that the United States was a former colony of the United Kingdom (there was no cultural and language barrier for British farms); third, the customs barrier made investment in American enterprises more attractive than in the enterprises of real British colonies. Therefore, British enterprises, instead of importing British exports to the United States, invested in American industrial enterprises—that is, in the enterprises of the decisive economy.

In any other country (that was not at the peak of the global economic pyramid), the need to strengthen the state would have resulted in the establishment of an authoritarian regime. This did not happen in the United States, because it had very peculiar conditions that no one else had. In particular, there was no pressure from the enterprises of the top of the world economic hierarchy, on the one hand, and large enterprises of the non-decisive economy (in this case, agricultural ones) were excluded from influencing the state, on the other hand. In other words, the enemies of the development of domestic enterprises of the decisive economy were excluded. Therefore, the situation did not require authoritarianism.

Therefore, the absence of external influence and the presence of numerous enterprises in numerous sectors of the economy determined the stability of American democracy.

AFTER THE BRITISH LION CRUSHED
THE EUROPEAN REBELLION

The United Kingdom, with all its might, defeated the European rebellion. But the receding wave of rebellion left behind an indelible mark—a new European industry. And although the joyful return of British goods showed the rickety nature of this industry, its presence had already become a factor in social life.

At the peak, there was a frank debate about how to keep other countries from industrializing. In 1816, Henry Brame explained in Parliament: "It is well worthwhile to incur a loss upon the first exportation, in order, by the glut, to stifle in the cradle that infant manufactures in the United States which the [Napoleonic] wars forced into existence."[177]

But after the first successes in "clearing the rubble of the Continental blockade," free-market measures began to stall. Industrial enterprises already existed, knew their interests, and achieved what they wanted everywhere—state protection. Of course, this protection no longer resembled the Continental blockade, but it nevertheless covered national economies with a protective fence of duties.

France

The state felt the pressure of private hierarchies as soon as it announced a large reduction in import duties in 1814 to please the victorious United Kingdom. This reduction caused concern not only among industrial enterprises but also among their workers, who feared losing their jobs. It was not difficult for the owners of these enterprises to organize joint efforts with the workers. The result was the abolition of customs duties as early as 1816.[178]

In addition, the restored monarchy could no longer rely on the power of large agricultural enterprises, as they had been destroyed during the revolution and it was no longer possible to restore them in full. Therefore, the new state sought, on the one hand, the support of industrial owners, and, on the other hand, it had already realized the importance of industry as such (after all, France had lost the war). Already in 1817, contemporaries noted that " [t]he progress of French industry is mainly due to protection."[179]

In parallel with encouraging private enterprise, the state (the July Monarchy since 1830) was directly involved in the construction of railroads, roads, and canals, making it easier for French products to penetrate the most remote corners of the country. During the 18 years of this monarchy, iron and textile production more than doubled.[180] New duties were already being actively discussed when the next revolution occurred in 1848.

Napoleon III continued and strengthened the economic policy of his predecessor—he introduced state support for large industrial enterprises and made special efforts to encourage the construction of roads, railways, and the electric telegraph as a means of the transport revolution.[181]

The railroads of the United Kingdom emerged as a consequence of the natural development of the economy—where and when the needs of the economy required it. The state was superfluous in this process. This was not the case in France. There, following the British example, some enterprises also started building railroads. However, France was not at the peak of the global economic pyramid and did not have a similar export sales; moreover, part of its own needs were met by industrial imports from the peak. That is why, at the time of Louis Napoleon's accession, the length of railroads per capita in France was still five times less than in the United Kingdom. However vigorous government intervention almost equalized this figure by the end of Napoleon III's reign.[182] Overall, the state invested a third of all the capital needed to build the railroad network.

The construction of railroads led to the development of a whole industry of mechanical engineering (locomotives, steam engines, machine tools for manufacturing parts, etc.), which in turn led to the development of the metallurgical industry. This boom was so strong that it exceeded the needs of the French railways, and in the 1860s, 40% of their production was already exported abroad.[183]

Louis Napoleon spent his years of exile in the United Kingdom. There, he observed how the United Kingdom was getting rich on the principles of the free market and became a believer in the benefits of such a market. He dreamed of introducing this miraculous mechanism for the benefit of his homeland. So, during the fifties, many duties were reduced. Under the July Monarchy, total imports were roughly equal to total exports. At the same time, exports of manufactured goods were ten times higher than imports. Napoleon III's reforms significantly increased total exports, and exports of manufactured goods began to exceed imports by more than 20 times.[184] These first successes confirmed his faith in his beliefs. Therefore, he probably saw a free-market agreement with the United Kingdom as just another step on this successful path. He simply did not take into account that in previous steps the French Empire had built an economic pyramid of countries that purchased French industrial goods, and with this next step, it was going to voluntarily become the base of someone else's pyramid. At the same time, he was well aware that this step would meet with resistance from industrial enterprises and therefore prepared it in complete secrecy. Only when the Franco-British trade agreement was ready for signature was it reported in the newspapers, where Napoleon III proclaimed that without international trade the economy does not prosper, industry without competition stagnates, and without industry, agriculture remains underdeveloped.[185] Without waiting for the opinion of the parliament, the liberal dictator Louis-Napoleon signed the agreement on January 20, 1860. The dissatisfaction of large industrial enterprises was manifested almost immediately, but Napoleon III adhered to his ideological views to the end—that is, until the end of his reign in 1870.

Faith (ideology)

But since this agreement, the French economy has been mal-functioning, which, among other things, was manifested by the fact that total imports exceeded exports. And especially sad was the staggering growth of the industrial part of imports, which over the next 10 years (1860–1870) reduced its lag behind industrial exports by about four times.[186] Napoleon III's first, successful duty reductions (except for agricultural products) concerned coal, cast iron, iron, steel, wool, cotton, and similar goods.[187] However, these industrial goods were only semi-finished products that were used by French enterprises to produce final products. These French enterprises were already well established and not only did they not need protection, but were eager to enter foreign markets. Thus, the mutual reduction of duties opened foreign markets to these enterprises. And, the reduction in the cost of inputs made their products cheaper. The reduction of duties was beneficial to France to the extent that France was the second most economically powerful country in the world (i.e., relative to all countries except the peak one).

However, the agreement with the United Kingdom was a qualitatively different phenomenon. First, this agreement was concluded with a stronger partner, and this determined its content. France received a reduction in duties on agricultural products (primarily wines and cognacs) and fashionable trinkets in exchange for a reduction in duties on steam engines, floating vehicles, acids, leather goods, etc.[188] Secondly, it was a <u>commitment, made for a certain period</u>, not to raise duties again. This is in contrast to the aforementioned previous voluntary French discounts, which could be canceled at any time when they proved to be unsuitable.

What proved to be fateful on a global scale was that the agreement contained a "most favored nation" clause. This clause obliged each party to the agreement to grant the other party such new customs exemptions as would be granted to any third party in the future.

This paragraph was extremely attractive to other countries that saw France as a market for their industries. Among the first were Belgium and Switzerland, which received almost the same discounts on duties on industrial products. Of course, these countries were happy to introduce this "most favored nation" clause into the agreement. By introducing this clause into the agreement, they automatically received the concessions that France had granted to the United Kingdom or other countries with which it was about to sign agreements. In return, they reduced duties on wine, cognac, leather, and silk for France.[189] In keeping with its belief in the free market, the French state no longer saw the need to subsidize exports, nor to continue bans on the export of certain goods from the country. All of this combined began to have disastrous consequences, which the heads of industrial enterprises never tired of pointing out.*

The overall result for France was that agricultural growth rates increased, industrial growth fell, GDP declined, and the level of capital investment also fell.

Agriculture	Industry	GDP		Level of capital investment
1826–1846	0,7	1,8	1,3	8,1
1846–1856	1,1	2,0	2,0	8,2
1856–1866	2,5	1,3	1,6	7,4
1866–1875	2,0	1,3	1,7	5,4
1875–1882	0,7	2,6	2,0	9.1

Source: Levy-Leboyer and Bourguignon (1985: app. A-IV) in "France"[190]

* It is interesting that developed European countries on this path to the free market were in no hurry to sign the same agreements with the United Kingdom. After all, in this case, they would only receive concessions in their agricultural exports equal to the privileges received by France

Although the years in the table do not coincide with the main events of Napoleon III's reign (1850—reduction of duties, 1860—signing of the Franco-British Agreement, 1870—loss of power), it still provides a good reflection of them. Government efforts to promote the economy in the first phase of his reign led to a marked increase in growth rates between 1848 and 1860. From 1860 onward, there was a decline in growth (except in agriculture), and only after he lost power did it pick up again.

The same is true of railroad transportation statistics. In the 1860s, the amount of goods transshipped from trains to ships in German ports began to exceed that in French ports. This was even though German ports were far from the Atlantic (and goods from America, Africa, and Asia were transported across the Atlantic). If we take into account that the land border of the German countries was much longer than that of France (and therefore more trade took place across it), it becomes clear that the decade of the 1860s was decisive in the economic superiority of future Germany over France[191].

From the point of view of Louis-Napoleon, he helped his country significantly—the overall growth of its GDP accelerated, and this is the main thing. The fact that the growth rate of the industry, taken separately, slowed down was not significant—according to the liberal approach. France simply adapted its economy to its 'natural' advantages.[192] That is, if France was good at making wines and not good enough at making steam engines, the economy was restructured so that more resources went to wine production at the expense of building steam engines.

A country under the cover of state protection
and a country in a free market situation—*Source: NSL Archive*

The government of the Second Republic (which came to power after France's defeat in the Franco-Prussian War) largely continued the liberal course of Napoleon III. It indifferently watched as ships from the other side of the Atlantic unloaded in the ports of Germany, Holland, and Belgium, bypassing the

French ports that were the first on their way. He knew that this was because those ports were better equipped and took less time to reload ships, and the German state railroads charged lower freight rates when picking up goods from those ports. French parliamentary commissions and research by individual MPs led to conclusions similar to the following: "French prices have not fallen as much as German prices; the fault lies with private companies."[193] In other words, French private enterprise was not up to the task of capturing the peak of the world economy on its own. The liberal decision of the state to refrain from interfering in economic processes was made at the wrong time (France was not yet at the peak) and proved to be fatal.

The consequence of this liberal approach was that <u>France began to lose its leading position in the economic world. If until then it had been the "eternal second," the one that was constantly breathing down the leader's neck since then it has begun to slip back to third place.</u>

New challenges

The second industrial revolution was approaching, and the main challenge was not the ratio of total exports and imports, as it had been in the days of mercantilism, but their structure.

France soon had to learn that the advantage of the peak is that it (the peak) has something that others do not have—certain industries (the decisive economy). A valley has the same as others. For example, France had a developed agricultural sector, but the import of cheap grain from Ukraine, which displaced local products, reduced the profits of French enterprises, which resulted in a drop in orders for industrial goods, which was another blow to French industry.[194]

And even more importantly, the Second Industrial Revolution brought other goods and other enterprises to the forefront. Even during the First Industrial Revolution, the structure of exports and imports was negative for France, increasing the export of agricultural products in exchange for an increase in the import of industrial products. This fact alone placed France at the bottom of the economic pyramid, not at the peak. But even worse for France was the fact that this was the time when the Second Industrial Revolution was beginning to cause *countries to rise and fall in the economic hierarchy, depending on what industrial and raw materials were imported and what was exported.*

By opening its market to foreign industrial goods, France lost the chance for the rapid emergence and development of new technologies of the Second Industrial Revolution. Its companies did not grow in sizeon industrial exports. Because companies did not grow, they did not acquire a complex structure and did not become carriers of accumulated experience and a source that generates and nurtures new ideas.

That is, what happened in the US and Germany did not happen in France.

COLLABORATORS

Europe would have been completely unable to conquer the East (either politically or economically) if it had not been for help in the East. Western European enterprises met local entrepreneurs there who were ready to cooperate and were looking for opportunities to make a profit in cooperation with Western enterprises. The circle of people willing to cooperate with Western companies consisted not only of entrepreneurs. They were sailors who wanted to be hired on European ships; they were translators and experts in local customs or roads; they were willing to be hired to work in European factories and simply stevedores who could be hired by the next European ship. Perhaps not all of them, but probably most of them, began to sincerely respect the West over time and became conductors of its influence (i.e., agitators of its benefits). After all, it provided them with income, and the further it went, the more it showed itself to be a more powerful and more promising hierarchy of socio-economic influence than their own states.

The same situation repeated itself over and over again in different places, with different peoples and countries, and at different times of Western European expansion: "A Western businessman would find himself besieged by thousands of native brokers pressing their services on him... lean and hungry auxiliaries who encircled the Portuguese when the latter made their first expeditions to the spice islands."[195] One Italian who lived in Africa from 1654 to 1667 noted that "for a coral necklace or a little wine, the Congolese would sell their parents, their children, or their brothers and sisters, swearing to the buyers that these were household slaves."[196]

It was this private local initiative, this vigorous search for profit, for opportunities to expand their enterprises, that made it extremely easy for European enterprises to build their pyramids of socio-economic influence in foreign countries. And from these pyramids of socio-economic influence of individual enterprises were formed large pyramids of political and economic influence of the countries of these Western enterprises. Local traders collected the necessary goods from the hinterland of a country and brought them to the coastal ports for the Dutch or the British, who had to pick them up and pay for them. They also distributed goods of the advanced economy in the same hinterland. In Africa, it was Africans bringing to the coast other Africans captured for sale as slaves to Europeans; elsewhere it was something else. "Thousands of . . . auxiliaries, associates and collaborators bustled around them—a hundred or a thousand times more numerous than the men who were not yet—but soon would be—the masters."[197]

Successful local businesses also saw their opportunity to "cooperate" with Europeans. For example, in India, the British needed capital for their operations, and local bankers were willing to provide it. Practice showed that loans to Western entrepreneurs were less risky than to local ones. Therefore, the available capital was more readily going to the Europeans. Thus, it was much harder for an Indian entrepreneur who wanted to expand his business or wanted to copy the best European practices to get money in India than for a Western one.

Local entrepreneurs were looking for opportunities for their businesses, and whether these opportunities were good or bad for their country was a completely different perspective. "And it was indeed these local minority groups who, partly under pressure, partly by their own accord, paved the way for European intrusion, teaching first the Portuguese, then the Dutch and English (and even the French, Danes and Swedes) the way through the labyrinth of the 'country trade'. The process had thus begun which was by the end of the eighteenth century to deliver more than 85 or 90 percent of India's foreign trade over to the English monopoly."[198] In the end, thousands of Indians who were simply looking for an opportunity and found it in the salary of a soldier in the service of the British East India Company (sepoys) conquered India for Britain.

AMERICAN CORPORATIONS

Private enterprises and risk

Rational entrepreneurship correlates the degree of risk with the rewards that can be obtained. The greater the risk, the greater the potential profit to motivate an entrepreneur to act. But there are circumstances when the risk cannot even be estimated. These are circumstances of extreme uncertainty.[199]

As long as the results of oceanic expeditions were characterized by extreme uncertainty, private households preferred to invest in other projects where it was at least possible to assess risk. When the state-owned expeditions of Portugal and Spain found ways to new markets and identified trade opportunities in the newly discovered markets and the dangers of sailing there, private enterprises became able to assess risk and make decisions. The decisions continued to be negative for about a hundred years. When the paths were already well-trodden and all the risks became much clearer and smaller, the first private expeditions began. Even then, private enterprises sought state support primarily in the form of securing their monopoly on their future trade or on the lands they were going to develop. Obtaining a monopoly from the state significantly increased the chances of good profits, and thus helped to outweigh (and survive) the risks that remained high. *And this is another pattern—when the risk is impossible to assess, the unknown in human history has been broken through by state action. This was followed by a private initiative backed by state aid. If state aid in the past consisted of granting a monopoly to those who followed the paths trodden by the state initiative, now, for example, Musk receives state orders to fly his rockets, which follow the paths trodden by NASA.*

Economy as a soup with Brownian motion

After 200 years, when information about distant lands, distances to them, approximate profits from trade with them, etc. became widely known, and when ships became much more reliable, faster, and carried more cargo, the risk became not only easy to assess, but most importantly, it became incomparably smaller. It was potentially a time to unleash the potential of private initiative. However, the monopolies of the companies licensed at the previous stage (mainly the East India Company) stood in the way. However, the point of their existence has already disappeared. Everything that only a large company could do before could now be done by small enterprises that entered into temporary contracts with each other and could quickly reorient themselves to other enterprises, other products, other areas of trade, and other methods of production. Because of this, they did what large companies used to do with incomparably greater efficiency. Such a dynamic, moving system of interconnections could only be formed at the peak of the economic pyramid in a diversified economy with diverse external relations. Such companies entered into contracts, extended them, or broke them, depending on the circumstances. They collided, stuck together, and repelled like particles in a Brownian motion.

The growth in demand for certain goods classically raised prices for them, the rise in prices increased potential incomes, and the increased incomes attracted private initiative to produce these goods—new enterprises were formed to meet the increased demand. When demand dropped, these enterprises, if they could, switched to producing other goods; if they could not, they closed down, and capital and people flowed to other enterprises. This was the classic economics of Smith and Schumpeter, made possible by an abundance of capital and opportunity, which in turn was made possible by being at the peak of the world economy.

Peak conditions further reduced risks for British companies. The concentration of global economic ties in one country brought about the concentration of almost all European export and import operations in warehouses in UK ports, as well as inflows of foreign capital from around the world. This concentration provided convenient access to all the goods in these warehouses, to information in local offices about the movement of world goods and supply and demand in other parts of the world, etc. The availability of this information allowed entrepreneurs to invest in the production of goods for which a new demand was emerging somewhere, reducing their risk. Less risk requires less capital. Therefore, many British entrepreneurs were able to open many small and medium-sized enterprises to meet international demand.

In a highly diverse economy at the peak, even the oligarchy could not be sure that the old, sluggish monster companies would bring it more wealth than the capital invested in small, nimble companies created to seize the current opportunity. That's why it didn't put up much of a fight when small and medium-sized enterprises started demanding the abolition of monopoly licenses. Without them, huge, structured enterprises with a variety of industries within them began to disappear in the United Kingdom. *Britain was the very first industrialized country in the world, and its unique conditions created an economy of "small and medium-sized businesses." All those who came later needed large enterprises.*

Concentration of production

The success of the British classical free-market model of economy in the United Kingdom depended on the success of the implementation of free-market ideas in the world. And by the mid-19th century the UK had succeeded in spreading free-market ideas to many other countries. But the United States, meanwhile, fenced off from British exports, was developing its own economy. Since this economy did not have such a diverse and abundant inflow of capital, knowledge, skills, goods, etc. from around the world, its development took on different forms. In this economy, only a limited number of enterprises that were able to acquire capital, knowledge, skills, etc. served local American demand. And most importantly, while in the UK many small enterprises emerged in different parts of the country to serve domestic and foreign demand, in the US almost the same circle of companies in the northeast, whose composition changed rather slowly, gradually increased their market. Their market grew due to a constant but gradual increase in demand created by "internal colonization." Much more limited sources of capital, knowledge, etc. (compared to the UK) led to the fact that new entrepreneurial people, inventors, specialists, etc., instead of trying to start their own business, brought their capital, knowledge, and labor to a small number of existing enterprises. As a result, a small number of enterprises grew in size as demand grew. The new enterprises that emerged later found it difficult to compete with the existing large enterprises. Often these new companies were bought up by the old large ones or went bankrupt.

Thus, an important American feature was developed—large enterprises, often with their own internal structure, which reflected the sectoral and territorial division of the economy. In other words, parts of the American economy (from different industries and in different territories) were combined within a single company, forming, so to speak, "sub-economies" of the overall US economy.

An example is steel production. Andrew Carnegie combined the production of several different businesses under one roof—coke production in furnaces, smelting of metal in blast furnaces, and rolling and manufacturing of rails, beams, bars, and structural steel. As a consequence, he received a significant increase in output and, as a result, a significant decrease in production costs (from $67.50 per ton in 1880 to $29.25 in 1889).[200] This allowed him to buy up other metallurgical enterprises in

Pittsburgh. By the end of the century, several mergers took place to form the United States Steel Corporation, the world's first company worth more than a billion dollars. This company is still one of the main oligopolists in its industry.

Corporations grew especially rapidly from the last quarter of the 19th century onward, acquiring new divisions in other territories and other industries. The growth of businesses was driven by the fact that the competition was won by those who were able to achieve greater economies of scale. "This was historically a necessary condition for those firms to become oligopolistic players in capital-intensive industries. Enterprises that subsequently integrated production and distribution accounted for a significant share of physical capital formation in the new scale-dependent technologies that were prime engines of growth particularly between the 1880s and World War I."[201]

Bureaucracy as a new inherent feature of private enterprise

In parallel with the growth, another feature of American enterprises developed: the bureaucratization of entrepreneurship. Colossal enterprises could no longer manage processes in far-flung territories in various economic sectors. They had to develop a management hierarchy, just as states had done before them.

State hierarchies grew from a small hierarchy of the emperor's slaves, the prince's close vigilantes, through the court of the king with his close nobles, then the hierarchy of noble local assemblies and royal governors, up to the trained professional bureaucracy of the modern type. Now, large corporations have followed the same path. Through a few relatives of the entrepreneur, then a few hired foremen, the managerial hierarchy became trained and professional and grew to a size no smaller than some state hierarchies.

As in states, the advent of professional bureaucracy has raised the efficiency of managing the complex pyramid of a corporation to new heights. Moreover, it was this advent that generally made possible the incredible complexity and subtlety of the interplay of parts that characterize both modern corporations and the developed economies of today.

The United States is coming out of its thieving age
At the stage of acceleration, American corporations mostly took existing foreign (mostly British) product samples as a model and put them into production. That is why "... from their very beginnings, large industrial firms concentrated, not on basic research but on development, not on inventing new products and processes, but on commercializing them, for national and global markets."[202] This sharply distinguished them from German concerns. But as the products of the Second Industrial Revolution became more and more science-based, it became increasingly important for the enterprises that produced them to cooperate with universities, private research organizations, and public research institutions. Toward the end of the 19th century, enterprises in the United States had already left the infantile period. A sign of their maturity was that they began to incorporate research into their internal structure, first by opening research departments within the enterprises, and second by hiring scientists and various specialists to oversee the production process and work in design offices.

It was only when they reached this stage that US corporations outgrew the childhood disease of unceremoniously stealing and copying British designs and began the path of their innovations and discoveries. Industrial enterprises grew so fast and so widespread that by the 80s of the 19th century, market saturation began to be felt and enterprises providing similar goods (or services) could no longer expand further without entering into competition. Competition naturally had to end with the victory of the fittest, best, strongest. The winner would take everything—the entire market. In other words, they became a monopolist. It often happened differently. Enterprises, tired of fighting each other and suffering significant losses, eventually agreed with each other. They divided the markets or agreed on high enough prices to suit everyone.

The different problem of monopolization

In the United Kingdom, huge monopoly enterprises were the result of a state act—granting a monopoly to certain enterprises. In other words, they were the result of state intervention in the economy. When numerous new companies achieved the ability to perform the functions of these monster companies, but because of licenses were still unable to perform them, their dissatisfaction was directed against the state and its interference in the economy.

In the United States, the picture was diametrically opposite. In the United States, huge, structured enterprises with a variety of industries within them formed monopolies as a result of the natural growth of their business operations and the absorption or displacement of competitors. In other words, they were a product of the free market. Therefore, in the United States, it was not the state that caused the dissatisfaction of new small enterprises that wanted to enter the market, but unrestricted competition. These new smaller companies did not want a free market—they demanded government intervention, they wanted a regulated market.

Since the British monopolies were the result of state action, their elimination had to be the result of state action, i.e., the abolition of state licenses. This part was easy to implement.

The only complication was that, for example, the East India Company had vast private territories and property in foreign lands (which it had acquired itself), and the elimination of the monopoly license for trade did not eliminate this property. So, in this case, the British state resorted to nationalization, and this option suited everyone. For example, the continuation of India's private ownership by the East India Company could have prevented other businesses from trading with India. The nationalization of India by the British state in 1858 made India equally accessible to all British enterprises. So, nationalization as a way to make the market freer and fairer* proved to be a good idea in this one of the first cases of large nationalizations in modern history.

The problem of American large enterprises could not be solved so easily. In this case, the state had to enter the market instead of withdrawing from it. Moreover, while large structured enterprises created unnecessary inertia at the peak (in the UK) where rapid adjustment to ever-changing situations was needed, in the US, these large structured enterprises were a necessary way of economic growth. The United States was not at the peak of the world economy, and it did not have such rapid changes in situations that did not depend on either American enterprises or the state. **The formation of such "sub-economies" of the overall American economy was precisely the essence of the American way.** It was disadvantageous to the Americans to destroy the concentration of production that had been nurtured, but it was worthwhile to put limits on it. One by one, state governments introduced laws aimed at limiting the monopolization of the market by individual enterprises. This pushed potential monopolists to go beyond the borders of

* from the point of view of British companies, not Indians

individual states and have their components in different states. The enterprise could thus continue to grow without violating antitrust laws. Over time, however, as they grew naturally, such enterprises began to acquire monopoly status on a US-wide scale. Thus, in 1890, the Sherman Act, an antitrust law, was passed.

This struggle between the state and the enterprises led to the next natural step in this situation. To grow further, enterprises needed to go beyond the borders of the United States. This course of action was, moreover, encouraged by the state. The state, for example, could provide enterprises with a subsidy in the form of a certain amount for each unit of exported goods. Such subsidies enabled these exporters to sell their products abroad at reduced prices and conquer foreign markets. The United States began to build its own American economic world in the Western Hemisphere, promising to reduce tariffs in exchange for allowing its goods to enter the markets of Latin American countries.

The United States begins to build an economic pyramid

American companies began their triumphant march across the world, with large branches opening not only in Latin America but also in key European countries, such as the United Kingdom, the German Empire, France, and the Russian Empire[203]. The huge American Standard Oil had few worthy rivals in the world, except for the Dutch Royal Dutch Shell. The same is true in the production of electricity—the American corporations General Electric and Westinghouse Electric already dominated the world markets in the production of electric lamps, power lines, generators, transformers, electric motors, etc. along with the German Siemens and Allgemeine Elektricitats Gesellschaft (AEG)[204]

General Electric built factories in the United Kingdom and France, and Westinghouse Electric in France, Germany and the Russian Empire. In the telephone industry, AT&T Corporation captured a monopoly in the United States and by 1914 already had branches in the United Kingdom, Germany, France, Canada, Italy, the Austro-Hungarian and Russian empires*.

By the beginning of World War I, the major American corporations had already crystallized and divided their markets. They maintained their dominant position thanks to their own large profits and prevented new companies from entering the market in every way possible.

American three stages

The US economy, like the British economy, grew in three stages, but with its own "specifics."

1. Building the national economy—the agrarian oligarchy in power in the American republic hoped that Europe (especially the United Kingdom) would not survive a pan-European war without its agricultural and raw materials—hence the American embargo, which gave rise to the British and French embargo in response. This provided a chance for American industrial enterprises, which did not miss it. Subsequently, these industries fought to maintain high customs walls around the United States. This provided an opportunity for the formation of the US national economy.

2. The formation of the "colonial empire" was carried out through the internal "absorption" of native American lands and the massive arrival of immigrants. The resulting economic growth was accompanied by the democratization of American society and the introduction of universal suffrage. This, in turn,

---

* the company was split into smaller ones by the state in 1982

gave rise to the phenomenon of the "spoil system". The state-spoil provided an opportunity for the formation of monopolies, which contributed to the development of large non-agricultural enterprises.

3. After the growth of the established monopolies was put to an end by the freed state, they were forced to start growing by opening their subsidiaries outside the United States. These subsidiaries captured new markets and transferred most of their profits back to the United States. In this way, a global economic pyramid was formed with the US at the peak.

RUSSIA ON THE EVE OF A REBELLION

Although the balance of Russian foreign trade continued to be positive during the 19th century, the industrial part of it (iron and alloys, finished products from yarn and linen) fell dramatically, and, as in pre-Peter the Great times, exports of wood, hemp, leather, etc. (mainly to the UK), as well as wheat and sugar from Ukraine began to prevail. The Russian Empire, having fallen into the trap of being a raw material appendage (and having accepted this role), began to discover the unpleasant aspects of this role. The industrial revolution in the West made the main raw materials of Russian exports, one by one, unnecessary. If the United Kingdom (UK) used to need huge amounts of rope and hemp for its fleet, this need was drastically reduced with the introduction of steamships. Lard exports declined as stearic candles were replaced by lamps and lubricating lard by petroleum-based oils. In addition, the UK began to favor importing bread from its colonies and the United States.

The owners of large agricultural enterprises (the nobility) were still interested in exporting their wheat and thus had no interest in Russia changing its status as an agricultural exporter.

The stunted industrial enterprises were unable to compete with Western products and exported only a little to China, Iran, or Turkey. And even there, their goods were being supplanted by Western products.

The state, which had previously been satisfied with the situation, had to change its point of view, especially because most of the declining industrial exports (iron, cloth, etc.) were products of state-owned factories. The defeat in the Crimean War was a vivid demonstration of the backwardness of the Russian Empire just 40 to 20 years after its decisive victory over Napoleon and its honorable position as the "gendarme of Europe," along with Prussia and the Austro-Hungarian Empire. The need for rebellion against fate became obvious. The Crimean War showed that while European countries could bring the necessary ammunition and provisions to their troops by ship, the Russian Empire could not do so on its territory due to the difficulty of transporting them by land by carts. The need for railroads became obvious and urgent. Therefore, Alexander II first of all eliminated serfdom and then began extensive construction of railroads. From this time on, we can count the rise of Russian industry caused by the reforms.

The fact that the vast majority of the population in the Russian Empire (85%) lived in rural areas,[205] reduced the demand for light industry goods (such as clothing and household items) and, as such, increased the risk of starting an entrepreneurship. After all, the rural community produced most of its consumption goods itself. The result was that "[t]he textile and food industries were not absent from this growth, but, given the limited domestic market for consumption goods, they did not have a great impetus."[206]

Thus, economic growth through the expansion of light industry production, followed by the expansion of heavy industry production, was difficult. Therefore, in the Russian Empire, the Anglo-Saxon model of economic growth was not promising. Instead, the German model had to work, i.e., the expansion of heavy industry, which would prepare the ground for the subsequent rise of light industry.

At the same time, the entrepreneurial spirit of Russian entrepreneurs was focused mainly on trade and, occasionally, on attempts to establish light industry, primarily weaving. Due to the weak activity of local entrepreneurship, the state had to take entrepreneurship into its own hands. First of all, the state began to build and operate railroads and ports at public expense or to guarantee private entrepreneurs compensation for their possible losses. For example, the state authorized the establishment in 1856 of the Russian Shipping and Trading Company, a joint-stock company with one-third of its shares owned by the state. This company made a significant contribution to the development of Russian exports to the Middle East and thus helped finance the state's economic endeavors[207]. To have the capital to stimulate the economy, the state also first sold part of its territory (Alaska) and then began to establish purely state-owned enterprises whose profits were used for these purposes. However, since this profit was not enough, the state had to follow the path of almost all European countries—the burden was placed on the peasants through taxation. This, of course, reduced peasant demand for light industry goods even further. But the state thus had the resources to stimulate heavy industry. Otherwise, the peasants' income would most likely have been spent on vodka or something like that. But concentrated in the hands of the state in large sums, this income was successfully invested in railroads, the development of metallurgy, etc.

Due to their vast territory, Russian railroads had to be long and thus required large investments from the start. Due to the lack of industry, they had to rely on imports of all equipment from abroad, and on the other hand, they could not expect large volumes of commercial traffic. Therefore, only the state could come up with the necessary large capital and step over the risk that was unbearable for private enterprise. An attempt to build railroads entirely on imported equipment in the 1860s and 1870s quickly led to a trade balance crisis[208]. To avoid going into debt, the Russian state placed orders for equipment needed by railroads and ports only with Russian enterprises, if they were available (even if of inferior quality).

Initially, low customs duties allowed British and then German industry to strangle the sprouts of Russian industry without hindrance. Only in 1877 were duties finally raised and the trade balance turned positive. This happened by reducing the import of consumer goods for the nobility, but not only. The industry of the Russian Empire, which could now develop under the cover of the customs wall, made it possible to reduce the import of sugar, tobacco, oil, cotton fabrics, etc.[209] Subsequently, duties gradually increased from an average of 12.7% in 1869-1876 to 33% in 1891-1900. Although the state often tried to raise its revenues rather than protect the industry, duties began to protect the emerging industry. At the same time, duties were reduced on goods needed by industrial enterprises or even canceled altogether, for example, on iron or machinery. High duties to protect domestic industry kept consumer prices high enough, and since three-quarters of the population were peasants, they were again the main group that bore the burden of the rise of domestic industry.

The other side of the high duties was that foreign businesses, which were losing the opportunity to import their goods to the Russian Empire, sought to open branches in Russia to continue to make profits on the Russian market. "For example, the increase in customs duties on imports of steel, iron, and coal led to the establishment of several joint-stock companies in France, whose goal was to build metalworking plants in Russia. The beginning of production activities of German electrical and chemical companies in Russia was also associated with the establishment of customs barriers."[210] To reinforce this trend, the Russian government further reduced the risks of Western investors by pursuing a policy of suppressing the labor movement, which reduced the costs of labor for entrepreneurs. All this was the reason why 40% of the capital of Russian joint-stock companies were foreign investments.[211]

It is worth noting this fact—as we have seen many times before, the increase in duties promotes the establishment of domestic enterprises of the decisive economy in the valley countries. Raising them even higher contributes to the establishment of such enterprises in these countries by enterprises of peak. (provided that the market is large enough or export opportunities are available).

Under the protection of customs duties, the industry of the Russian Empire grew mainly around St. Petersburg, Moscow, and in the Urals in Russia itself, as well as in Ukraine and Poland. For example, in Ukraine, in 1872, a pig iron smelting plant was built by a British entrepreneur, John James Hughes, not far from rich coal deposits. The settlement was called Yuzovka and later became the city of Donetsk. As early as 1795, not too far away in Luhansk, there was a state-owned factory producing cast-iron cannons for the Black Sea Fleet. Soon after, not far from there, in Mariupol, two huge metallurgical enterprises were founded, one by the Belgians and the other by Americans, French, and Germans in a joint-stock company. While in the 70s of the 19th century, the Urals plants produced 67% of the empire's metal, and Donetsk's 0.1%, by 1900 the share of the Urals had dropped to 28%, and the share of Donbas had increased to 51%.

"Russia, the least developed part of Europe." had "a very slow growth until the mid-1880s followed by a sudden acceleration that lasted until 1900. The so-called heavy industries led this 'spurt' with exceptionally high growth rates in such sectors as steel-making and engineering."[212] This "sudden acceleration" is easily explained by the fact that "this period was characterized by intensified involvement of the government... in the economy."[213] This period was characterized by the state buying up private railroads, Witte's measures to eliminate railroad delays, and the promotion of the construction of the Siberian Railway (the longest railway at the time, and perhaps still today).

Thus, state measures played a key role in the beginning of the economic growth of the Russian Empire. But by Western standards, the stimulating role of the Russian state was more than modest. The Russian state did not care much about education—72% of the population was illiterate,[214] not to mention higher education. Furthermore, apart from loan guarantees, mainly for the construction of private railroads, the state did not provide any other assistance, especially state subsidies, which are so common in the West. The range of state-owned enterprises was limited mostly to railroads, postal services, telegraph, and the sale of alcohol (until the monopoly was abolished in 1863). In addition, the purchase of arms, a classic measure of the Western powers to indirectly stimulate heavy industry, was so meager that it could not play a stimulating role[215]. All of this proved to be decisive in the insufficient acceleration of the economy. This, in addition, was the central reason for the loss in the Russo-Japanese War of 1904-1905. And this defeat caused the breakdown of even the uncertain economic acceleration that had already begun. This, in turn, became the catalyst for the 1905-1907 revolution, which further depressed economic development.

Being at the bottom of the Western European economic pyramid distorted the empire's development trajectory from the very beginning. The 3.3% annual growth was half due to growth in the agricultural sector. Efforts to build railroads only partially led to the stimulation of domestic industry—the penetration of railroads far into the interior of the continent enabled the hinterland to export its grain.[216] This, in turn, made it possible to use foreign currency to purchase the necessary Western industrial products, thus reducing demand for domestic industry.

Eventually, the embeddedness of the Russian economy in the Western European economic pyramid led to the fact that the state, trying to develop heavy industry, was forced to further promote embedding in this pyramid. To bring foreign currency into the country, the government encouraged exports. Loans were even granted at low interest rates for exports, and exporting enterprises received other privileges. But exports consisted mainly of grain, coal, and some oil and metal. Supporting such exports (in the late 19th and early 20th centuries) consolidated the embeddedness in foreign economic pyramids.[217]

JAPAN—THE BEGINNING OF THE REBELLION

From the middle of the 16th century to the second half of the 17th century, when Europeans were building pyramids of their economic worlds in Asia, the Japanese state, seeing no other way, decided to preserve the country's independence by closing itself off from the outside world. Trade and even leaving and entering Japan were prohibited. The only window of contact was Nagasaki, through which a limited number of Chinese and Dutch merchants were allowed to trade. In this state, Japan was able to maintain its economic independence, but only for as long as the West allowed it. While British and French guns were destroying the self-confidence of the Russian Empire at Sevastopol, the guns of American warships in 1854 forced the Japanese state to open its ports. The Japanese state even lost control of its customs duties. The situation presented Japan with a choice: either to be built into the base of the Western economic pyramid or to be on par with it. It was a choice similar to the one that the Russian state faced after its defeat in the Crimean War, only Japan's lagging at that time was incomparably greater and the task more difficult.

In Japan, transformations began after a coup d'état (Meiji Restoration in 1868), which abolished feudal rights, eliminated feudal lords, and introduced universal military service. But the most important thing was the strengthening of the state. "The previous government was decentralized and reliant on local authorities which needed to be replaced by a central government. The Meiji government completed a spectacular starting feat, creating a centralized government in roughly half a century."[218]

Having barely achieved the first successes in its strengthening, the Japanese state took up the economy. The goal was industrialization. Japan could not wait for Japanese private enterprise to stand on its own, and since there were no forces in the country that knew what to do and how the state began to establish the first industrial enterprises and infrastructure itself. It began by expanding armories and building shipyards. The telegraph connected the country's main cities by 1880. When the state planned to build the first railroad, it began to encourage private capital, following the Anglo-Saxon model. To do this, it guaranteed 7% dividends on the invested private capital. When it turned out that the private initiative was not up to the mark, the state founded the company itself and the first railroad was built in 1872. State investment in railroad construction accounted for one-third of all public investment in 1870-1874.

In addition, loans were taken from the UK[219]. As the railroads demonstrated profitability, further projects were able to attract private capital, but still under state guarantees of 10% dividends (and assistance by 256 engineers). By 1892, Japan already had 550 miles of public and 1,320 miles of private railways.

The industry needed iron, and since the existing private mines were small and equipped with outdated machinery, the state had to step in, opening six large-scale mines of its own with modern equipment. The mining industry was not new, so things were more cheerful here—even though some state and private mines went bankrupt, former feudal lords began to establish new mines together with Western capital. When things picked up, the state sold its mines to private companies that has already gained strength.

In parallel, efforts were made to boost private enterprise through government financial support. In Japan, there were no other forces with sufficient power to establish private industrial enterprises other than the former feudal lords. They were the ones who responded to state incentives. (Another source was traders, who, however, could themselves be descended from small samurai).

Shipbuilding and shipping are a good example. The state established a company to transport mail, cargo, and passengers on short sea lines. Soon, however, there was a private company that began to compete with it. This company (Mitsubishi) was an industrial enterprise founded by a samurai. Its owner, Iwasaki Yataro, gathered around him former samurai who treated him and his enterprise according to the samurai spirit of devotion to his master and his fief. The "morality of solidarity" of these samurai was one of the reasons for his success. The state did not interfere with private enterprise and began to transport mail on its ships. In 1874-1875, the state purchased

11 metal steamships and leased them to Mitsubishi (eventually donated them) so that it could compete with foreign companies on the Japan-China transportation line. Considerable government subsidies came later. By 1877, Mitsubishi had met expectations.[220]

The state also promoted the textile industry, owning two of the three cotton spinning mills in 1877. But in general, the Japanese state focused its efforts only on capital-intensive and technologically sophisticated industries, leaving the rest to private initiative. In the end, funds were limited. After all, the state was simultaneously establishing model enterprises for the production of cement, glass, and various machine tools. Not all state-owned plants and factories were successful. Some of them eventually went bankrupt. But they raised new Japanese cadres—engineers and professional workers. Roads, ports, and banks were also built alongside by the state.

Seeing the economic shifts caused by the state, the samurai were more willing to engage in entrepreneurship. They often started with trade and then, having accumulated capital, invested it in industry. One of the first examples of such entrepreneurship is the Mitsui Bussan Company, founded by one of the barons (Takashi Masuda). It was one of the first domestic trading companies that exported agricultural products and purchased necessary technological goods in the West.

The Japanese Empire began its industrialization almost simultaneously with the Russian Empire but achieved incomparably greater success, which was convincingly demonstrated in the Japanese victory in the Russo-Japanese War in 1905.[*]

This is because the Russian Empire was already built into the base of the Western European economic pyramid, while

* It was the first victory of an Asian country over a European country in modern times

the Japanese Empire was not. Because of this, in the Russian Empire, former feudal lords were already accustomed to making a profit from their economic activities aimed at exporting agricultural products to Western Europe, while in Japanese self-isolation, this path had not yet been paved. Therefore, for the Japanese former feudal lords, any way to expand their business activities was equivalent. And the state's task was simply to direct it in the right direction.

In addition, unlike the process in the Russian Empire, the process in the Japanese Empire took place not only with much greater direct state involvement in entrepreneurship but also under much greater state control as far as Western investment was concerned.

Creating a foreign economic pyramid
During this period of industrialization, the Japanese state also helped domestic enterprises in other ways. Since Japan was short of raw materials, the Japanese state began to conquer new territories where such raw materials were available and where there was a population to consume Japanese goods. The conquests began with the capture of Chinese Taiwan in 1895, followed by the annexation of Korea in 1910. The loss of the war cost the Russian Empire part of Sakhalin and the Kuril Islands. The fact that as a result of this war, Japan took over Manchuria from the Russian Empire "was very important for the zaibatsu in several ways, firstly, it was the arrival of an American railroad magnate (E.G. Harriman) in Japan to bring American economic interests to the development of Manchurian resources. Second, it gave the Japanese access to resource-rich North China."[221]

With these conquests came a new stage in the development of Japanese industry. Along with the boom in light industry, shipbuilding and coal mining continued to grow, and the chemical and power generation industries began to develop. Successes in the development of metallurgy made it possible to produce locomotives and other heavy equipment alongside steamships.

One-sided solidarity

Such a great involvement of the Japanese state in industrial entrepreneurship contributed to the fact that the Japanese nobility (unlike, say, the Russian nobility) not only did not shy away from it but began to actively get involved in it. Already at these early stages, Japanese entrepreneurship developed along the lines that later came to be regarded as inherently Japanese: the spirit of solidarity in the economy; the tendency of enterprises to develop as conglomerates, buying up enterprises in other industries; and, most importantly, constant cooperation between the state and private enterprises. The nobility seemed to follow their emperor in battle. In addition, the state intervened in the relations of private enterprises, trying to resolve competition in a spirit of harmony, just as it had previously tried to settle the discord between warring feudal lords. In other words, the corporate structure of Japanese feudal society was smoothly and seamlessly transferred to industrial society.

At the same time, the solidaristic spirit that had no time to be killed by the liberal spirit of free-market capitalism encouraged the emergence of cartels in Japan even more than in the Germanic countries. Cartels, with the assistance of the state, not only dampened competition but also saved efforts. The work that was common to all, which each enterprise would have to do on its own, could be done by the cartel for everyone at once. Cartels published technical publications and facilitated the exchange of engineers between enterprises, which contributed to the overall accumulation of knowledge.[222]

Creating an economic empire

Japan, having started industrializing, quickly found that it had to buy not only Western technological equipment but also raw materials for production. Thus, the need to produce for export (to have the foreign currency to buy imports) was in full force from the very beginning. This is what distinguished Japan from the Russian Empire, which, having almost any raw material and a tradition of exporting agricultural products, had a much smaller need for export production. In addition, lesser involvement of the state of the Russian Empire in industrialization prevented the state from focusing foreign exchange earnings from the sale of raw materials on rapid industrialization, as was done in Japan by its state. Among other things, this situation pushed Japan to take an original step that later became common—the Mitsui Corporation raided American companies shortly before the outbreak of World War I, buying the Standard Aircraft Corporation, which gave it approximately $14 million in profits and immeasurable experience in the production of airplanes.[223]

In insular Japan, the need for exports led to efforts to establish shipbuilding to avoid having to pay for Western services in exporting exports outside Japan. This was also an indirect reason why the Japanese navy was able to defeat the Russian fleet off Tsushima in 1904. Exports began with silk. The state made special efforts to help this sector improve its equipment.

Unlike Russia, Japan was forced by the United Kingdom and the United States to lift customs restrictions on imports. Thus, its markets were open to Western goods. In such circumstances, Japan had to become the foundation of Western economic pyramids or do something unexpected. The state tried to limit the inflow of foreign investment by providing subsidies, and most importantly, guarantees for income from domestic private investment. But even more important was the fact that the Japanese state from the very beginning began to encourage private households to "buy Japanese." Wherever possible, the state wove national pride into a free market open to the western winds. Traditions of social solidarity were invoked to ensure that Japanese enterprises helped each other wherever they could. This tradition of solidarity is still a distinctive feature of the Japanese economy today, and it still gives Japan the ability to maneuver and win where the economic superpowers manage to impose liberal rules of the game.

Thus, Japan went through its first two stages—building a national market and its separate economic pyramid within the framework of its conquests. Japan failed in its third step—an attempt to capture the global economic pyramid, which resulted in military defeat during World War II. Nevertheless, Japan continued to expand its economic pyramid to the best of its ability after World War II. The "secret" of its success, among other things, was a pragmatic attitude to its goals: after losing the war, the Japanese began to trade peacefully with their victors. Moreover, Japan even traded with the USSR, with which it remained at war until its collapse.

THE DOOM OF THE PEAK

The lordly fate of the leaders
In 1850, 93% of British exports consisted of manufactured goods and the same share of imports consisted of raw materials and agricultural products. At that time, the United Kingdom produced 40% of the world's industrial products for export. At the same time, about 25% of world trade passed through British ports.[224] The UK, having placed itself at the peak of the global economic system, obtained the best or cheapest raw materials for its industry from all over the world and shipped products

to the places where it could get the highest price. It was a well-established and already stable system. The presence of such a peak in the world economy made the new enterprises in the valley, which had succeeded with the assistance of their states, want to take advantage of it. Instead of taking on all the complexity, and most importantly the risk, of finding customers in the world and concluding agreements with them (which could easily be violated by the weak and unreliable businesses of the newly industrialized countries), these enterprises took their products to Britain. From there, these products were sold by British intermediaries. If a buyer changed his mind or was unable to purchase the product, it would eventually be purchased by another enterprise, possibly from a completely different part of the world. The same applies to purchases: instead of looking for the necessary raw materials somewhere in the world, the buyer would go to the United Kingdom, where he would find raw materials from different parts of the world and could slowly choose the right price and quality.

The whole world was enveloped in networks of British banks and insurance companies, where British traders could always conveniently borrow and insure their operations. There were British wholesale agencies everywhere and the opportunity to use British merchant ships to transport goods. Foreign traders also took advantage of all these already existing enterprises, which were willing to open their doors to them. Part of their trade also increased the income of the United Kingdom. In addition, we should add the income from freight—the services of transportation of goods from other countries by ships, insurance by British companies of foreign entrepreneurs, and other services,[225] which were the result of the UK's position at the peak of the economic pyramid and increased the profits of British trade and reduced them for other parties. This global dependence on British trade and finance remained intact despite the decline in the profits of British industry.

Everything said about goods also applies to capital. During its time at the peak of the global economic pyramid, the United Kingdom accumulated a lot of capital. And they were invested in other countries of the world in the businesses that the British needed. Start-ups around the world knew that if they needed capital to realize their ideas, Britain was the best place to look. The fact that capital seekers came to London first led to the fact that enterprises looking for a place to invest their excess capital also came to London first. Thus, London became a global center for financial services. The fact that other countries were industrializing and pushing Britain out of their markets did not affect this fact—a convenient place for borrowers and lenders to meet had already been established and it was impossible to move it elsewhere. All of this reduced risks, which is very important, especially for start-ups. As Halford John Mackinder, who is considered the father of geostrategy, noted in an address to the Institute of Bankers in 1899: "It seems inevitable that there should be a relative fall [of British industrial activity]. But the world's clearing house* tends, from its very nature, to remain in a single position, and that clearing house will always be where there is the greatest ownership of capital. This gives the real key to the struggle between our free trade policy and the protection of other countries—we are essentially the people with capital, and those who have capital always share in the activity of brains and muscles of other countries."[226]

* one that deals with interbank netting

The slave fate of leaders

While the United Kingdom was building its economic pyramid out of the world economy, subordinating it to the needs of its industrial production, it was, at the same time, increasingly embedding itself in the global flows of goods and capital. It could be said to have become a victim, or a slave, to these flows. In any case, it became extremely difficult for them to escape from their captivity. The largest market, the world market, was opened to British enterprises. And the availability of any goods, services, and, most importantly, subcontractors reduced the risks that were inevitably present in other countries. These risks were the driving force in other economies that pushed businesses to merge or establish new divisions engaged in related operations. A metallurgical enterprise could establish another unit that would manufacture products from its metal to ensure the sale of that metal. It could also buy up coal mines and iron ore mines to ensure that it always had raw materials, and maybe even a transportation company to avoid the hassle of shipping raw materials and finished products. These trends existed because of limited sources of raw materials and services and underdeveloped demand. So enterprises had to take care of securing all the market elements that were important to them. The acquisition of these elements created the greatest guarantees and gave rise to multi-unit enterprises (Mform), which, due to the complexity of their structure and management, generated new management skills that were retained within the structure of these companies. Such enterprises were capable of making large investments in their own scientific and technological research, and the knowledge gained was also retained in the structure of these enterprises. Such enterprises became capacitors that made it possible not only to accumulate knowledge and skills but also to expand and increase them, which facilitated progress, despite all the obvious shortcomings. The absence of these "capacitors," accumulators of knowledge and skills, i.e. large companies, was one of the main reasons for the economic lagging behind of the UK, which began in the late 19th century.

Moreover, being at the peak of the global economic pyramid gave rise to concerns about government intervention as something that could spoil the system that had worked so well under the free market. This fair and well-founded concern naturally extended to the "artificial fruits" of this intervention—the huge foreign trade companies whose profits kept many smaller enterprise owners awake at night. The consequence was the cancellation of licenses for such enterprises and the virtual destruction of these multi-unit accumulators of knowledge and skills.

After the abolition of the East India Company's monopoly on trade with India, a lot of small companies rushed into this trade and the export of cotton products from the United Kingdom increased 56 times in 18 years.[227] Accordingly, the lucky ones who now have access to the previously unavailable trade quickly found themselves with only pennies. The unrestrained, now unregulated, influx of British products reduced the profitability of British trade by half from 1800 to 1860. That is, without the East India Monopoly, the United Kingdom had to export twice as much product for the same profit.

But the main thing is that exports were mainly driven by light industry, i.e., those whose products satisfied the final consumer demand.[228] This was the type of product that the British global trading network needed. It was a type of mass-demand product. Steam locomotives, engines, mechanized machines and seeders, hydro turbines, etc. were not adapted to the traditional value chain that brought the UK its global economic dominance. But in the field of light industry, the British enterprises still found their safe harbor, their cozy corner, where they were still masters and where their capital still brought them guaranteed profits. So, they saw no need for change.

Because of this, heavy industry suffered. And its rise "would have provided a greater long-term asset to the economy than a large, efficient jam-making or chocolate industry."[229]

At the same time, more and more of the profit from exports was consumed by goods and services that served the increasingly high standard of living of the population—jewelry, exotic goods, and overseas fruits. This situation was even welcomed by the enterprises because it "allowed the backward countries to earn foreign currency to purchase British industrial exports." The dismissal of the state, "because it can only get in the way," left no hope for the visible, enforcing hand of the public interest. In 1913, imports (600 million pounds sterling) already exceeded exports (500 million GBP). Only the profits from foreign investments, amounting to 200 million GBP, helped the UK to still be in the black and maintain its position at the peak of the world.[230]

The United Kingdom fell victim to its position at the peak of the global economy, did not rethink the free market ideology that had been beneficial to it for the time being, and did not rebel, did not try to break free from the waves that were carrying it into a minor future. The UK did not have a state that would take the helm with a firm hand and steer it against the will of the treacherous waves. Like the United Provinces in the 18th century, the United Kingdom was increasingly switching from manufacturing and trade to financial transactions.

A NEW LEADER—HISTORY REPEATS ITSELF

Once upon a time, at the initiative of the British state, the British economy gained such momentum that money invested in the United Kingdom began to generate returns at least as high as the Dutch had from their overseas trade. Because of this, Dutch money began to flow inexorably into the British economy, further strengthening it. Inexorably, because the private interest saw this as a direct benefit, and the Dutch state saw no point in hindering the movement of capital, since it was in the freedom of this movement that the secret of the fabulous prosperity of the "open to all winds" Dutch economy had been.

At the end of the 19th century, British private capital also found a fabulous place to invest, where it brought unspeakable profits. This place was the United States of America. The British invested in American railroads and other businesses, just as they did in other countries. But while elsewhere in the world, the British built railroads to bring cotton or ore to ports for further transportation to the United Kingdom, this was not the case in the United States. Here, railroads (like other British investments) followed the lines of the American economy, going where local enterprises needed them. In other words, British investments in the United States were not determined by the needs of the British economy, as in other countries, but served the needs of American corporations or simply became part of the share capital of local corporations. This did not prevent British enterprises from achieving their main goal of reliable profit. "The United States happened to be the country that received the largest share of these investments, and this gave British investors the greatest rights to foreign assets and future profits. Thus, between 1850 and 1914, foreign investment and long-term loans to the United States reached three billion"[231]. But during the same period, the United States paid 5.8 billion in interest and dividend payments, mainly to Britain. The result was an increase in American foreign debt from 200 million dollars in 1843 to 3,700 million in 1914. Thus, between 1850 and 1914, the relationship between the United Kingdom and the United States remained the usual relationship between the peak of the economic pyramid and its base. By the beginning of the 20th century, the U.S. GDP had long since surpassed that of Britain. But the reality was that it largely belonged to the United Kingdom. This situation could have lasted indefinitely, given the lack of a defined state policy regarding domestic ownership or foreign investment in the United States.

However, the failed German rebellion of 1914 against Anglo-Saxon domination of the world had consequences that were not counted on. Instead of toppling the United Kingdom from the world's pedestal and putting Germany in the lead, the revolt freed the United States from British economic shackles. Fighting this rebellion required an effort from the United Kingdom that was excessive even for the peak of the economic pyramid. Loans to its allies and spending on its military operations exhausted the country's financial reserves and began to bite into its property holdings abroad. "British assets in the United States were liquidated on the New York Stock Exchange at heavily discounted prices."[232]

As a result, after the war, the profits of American businesses began to stay at home. In addition, while the UK's hands were tied by the war effort, the United States pushed it out as a major investor and financial intermediary from Latin America and parts of Asia. When the war ended, the United Kingdom had a huge debt to the United States.

The United States rose to the peak, but did not displace the UK, but shared it with it. The British private sector (despite the instructions of their government) had already contributed decisively to the rise of the US economy and was now reaping the rewards of their "free market" actions.

THE TIME OF AUTHORITARIANISM

US ECONOMY AFTER THE FIRST WORLD WAR

The days when the American economy was driven forward by population growth and settlement in new uninhabited territories were coming to an end. America had reached the shores of the Pacific Ocean and newcomers were already settling among the previous settlers. The time of frenzied demand for shirts and axes, for all the simple but necessary goods in the pioneers' everyday life, was inexorably waning. Roads and railroads, which were constantly being extended to new settlements, were also slowing down, exhausting their destinations. In the United States, the time was coming when everyone had almost everything and only needed a small replacement for goods that had broken down. But although the circumstances began to resemble those in Europe, the large enterprises themselves were not like European enterprises. European (at least northern) enterprises, which were on the defensive against British pressure, formed cartels and played along with each other, avoiding competition. American corporations, growing in an economy that was fenced off from the world by perhaps the world's highest customs walls and rapidly expanding in scale, did not develop solidarity skills among themselves. On the contrary, when they entered new territories, they immediately entered into competition with other similar profit-seekers. Competition became the way American corporations existed, shaped them, and dominated their activities.

The conditions for American companies in the United States have changed. But in these new conditions, American corporations could not follow the path of European enterprises and divide markets among themselves. This path was closed to them by anti-trust legislation. <u>One of the workarounds was to invent new products</u>. Since the market was saturated with goods, new goods were needed, the demand for which would enable further growth. Thus, the introduction of new products—innovations—into production became the way large American corporations existed. Innovations require inventions and discoveries. For this purpose, special workshops were needed. These workshops were research and development departments, where scientists and engineers were paid not for the production of goods, but for the invention of new goods or new applications for already known goods, or the improvement of these goods. In other words, the production of knowledge became the raison d'être of these departments, and then of the corporations themselves, as had happened earlier in the German Empire. However, the American path was different from the German one. Processes in the German economy began with fundamental science, where inventions were made. These inventions were used by heavy industry to create more advanced technologies for light industry. Based on these technologies, the light industry could more efficiently meet the known needs of people and other enterprises. The processes in the American industry proceeded the other way around, inventing new products for consumers (or new uses for old products) and trying to put them into production in the light industry. To do this, it put forward new requirements for heavy industry products (machines, materials, energy sources, etc.). In an attempt to meet these requirements, heavy industry resorted to the services of applied science.

Another workaround was to expand abroad. Taking advantage of the fact that German companies had disappeared from the scene as a result of the German rebellion, American companies began to fill the niches that had been created. In many cases, they were now free to use the discoveries and technologies of the defeated rebel. This was especially true in the electrical and chemical industries. General Electric became the dominant power in the electrical equipment industry in all parts of the world (seizing the moment, it even bought 25% of the German AGE). In the chemical industry, American corporations were now able to launch an offensive in the markets for dyes, medicines, fertilizers, etc. Du Pont became the world's leading producer of explosives.

Scale and scale again!
Those enterprises that were the first to make the necessary large investments in the means of production, in the knowledge and skills of their people, and in the organizational structure necessary to fully exploit economies of scale quickly became oligopolies.

These oligopolies could no longer compete with each other by lowering prices. The firms tried to drive out competitors with lower production costs by identifying more suitable sources of supply. They also beat competitors by moving faster than them from declining markets to expanding ones[233].

Hierarchies
The growth of corporations reduced risk. Enterprises opened new branches in other territories and tried to displace or buy

up other companies that produced similar products (*horizontal expansion*). The risk was reduced by monopolizing the market—rivals were eliminated and their profits were taken over. The higher profits of some branches allowed the company to support other, declining branches. At the same time, risks were mitigated by diversifying products with related products—for example, when a furniture company buys a paper company and then establishes a branch that produces railway sleepers. Another way was to take over companies from which the company had previously bought or sold products (*vertical expansion*). In this way, the corporation reduced the risk of a supplier changing its price or switching to another company. The same applies to consumer enterprises: they will no longer switch to competitors, undercut prices, or go bankrupt unexpectedly by failing to fulfill all contracts.

These types of corporate expansions continued to maintain competition in a world of giant corporations. Since the entry into the market where these companies operated was virtually closed to newcomers, the relative calm of oligopolistic competition was only disturbed by the arrival of other giants from other related industries or other territories.

Hierarchy of hierarchies

"The functional, technical, and managerial capabilities, honed by oligopolistic competition, provided a dynamic not only for the continuing growth of the firm but also for the industries which they dominated and the national economies in which they operated."[234]

Large corporations have become the peaks of hierarchical pyramids, with smaller companies at the bottom, ready to fulfill their various orders. They are ready to produce the semi-finished products required by the giants and provide the necessary services, such as repairs, investigations, transportation, obtaining certain equipment (and its maintenance), and even maintaining their buildings, not to mention infrastructure. Such pyramids are also related to scientific and technological research. After all, these enterprises, having become centers of such research, unite the efforts of teams at universities, special research institutes, and specialized companies. Such large corporations have become the drivers of scientific and technological progress in the United States.

DEMOCRACY AND ECONOMIC HIERARCHIES

Economic diversity

The economy at the peak of the economic pyramid, like the icebreaker, is the first to move forward in a sea of scientific, technological, and ultimately economic change, leading the caravan of other economies in its economic hierarchy. It has everything it needs to move forward. Its enterprises and entire industries are in a state of constant change. This is due to the interaction of industries with each other, the emergence of new industries, the interaction of new industries with existing ones, and the addition of new economies to the base of the economic hierarchy. The economy at the peak of the economic pyramid becomes very diverse due to its very "centrality". After all, such an economy has toenter into relations with a very diverse set of other economies in the world.

Economies at the base of the economic pyramid, in a free market, become highly specialized in a few (or even one) sectors of the economy. This happens because local economies, trying to maximize their profits, invest in what they are best at or what makes their country stand out from the rest (in terms of geography, geology, or climate). This could be the extraction of some special ores, wood, etc. The country's industry begins to build around these products—extraction, processing, packaging, delivery to the borders, and provision of various services to Western companies that come to buy these products. The governments of such countries, seeing the easiest opportunity to earn foreign currency by exporting these products, contribute to the development of events, and thus consolidate the presence of only a few industries in the country's economy.

Moreover, these countries find confirmation of their course in Adam Smith's free-market theory, which shows that all countries of the world, and the world economy as a whole, will achieve the best results when countries specialize. Everyone should do what they do best. Then they will have the highest profits. And with these profits, they will be able to buy more of what they need than they could do on their own, and even then, ineptly, poorly, and over a long period of time.

Level of democracy as a consequence of place in the economic hierarchy

1. Countries at the base of economic pyramids remain specialized in a few industries. The countries at the peak, however, become diversified. The presence of many industries in one center promotes their interaction and mutual influence, which gives rise to new ideas, innovations, and ultimately new industries. This process does not occur in valley countries, where only a few industries are available. Thus, the peak rises above the valley even more, its standard of living becomes even more detached from the base countries, and its level of living becomes less and less attainable for the base countries.

2. Due to concentration, production in most industries eventually becomes concentrated within a small number of the largest enterprises (perhaps even two or three). Since there are

a large number of different industries in the peak countries, a few large enterprises per industry yield a large number of large enterprises. Such large enterprises compete with each other for influence on the state, and in this struggle, they neutralize each other. Just as the state once gained independence based on the struggle between cities (artisanal enterprises) and feudal lords (agrarian enterprises), so in the modern world, the states of the peak countries can have real (up to certain limits) independence, rising above the struggle of interests of various large enterprises. That is why the peak countries can have a true democracy.

At the same time, the countries at the base of economic pyramids have only a few industries. Enterprises belonging to different industries do not neutralize each other in the struggle for influence on the state. A small number of large enterprises of these few industries gain irresistible influence on the state. This is the reason why the countries at the base of economic pyramids naturally come to oligarchic democracy. That is a democracy in which a small number of owners of large enterprises put their proxies up for election and have a gentleman's agreement among themselves to recognize the victory of the proxy for whom the majority of the people vote.

REVOLUTION IS A REBELLION

"On the eve of the First World War, Russia remained a very backward nation with a per capita income less than a third of that of Britain; 75 percent of the workforce was still engaged in agriculture (compared to 59 percent in Italy and 62 percent in Japan), 72 percent of the population was illiterate (compared to 48 percent in Italy), and only 15 percent of the population settled in urban areas."[235] But its industry developed quite rapidly. The main feature (and one might say means) of its development was a high concentration of production, which, to some extent, resembled the development of German industry. In 1910, 53.4% of all workers in the country worked in factories with more than 500 employees (33% in the United States at that time).[236] The entire industry consisted of a limited number of enterprises that were concentrated in only a few areas of the empire. Therefore, the Marxist socialization of industry should have been a relatively simple task for the Bolsheviks who took power during the war. Apart from the ideological side of the matter, such nationalization could potentially bear practical fruit—economies of scale, within such a large state conglomerate, were expected to bring great savings and lead to extraordinary efficiency. The possibility of transferring funds of this unified economy from one industry to another, in the direction that was most important at that moment, made it possible to raise one industry after another by means of all the enterprises. As Lenin used to say, "pulling the main link." However, the Bolsheviks' ideological fervor did not allow them to start building the economy. Instead, they began to implement ideological schemes of universal socialization, where the bakery on the street corner and the weak horse of a street cart driver were to become public. Revolutionary enthusiasm diverted the country from economic development and led it down the path of war, riots, uprisings, executions, and famines.

Ideology
The first post-revolutionary years were a time of attempts to implement the bare schemes of communism (which, by the way, did not even exist in the works of Marx-Engels, and which were only very schematically outlined in the works of Marxist leaders available at the time). The Civil War only spurred the

Bolsheviks to take more hasty and decisive action. The period of "war communism" was an attempt to implement communism, for example, by abandoning money. The product simply had to be taken by the state from some enterprises for free and delivered to others and consumers.

Holodomors swept across the former empire, accompanied by peasant revolts. The green wave threatened to overwhelm both the white and red waves (green at the time was the name given to peasant militias spontaneously formed to resist both white and red plunder; Makhno's anarchist army in Ukraine also fed off this same wave).

But the Bolsheviks' belief in their truth pushed them further and further, preventing them from stopping and looking around. Belief in their truth bit the reins. All industrial enterprises were to be socialized, regardless of whether the state was ready to take over their management or not. The factories that were taken away from their owners and left unmanaged were shut down because the workers did not know where and what to buy where to send it and how much of it was needed. It turned out that at a time when people had nothing to eat, it was very important to change the names of all streets or entire cities. Worse, the old administration had to be immediately dismissed and a new one introduced. As a result, cities were left without food and heating in the cold of winter, because the new administration simply did not know that it was necessary to take care of coal and firewood supplies. The Bolsheviks already knew the truth and the path to it was clear. Revolutionary enthusiasm demanded that they go further, and further.

NEP

There had to be a revolution within a revolution to suddenly turn the wheel and go backward instead of forward. There had to be a realization that most people went to the revolution not because they preferred public to private enterprises, but because they hoped for a better standard of living.

Thus, for Lenin, the construction of a new system was now combined with the task of achieving faster economic development than the leading European countries. "the struggle has been transferred to a global scale. If we solve this problem, then we will have won on a global scale for sure and completely."[237] "The winner is the one who has more advanced technology, organization, discipline, and better machines."[238]

Thus, Lenin turned the ideological struggle into a practical economic competition. The NEP became an expression of this turn. Instead of stubbornly following the "blueprints," he began to implement those elements of socialism that would help win the economic competition and to retain those elements of capitalism that could help the same goal.

Interaction between enterprises was left to the market, but large enterprises, banks, and foreign trade were placed in the hands of the state. Foreign investment and cooperation with foreign companies were allowed. By 1927, enterprises concessioned to foreigners accounted for about 1% of industrial output[239].

The very high concentration of industrial production in the Russian Empire was surpassed not so much because of ideological reasons as because of necessity: the factories, at the end of the Civil War, were half empty and half worked out, and there was a shortage of engineers and workers with the necessary specialization. Therefore, some of the large industrial enterprises were simply mothballed for the future, while others were sold or leased to willing private entrepreneurs. Only the most promising and most necessary for the country's economy were left in the hands of the state and were given both equipment and labor from the mothballed enterprises. They were organized into 421 trusts[240]. These trusts can be considered separate corporations. Their activities were subordinated to achieving the highest possible profit. But at the same time, they gave 80% of their profits to the state. Thus, the trusts were able to maintain and only slightly expand their activities with their funds. It was as if they were maintaining the level of development achieved by the country. The concentration of 80% of the profits in the hands of the state allowed it to take measures to break through to a higher level. For this purpose, it was able to make quite significant investments in areas recognized as strategic (at that time, these were mainly large power plants).

As a result, within a very short period (1921-1926), the level of industrial production of the Russian Empire before the First World War was reached and surpassed. Economic growth rates reached almost 40%* per year![241]

Thus, state-owned enterprises operated in a market environment, and the concentration of profits in the hands of the state allowed it to influence the economy by increasing the number of enterprises without distorting market relations too much.

Rebellion against the Peak

The NEP allowed the country to restore economic order and meet the basic needs of its citizens. It also brought about a period of rapid growth. Once the pre-war level of production was reached, further growth had to be much slower. The communist leadership, accordingly, plunged into a heated, destructive debate over further development. Behind the ideological

---

* The data may have been exaggerated by Soviet propaganda. However, judging by the number of new industrial enterprises founded, the pace was certainly amazing.

struggle, quite frankly, was a power struggle. But the obviousness of this fact does not negate the importance of the discussions that took place. The USSR, in its relations with the West, was acutely aware of the humiliated position in which the Russian Empire had left it—an exporter of grain and other raw materials in exchange for manufactured goods. The price of grain on world markets was falling, and the Soviet Union was able to buy fewer and fewer industrial goods for the same amount of grain exported[242]. So, with this in mind, the debate in the CPSU was not just a primitive power struggle or a great struggle for understanding ideological principles. From the point of view of the political economy of the rebellion, they were looking for ways to get a less developed country out of economic dependence on more developed countries.

In the end, the course of accelerated industrialization of the country, which was to take place through more active state intervention in the economy, won out.

When ideology rules the day

In all nations, industrialization took place at the expense of agriculture and the living standards of rural residents. In this case, however, the desire for industrialization additionally coincided with the ideological attitude of collectivizing agriculture according to communist principles. Those who were unwilling to join collective enterprises were seen as enemies of the collectivist ideology. "For seven years, between 1929 and 1936, a war raged in the Soviet republics between Communist officials and peasant resistance, leading to famine and devastation... Gradually, by using terror—confiscation of land and supplies, mass arrests, deportations to labor camps, executions—the Bolsheviks turned the tide of opposition"[243]. Most importantly, such an ideological desire for socialization, collectivization of enterprises, and ideological hatred for those who stood in the way of ideological goals resulted in the Ukrainian (mostly) Holodomor, which claimed millions of lives. The ideological stiffness did not allow for the correct perception of negative feedback signals, which allowed such tragedies to occur.*

Despite the enormous damage caused by ideological blindness and the fact that foreign capital left the country, net national income increased by 60% during the first five-year plan (1928-1932)![244] *Of course, no amount of success can justify even a small fraction of the unimaginable sacrifices made by Bolshevik violence. Nevertheless, it is important to understand what caused these successes. Violence alone did not make people work better or harder. The success was due to the state's establishment of a large number of industrial enterprises, which, to begin with, freed the country from the need to spend foreign currency on importing important goods.*

The global economic pyramid

By this time, the global pyramid had undergone significant changes. In the Dutch pyramid, trade was at the peak and it gave orders to the industrial enterprises in the Northern European countries that depended on it. The economic pyramid of the United Kingdom (UK) eventually inverted this dependence, with industry at the peak, providing trade with goods for distribution around the world. Over time, when other countries' economies began to produce goods that were previously purchased from the UK, they continued to be dependent on the UK because they had to buy the machines for such production from British enterprises. Thus, the heavy industry consolidated its position at the peak of the world economic hierarchy and further tied other countries to it.

* The reaction did come (food began to arrive in Ukraine), but with a tragic delay

Therefore, to break out of the bottom of this pyramid, i.e. to gain independence, it was necessary to build a domestic heavy industry. And that is why the USSR directed its main efforts in this direction. In fact, from the point of view of the political economy of the rebellion, the USSR was going through the first stage of reaching the peak—building a national economy.

It was too early to talk about the second stage, the construction of its economic pyramid. But as the first socialist state, the USSR found itself at the peak of another, ideological pyramid-the pyramid of the communist movement, in which it acquired clients whom it helped financially, ideologically, and diplomatically. However, these clients (communist parties and movements) saw the CPSU as a pioneer on the path to world communism, and within this approach, they saw the USSR as a leader for the duration of the common struggle. As for a separate new economic pyramid, it was simply out of the question.

Not on the Rhine, not on the Marne—We will do everything ourselves and at our place![*]

The structure of the economy began to change rapidly. While in 1928, 49% of the net national product (NNP) was produced by the agricultural sector and only 31% by the industrial sector, in the first two five years plans the share of the agricultural sector in production fell to 28%, and the share of the industrial sector rose to 45% (the rest was the service sector)[245].

Since the goal was to gain technological independence from the West, the "German approach" to economic development through heavy industry, which was inherent in the Russian Empire, gained even more strength in the USSR. The share of consumption in the NNP fell from 82% in 1928 to 55% in

* Pavlo Tychyna, poem "The Party Leads"

203

1937[246]. Although the plans of the first five-year plans, despite statements of fulfillment and over fulfillment, were implemented with a delay of two or more years, the results were still impressive: from 1928 to 1937, steel production increased from 4.3 to 17.7 million tons, electricity production from 5 to 36.2 billion kilowatt-hours, and cars from 0.8 to 199.9 thousand.[247] Thus, in one decade, this country managed to break into the category of industrialized countries of the world.

Industrialization in a fairly short period created a powerful complex of enterprises in the USSR in all sectors necessary to support the independent existence of an industrial country. Each link of all production chains had its enterprises, which allowed the country's economy to exist in a virtually isolated mode (similar to the American economy in the 19th century). From the very beginning, this entire complex was planned and implemented as a system of enterprises, each of which had to make full use of economies of scale and scope. Soviet enterprises did not have to compete with each other for oligopolistic market capture (which created the possibility of efficient production for American corporations). They were initially (by design) allocated a market sufficient for efficient production. The scale of some plants exceeded any other in Europe or even in the world. For example, the Moscow and Gorky automobile plants, the Stalingrad Tractor Plant, and the Ural Machine-Building Plant.[248]

As a newly industrialized country, the Soviet Union was not capable of designing and organizing the production of the huge number of goods that was necessary for the successful functioning of a closed economy. It was necessary to put into operation all types of enterprises almost simultaneously and in sufficient quantities. Therefore, key factories were set up with the help of foreign enterprises. For example, the Moscow and

Horky automobile plants were built with the help of Ford, and the first cars (in 1930) were produced from Ford components and according to Ford drawings, but three years later Soviet components were introduced. The Stalingrad Tractor Plant was bought in its entirety in the United States, disassembled, transported, and reassembled in Stalingrad, but two years later, a design bureau opened there and began designing tanks, which were produced at the plant alongside tractors. Equipment for Uralmash was purchased in Germany and the United Kingdom, and a large number of foreign specialists worked there, but only at the beginning. The main principle was to quickly master technologies and try to develop them independently. In addition, foreign companies were not allowed to open their branches and invest their capital in the development of new enterprises. Their help was always bought and the factories they created were entirely Soviet. Consequently, the income from them was to belong only to the USSR state and it could use it all to further develop the economy.

The entire economy was being transformed into a single "People's Economy." And this economy developed and worked according to a single plan. All industrial enterprises in the Soviet economy now worked as workshops of one enterprise— producing what this enterprise needed, and in the quantity it needed. Soviet factories scattered throughout the vast country were able to produce for each other according to an hourly schedule*! Entire industries popped out of nothing within a few years (for example, when the aviation industry was introduced). In a short period, about 10,000 factories appeared.[249]

Thus, from an economic point of view, the Soviet approach was a cross between the American approach of growing enterprises and

---

* what was convincingly demonstrated during the Second World War

the German approach of forming concerns and leading heavy industry leadership.

The USSR in the Second World War

The strength of the emerging system was tested in World War II. During the first five months of the war, along with the lost territory, almost half of the country's industrial potential was lost—from 58 to 63% of iron, steel, aluminum, and coal production, 40% of grain production, 32% of the industrial workforce and 40% of the total population, more than 31850 industrial enterprises.[250]

The country's economy was rebuilt in a matter of months. Thousands of factories were dismantled and transported to the Urals, Western Siberia, Kazakhstan, etc. All of this required immediate large-scale construction of roads, railways, power lines, water supply, and everything else necessary for people's lives and the functioning of factories in the almost deserted eastern territories.

The reorientation of resources and budgetary expenditures from consumption to military needs resulted in an increase in military spending from 11% in 1940 to 44% of national income in 1943.[251] Among other things, the financing came from deferred consumption—living conditions were such that they did not allow for widespread consumption—the working day was extended by three hours, vacations were canceled, as well as holidays. In addition, in such a difficult situation, no one paid attention to the elements of the market that were reviving again, especially in agriculture, which also worked to increase GDP.

The Second World War was a war of economies. The winner was the one who was able to produce more and better tanks, airplanes, guns, machine guns, and all other weapons and ammunition. And in this competition, the Soviet economy won. At the same time, however, "British and American land-lease aid amounted to a mere 4 percent of total Soviet war production...however, it was unevenly distributed, with most of it coming in during the last two years of the war, while only a small fraction of it came to Soviet ports during the Soviet Union's darkest months before and during the battle of Stalingrad."[252] At the same time, the Soviet economy was opposed not only by the economy of the much more powerful German Empire but also by the economies of its allies and the economies of the countries it conquered. From the conquered countries alone, Germany received resources equal to 16-17% of its GDP, which was incomparably higher than that of the Soviet Union.[253] Thus, the economy of the Soviet Union was confronted by the economy of almost all of Western Europe.

The victory, in such circumstances, was <u>due to the opportunity provided to the Soviet Union by the organization of the entire economy into the hierarchy of a single economy, namely, to effectively concentrate resources on achieving the main goal of victory</u>.

So the rebellion against the West looked quite successful (which does not mean "quite acceptable" if we remember how bloody it was).

A REBELLION THAT BECAME A WORLD REVOLUTION

The uprising of the peoples of the former Russian Empire brought them off the periphery of the world and caused tectonic political changes in the world. In those countries where socialist parties already existed, these parties became stronger and new ones emerged. In countries where they did not exist, they emerged. In these latter countries, these parties were particularly reminiscent of Leninist-type parties-disciplined and committed to a single idea and goal, with a firm hierarchy supported by voluntary discipline. Thanks to this revolt, Marxism became a global ideology. This had two consequences. In some countries, pro-socialist forces grew stronger and later came to power. In other countries, their growth caused a backlash, with the rise of fascist regimes. The English-speaking countries were the only ones in the world that remained liberal (the United States and the British Empire). And even there, liberalism was significantly distorted by a more decisive and active role of the state.

Outside of the United States, Europe with its colonies, and Japan with its newly acquired territories, only Latin America and China remained. Latin America's goods (copper, coffee, bananas, etc.) were no longer in demand during the world wars and the Great Depression. Thus, it lost the ability to acquire foreign currency for the purchase of industrial goods and was pushed to import substitution. Latin America knew that this was the path that the United States and the Soviet Union had taken, and it saw that this path had brought them fabulous results. So its countries set up high customs barriers and began to build domestic industries. At the same time, entire industries were nationalized—primarily mines, communications, electricity, and some metallurgical and other industries ("These were often too large for local capitalists to finance.")[254]

The 1917 revolt in the Russian Empire was a real threat to liberalism and the free market. However, they were saved by the fact that they were preserved at the peak. And the peak managed to pit its rivals—fascism and communism—against each other.

BRITAIN AFTER THE FIRST WORLD WAR

A raw material appendage at the peak of the global economic pyramid?

The global demand for British coal, and most importantly for cloth and other products, fell further. Both because European countries and the British colonies were learning to make them themselves and because of the Second Industrial Revolution. As the United States continued to drive British locomotives out of Latin America and Japanese shipbuilders drove British ships out of the Asian market, the increasingly powerful customs barriers of other countries on industrial products only worsened the already deplorable state of the British economy.

During the second industrial revolution, the chemical, pharmaceutical, and electrical industries became the defining ones. While continuing to produce the goods of the first industrial revolution, the United Kingdom was putting itself in the position of a supplier of "raw materials." It transported coal, steel, fabrics, etc. as raw materials for chemical, pharmaceutical, electrical, and other industries in other countries, and also provided them with transportation services and finance.

For a long time, Britain was unable to replace its gas streetlights and steam locomotives with more modern electric lights and diesel locomotives. Already in 1900-1914, the main lines of the London Underground were laid by American engineers with more American products than British ones and with mostly foreign financing.[255]

The problem was that the private initiative did nothing to bring the United Kingdom out of this situation. On the contrary, the enterprises were trying to follow the well-trodden, familiar path. Waiting for the enterprises to take over and fix the situation was like waiting for citizens to buy their weapons, organize themselves into companies and regiments, and organize a worthy response during an enemy invasion.

Struggle for an independent state

Thus, the loss of the United Kingdom's exclusive position at the peak of the world economy pushed its state to take more active actions. Moreover, the events of the World War showed that state action, will, planning and organization of national processes on a huge scale were not only possible but quite successful. The acquired skills and experience could and should now be used in a peaceful life.

To be able to have a more active influence on the economy, the state had to be independent from the influence of private interests. In the conditions of the UK, which was still at the economic peak of the world, at least sufficient autonomy was enough. And its possibility could be provided by the economic independence of the state.

At the end of the 19th century, at the same time as the United States and the German Empire were openly nipping at the heels of the United Kingdom, the UK state acquired a state telegraph (in 1868, in addition to the always state-owned post office) and in 1914 bought a controlling stake in the future BP (British Petroleum). In 1926, it made radio broadcasting (BBC) state-owned. This movement from the peak was met by a movement from the valley—local government authorities were even more active in acquiring their property.

Free-market incentives for state ownership

Infrastructure, in many cases, is a natural monopoly. For example, it is difficult to imagine three canals laid side by side (for competition) if the capacity of one is sufficient. The same applies to water pipelines, hydroelectric power plants, etc. That is why railways, parts of electric, gas, and water supply networks, tram lines, etc. were private enterprises, but under strict state supervision as far as their prices were concerned[256]. Also, the need to buy up private land along the route required state consent and assistance. In addition, cases of cholera spreading through clogged water lines also forced the state to take care of such matters of private enterprises.

However, the main reason for the constant growth in the number of infrastructure enterprises owned by local governments during the 19th century was the need for revenue for most cities and towns. In cities with a developed private economy (such as port cities), tax revenues from private enterprises were sufficient. But where the private sector was weak, it needed to be promoted. When local governments built a local gas pipeline and a hydroelectric power plant with power lines, paved a road, etc., they achieved the following. First, state enterprises kept prices reasonably low, which reduced the cost of local private enterprises (and almost all enterprises need roads, gas, electricity, etc.). Secondly, this infrastructure, being in state ownership, brought revenue to the state authorities, based on which they could reduce taxes on private enterprises. Thus, state enterprises allowed the state to have more income, enterprises to pay lower taxes, and people to pay lower prices for goods. <u>State enterprise, simply by its presence, helped private enterprises</u>. *The other side of the situation was that the state pyramid was generally more stable and independent in its relations with private enterprises.*

The state is trying to return the rudder
In 1932, the United Kingdom abandoned its free trade policy and introduced general import duties. This measure continued the measures started in 1921 when, after the war, import duties

on products of "key industries" such as automobiles, precision instruments, and dyes were not canceled. In addition, the absence of large enterprises was recognized as the reason for the lagging development of the British economy, and the state began timid steps to improve the situation.

Various governmental and parliamentary commissions have concluded that it is necessary to merge various separate private enterprises, especially in the field of infrastructure. For example, the construction and maintenance of a single large hydroelectric power plant on a large river or a large thermal power plant was much cheaper than the construction of many small power plants by different firms. In addition, the latter could produce electricity of different voltages and frequencies. It was decided to promote the unification of electricity, water, and gas supply into single networks standardization of their products, and centralization of coal mining (after 1945 it was completely nationalized). In 1926, the Central Electricity Board was established, which introduced a UK-wide voltage and frequency standard. This enabled the board to connect the disconnected islands of electricity networks into a single National Grid in 1938. The result was to close the efficiency gap with the United States.[257]

At the beginning of World War II, two British airlines were merged and nationalized as British Overseas Airways Corporation.

The curse of the peak

Many voices, including Keynes, began to call on the state to act more decisively. The main points were as follows. "The structural changes taking place demanded massive government intervention... The problem of the major industries, which had of necessity to be contracted, rationalized and re-equipped, could only have been solved by a large degree of central planning, unofficial nationalization to some extent... and large injections of capital"[258]. These recommendations were not implemented for political reasons. They were too much like the Soviet way.* The powerful appearance of the working class on the scene with mass demonstrations, strikes, and clashes with the police in the 1930s induced purely ideological (not rational) opposition to change. This was in addition to the justified distrust of a country at the top of the economic hierarchy towards state intervention in the economy. The fact was, however, that the United Kingdom was losing its position at the peak and only this state intervention could change the situation.

Starting with the Great Depression of 1873, the productivity growth of British enterprises slowed down dramatically, as the low value added of the late Victorian British economy "was unable to deliver the productivity gains of economies such as Germany and the United States which had a more "high-tech" orientation. The British productivity performance improved after the mid-1920s, but still left Britain lagging behind the United States, Germany and France."[259]

The British state's rebellion against fate was too indecisive. Therefore, it was only a matter of time before it lost its leadership.

THE US STATE AFTER THE FIRST WORLD WAR

European countries resorted to stricter state power because they were dissatisfied with the situation they were in. However such dissatisfaction did not exist at the peak of the economic pyramid of the world. Since the peak was occupied by two

* The rebellion in the valley, in Eastern Europe, was already exerting its influence even at the top of the global economic pyramid, where it eventually began to layer on the local rise of the labor movement caused by the Great Depression

predominantly English-speaking countries, the idea of a special Anglo-Saxon path has since emerged.

Being at the peak of the world developed a largely Anglo-Saxon perception of the world, which was that if you do not interfere with the free market system, it will bring prosperity to everyone—both those at the peak and those in the valley. Practice confirmed this belief—American corporations grew, the economic power of the United States grew, and the standard of living of its population grew. The free market generated progress, and progress gave everyone a higher standard of living.

However dramatic changes occurred in the 1932 elections. "Unrestricted control over labor, finance, and capital was withdrawn from the private sector and the skittishness about concentrations of public power in a central authority away from the local community suddenly evaporated."[260]

Keynesian approach

The United States was already at the economic peak of the world and it made no sense for it to resort to the economic measures of the rebels in the valley. But the United States, like the countries below it in the global economic hierarchy, suffered the devastating effects of the Great Depression. The economic downturn and bankruptcy of a large number of enterprises multiplied the risk of entrepreneurship, and the fall of the stock market made it impossible for enterprises to get investments through the classically American method of selling options or shares. The situation was complicated by the rise of Marxism in the world. Until now, the United States, as the country at the peak, had avoided this influence, but the steep decline of the economy threatened to combine workers' discontent with Marxism or fascism (as had already happened in Europe). Even in the United Kingdom (UK), the socialist party, Labor, managed to take power. But the UK was a descending peak, and the US was an ascending peak. It had to find its own way.

For the United States, abandoning liberalism at a time when it was successfully occupying the peak of the world was inexpedient. Therefore, another liberalism, Keynesianism, was adopted. "Keynesian economics sees government as being critical to a well-functioning economy. Keynesians believe the government should provide a wider range of public goods (such as healthcare) and that government spending is needed to move economies out of recession or depression. Their view is that when business fails to invest for economic growth, government must step in"[261].

Usually, a peak economy is at the peak because its private sector is at its best and provides capital where it is needed most. The state, when engaged in direct investment, can "miss the mark" and invest in unpromising projects. But in the face of such a deep crisis as the Great Depression (with the labor movement growing stronger), the state still could not stand aside. And Keynesianism "was the least evil" for the United States. It gave Franklin Delano Roosevelt not so much a strict set of actions to implement as a general ideological excuse for his active intervention in the economy. To inject additional funds into the economy, the Roosevelt government expanded credit, increased unemployment benefits, and most importantly, began direct government investment in the economy.

New Course

Reacting to the severe consequences of the Great Depression, Americans ". . . overwhelmingly voted in favor of the Democratic promise of a "new deal" Opposed to the traditional American political philosophy of laissez-faire, the New Deal generally embraced the concept of a government-regulated economy aimed at achieving a balance between conflicting economic interests."[262] The experience of successful organizational activities of the state during the First World War had a powerful influence.

Since private enterprise was no longer able to provide jobs, the state began to provide jobs for millions of people. It was then that the state began to build highways on a large scale. 8.5 million people built them at the expense of the state treasury. 1046,000 km of roads, 125,000 public buildings, 75,000 bridges, 8,000 parks, and 800 airports were built.[263] The state provided jobs for thousands of artists who worked on the decoration of state buildings, in communal theaters and museums that were widely opened at the time. It also provided jobs for 3 million people in state forests—planting new trees, building flood barriers, maintaining forest roads, etc. The dire state of the economy and the people who lost their jobs required decisive and quick action—workers were provided with housing in semi-military camps.[264]

New bodies were established to control the market processes to prevent a repeat of stock market crashes and massive bank failures. Great efforts were made to revitalize the economically lagging regions of the United States. In 1933, the Tennessee Valley Authority, a state-owned corporation, was founded. This corporation was engaged in the production and delivery of electricity in a vast territory of seven states: part of Tennessee, parts of Alabama, Mississippi, and Kentucky, and some parts of Georgia, North Carolina, and Virginia. In addition, its responsibilities included (and still include) shipping, flood control, fertilizer production, and general economic development of the entire Tennessee Valley region. As President Roosevelt himself explained: "It is time to extend planning to a wider field, in this instance comprehending in one great project many

States directly concerned with the basis of one of our greatest rivers."[265]

Since 1935, the New Deal has also sounded notes of solidarity that were not typical of the peak. The National Labor Relations Act (Wagner Act) greatly increased the scope for state intervention in labor-employer relations and strengthened the organizational power of trade unions by establishing the National Labor Relations Board. Until the mid-1960s, although to a lesser extent than in Europe, class peace in the United States was maintained by organized negotiations between workers and businesses, with state mediation when necessary.

Finally, it was at this time, within the framework of the New Deal, that the American state finally came to what all European states-liberal, socialist, and fascist-had long since come to. Between 1935 and 1939, old-age and widow's pensions, unemployment benefits, and disability insurance were established. In addition, maximum working hours and minimum wages were introduced (in 1938). Besides that, the American rejection of the federal "imposed" government was overcome through joint initiatives with states and cities. Also, there was less resistance to mixed-ownership enterprises with the federal state on the one hand and private capital or states and cities on the other.[266]

The rebellion of the US state was more decisive than the rebellion of the UK state, and it was the future.

The world was plunging into a global, universal revolt. After the fall of the French Republic, it was sharply divided into the peak, where two English-speaking countries (the United States and the British Empire) were located, and the rest of the world. The sharpness of the division was that only the peak retained and allowed democracy. The countries of the valley, led by more or less authoritarian states, were pushing their economies in a new revolt against the peak (or at least in silent opposition to it). But even the countries at the peak did not escape the growing state influence on the economy.

THE AGE OF IDEOLOGIES

At the beginning of the French Revolution, those on the right in parliament supported the monarchy, while those on the left favored a republic. In practice, those on the right wanted the state to continue to manage the economy, meaning that the king's power was above the landowners and manufacturers. But for better management, they recognized the need to have feedback from the enterprises. And this feedback was to continue to exist in the form of the parliament, which was to continue to be an auxiliary, advisory body to the monarch (under the king). Those on the left wanted to use the state as a tool in the hands of the enterprises, so they wanted to put the parliament above the king and reduce the king to the level of executive power.

The kings gathered the owners of large agricultural enterprises, as well as representatives of cities as representatives of craft and industrial production, in the first parliaments. This was because the monarch needed finances from these enterprises, as well as people for war. Agrarian and urban enterprises were ready to give them to the king but in exchange for some concessions[267]. Thus, the decisions of the parliament were made on behalf of the state and private enterprises, which reflected the reality itself—after all, they were the real social forces, as centers of socio-economic influence.

When industrial enterprises came into existence, they found a state that was closely tied to agrarian enterprises: the landowning aristocracy supported the king and was supported by the king. All public offices were also held by large landowners.

Attempts by the bourgeoisie to squeeze landowners were met with resistance not only from landowners but also from the state. Therefore, the ideology of the enterprises, a liberal ideology, saw a threat in strong state power and called for equality of all individuals and popular control over the state to eliminate the danger of dictatorship and moral decay of state officials. The ideology that came to battle with liberalism was called conservatism (because it wanted to preserve the power of the state).

The victorious march of liberalism began with bloody revolutions, but later the liberal struggle was to extend the right to vote to the entire population. On the one hand, this was in line with liberal principles of equality. On the other hand, it quickly became clear that large enterprises were able to influence elections through their influence on the media (either by owning them or simply by having money to advertise their candidates). Thus, candidates supported by them have much better chances. Therefore, the control of the people over the state, proclaimed by liberalism, has resulted in the control of the enterprises over the state.

As consequence, the extension of the right to vote to the entire population has involved the people in socio-political decisions that were previously entirely in the hands of the state and large enterprises. The role of the people was that of an object of influence from powerful pyramids of the socio-economic influence. But this very universal suffrage created an opportunity for the people to organize themselves—to create new pyramids of the socio-economic influence, independent of the state and large enterprises. They took the form of trade unions and various parties of workers, peasants, and small businesses. The most powerful were the labor parties of various Marxists and other kinds of socialists.

While for the liberals, the main interaction was between

the state and private enterprises, for the labor parties, the main link was between workers and private enterprises. The state was viewed as a mere tool in the hands of private enterprises. Therefore, if the left wanted to control the state, the "leftists" wanted to abandon the state altogether. The Marxists believed that a transitional period, socialism, was necessary, during which the state should still exist (to organize self-destruction). And then communism was to come, the complete absence of the state. Anarchists were even more leftist, as they wanted the immediate abolition of the state.

Faced with the need to organize society for economic growth and confrontation with other states, the communists, upon coming to power, not only did not set about destroying the state but, on the contrary, made efforts to strengthen it. Their state, in the absence of large private households in society, gained such comprehensive power that conservatives had never dreamed of.

Thus, four ideologies were formed:

1. Communist, which believed that only the state (with its state enterprises) was needed and that private enterprises should be eliminated,

2. Conservative, which believed that both the state (with its state enterprises) and private enterprises were needed, but the state should control private enterprises,

3. Liberal, which believed that both the state and private enterprises are needed, but private enterprises should control the state* and state enterprises are not very necessary, and finally,

---

* the state is controlled by the people, but the people themselves are controlled by enterprises through the socio-economic influence of large enterprises

4. Anarchists believed that only private enterprises were needed and the state should be eliminated.

Therefore, the correct location on the "right-left" scale should be as follows: communist (in power), conservative, liberal, communist (in opposition), and anarchist.

Hence the difference in attitudes toward globalization. Since the left is more concerned with private enterprises, globalization is the norm for them—enterprises, under weak states, freely enter into relations with each other, forming a global free market. The right wing, in favor of a strong state, tried to avoid globalization processes, because the global free market includes any country in one or another economic pyramid. This leads to the influence of foreign enterprises and countries higher up the hierarchy on the state. So, conservatives naturally gravitated toward nationalism. However, there is a notable exception. Since the influence of other states on the peak state is less than its influence on other states (and the same applies to enterprises), the peak conservatives are, on the contrary, free-marketers. And this difference in the situation is the essence of the difference between European and American conservatives.*

* Of course, another significant reason for the difference is the following. Whereas European conservatives have always wanted to preserve (and now revive) the system of a strong state, American conservatives have always wanted to preserve (and now revive) the system of free small farms that do not need the state to rule over them. In other words, the reason is the different pasts of Europe and North America, which existed before the advent of industrial enterprises.

THE COLD WAR

POLITICAL AND ECONOMIC HAPPINESS

Both economics and politics exist to meet the needs of the people. This is the goal of the economy, the state, and the people themselves.

Some people try to achieve happiness by reducing their needs to the level of their capabilities. But most people try to increase their capabilities to the level of their needs. The moment when a person's basic needs are satisfied should be considered happiness. But achieving happiness does not last long. People get used to their "happy" state. Having satisfied some needs, a person wants to satisfy others, or the already satisfied needs suddenly demand more and cease to be satisfied. If the person manages to satisfy the new needs that have arisen, the feeling of happiness comes again, and everything repeats. Happiness (sharp, joyful, colorful) never lasts long. A person, having "got everything," finds that his level of happiness is no higher than it was at the beginning of the journey. But the feeling of satisfaction sometimes reminds him of himself again when he compares his situation with the situation of other less successful people. The absolute value of the standard of living was important in the past until people achieved sustainable satisfaction of basic needs—food, basic comfort, and security. Since then, a person's level of satisfaction has been determined more by their relative position in the hierarchy of living standards.

This kind of satisfaction is also inherent in entire nations. The higher the standard of living of a people in the world hierarchy, and the ability of its state to guarantee security, order, and opportunities for entrepreneurship and earnings, as well as its influence on other states, the higher the level of satisfaction of such a people.

The level of happiness of the Germans living in the villages of central Europe in the first century AD was not lower than that of modern Germans, although objectively their standard of living was incomparably lower. The level of satisfaction of the Romans must have been high because they compared their standard of living to that of the Germans. But, if the Romans somehow learned about our current standard of living, their level of satisfaction would inevitably drop.

THE UNITED STATES AFTER WORLD WAR II

The first struggle to keep the peak

The Second World War called on U.S. resources, first to supply all the belligerents and then to equip American troops on two fronts. The flow of government funding for military development not only quickly brought full employment, but also became a powerful stimulus for scientific and technological progress. All the belligerents were also straining their forces in this area. However, it was the American state that now had the world's largest financial resources, and American businesses had the greatest experience, capacity, and already developed research and development units that only had to be

strengthened and expanded. The state's need for military aircraft created an entire American aviation industry (Thanks to
the same state investments). State funding for the development
of technology for the industrial production of the world's first
antibiotic, penicillin, led to a revolution in the pharmaceutical
industry in the postwar years. State funding for the development of high-octane gasoline and artificial rubber gave impetus
to the production of polyethylene, polypropylene, etc. developed
recently. Finally, research in radio, radar, etc. led to the emergence of many technologies that were the basis of the postwar
information revolution.[268]

State influence was not limited to science. New factories
for the production of steel, rubber, aluminum, magnesium, airplanes and ships, etc. were rapidly built with capital provided
by the state. Gas pipelines were quickly laid to supply gas to the
east coast, etc. The result was that by 1945, three-quarters of
all new factories and equipment were owned by the state. "The
government's power over private firms was as complete as an
elaborate network of controls over prices, wages, raw materials,
and transportation could make it."[269]

After the Second World War, Western countries reduced the
scope of their intervention in economic processes. However,
in Europe, state control over prices and the widespread use of
state enterprises were preserved as they had to rebuild their
destroyed economies and try to get back to the peak. But at the
very peak, in the United States, state control over prices and
enterprises, and thus state ownership, receded quite quickly
and decisively. However, the state did not completely withdraw
from interference in economic processes. The reason was that
the United States had seized the peak of the global economic
pyramid at a very tense moment when the actions of the new-
born world leader had to be determined by the need to defend

and strengthen the captured pyramid. After all, the Soviet threat was not so much to push the United States off the peak of the world economic pyramid as to destroy this pyramid. *But being at the peak necessitated a different kind of intervention in the economy.*

The American giving pyramid

While continuing to take a large part of private capital through taxes, the state continued to concentrate it in those areas that it considered necessary for the interests of the whole country. It concentrated a large part of these resources on helping other countries, which was the way to build its global pyramid of political influence. This influence of the state made it easier for American corporations to penetrate other countries, and thus strengthen the new economic pyramid.

"Just as the New Deal government increasingly took active responsibility for the welfare of the nation, US foreign policy planners took increasing responsibility for the welfare of the world... In the lexicon of the New Deal, taking responsibility meant government intervention on a grand scale."[270]

The American corporations that quickly followed the American troops into Western Europe found that they could not sell their goods there because of the lack of money in Western Europe. The U.S. government had to make Europe able to buy American goods again, and for this purpose, it provided Europe with funds under the Marshall Plan. Europe and Japan had lost close to greatest part of its production and American goods had almost no competition. Although Europe was buying American goods with American money, it still helped 1. the growth of American enterprises and 2. the consolidation of Europe as a market for their goods.

The Marshall Plan could not last forever. It was important only for acceleration. Then European countries had to turn on their engines. From then on, access to the American market became critical for them to acquire the currency to be able to buy the products of American enterprises to which they were now accustomed. American permission to access its market became a matter of prosperity or decline. It was a new world—the world of the giving American economic pyramid. Only the dependency in this pyramid scheme was taken to a new level. In it, aid was not given as a reward for "right" actions—it was given by default but taken away in response to "wrong" actions. It was a new world—a world of US sanctions in which those who disagreed with the US were punished by a ban on trade with the US.

THE UNITED STATES AND THE PECULIARITY OF THE FATE OF THE LEADER

Continuation of the third American stage

American enterprises moved their divisions to other countries and grew further, bypassing the limits of anti-trust legislation, and this became a determining factor. More and more of the economic exchange with other countries took place within the enterprises as exchanges between their divisions. U.S. exports and imports increasingly became a flow of semi-finished products from one enterprise branch to another and finally to the final product assembly site.

Over time, U.S. corporations have learned to capitalize on the competitive advantages of different places in the world. First, they locate units that require a lot of workers in countries where wages are lower, those units that require a lot of certain materials as input in countries where these materials are available. Research and development units are in countries where there is a large number of relevant specialists (but mainly in the United States). And finally, management units remain in the United States. Adam Smith argued that each country should use its competitive advantages. However American corporations have learned to use the competitive advantages of many countries simultaneously. Secondly, these corporations, having export-import operations as their interdepartmental exchanges, set prices for them according to their needs. If the income tax in country A is lower than in country B, then it is advantageous for some of the company's products produced in country A to be artificially assigned a greater share of the value added to the company's final products. In this case, the branch in country B will have less income than it has and will pay less taxes.

Still, the main thing was the possibility of further growth and an increasing concentration of capital at the peak of the economic pyramid of a large corporation. The centralization of production was also important, bringing economies of scale and scope to a new level. In this way, American corporations successfully ousted other competitors from world markets, and so the pyramid of the American economic world grew and strengthened. Such monster corporations were simply doomed to dominate the world. This stage began after the First World War, but after the Second, the expansion of American corporations was greatly facilitated, and the risks were greatly reduced by the measures of the American state.

Reducing risks

The newest large American corporations no longer needed government protection from the terrible foreign monsters-they had become monsters themselves. Now they were already hindered by government duties—after all foreign countries retaliated with their own duties and prevented the penetration of American corporations into them. They were no longer satisfied with subsidies, whose extension was subject to approval by state commissions and had to be in line with the economic policies of successive governments. All that corporations needed from the state now was to reduce their risks. But in a different way.

The conscious reliance of enterprises on economies of scale brought lower unit costs, which gave them a competitive advantage. At the same time, it also brought vulnerability. The technologies involved required large expenditures on both equipment and specialists. These high costs are profitable when production is operating at full, calculated capacity. If, for example, due to a temporary decline in demand or a shortage of raw materials, output decreases, then unit costs immediately increase, making production less profitable, or even unprofitable. In other words, such technologies were "scale-dependent." The volume of production required to maintain optimal production throughput can only be sustained if the flows of raw materials, semi-finished products and information within the company are carefully coordinated, as well as the flows of inputs from suppliers and outputs to distributors and end users.[271]

In the struggle to reduce risks, corporations have already done everything they could—they gradually bought up their suppliers and customers to guarantee the purchase of semi-finished products and sales at "acceptable" prices. Then the task repeated itself—now they had to buy up the suppliers of their former suppliers and the customers of their former customers. The process ultimately had to rest on the extraction of raw materials at the input and sales to the end consumer at the output, which could no longer be guaranteed.

The state as a guarantor in the citadel
of the free market

Where private enterprises were able to present their interest as a public interest, they were able to "embed" their production process in the state capital circulation. In other words, such corporations were included as permanent and inseparable links in the annual flow of public spending. "This is the case in the development and supply of modern weapons, in the exploration of space, and the development of a growing range of modern civilian products or services including transport planes, high-speed ground transportation, and various applied uses of nuclear energy. Here, the state guarantees a price sufficient, with a suitable margin, to cover costs. And it undertakes to buy what is produced or to compensate in full in the case of contract cancellation. Thus, effectively, it suspends the market with all associated uncertainty. One consequence, ... is that in areas of the most precise and advanced technology, the market is most completely replaced, and planning is therefore most secure."[272] This applies primarily to large corporations, but not exclusively. Start-up companies formed around new ideas have a chance to reduce their risks through government subsidies. For this purpose, there are programs with clear application conditions.

Saving the drowning is the work
of the drowning themselves

However, not all corporations' products are considered strategic by the state and worthy of support. In all other cases, an enterprise can reduce its risk in starting a new project by predicting the demand for its new product. With the saturation of the market with goods, American enterprises have encountered difficulties with sales. Therefore, their research and development departments began to invent new products more actively, and their sales departments began to convince consumers of the urgent need for these products. The place of these departments in the business hierarchy has risen, while the place of the production department itself has fallen. An increasing share of resources, both human and financial, is allocated to them. At times, sales departments begin to exceed production departments in terms of the number of employees and salaries. The result is that "the general rule, with fewer exceptions than we would like to think, is that if they make it we will buy it."[273]

This ability of enterprises to secure sales of their products enables them to plan future demand and, based on this, to plan the purchase of semi-finished products and raw materials, thus reducing the enterprise's risks.

Pioneers take more risks and therefore their situation is different from those who follow them

Buying up suppliers and distributors, as well as taking over competitors, creates certain sub-economies of the overall US economy. And each of these sub-economies plans its activities. In other words, the overall economy of the country consists of sub-economies regulated and planned from their centers. And the greater the concentration of production and capital, the fewer such sub-economies there are (i.e., fewer large corporations occupy 40-60% of the total economy). Consequently, the larger parts of the economy operate under a plan or at least general central coordination.

By the end of the 1960s, the products of 2000 US industrial corporations accounted for half of the country's non-governmental GDP. It was these 2000 corporations (and if you look closer, no more than 500) that made up the peak of the economy and formed a pyramid of dependent companies around them that consumed their products and innovations and supplied them with semi-finished products and various services[274]. In addition, many smaller companies that formed pyramids of dependence around them also had to obey the plans of these huge sub-economies, although less strictly. Thus, the American economy was (and still is) a combination of the plan and the free market. Giant islands of planned sub-economies float in a sea of free markets. And in this combination, both parts are important.

The British economy managed to do without large corporations. But this is because it was the first industrialized country in the world. For the United States, huge, closely-knit sub-economies were essential for the mass production of already-known goods (adopted from the United Kingdom). They could build large factories to produce a well-known product in large quantities and to organize its sales. At this stage, the market was less important. Monopolization was the engine of the American rise in the second half of the 19th century. Oligopolies use their resources in the most optimal way to produce a given product. They provided the US economy with the opportunity to introduce into production everything that the United Kingdom could produce and outsell it.

But when the United States came to the peak, there was no model to follow, no products to copy. On the contrary, the optimality provided by the plan and organization of a large enterprise contradicted the production of the new, because the new breaks the old optimality tries to redefine the connections between structural units and tries to change the plan in connection with the new properties of the product. And soon another innovation tries to change the new optimality. The economy of innovation becomes the enemy of optimality. For the peak, the freedom of the market is more important—for the generation of new things based on the principle of "natural selection of the fittest." Natural selection is wasteful and cannot be optimal. But it allows the country at the peak to continue to stay there. The planned sub-economies were still important to enable the implementation of large projects. Still, for the peak country, it was more important to produce a wide variety of new things.

Precisely because the importance of the planned component outweighed the free market component for a country at the bottom of the economic pyramid, the transformation of the entire economy into a single planned continent could have yielded amazing results in the case of the USSR. *For the valley, it is more important to be organized to produce a given list of goods and services "like those at the peak." But for the American peak, natural selection became more important, giving it new goods that the rebellious valley was forced to reproduce by breaking its organization and breaking its plans.* This is why the struggle against the socialist economic pyramid was won.

The special situation of the leader and democracy

In the valley countries, the presence of large enterprises leads to the subordination of the state to their interests. On peak, innovations and the constant reorganization of large enterprises greatly weaken their ability to defend their interests in relations with the state. Broad introduction of innovations is constantly changing the configuration of the economy—sub-economies change their composition and essence. They sell divisions in some industries and buy in others; they leave one area and appear in another; they increase and decrease the number of their factories and their employees, etc. This constant bubbling soup not only makes it impossible for large businesses to organize to jointly oppose the state in defending their interests, but this constant bubbling soup does not even allow, in most cases, to define what those interests are.

But more importantly, the new also gives rise to new enterprises whose interests do not coincide with those of the old enterprises. The constant introduction of innovations guarantees the diversity and contradictory interests of large enterprises, making it difficult for them to form a united front.

In the past, the state was opposed agrarian enterprises. These enterprises had similar interests, and this made it easier for them to form a united front against the state. Therefore, the state was not so much opposed to them as dependent on them. In today's world, the countries n the foundations of economic pyramids have predominantly lopsided economies, with pyramids of a few large enterprises rising strongly among a sea of small ones. In such conditions, the states of these countries are completely subordinated to the oligarchy that owns these large enterprises. Just as the European states of the Middle Ages were able to gain independence based on the contradiction of agrarian and artisanal enterprises, it is much easier for modern states at the peak to maintain independence in a sea of various powerful enterprises whose interests contradict each other.

This is, in fact, the key to democracy in the countries at the peak. The valley states desperately need to rely on state property and organized labor to avoid dependence on oligarchy. However, the states around the peak can successfully maintain their independence without the support of solidarism or state ownership.

Independence of the US state

Nevertheless, the U.S. government used both. In the postwar years, the labor movement in the United States gained a wide scope and achieved higher and higher salaries through regular strikes. These wage increases, due to the increased purchasing power of the population, translated into higher prices for goods. Thus, inflation regularly "ate away" the gains of the class struggle. Therefore, every year it started again. This state of constant social tension required the U.S. government to take legislative action to improve the lives of workers and to direct their struggle in other, non-communist, directions. To this end, the state did introduce elements of solidarity that were not typical of the United States: it promoted the trade union movement and even organized sectoral negotiations between unions and business representatives.

Regarding state ownership, Galbraith wrote the following in the 1970s: "The services of federal, state and local governments now account for approximately one quarter... of all economic activity. This far exceeds the government share in an avowedly socialist state like India, considerably exceeds that in the anciently social democratic kingdoms of Sweden and Norway, and is not wholly incommensurate with the share in Poland, a communist country which, however, is heavily agricultural and which has left its agriculture in private ownership."[275]

In the 1960s, private railroads announced the impending closure of their railroads in the western United States. The reason given was the competition of private road and air carriers, which was killing rail transportation, and the state was to blame because it was the state that built highways and airports. In addition, the state was increasingly transferring mail transportation (which was very profitable for railroads) to the same road and air carriers. Therefore, in 1971, the National Railroad Passenger Corporation (Amtrak) was founded, which, unlike many other state-owned companies, was put on a self-financing and self-sustaining basis. Today, this railroad is 30-40% more efficient than private road and air carriers[276]. In other words, this state-owned enterprise managed to survive in conditions that private companies considered "not viable".

The state continued to own vast reserves of land and all underground resources. The management of this economy required billions of dollars (15 billion in 1949) and 100,000 state employees. The state paid special attention to the development of the lagging Midwest, where the CGPA continued to operate. "[T]he West had found in the federal government the engine for development it had long sought: the growth it so cherished seemed to stretch endlessly before it."[277] Cities and states continued to acquire new businesses and became more and more involved in housing construction. The most prominent example of this kind of state enterprise was the Port of New York. The port owned bridges and charged tolls for crossing them. It built an airport and a railroad line to connect it, new bridges, and tunnels. The port also owned the tallest skyscraper in New York—the World Trade Center.

At the same time, the resilience of the US state in its relations with the enterprises continues to be supported by the fact that the peak state (unlike others) can be useful to its enterprises in a very special way. For example, when Japanese steel began to displace American steel on the American market, the US state managed to reduce the import of this steel without raising duties (and thus without increasing its price). In 1969, the U.S. government "persuaded" Japanese enterprises to "voluntarily limit their steel imports." The same applies to European enterprises[278]. However, when it came to the flagships of the industry, the state rescued them with the simplest and most crude intervention in the economy—for example, direct financial support, as in the case of Chrysler, which was on the verge of bankruptcy in 1979 or during the financial crisis of 2007.

It is impossible to copy the conditions of the peak in the valley. Therefore, the fates of the peak and valley countries are different.

THE USSR AFTER THE SECOND WORLD WAR

According to the Organization for Economic Cooperation and Development (OECD), despite all the enormous human and economic losses, the USSR managed to reach the level of 1940 by the end of 1948[279]. In 1947, the system of rationing was abandoned because the production of food and everything necessary for life had reached acceptable levels.[280] The war largely destroyed the economic potential and lowered the economic level of the Soviet Union. In such circumstances, such a rapid recovery of economic potential indicates nothing more than that the lower the economic level, the more effective the state's influence on the economy can be.

New state efforts were aimed at boosting all major industries, including chemical production, raw materials extraction, electricity, and metals production. The new "leading megascale projects of the century" again gave new impetus to development: the Volga-Don Canal, nearly 20 hydro and thermal power plants, and numerous new factories and plants. The economic boom was also undoubtedly fueled by population growth, from 160 million in the late 1930s to nearly 300 million in 1991[281].

All this could not but affect the rapid growth of the economy. During the fifth five-year plan (1951-1955), the GNP grew by 5.5% per year, industry by 10.2%; during the sixth (1956-1960), the GNP grew by 5.9%, industry by 8.3%; during the seventh (1961-1965), the GNP grew by 5%, industry by 6.6%.[282] This is even though the influence of ideology continued to impede this very development—under Khrushchev, even the small private businesses that had survived Stalin began to be eliminated from the economy. Such reforms were driven by the belief that the planned economy would make it possible to plan even the production of small enterprises (or to produce it through the efforts of large enterprises).

Making the valley economy like the peak economy

After World War II, the Soviet economy experimented with reorganizing the economy on a different organizational basis. In other words, processes like those that took place in American firms, known as restructuring, were taking place. The point was to find the most efficient structure for the big enterprise.

After the experiments in the Khrushchev era, under Brezhnev, factories began to unite into so-called "production associations," which were groups of related factories. Such units could (to a certain extent) determine their sales and demand and organize connections within the association. The first such associations emerged in Ukraine in the Lviv region and were called "Soviet Firms." The very first one, Progress (in Lviv itself), united five shoe factories. Each factory specialized in a different type of footwear, with the main factory opening its laboratory, launching trial products, and supporting services on behalf of the entire association.[283] Such associations, in addition to production units, usually also had their construction units, repair shops, and printing houses, as well as units entirely dedicated to improving the living conditions of employees— kindergartens, health resorts, clinics, and hospitals. Moreover, such associations had large agricultural enterprises in their structure, from which they provided their employees with food. In the 1980s, it became common for such associations to have their railroad cars and containers to transport their products, and workshops to repair these cars.[284]

It is possible that the connections between factories and the planning of production that existed in 1917 could have been organized from a single center. However, scientific and technological progress brought such a staggering increase in the range of goods, the number of factories, and various industries that management from a single center became less and less accurate, giving rise to the famous over-stowing and "shortages." The task of drawing up plans, especially for five years ahead, was becoming staggeringly difficult. Therefore, a step was taken toward the market. Production associations were given the right to make their investments in the amount of 14-21% of their profits. In addition, they could partially change the salaries of their employees and contribute to their living conditions.[285] These units can be considered Soviet enterprises of the late period. As a further tactic to avoid miscalculations in comprehensive planning, such enterprises established their production of semi-finished products, the supply of which was often disrupted[286]. In such a vast economic "empire," it was possible to do their internal planning. *Thus, from a purely economic point of view, the Soviet economy was a way of developing the advanced capitalist countries—the United States, with its huge corporations, Germany, with its concerns, and Japan, with its keiretsu—taken to the extreme. From this perspective, the events that began with "perestroika" were simply a return to the organization of the economy along the lines of the valley countries, that is, return to capitalism, but the capitalism of Bolivia, the Philippines, or Chad.*

SELF-CONSTRUCTION OF THE SOVIET PYRAMID

The task of building an external economic pyramid

By the time the Second World War ended, the USSR had already completed the first stage of its growth, the construction of the national economy. Now it was facing the second stage—an innovative move to accelerate the economic growth. The unification of all enterprises in the country into a single enterprise with a single internal production plan can be regarded as such a move. To a certain extent, this approach worked. "In the 1950s, the Soviet Union experienced growth rates equaled only by Japan, approximated only by West Germany during its "miracle" of that decade, and far above the growth rates clocked by Great Britain and the United States"[287]. In other words, this move can be seen as a substitute for internal American colonization—the country was developing rapidly without going beyond its borders. But in the United States, the next step was for large businesses to take their branches abroad, i.e., to begin building an external economic pyramid. The Soviet Union had problems with this construction. The main one was the lag in the quality of Soviet goods compared to Western models, which impeded the export of Soviet industrial products to Western countries. For example, the USSR exported printing presses to Italy, France, Belgium, and Argentina, but due to low quality, it was increasingly losing its markets[288].

This was not the only reason for the difficulties in expanding exports. The USSR, for example, supplied glass to Canada, Italy, Burma, Indonesia, Pakistan, Sudan, Ceylon, and other countries. "New opportunities arose in the United States... However, American companies would only accept glass from the Lisichanskii factory in Ukraine."[289] However, this factory was not able to satisfy all American demand. The opportunity was largely missed because the Soviet planning system was not designed for unexpected opportunities, as the massive economic machine could not rapidly turn around to meet unexpected demand. Therefore, in such cases, delays often occurred, such as with the delivery of equipment for steel mills in Finland and Cuba in 1963. If the quality was satisfactory and the throughput was sufficient, then a systemic weakness came into play: in the Soviet system, individual enterprises did not have their repair shops but rather had universal workshops where specialists repaired the equipment of any enterprise. Moreover, production enterprises were not able to help repair their products abroad. Japan began purchasing Soviet metal-cutting machines in 1962. Its purchasing enterprises were forced to open their repair shops for these machines, but it took a long time to get spare parts. When they arrived, they were unsuitable. When the good parts finally arrived, the sour attitude toward Soviet products had already been established. Imports of Soviet machine tools to Japan began to decline in 1964.[290] On the other hand, exports exceeded the capacity of the infrastructure. For example, the capacity of roads and ports in Soviet Ukraine was not able to handle all the available exports. In 1961, the port of Odesa was so overcrowded with goods for export that to "clear" the congestion, the Ministry of the Merchant Marine had to refuse to export heavy industrial equipment and agricultural machinery, and the Ministry of Railways stopped all transport moving to Odesa with equipment for a stadium in Jakarta, an airport in Guinea, and a power plant in Nayveli (India). Although there were high-profile successes, such as the construction of the Bhilai Steel Plant in India, where the Soviet part of the plant was completed faster than the West German part (which was started earlier), cases like the above were more frequent.[291]

All these factors complicated the task of building the soviet external economic pyramid. But no such task existed. Such a pyramid did not correspond to the planned future in which all countries were to be closed economies in which production was subject to their plan-law. A country's plan could not be a law extending to trade with unpredictable capitalism. Such a pyramid was seen as a burden rather than an asset. A representative of the Comintern said in 1921 in Ulaanbaatar: "Within ten years we must have built up socialism in Mongolia. To fulfill the instructions... to completely end the importation of flour from the USSR, it is urgently necessary to develop agriculture."[292] The USSR encouraged a model of self-sufficient planned economy in its clients (for this purpose, it concluded agreements with states and assisted state-owned enterprises, not private ones). There was no place for economic hierarchy in the union of such economies because of their independence from each other. Such countries could continue to be in a patron-client relationship through the economic or military assistance of the patron. But, as in the Roman patronage networks, the client could easily move from one hierarchy to another, looking for his benefit. None of the Soviet clients ever paid the price for joining the enemy pyramid. This was not the case with the clients of the American economic world. The U.S. government encouraged American enterprises to establish economic ties with Third World countries and provided aid primarily to private companies in those countries. These ties had to inevitably become peak-to-valley ties, i.e., the exchange of manufactured goods for raw materials and agricultural products. And it was very painful to break these ties once they were established. The Soviet Union, having built a metallurgical plant for a customer country and received full repayment of the loan for this plant, lost any leverage over it. The United States, by exchanging its metal-lurgical goods for those of the client country, kept that country dependent, and in case of disobedience (for example, interaction with a competing pyramid), the embargo became an effective weapon. "In India, they [the Soviets] were building refineries without stipulating increased crude deliveries to that country, and what's more, their management was being handed over to Royal Dutch Shell. In Turkey, a glass factory built by the Soviets was being supplied by Americans. In Cambodia, Indonesia, and Burma, the Soviets built hospitals without insisting that they

supply the medicines as well."[293] The Soviet Union, building factories in the Third World, obviously hoped that the emergence
of factories would lead to the emergence of a large working
class, and thus the emergence of the communist Parties, which
would bring the emergence of communism in these countries
closer. Hardly anyone thought about what would happen after
the worldwide victory of communism. There was supposed to be
a non-hierarchical brotherhood of communist countries.

The pyramid was built on its initiative

The Eastern European economic rebellion after World War II
was superimposed on another rebellion against the peak: the
colonies of the European empires began to separate from their
metropolises. Having raised their rebellion against Western
collective supremacy, they perceived American attempts to get
closer to them as an attempt to replace one domination with
another. And a large part of these rebels began to turn toward
the rebel already known to all—the USSR.

"A quick look at the Soviet archives from the mid-1950s
reveals the beginnings of what would become a constant flow
of petitions from the poor nations arriving to Gosplan and the
Council of Ministers for aid and advice, not all of which could
be fulfilled. When the Afghans were not asking for the Soviets
to make haste in helping to organize the production of elevators and mills, it was the head of Burma (now Myanmar)
asking for architects, or Guinea asking for whatever the Soviets
could offer. As time passed, the flow would grow ever wider,
geographically, and in volume."[294] In 1951, Indonesia offered its
rubber, tin, and jute in exchange for agricultural machinery,
sewing machines, and more. With the development of relations,
the Soviets built a steel plant, a phosphate fertilizer plant, etc.
in Indonesia. In 1955, Burma turned to the Soviet Union, and

soon construction began on a hospital, technical institute, and sports center in exchange for rice. "Along with other countries bordering the Soviet Union—such as Turkey and Mongolia—Afghanistan had been a recipient of Soviet aid already in Stalin's time."[295] In 1954, Afghanistan requested assistance in building four factories, a bakery, and grain elevators, and the Soviets began building a major highway and searching for oil.

For many of these countries, it was not only Soviet assistance in the form of loans or supplies of industrial equipment that was important but also the services of a sea carrier. After all, shipping was the very first tool by which Western Europe economically conquered the Indo-Pacific economic world. The Soviet Union was rapidly building up its cargo fleet (primarily in the Black Sea and the Far East), which became an important element of the offensive against Western European domination in the former colonies, for the newly emerging countries. On the other hand, it allowed the USSR to carve out an increasing share of world freight traffic, which brought in more and more foreign exchange earnings. From 1958 to 1967 alone, the USSR's maritime trade grew from 26 million tons to 109 million tons. An extensive shipbuilding program was launched to achieve this. While in 1961 the Soviet merchant fleet was the twelfth largest in the world by tonnage, in 1968 it was already the sixth largest (its tonnage tripled). To a large extent, the USSR's success was driven by the American embargo on maritime trade. For this purpose, not only large shipyards were built (for example, the Kherson shipyard is one of the largest in Europe), but also the production of huge marine diesel engines, gas turbine engines, and other equipment was established[296]. In the 1980s, the Black Sea Shipping Company alone was already the largest in Europe and roughly the third largest in the world. The USSR was also valued for providing other services that Western economies considered unprofitable or strategically unprofitable, such as oil exploration.[297]

Thus, an economic pyramid began to be built under the Soviet Union on the initiative and activity of the Third World countries. However, this pyramid was nothing more than a patronage hierarchy, with no firm commitments between the parties. From the point of view of nationalist parties, the orientation toward the Soviet peak was attractive, even if they did not accept communist ideas themselves. There was always the hope to "take advantage of the help, and then it will be seen." On the Soviet side, there was a similar hope: to use the help of nationalists in the fight against global imperialism, and maybe the local communists would grow stronger.

Import substitution as an act of rebellion

The Soviet experience was therefore illustrative and attractive to many countries, as it showed the possibility of development without foreign investment. To save currency for imports of only advanced Western technologies that promised the country's future economic independence, the USSR had to reduce imports of other goods. Thus, the country created domestic enterprises to meet the household needs of its citizens. The goods were of low quality, but they were able to satisfy people's needs.

Import substitution has become a sign of the times and the most common form of rebellion against the peak. And it not only promised the rebels a reorientation of foreign exchange spending to purchase new technologies, it promised more—a reduction in the loss of population. And the most valuable population. The presence of domestic (albeit low-quality) production made it possible to keep in the country those for whose education the state spent substantial money and with whom it hoped for economic development—specialists. Moreover, the population decline generated a process opposite to the American internal colonization: the outflow of consumers reduced the demand for industrial products and made them less profitable.

Import substitution gave hope. But, since it was a rebellion against the peak, it naturally generated opposition from the peak. In addition, since rebellion requires effort and sacrifice, it generated internal opposition from those who were not ready for it. And this internal opposition was looking for opportunities to get help from the peak. Once caught in this grip, the rebellious states threw themselves into the arms of the other superpower, i.e., voluntarily mounted into its political pyramid of political and economic influence.

Willpower

Import substitution offered imperfect domestic goods, which were often more expensive (both because of imperfect production techniques and small economies of scale). It demanded that those who had already tasted Western goods give them up. As a result, this policy faced opposition from a large part of the people in the cities, who were not ready to "give up." In addition, import substitution destroyed the trade enterprises associated with Western imports, which had already acquired sufficient socioeconomic influence.

Therefore, such a policy aimed at independence could not be implemented without a certain degree of political coercion of the dissatisfied (just as violence had been used to gain political independence before). As long as there was an attraction to the American standard of living and it goods, dissatisfaction with import substitution could not pass.

The Soviet pyramid of socioeconomic influence grew because the Soviet approach, which did not imply economic dependence, continued to attract rebel countries. But the advantages of the

American pyramid, such as product quality and much more extensive free aid, were no less attractive. Therefore, the rebel country had to decide every day whether it was still a rebel or had already agreed to more extensive aid and quality. In other words, the situation was such (as it always is with rebels) that the continuation of the rebellion was determined by the strength of will. And the willpower of a country is the determination of the state. And the ability of the state to enforce its will is determined by the power of the state pyramid of the socioeconomic influence. And the problem of the Third World countries was precisely that their newly emerging states were weak.

To be inspired to make efforts to lead the economy and the people, the state must have its willpower. And this willpower is the party. The ruling party constantly keeps the goal of the movement in sight and does not allow the state to be distracted by secondary (from its point of view) goals, and most importantly, to turn off the path due to difficulties.

The weakness of the state led to a complete inability to control state-owned enterprises. The result was rampant corruption in these enterprises. The Soviet Union, which built turnkey enterprises for these countries, went through the terrible abyss of repression in the 1930s to more or less stabilize the behavior of its bureaucracy. No wonder Soviet repressions were mainly aimed at members of the party, state, and military apparatuses. A considerable number of people who were imprisoned in the Gulag camps were officially there for economic crimes (embezzlement, theft of state property, etc.). An even larger number were imprisoned for "sabotage," which was often a politicized form of accusation of economic mismanagement. In the end, the Soviet state apparatus, permeated from within by the party hierarchy, managed to perform its functions quite successfully. The same goes for state enterprises. They were permeated by both the party hierarchy and the trade union hierarchy. In such conditions, it was not as easy to quietly plunder the enterprises as one would have liked, and thus the enterprises were able to function and even rapidly raise the economy of the Soviet Union for some time.

This was not the case in the Third World. Their state pyramid was weak, and the party system did not extend to the enterprises. These states often resorted to terror. But the terror was directed against political rivals and, despite its gruesomeness, did little to reduce economic crimes. The consequence of such dictatorships was despondency. A significant part of the people concluded that this country and this people were not capable of achieving success. The enthusiasm of the first years of independence was replaced by pessimism and even the belief that the only real way out was to return to the external governance of other nations that had proven themselves.

Disciplined parties
Rebellion has always been more stable where independence was gained through a long underground or guerrilla struggle, or at least through an organized and widespread movement of national disobedience to the metropolis. The point was that a force came to govern the state that was already organized in its pyramid and had been hardened in the struggle against the forces that tried to break it down (bribery, among other things) and had to acquire a structure of self-purification. This force was a disciplined party. Its presence was decisive in continuing the course of independence, both political and economic.

The strong frame of the Soviet pyramid was also formed on its own initiative
As communist ideas spread in the newly emerging countries, the Soviet Union gained more and more supporters in them.

For them, the USSR was proof that socialism was possible. It also attracted them as an example of rapid development without Western assistance. Finally, they were interested in the assistance the Soviet Union provided to communist parties in other countries.

Thus, within the patronage pyramid of the Soviet Union in the Third World, a stronger framework was formed, with ideological ties as its links. These ties were also partly patronage ties. But they were also partly tied to voluntary submission to the discipline of common struggle.

Ideological obstacles to the construction of the pyramid

Marxism prevented the USSR from building not only an economic pyramid of socio-economic influence (SEI) but also an ideological one. The USSR held the view that the Third World countries were not ready for socialism and needed to build capitalism first. To the frequent appeals of communist movements in these countries to help them come to power, the Soviet state replied that first a large and conscious working class must grow in that country, and this class will take matters into its own hands. For example, when the Chinese Communists asked Stalin to help them build their armed forces, he replied: "We need the [Guomindang] Right. It has capable people who still direct the army and lead it against the imperialists"[298]. Similarly, during World War II, Iranian communists "stressed the immediate potential for revolutionary uprising in Iran, Stalin strongly disagreed with that perspective. His main preoccupations were defensive—denying the imperialists access to the oil resources in northern Iran and securing a treaty with the leftist bourgeois nationalists in Tehran."[299]

Thus, the USSR refused to help the Third World Communist Parties, considering their movement premature and therefore doomed to failure. This meant that the USSR deliberately refused to build its ideological pyramid of the socio-economic influence. Thus, in April 1927, the Communists, who had not waited for Soviet help, were crushed by the Kuomintang army under Chiang Kang-shek and their main leaders were arrested or killed.[300] Similarly, after World War II, with the gradual rapprochement between the Shah of Iran and the United States, communists there were persecuted and had to go underground.

Even later, when the victory of the Chinese Red Army over Chiang Kai-shek's forces was certain, Stalin continued to instruct the Chinese Communists not to rush to introduce socialism. Stalin insisted that after the victory, the Communists should form a coalition government with other parties, not declare it a communist government, but a national revolutionary democratic government, and refrain from nationalizations for a time (the duration of which is difficult to predict).[301]

The unification of all the country's enterprises into a single planned economy gave the USSR unprecedented advantages in using economies of scale and scope and in the ability to concentrate resources in "breakthrough" areas. For a time, these factors were decisive. But the higher the USSR climbed in its political and economic pyramid, the more significant other factors became. In the economic sphere, the fact that its products were imperfect alienated its followers (or made life difficult for them); in the political sphere, its inflexible adherence to ideological conclusions made it overlook obvious opportunities. In general, the USSR saw the acquisition of clients as a "noble, but compelled, burden of helping comrades-in-arms" rather than as constructing a political and economic pyramid that could potentially establish its dominance in the world.

And nowhere was this more clearly demonstrated than in relations with China

Assistance in the industrialization of China

The Soviet economy, assembled into a single-managed pyramid of enterprises, was moving forward at full steam ahead. The Soviet Union not only proved capable of lifting itself out of the terrible destruction of World War II without foreign aid in these difficult times but also helped others. The USSR helped many countries, but its efforts to rapidly industrialize China were exceptional in history (even if we consider the unheard-of American Marshall Plan).

After the Soviet troops defeated the Japanese army in Manchuria, they handed the Japanese trophy weapons to the Chinese Red Army. Then Soviet weapons were added to it. Soviet troops withdrew from Manchuria in May 1946. However, during 1946 and 1947, the Chinese Red Army continued to receive modern weapons from the Soviet Army. In 1950, the Soviet Union handed over to communist China the China-Eastern Railway, built under the tsar, which the USSR had agreed with the Kuomintang to be jointly owned. The same was true of the military base in the former Port Arthur. Under the same agreement, the USSR provided China with a large loan to pay for the supply of equipment and machinery from the Soviet Union. On May 15, an agreement was signed to assist China in the construction and reconstruction of 141 large enterprises. The list of enterprises included several groups of metallurgical enterprises, non-ferrous metal production enterprises, coal mines, oil refineries, car factories, tractor factories, and power plants.[302]

More followed. A memorandum from the Soviet government on August 10, 1954, stated that the Soviet Union was ready to carry out design work, supply equipment, assist in the construction of fifteen new defense enterprises, and help build a further fourteen new industrial enterprises, including a plant to produce up to 600 anti-aircraft missile control devices per year.

The USSR also agreed to contribute to the development and supply of equipment for heavy ground and anti-aircraft artillery, including new types of artillery. In addition, Moscow presented a number of its proposals for the modernization of certain types of weapons (MiG-17 jets, anti-aircraft guns, and tank diesel engines). In some cases, Chinese factories could begin production of such advanced weapons before the Soviet Union itself. Khrushchev's visit to China led to several new agreements. On October 12, 1954, he signed a protocol to increase the supply of Soviet equipment to Chinese industrial enterprises... and to assist in the construction of fifteen more enterprises... After the twentieth Congress of the CPSU, in April 1956, Mikoyan visited China and signed new agreements to promote the development of advanced industries, including the construction of fifty-five new large enterprises. In addition, Soviet assistance was provided in the creation of three research institutes for the military industry and the construction of a railroad from Urumqi to the Soviet border[303]. In March 1956, the Soviet Union, China, and nine other socialist countries organized a joint Institute for Nuclear Research in the town of Dubna near Moscow. The Soviet Union covered half of the costs of establishing the institute, and China 20 percent. The newly created institute included the main centers of Soviet nuclear research: The Institute for Nuclear Research and the Electrophysical Laboratory of the USSR Academy of Sciences. The laboratories of the Dubna Institute were the best that Soviet science could offer; they had giant accelerator facilities for nuclear research, the world's largest synchrophasotron, and synchrocyclotrons. For the first time, Chinese scientists had a real opportunity to conduct advanced nuclear research at this institute... According to the agreement, in 1955-1956, an experimental nuclear reactor and an elementary particle accelerator were designed and delivered to China;

China also received free of charge in 1958 scientific and technical documentation related to the nuclear reactor and accelerators, as well as assistance in the assembly and commissioning of the reactor.[304]

In March 1955, Moscow and Beijing signed a new aid agreement that provided for an additional 16 industrial projects to be fully funded by the Soviet Union. Under Beijing's first Five-Year Plan (1953-1957), the Soviet Union helped China build as many as 166 industrial plants. In the 1950s, Moscow also helped Beijing obtain significant assistance from Eastern European countries, including East Germany, Czechoslovakia, Poland, Romania, Hungary, and Bulgaria. These countries agreed to take responsibility for building 116 fully-equipped industrial plants and 88 partially-equipped plants. While Eastern Europe was focused on agriculture and forestry, the Soviet Union was responsible for supplying advanced technologies, including metallurgy, ore dressing, oil exploration, locomotive production, hydraulic and thermal power plants, hydro turbine production, machine tool building, high-grade steel production, and vacuum installations. It is also interesting to note that China simply compensated for the costs of duplicating and copying the drawings; it did not pay anything for patent rights and thus received these technologies for almost nothing. In addition, for the Chinese to master production methods and scientific knowledge, the Soviet and Eastern European states sent more than 8,000 advisors and experts to China and received up to 7,000 Chinese for training and education in the 1950s.[305]

Of course, the Soviet state sought to spread communist ideology in the world. Of course, it was happy to see another implacable enemy of the United States emerge in Asia. At the same time, it did not attempt to secure China at the foot of its economic pyramid. On the contrary, the USSR was in a hurry to bring China to a developed industrial level as soon as possible so that it would not have to bear the burden of helping and protecting it. After all, for the USSR, "the construction of enterprises in China accounted for approximately 7 percent of the Soviet annual national income"[306]. *Neglecting economic opportunities in the name of ideological principles never allowed the USSR to fully enter the third stage of economic growth.*

THE COLD WAR

At the end of World War II, the United States found itself alone at the economic peak of the world. Other once-powerful economies had fallen far from the peak as a result of the war. It was a world where the United States, in theory, could continue to grow domestically (especially since immigration from destroyed Europe and Asia was enough for domestic growth) and simply increase its exports to the rest of the world. If the United States had followed this path, it would have built a global economic pyramid similar to the one built by the United Kingdom. But there were several "buts" that changed the course of events. In addition to the inability of the destroyed Europe to buy large quantities of American exports, there were other problems. 1. Since the Soviet economy was developing at a good pace, no one could know how fast and how well the countries that chose the socialist path of development would develop and what consequences this would have for the US position in the world. 2. World communism was on the rise, and now it had a powerful center that was becoming the ideological peak for millions of people in different countries. And since the Western European countries all had their Marxist movements, it was not at all clear how far this process could go if nobody stood in its way. 3. Finally, since pro-socialist movements came to power, or had a chance of coming to power, in many countries that emerged from the ruins of the European colonial system, the entire raw material base on which the Western world had been built and had been growing until then was called into question. "The immense rise in Soviet power as a result of World War II...would have posed a challenge to any great power engaged in Europe or Asia. But it was the American ideological insistence that a global spread of Communism would, if unchecked, result from the postwar extension of Soviet might that made the rivalry between the two powers into a Cold War."[307]

The Marxist movement in Europe has been on the rise, due to the quantitative growth of the working class during the industrial revolution, since the end of the 19th century. Its first surge can be attributed to the first Great Depression and all subsequent economic difficulties gave it greater strength. The victory of the socialist revolution in the Russian Empire was certainly a powerful reinforcing factor for Marxism. After the end of World War II, Marxist parties in some cases gained even more influence (especially in France and Italy), due to their implacable struggle against the Nazis and the German occupation. The high rate of development of the Soviet Union in those years, and the unexpected ability of its economy to overcome the incomparably stronger world third economy, made its example attractive to many and further contributed to the popularity of communist ideas in the world. The first postwar elections began to show their influence in all its dangerous power for the newly acquired American economic world.

The American response was the Marshall Plan. Assistance to impoverished countries in Europe (and later the Third World) "...would have the same effect as social welfare programs within the United States—it would give them the security to overcome chaos and prevent them from turning into violent revolutionaries. Meanwhile, they would be drawn inextricably into the revived world market system."[308] The United States poured huge amounts of money into Western Europe and significantly helped rebuild it and reduce human deprivation. The United States was at the peak of the giving pyramid and won the hearts of both European economies and peoples. The enormous authority and wide membership of the Communist Parties and other varieties of Marxists, with even more sympathizers, could not work a miracle. People went for help, which was provided free of charge by the United States.

A little later, with the same goal of weakening the communist movement, which was gaining strength in Japan in the poor conditions of postwar life, it was given similar assistance. Fighting like a knight "without fear or reproach" against the communist offensive in Korea, the United States poured a flood of money into Asian countries for troop stations, supplies, repairs transportation, etc.* Access to the U.S. market was even more important for these countries because of their smaller export capacity.

The United States had the capacity for such generosity. "Its economy, dominant already in 1939 at about half the size of the combined economies of Europe, Japan, and the Soviet Union, was larger than all of them put together seven years later."[309] By the late 1940s, the United States produced half of the world's industrial output, and American exports accounted for 20% of world exports.[310]

In Eastern Europe, the USSR did not have the resources to resort to anything remotely similar to the Marshall Plan. Unlike the United States, the USSR had a decimated economy in the European part. Moreover, most of the countries of Eastern

---

* We can say that the communists did manage to raise Asia, though not in the way they thought.

Europe were allies of the German Empire in the war with the USSR. Therefore, the Soviet Union did not feel much remorse for imposing a contribution on them, which consisted, in some cases, of complete dismantling and transferring entire factories from their territories to the USSR. But even before the Marshall Plan began, the Soviet Union began to slow down this policy and eventually abolished the contributions altogether in 1947.

Moreover, the Marxist wave was on its side. Marxists in Eastern Europe, as well as in Western Europe, were "rushing to battle." Confident that if they failed, the USSR would protect them, they acted much more boldly and decisively. In any case, by February 1948, all countries in the Soviet occupation zone were led by communist parties. In April 1949, NATO was formed to counter a possible communist offensive, and in May 1955, a military alliance of socialist countries, the Warsaw Pact, was created to counter a possible NATO offensive. We now know from the disclosed documents that neither side had actual plans for an attack, but at the time both sides were filled with distrust of each other.

The wave of secession of former colonies and overseas territories threatened to combine with the wave of the rise of communism. More and more leaders of liberation movements were using Marxist vocabulary and talking about collectivist reforms. To stop this wave, the American state had to extend its giving pyramid to these countries too. So, the United States, like Don Quixote, raised its visor and rode into battle. It was a battle in which the United States sincerely wanted to help the world follow a better path of liberal freedoms and accelerated development, in which it offered itself as a tugboat that would pull everyone along with it into the Prosperity it believed in and was headed for.

The Marshall Plan helped liberal European countries strengthen the state pyramid of socio-economic influence and reduce the authority of the Communist Parties. Based on this experience, it was easy to assume that similar assistance to the states of backward countries could stop the strengthening of communist ideas in them. " . . . aid was tied to the recipient's acceptance of market access and export of profits . . . and the exclusion of communist and left-wing socialists from government."[311] Americans taught the world to open its borders to their exports.

But already in the early stages of the Cold War, the experience of involvement in the political life of the Third World left a bitter taste in the minds of the US government. "The Chinese Communist Revolution, the US-supported wars against Communist guerrillas in Vietnam, Malaya, and the Philippines, the radical orientation of the post-independence regimes in Indonesia, India, and Egypt, and even the successful interventions in Guatemala and Iran convinced the Eisenhower administration that the Third World may not be ready for democracy—the ingratitude shown by the Chinese and Indonesians to US efforts to secure their freedom during and after World War II signified a lack of appreciation for the principles America was trying to further."[312]

Having met an opponent whose economic challenge to the peak was supported by political and ideological means, the United States was forced to become the peak of the economic, political, and ideological pyramids. This led the United States to break out of its political isolation on the American continent, which had characterized its previous development. But it is unlikely that this "going outside" would have happened if the "going outside" of American corporations had not happened earlier.

EASTERN EUROPE—REBELLION AND SOCIALISM

On January 5, 1949 (8 years earlier than the EU), the Council for Mutual Economic Assistance (CMEA) was formed. Since each country was conceived as a closed economy, subject to a plan-law, the economic hierarchy was alien to communist thinking. Trade within the bloc was not supposed to contradict the planned economy, as imports and exports within the CMEA were included in the countries' plans. But economic realities soon became fully apparent. The more developed socialist countries gradually took up positions at the peak of the economic pyramid that naturally began to build. The USSR, although not at the very bottom, was not at the peak either. The USSR was only the political peak of the ideological socialist world.

The USSR imported agricultural products from Bulgaria and Romania in exchange for industrial machinery, and equipment (and oil). But, at the same time, the Soviet Union, within the framework of this "its" economic union, exported mostly raw materials, coal, metal ore, cotton, agricultural products, etc. to Czechoslovakia, the GDR, Hungary, and Poland. In exchange, it received equipment and consumer goods. Prices for goods were set by world prices, and since industrial products in the world were constantly rising in price relative to raw materials, Soviet exports to the CMEA were steadily falling in value relative to their imports from there. From 1958 to 1970 alone, this proportion fell by 20%.[313] In addition, to maintain its influence (as well as out of an understanding of "brotherly relations"), the USSR supplied oil to the CMEA countries at reduced prices (relative to world prices), which became especially noticeable after the oil crises in the West in the 1970s. The USSR's economic position was thus steadily sinking.

Economic laws are therefore laws that break through any schemes that ideologies try to impose on them.

A doomed struggle

The leading socialist countries, having accelerated their economies in the economic spaces of the CMEA and having a guaranteed market, decided to try their hand at the West. They began to borrow from the West to purchase new technologies from the West, hoping to create a sufficiently competitive production using relatively cheap labor and still cheap oil from the USSR. But socialist economies, by their very nature, are not designed to compete, but to best meet the current needs of their population.

Western enterprises sought greater technical sophistication in production to reduce production costs (and thereby gain a competitive edge). An integral part of this continuous technological re-equipment was the reduction of the labor force (and thus wage costs). The socialist countries were "workers' countries" and could not, by their ideological nature, reduce the labor force in favor of efficiency and optimal production. Therefore, their "competition" with Western economies was doomed from the start.

In addition, the giant industrial enterprises of the socialist countries were designed to produce the same products on a massive scale for a very long time. They were a worthy competitor to the capitalist economies in the production of the products they were designed to produce. However, since Western enterprises were constantly working to create new products, this "worthy competition" could only last for a limited time.

Some socialist countries began to give their enterprises more freedom of action and limit the plan to generalized guidelines. This allowed any enterprise to try its hand at the West. Therefore, the state did not organize efforts in the most promising areas. In other words, these countries acted like any other country at the bottom of the economic pyramid, whose private enterprises are trying to break into Western markets at their peril. *In some miraculous way, the socialist countries were trying to jump from a complete command-and-control approach to a completely free-market approach (albeit based on state-owned enterprises).*

A natural result

Ideology has stiffened socialist countries. In Yugoslavia, the fact that the workers who worked at the factories were considered to be the owners of the factories discouraged long-term investment. Since ownership ended with a change of job, employees were interested in distributing profits as quickly as possible to pay salaries rather than investing in long-term, promising projects to re-equip the enterprise. Similar situations existed in other socialist countries that experimented with their varieties of socialism (Poland, the GDR, Hungary, and Czechoslovakia).

The withdrawal of U.S. troops from Vietnam gave rise to a surge of confidence in the exhaustion and "decay" of the United States, and the oil crisis of the 1970s in the West promised even greater prospects. The socialist camp, led by the USSR, finally decided to actively help build a pyramid of political and economic influence in the Third World. However, this assistance required an increased diversion of resources from economic tasks, even though the oil crisis of the 1970s further reduced the demand for exports of the socialist countries and their states had to take over the enterprises that were on the verge of bankruptcy.

Since the socialist countries were unable to export competitively, they began to sink further into debt. Poland owed 25 billion to the West at the beginning of 1980, Hungary—10 billion, and Romania more than 1.3 billion at the end of 1981. Yugoslavia owed 20 billion by 1982[314]. Debt service ate up between 40 and 70% of all foreign exchange earned by export operations. The

Soviet Union, trying to save its political-economic-ideological pyramid, provided these countries, such as Poland, with hard currency for their goods instead of bartering for their own goods. However, the decline in world oil prices in the mid-1980s caused the USSR itself to lose its export and import balance. In 1991, its debts reached 66 billion dollars[315].

The socialist countries were forced to move to a regime of self-restraint, which caused popular discontent. In the context of the Cold War, this dissatisfaction could not but be reinforced by the other camp and inevitably turned anti-socialist. This trend also resulted in a lack of confidence in the capabilities of state-owned enterprises. But the main thing was their anti-state orientation-the *people no longer wanted the combat discipline of the insurgent camp-they wanted freedom, like at the peak!* This dissatisfaction resulted in the emergence and strengthening of the Solidarity movement in Poland, the beginning of the processes that led to the war in Yugoslavia and the uprising in Romania.

THE BEGINNINGS OF CHINA'S RISE

How Europe broke into China

Aside from arms, Europe had nothing to offer China up to the 19th century to draw it into trade, and through it into the foundation of its pyramids. But finally, such a product was found—opium. Opium, which was being exported from British-controlled India, found many people in China willing to consume it, and with it, European trade could finally penetrate China. However, the Chinese state suddenly banned the import of opium and began to crack down on smugglers. In response, in 1840, the United Kingdom Navy blockaded the port of Canton (Guangzhou), starting the First Opium War. After two opium wars, the Chinese state softened its position and allowed British traders to trade in China on British terms.[316]

Thus, government intervention ensured that Western European enterprises had free-market relations with China. And by the beginning of the 20th century, almost all of Europe, as well as the United States and Japan, were already trading in China as if it were their home. This led to the massive penetration of their goods into the Chinese market, and thus to the ruin of Chinese enterprises and the loss of jobs for many people. The blind and terrible popular uprising resulted in the killing of Christians and attacks on embassies. In 1898-1901, the troops of the Austro-Hungarian, British, German, Russian, and Japanese empires, the French Republic, the United States, and the Kingdom of Italy suppressed the Boxer Rebellion of the Chinese people and enterprises for China's economic and political independence.

Therefore, the Chinese state was forced to embark on transformations designed to modernize China. The reforms began in the 1860s (after the defeat in the Second Opium War), almost simultaneously with the Russian and Japanese empires. State-owned and joint public-private enterprises were to lead the way in economic transformation. The state also founded new higher education institutions and began building railroads. But all these projects required national efforts, which at least had to be expressed in higher taxes. This triggered a new blind and terrible popular uprising in 1911 that led to the fall of the imperial government. The unwillingness to pay higher taxes and dreams of democracy gave rise to a long period of civil wars, revolts of generals, the breakup of the country into separate territories governed by local chieftains, and the almost complete paralysis of the state.

The arrival of parties

The Kuomintang Party was born out of the organizations that participated in the overthrow of the Chinese imperial state in 1912. It had to follow the difficult path of fighting the pyramids of socio-economic influence (SEI) of local chieftains, organizing a rebuff to the Japanese invasion, and entering a civil war with the Communists. Its economic policy was conceived and, whenever possible, implemented in such conditions.

In the early 1920s, Sun Yat-sen (the first chairman of the Kuomintang) realized the importance of a cohesive, disciplined organization and made efforts to rebuild the Kuomintang into a disciplined revolutionary party, for which he invited advisors from the USSR[317].

And it was this organized, ideological party that began to reforge the ruined country. And it was this party that had good luck. In the end, ideology is the cement that holds the bricks of the pyramid of socio-economic influence together into a powerful whole. The hard generals in power in the central government and the seceding lands, lacking such ideological cement, lost the struggle for influence over the people, and subsequently the military struggle, to this party.

When the Communist Party of China emerged, the Soviet Union, like a Buridan's ass*, could not choose between it and the Kuomintang for a long time. One of the Soviet advisors to the Kuomintang, Marshal V.K. Blukher, participated in the development of the plan for the Northern Campaign, which resulted in the Kuomintang's seizure of power in China. During the campaign, Chiang Kai-shek, the commander-in-chief of the Kuomintang troops, resorted to mass extermination of communists. At the same time, Chiang Kai-shek's son, Chiang

* Buridan's ass—a catchphrase. It means that someone can't dare to do something because they don't know which choice would be better

Ching-kuo (蒋经国), under the name Nikolai Vladimirovich Elizarov, lived in the USSR for 12 years, where he joined the Communist Party. For some time, he lived with Lenin's older sister, Anna Ilyinichna Elizarova-Ulyanova, from whom he took the name Elizarov. He participated in the collectivization of agriculture in the Moscow region in 1931-32. At the Comintern school, his fellow student was the future father of modern Chinese reforms, Deng Xiaoping. On the other hand, during the Kuomintang repression of the Communists, the CCP held its congress near Moscow. Stalin made every effort to reconcile the two parties but without success. The final choice was made only at the end of World War II.

THE COLD WAR—ATTRITION

USA: Clients rebel against client fate

The level of "giving away" on which the US pyramid of socio-economic influence was based could not be sustained for a long time. And not even because countering the Soviet pyramid required a lot of money. The clients of the US economic pyramid were increasingly adept at turning the pyramid upside down— their enterprises became the peak of the pyramids, the bases of which formed the American enterprises in the United States.

Like the British economic pyramid before it, the American economic pyramid had to stand firmly in a world sea of enterprises that would form the base of the American economic pyramid. But to be the base of the pyramid, these enterprises had to find a specialization that would be useful to the enterprises at the peak. That is, instead of competing with the enterprises at the peak (producing similar goods), they had to supply the enterprises at the peak with the raw materials and semi-finished products the later needed. And in a free market, where enterprises interact directly with each other, this has always been the case. "Disharmony" was introduced by the actions of "unconscious" states that desperately wanted their countries' enterprises to produce the goods produced by the peak and, if possible, earn foreign currency by exporting their goods to the peak. The enterprises of the base usually lack the finances for such endeavors, and the risks of losses in competition with the enterprises of the peak are too great. The lack of experience in the peak market the absence of repair and maintenance centers for their products, the outdated home technology, and the resulting low quality of products only raise the probability of losses to unbearable heights. But when governments intervened, with their export incentives and measures to compensate for possible losses, the threshold for risk avoidance was overcome. The flow of exports of European and, above all, Asian enterprises was gaining strength. The trade surplus of the peak economic powerhouse has turned negative. In such a situation, it was no longer sensible to continue the policy of the giving pyramid. The pyramid of the U.S. economic world began to crack and wobble. On the other hand, in the struggle against the expansion of the Soviet pyramid of political and economic influence, the base area of the American pyramid was slowly, with indents, narrowing. The number of countries that joined the Soviet pyramid or tried to stay away from both pyramids was growing. American intellectual circles were concerned that this situation was reducing the opportunities for American enterprises, the raw materials available to them, and the markets open to them. They seriously feared that this trend could eventually reach a critical level.

The Soviet problem of the country of the peak

The Soviet Union, for its part, had its difficulties. It did not realize the usefulness of building an economic pyramid of dependency underneath itself. On the contrary, it was always in a hurry to strengthen its clients so that they would no longer burden it with their requests for help. In confronting the world's first superpower, he needed a strong ally and set about making such an ally out of China. However, no amount of aid could eliminate China's dissatisfaction for the simple reason that China continued to feel its objectively low position in the economic hierarchy of the Soviet pyramid. It was concerned that "The second half of the 1950s saw a rapid increase in Soviet exports of manufactured products to China. More importantly, over 30 percent of China's exports to the Soviet Union were of raw materials."[318] In addition, agricultural products accounted for more than 48 percent of Chinese exports to the Soviet Union.[319] China expressed indignation that "[a]s low-priced commodities . . . a large amount of Chinese agricultural products and raw materials could be bartered for only a small number of Soviet machines and other industrial goods."[320] In almost all of these cases, the USSR made concessions, possibly feeling a guilt complex over the near-annexation of Manchuria by the Russian Empire. However, Chinese demands were not satiated, but rather increased over time. For a long time, despite Soviet refusals, China asked the USSR for nuclear technology. On September 27, 1958, China's first experimental nuclear reactor together with a cyclotron was put into operation.[321] But this could not satisfy China, given its desire to have its atomic bomb for defense. The proposal to create instead a joint flotilla of nuclear submarines with China "for joint defense in the Far East" only angered China. In a conversation with the Soviet ambassador, Mao said that relations between the USSR and

China resembled those between a father and son and recalled that Soviet leaders, "all recognized that such a father-son relationship" was unacceptable.

But irritation was also growing on the other side. The Soviet Union believed that Mao, with his intransigence toward the Americans, was simply provoking the USSR into war with the United States. In addition, having gone through the bloody carnage of its class struggle, the USSR was probably suspicious of various extremes in the introduction of socialism. On the eve of the Great Leap Forward, CCP leaders were alarmed to learn that Moscow doubted their achievements and that "'[t]he idea [of] getting food without paying for it, and our current propaganda on Communist ideology,' were 'incomprehensible' to them."[322] "A further irritation arose when Khrushchev "suddenly" went to Beijing in late September. At a seven-hour-long meeting with Mao and other top CCP leaders on October 2, the Soviet leader accused Mao of his "risky" policy toward the Taiwan Straits and Beijing's belligerent attitude toward the Sino-Indian territorial dispute. Khrushchev pressed Mao to consider the possibility of an independent Taiwan and adopt a more accommodating policy toward the United States... It is hardly surprising, ... that Mao felt bitter because the meeting 'severely damaged the Sino-Soviet relations.'"[323] Finally, in "1960, the Soviet Union "suddenly" notified Beijing that all Soviet advisors and experts in China would soon be withdrawn."[324] It is difficult not to see that the USSR finally realized that by failing to secure China at the bottom of its pyramid through a deliberate policy, it was simply raising its rival.

Thus, in their mutual struggle, the two superpowers created their rivals. Just as the United States grew the economies of Japan, South Korea, and Taiwan, which soon caused them major problems, the USSR contributed to the rise of China, which eventually became its irreconcilable adversary, and in the global battle of the two pyramids was more often on the American side than the other way around.

THE US GOVERNMENT IS TURNING THE WHEEL

Someone had to fall first or make decisive changes. And the United States turned the wheel first. This happened after the deviation from free-market principles in the United States reached its greatest extent under Nixon, and the state, for the first time in peacetime, introduced state regulation of prices and wages. Inflation in the United States then began to spiral out of control even before the oil crisis. To curb inflation, Nixon froze prices and wages for 90 days in August 1971 and abandoned the dollar's conversion into gold on that very day. This was only the beginning of three years of active regulation in 1971-1973. And although these measures are generally considered successful, their implementation and maintenance disrupted the well-established self-regulating system of the peak. Meat even disappeared from store shelves, and wage restraint eventually began to cause workers to become angry. The people at the peak of the world economic hierarchy saw no justification for the increased labor and decreased living standards; they became more amenable to enterprises' agitation against state interference in economic affairs. Rising wages and environmental protection costs have greatly increased the cost of American production and caused large corporations to seek to keep their profits abroad. The oil crisis has only exacerbated the situation.

It was after this that Ronald Reagan's reforms began. Under his watch, the government cut social assistance programs for the poor and also cut funds for the U.S. Environmental Protection Agency. At that time, American labor unions were also crushed. So, to a certain extent, the state freed enterprises from the need to take care of their employees and thus cut the ballast from the feet of the bird-enterprises that were rushing to the sky.

The government reduced taxes and increased bank interest rates to encourage companies to stop taking cheap capital out of the country. Moreover, a long process of reducing restrictions on the activities of enterprises began, which was essentially a removal of the state from interfering in the economy.

A side effect of the fact that rational actions were justified by ideology (neoliberal) was a particularly fierce attack on state-owned enterprises. Hundreds of companies were privatized in whole or at least in part. Finally, a decisive attack was launched on state ownership of land, water, and mineral resources.

On none of these points was the victory complete. Social programs survived, albeit in a damaged form. Not the entire public sector was privatized. The Tennessee Valley Authority, for example, remained in charge of the rise of the American West, just like Amtrak. Nevertheless, state agencies and enterprises that failed to be privatized were restructured. In many cases, these agencies and enterprises were forced to reduce their labor force and become more efficient. Thus, they no longer play the role of a lifeline to reduce unemployment.[325]

The refusal of the state to be a giving pyramid at home could not but lead to the refusal of the American state to continue to be a giving pyramid of political and economic influence in the world. European (primarily Germany) and Asian (primarily Japan) states now succumbed to American pressure. They were required to self-restrict their exports to the United States and were threatened with a ban on exports to the American market. European and, above all, Asian states, which had organized the offensive of their enterprises on the US market, were now forced to organize voluntary self-restraint of their enterprises from attacking the US market. The US state forced Japan and Germany to pay for their rise (very partially). To do this, they had to voluntarily and at their own expense provide an artificial rise in the exchange rate of their currencies against the US dollar. This forced "gesture of goodwill" raised the price of their goods on the American market and lowered the price of American goods on their markets. The pressure on U.S. corporations fell, and previously inaccessible markets and new prospects opened up before them.

The reforms worked. Under Reagan, GDP per capita began to grow faster. And, most importantly, the share of industry in GDP increased and returned to the levels of the 1960s. The people of the United States, deprived of the elements of solidarity and social protection introduced earlier, began to feel the improvement in living standards caused by the accelerated growth. And apparently, they did not lose. The reason was the fact that the United States was at the peak of the economic pyramid. And there, the best conditions for economic development are created when there is minimal government interference in its processes. The distortion of the natural free-market approach in the United States cannot be explained except by the confrontation with the USSR and world communism. It was this confrontation that made the peak of the economic hierarchy also the ideological and political leader, with all the obligations that this implies. But Reagan's "revolution of common sense" was about abandoning the ideological approach, in which the United States tried to show that "under capitalism, you can also have the social protection that attracted people to socialism."

Until the mid-1970s, the USSR was a model for others because, on the one hand, it had higher growth rates than the United States, and, on the other hand, it had better social protection. Higher growth rates were explained by much greater economies of scale, supported by planned economic management. The United States, on the other hand, suffered from the consequences of unplanned capitalism in the form of the Great Depression. In these conditions, it was imperative to show that social protection under capitalism could be no worse, and even better, given that the peak had enough resources to do so. This had to be shown both inside and outside the country. From the mid-1970s, however, it became apparent that the pace of development in the USSR had slowed. And the reason was the lack of innovation caused by the absence of free enterprise.

This opened up the possibility for the peak to return to its natural free market policy. For the same purpose, it was necessary to change the ideological rationale. Until now, the tone has been set by moderate varieties of Marxism represented by social democrats and socialists. Countries were competing with each other in terms of the best organized tripartite (state-organized negotiations between sectoral organizations of businesses and trade unions) and the widest range of social programs—pensions, unemployment benefits, free health care, etc. The general idea was to redistribute the resources of each country from those who had more to those who had less. In such a country, everyone was supposed to be happier, because everyone who lost their job, fell ill, gave birth to a child, or retired felt the care of the entire society, which was ready to support them. And since the richer ones voluntarily shared with the poorer ones, it was supposed to bring a sense of common elbow to the whole nation—everyone was in solidarity, and everyone supported each other.

Now it was time to change horses in the ideology. The new ideology asserted that instead of taking from the rich to improve the lives of the poor, it was better to leave them all the profits. The rich are rich because they are inventive and know how to organize production. Therefore, the more profit they keep, the more innovations they will introduce, and the more jobs they will provide with higher salaries. So, in the end, the poor and unemployed will benefit. And they will win more and more because the growth of wealth through innovation is unlimited, while redistribution is limited by the wealth that is currently available and thus prevents it from growing.

The welfare of those countries that followed the leader and found themselves in his economic pyramid had to grow in the same way—through faster overall development of all economies in the leader's pyramid.

Thus, the US state refused to be a "giving" one to the people of the United States and the client countries of its global pyramid of the political and economic influence. The change of horses worked, and the American economy felt a second wind— it went forward again.

The effectiveness of neoliberal measures in the former and current peak economies (the UK and the US) was a very influential argument for the market transformation that eventually began in Eastern Europe. The fact that this effectiveness manifested itself in the context of an economic peak did not attract attention.

EASTERN EUROPE—THE END OF THE REVOLT

In socialist countries, at first, the majority was satisfied with the fact that they had improved their living standards at the expense of former private enterprise owners. Later, the rapid pace of economic growth became a factor that quenched popular discontent. However, since the production of innovations in the West began to make the socialist giant enterprises obsolete and unable to compete, social peace has been shaken. In addition, the example of the "Asian tigers" showed the much greater potential of other ways. Hopes of catching up and overtaking (and thus raising their living standards to those of the peak countries) began to evaporate.

According to its scheme, a socialist society was a state that owned all the enterprises and a people that were the aggregate of the workers of these enterprises. In this bipolar system, the state could not position itself as an arbiter in the relations between enterprises and workers. Therefore, all the people's dissatisfaction could be directed only at the state, and it took the form of dissatisfaction with the Soviet-style totalitarian system.

The first wave

The most organized and first cessation of the riot of the East's rebellion took place in the German Democratic Republic (GDR). And it was the most classic. Had other socialist countries had the patience to watch longer, they would have seen the basic elements of the process they had rushed to embark on in such fever and such hope.

The accession of the GDR to Germany was the return of the prodigal son—the return of the agrarian eastern lands to the industrialized German west. Before the division of Germany, the exchange of industrial goods for agricultural products was the link between the two parts. The significant migration of workers from eastern farms to western factories contributed to Germany's rapid industrial rise. The reunification of East Germany resumed the process of migration of East Germans to western industrial areas, which had been interrupted by the Iron Curtain, and restored its agrarian status (relative to the western part).

The "country of workers"—the GDR was united with the traditionally solidaristic Germany. Quite naturally, it was decided "[i]t should be left to employees to run the companies because they have never enjoyed the fruits of their labor before . . . There are numerous cases in which, under the guise of self-management, only former managers have profited by acquiring ownership and laying off employees while embezzling large sums. This criticism should not obscure the fact that foreign investors have also greedily participated in corrupt practices often bypassing the very regulations they had called for."[326] The Treuhandanstalt, the agency created to carry out privatization, has prudently managed to exempt its employees from liability for the consequences of their decisions.

So, East Germans, just as they did during the German Empire, and just as they did when they climbed over the Berlin Wall during the Iron Curtain, continue to head to the western lands.

The second wave

As the wave of abandonment of socialism swept across Eastern Europe, just as in the GDR before it, privatization was carried out using "dubious practices" conducted by privatization committees that "became thoroughly opaque"[327]. The elimination of excessive regulation, which was characteristic of socialist economics, simultaneously removed many of the dams that stood in the way of corruption. One of the most widespread privatization schemes was the buyout of an enterprise by its management. This scheme originated in the West and had already been criticized there. Since the management always knows the state of the company (and thus its true market value) better, the owners of the enterprise who sell it to the management are at a disadvantage. The problems of this approach have been manifested on a much larger scale in post-socialist countries. In many cases, enterprise management managed to concentrate the majority of shares in the enterprise that was subject to privatization. In other cases, the state-owned enterprise was exploited by opening private enterprises that "rented" the state-owned space or in other ways. Such actions by the directorate of enterprises were impossible without the support of officials, which indicated that new anti-communist politicians easily colluded with the old economic leaders.

Throughout Eastern Europe, just as in the GDR, large enterprises "were very rapidly dismantled in the process also destroying their potential in terms of networks, exchanges, and. What replayed them were small, often very small units that proved incapable not only of generating synergies among themselves in the long term but of partnering with the German and European companies that emerged in the new economic landscape. [the widespread predominance of small enterprises was one of the root causes] is one of the root causes of inefficiency, whose ongoing effect has been heavy dependence on the West."[328] Western companies have been vigorously buying up these now weak fragments of formerly large enterprises, both because they wanted to acquire what still had value and because they wanted to deny these potential rivals the opportunity to recover.[329] Finally, as the customs gates were opened to foreign goods, these fragments of the economy lost all economic prospects.

Pure, sincere ideology

Neoliberal theory predicted the undoubted success of privatization in socialist countries because it saw society as consisting of individuals. Individuals, having received small shares of enterprises, were to become numerous and almost equal owners of every enterprise in the country. This theory did not want to see the hierarchy of the global economic pyramid, which causes the processes at the peak to differ from those in the valley. Nor does it want to see hierarchies in which the same individuals within each country inevitably organize themselves. If one hierarchy collapses, people will organize themselves into other hierarchies.

The Czech Republic is an illustrative example of real practice. There, rapid voucher privatization was carried out (when everyone was given a voucher for "their part of the economy"). Everyone had to invest this voucher in an enterprise. To help people who were far from the economy, investment funds were set up to collect these vouchers from people and invest them in enterprises on their behalf. At first, Czech privatization resulted in rapid economic growth, and the transition to a free market was declared complete in the mid-1990s. But in 1997, GDP growth fell by 40% and remained depressed. Analyses showed that investment funds had become the owners of enterprises. They were the very pyramids of the socio-economic influence, the very "vested interests" to avoid the formation of which, it was advised to carry out privatization at a rapid pace. Therefore, the hierarchy of individuals that they were trying to avoid came from the other side.

Before that, the Czech socialist state wanted to oppose the capitalist West. To do this, the state created new enterprises and supported old ones to catch up and overtake the West. The power of the communist leaders was secured by the constant growth of the economy. Falling behind the West threatened (and, as events have shown, threatened quite realistically) the loss of power. Therefore, the communist state fought for the survival of its enterprises. It was not the same with the new dominant private owners. They saw the enterprise as a cash cow in whose future they did not believe. After all, in the end, domestic enterprises lost to Western enterprises. If so, wouldn't it have made more sense to invest in Western enterprises? Therefore, the enterprise in their ownership was seen simply as a source of this capital. More than that. These investment funds relied on the support of state-owned banks. These banks continued to financially support the enterprises that were being ripped off by their investment funds. In this way, not only the lifeblood of the enterprises was being sucked out, but also the funds of the state-owned banks. The situation was so obvious that it was criticized by the Organization for Economic Co-operation and Development (OECD).[330] Thus, the very first successful privatizations, like all the others, showed the formation of new pyramids of the socio-economic influence from the wreckage of the former pyramids of the state, economic, and party apparatuses, rather than the formation of a society of free individuals.

At the same time, analyses show that the surviving state enterprises, after adjusting to market liberalization, began to operate quite profitably,[331] while Czech data on the success of privatization concealed the huge losses that privatized enter-prises made for many years after privatization[332].

Return is the end of the rebellion

"Although the CMEA was based in Moscow and followed agen-das set there. the Soviet Union, unlike the United States, was never able to persuade its allies to accept its commercial lead-ership. The reason was simple; as political scientist Randall Stone argued, "The politics of trade in the Soviet bloc swirled and eddied around opportunities created by the distorted prices mandated by the Council for Mutual Economic Assistance." Also loosely based on prices quoted in world markets, CMEA prices largely benefited Eastern European countries. That, coupled with the institutional disorganization in the Soviet Union meant that the smaller satellites were able to consistently resist Soviet pressure for fairer trade. The satellites were effectively subsi-dized by a country that was, in fact, less developed than many of them."[333] "In the struggle for the commodity structure of trade, a struggle that arose from the logic of the artificial prices used in communist trade, the East Europeans were consistently able to outmaneuver the Soviets, thus exchanging their relatively overpriced machinery products for relatively underpriced Soviet raw materials. Moreover, the Soviets tried time and again to raise the quality of Eastern European exported goods, an effort that, much like efforts to improve accountability and promote common objectives, was effectively defused by the satellites."[334]

Planning within the CMEA was carried out in such a way as to utilize all the capabilities of all enterprises in each country. Under such conditions, there could be no capture of foreign markets by squeezing out local enterprises. The abandonment of socialism in all CMEA countries had to give the GDR, Hungary, Czechoslovakia, and Poland the opportunity for rapid growth by suppressing the weak productions of the other countries of the economic bloc. These countries have always tried to sell to the USSR what they could not sell to the West. The USSR was a reserve reservoir where they could dump low-quality goods and still make a profit. The continued existence of such a "reservoir" for Eastern European enterprises would reduce the risk of entering the Western market and would bind the USSR to them with lower prices.

But this could only happen if states firmly managed their economies. This required further effort and restriction of consumption in favor of economic development. However, the popular discontent did not allow the states to follow this path. "The guard is tired"*—The people wanted an end to the struggle in which the state was leading them in order to "catch up

---

* The phrase was said by the commander of the guard to the members of the Constituent Assembly, who were to elect a new revolutionary government in Russia in early 1918. Apparently, seeing that they did not have the slightest influence on the armed forces, the deputies decided to leave. The "state" did not take place. Itcan be considered as a symbol of the fact that a state that is not supported by the people is powerless.

and overtake" and wanted the fastest possible improvement in their lives, which was promised by returning to the abandoned Western European economic world.

The Eastern European countries, which had been at the peak of the economic pyramid of the socialist camp (CMEA), took a modest position at the bottom of the EU economic pyramid. Their role in Eastern Europe, accordingly, began to decline. For example, the percentage of intra-Eastern European trade accounted for by the Czech Republic, Slovakia, Hungary, and Poland fell from 82% in 2000 to 76.8% in 2004 and 72.5% in 2007.[335] An increasingly large share of these countries' trade is now with Germany and other leading EU countries.[336] In other words, the peak has moved to Germany, and the center of the network of economic ties has moved there as well.

The same goes for trade with third-world countries. This is the type of relationship that has traditionally enabled European countries to climb up the economic pyramid. With the collapse of CMEA, Eastern European countries' trade with the former Third World began to fall from 15.8% of their total trade in 1980 to 8.8% in 1995 and 5.8% in 2004.[337] While in 1980 the economies of the socialist Eastern European countries plus the USSR accounted for 15% of the world economy, in 2016 they accounted for only 6%. The share of Eastern European countries, taken separately, fell from 4.1% to 2%.[338]

Throughout the millennia-long process of Eastern Europe's absorption into the economic and political pyramids of Western Europe, the peoples of Eastern Europe, losing their economic and then political independence, believed that if they were given the chance to take their destiny into their own hands again, they could build countries as good as those of the West. The arrival of the East in Berlin in 1945 seemed to confirm this belief, and following the "advanced scientific" theory of communism seemed to give them a chance to even catch up and overtake. The initial high rates of development seemed to confirm this, but the subsequent lagging behind led not only to disillusionment with communism (which tended to hinder their development) but also to a lack of confidence in their ability to even "catch up." The result was the idea that returning to the bottom of the Western European political and economic pyramid was desirable and the only way to improve their living conditions. The rebellion has exhausted itself.

An example from the automotive industry

With the accession to the EU, the automotive industry in Eastern Europe gained strength. It did not appear out of nowhere but is based on those enterprises that were founded during the uprising or even earlier. Their presence has now allowed Western companies to use these enterprises as a base. Poland exports about 90% of its cars both because there is demand in the West and because demand at home has fallen[339]. At the same time, while China, for example, is developing its domestic automotive industry, which was founded in the Maoist era, Eastern European countries, in their "return to Europe," have lost ownership of their industry. 93.1% of the Czech, 93.2% of the Hungarian, 97.3% of the Slovak, and 90.8% of the Polish automotive industry are now in foreign hands.[340] And the automotive industry is just an example.

At first, Western corporations bought up existing plants and organized production of their models there or opened completely new plants to assemble cars from imported parts. The biggest incentive was to avoid import duties on finished cars. Among other things, the existing design bureaus with their specialists were also used. Previous presence of these design bureaus made it possible for a certain (albeit rather modest) part of the research work to gain a foothold in Eastern Europe.

The situation changed with EU accession. In those new plants, where before only assembly took place, actual production began. And as more and more vehicles are sold from these plants to Western markets, to take advantage of economies of scale and scope, more and more production is being allocated to local plants. In the Czech Republic, Poland, Hungary, and Slovakia, "employed 1.3 million people directly or indirectly in the auto sector and accounted for almost a fifth of EU vehicle production."[341]

However, the design functions that are transferred to Poland, the Czech Republic, or elsewhere are of a low level (to be discussed later). Higher-level development continues to take place in Western countries. Research and technology institutions there are located close to company headquarters, which is convenient for high-level developments in close contact with enterprise management. In addition, they already have qualified staff and laboratories. And most importantly, after joining the EU, there were no obstacles to employing Eastern European specialists in these Western European research institutions and there was no need to involve them in design bureaus in their home countries. Overall, the volume of non-production functions remains modest.[342] *Eastern Europe stopped fighting and accepted its position at the base of the Western European (German) economic pyramid. The cause of rebellion ultimately aims to catch up and overtake. This means overtaking in terms of living standards. The people of these countries have certainly improved their standard of living, but they have also accepted the fact that they will never reach the standard of living of the German population. Did they have another way? There were intense debates about the possibility of other ways before and during the initial stage of those privatizations. They were dismissed as purely theoretical and unproven fantasies. However, today's China shows that those proposals were quite rational, and this will be discussed further.*

TIME HORIZONS

The "state-economy-people" relationship can be represented as a hierarchy of influence and control. The higher the level in this hierarchy, the greater the time horizon. And therefore, its plans are more far-sighted. But because of the difference in horizons between levels, contradictions arise: "workers-enterprise", "enterprise-state" and "people-state."

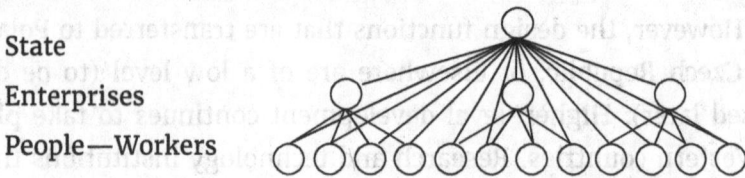

State
Enterprises
People—Workers

The planning horizon of an enterprise is a year or several years. An enterprise is unable to accurately predict the distant future and tries to reduce risks by returning as much of its profits as possible to production. The same is true for setting aside reserve funds. Securing the future requires allocating funds for production expansion, advertising, research and development, more capable (and therefore more expensive) management, spying on competitors' inventions, etc. All of this dictates an effort to reduce the share that is paid out in the form of wages, which is how a business makes its future more secure and protects the jobs of its employees.

But the workers' horizon is closer—they know that profits are here and now, and they want to get as much of them as possible as soon as possible because this larger share is their reserve fund. In addition, risk aversion tells them that if an enterprise goes bankrupt due to mistakes or inability, they will have nothing. From this level, it is difficult to accept that the money they need to live daily is being squandered on failed research and development, annoying advertising, and insanely expensive managers. Employees see more important goals for investing money: their children and elderly parents, their health, perhaps the needs of their social activities, etc.

The state-enterprise relationship is similar. The state plans for the long term. If the funds are taken from the current turnover of enterprises, they are invested at least in strengthening the defense. But often the state also plans to develop the country's economy. The goal of "catching up and overtaking" requires the redistribution of funds to key sectors. In the end, the state is not only concerned with economic problems; it also assumes responsibility for the health care of the people, their education, and assistance in difficult times (loss of work or ability to work, raising many children, etc.). It is obliged to set aside funds in case of plagues, natural and enterprise-related disasters (oil or toxic spills, etc.), in case of riots and ethnic clashes, etc.

But from the enterprises' point of view, paying money to the state, same as to paying it to employees, reduces their sustainability and increases their risks. In addition, the difference in horizons is that each enterprise is trying to preserve itself, regardless of whether its activities are promising in the long-term state perspective. And no enterprise wants other enterprises to be supported at its expense.

Multilevel problems of democracy

Where the influence of the lower level on the higher level is strong, it is difficult for the higher level to work for a much longer term than the lower level. Enterprises in countries with a strong trade union movement have always been at a disadvantage in standoff with their employees, which negatively affects their competitiveness in world markets.[343] The experience of those socialist countries that have tried to introduce the participation of employee representatives in the management of enterprises also shows a similar problem. Enterprises in such countries rarely had enough funds to expand production and to conduct research on production improvements (especially automation, which leads to a reduction in the labor force).[344]

A similar situation often occurs in "state-enterprises" relations in the valley countries (if a country has powerful enterprises). There, the enterprises can organize popular opinion in a way that favors their nominees through their powerful influence on the media. An undisguised oligarchic democracy is one of the extreme manifestations of this situation, in which there is no independent state voice at all. This situation makes it impossible for the state to take measures aimed at boosting the economy.

If a country does not have powerful enterprises, then the "state-people" relationship manifests itself in it's purest form, and independent state policy is complicated by the difference in the horizons of the state and the people. Fashion and changing voters' moods, their swings from willingness to die for a president they like to complete hatred of him, make it difficult to have a well-thought-out policy for a long time. The goal of a general economic rise dictates that people's living standards be limited, just as a small businessman's self-restraint on consumption leaves him with more capital for his business plans. The lower a country is in the economic hierarchy, the longer this period of national effort must be, and voters are generally not inclined to go through with it. Election candidates are forced to adapt to the changing moods of the people and abandon their plans or outright lie to them to get their plans through (so politicians' cynicism is sometimes forced).

TIGERS

The essence of the Asian way was to outplay liberalism. Japan and South Korea were able to play with the peak (the United States) by its rules and beat it because their private enterprises cooperated and showed solidarity with each other. They preferred to interact with each other rather than with the Americans, and this allowed these countries to keep their domestic markets free from American economic invasion. Also, demands to stop subsidizing domestic export enterprises were easily met. Since the chaebol and keiretsu consisted of both exporting enterprises and companies that worked exclusively for the domestic market, the latter could easily receive government subsidies, which flowed to exporting enterprises through the interaction of purchases, sales, and loans.

Taiwanese enterprises have not had this level of "natural' solidarity, they are not organized into similar concerns. Their interaction is more free-market—every man for himself. Instead, the Taiwanese state, to a certain extent, has introduced state solidarity—there are sectoral associations of enterprises and trade unions in society. The state interacts with such industrial associations through its body, the Bureau of Industrial Development (BID). The associations draw the BID's attention to certain industry problems, and the BID, through them, knows better the capabilities of each industry and their needs. The Bureau also contacts such associations to find out whether it is possible to purchase goods in Taiwan for which a company is seeking permission to import. It also finds out whether it is possible to start their local production[345]. In some cases, the Bureau of Industrial Development pushes industry associations to act like concerns. When a part of the textile industry faced the problem of overproduction several times, the BID pushed the relevant associations to agree on the distribution of each enterprise's share in production, and organized inspectors to check compliance with the agreement.

This solidarity differs from European social democratic solidarity in that sectoral associations of workers and employers are formed and approved by the state, not by their own will. And of course, in the social democratic version, the most important element is the coordination of the interests of enterprises and workers, an element that is almost completely absent in Asia after the defeat of communist parties. However, large enterprises themselves take on the task of providing social assistance to their workers, making state aid redundant. (The vast majority of workers, however, are employed on medium and small enterprises.) Although Taiwan's solidarity will probably start to shift in a European direction the more Taiwan feels "at home" at the peak.

Protection of domestic enterprises "from investments"

In Taiwan, during its rise, foreign investment in industry was allowed only in free economic zones. Foreign enterprises in these zones were allowed to produce only for export. Thus, they could not compete with domestic fragile companies. (These restrictions were very gradually lifted starting in the 1970s, and yet the share of foreign capital in the formation of domestic production capacities continued to be relatively small).[346] The same restrictions were applied to the zone of foreign enterprises in South Korea. There, however, they still had meager access to the Korean market but were not allowed to enter several industries until the 1980s.[347]

State enterprises

In South Korea, although state-owned enterprises were used to "kick-start" the rise, but as in Japan, not widely, only in a limited number of industries. Taiwan used state-owned enter-prises extensively as one of the main ways to kick-start the rise. They were thought of as pioneers, as those who staked out a territory and held it while private enterprises grew. In order not to disrupt this process, not only foreign but also domestic enterprises were restricted in their access to several sectors reserved only for state-owned enterprises, such as the financial sector or telecommunications. These sectors were gradually opened up during the 1980s and 1990s[348]. State-owned enterprises, especially in the early stages, generated substantial revenues for the state (on average, 10% of state revenues[349]). As a result, the state could afford lower taxes on enterprises and people.

Later, the state found that state-owned enterprises gave it independence from the influence of private interests. Moreover, they give it the ability to push private enterprises in the desired direction because private enterprises know that the state can withdraw its assistance and complete the project with its enter-prises. This must be the reason why the Taiwanese state has been less involved in direct administrative management of large private companies than the South Korea or Japan before the 1970s[350]. On the opposite, the South Korean state has from time to time assertively directed the activities of 'private' firms. And sometimes it simply told them what to do and what not to do.[351]

Adoptions-thefts

All the countries of the valley of the global economic pyramid that tried to rise resorted to borrowing and simply stealing technologies and products from the countries of the peak. But the Asian tigers took this to a whole new level. The United States, Germany, the USSR, Japan, and others did not export "borrowed" products. Borrowing allowed them to "cut corners" in their development and to master advanced goods and technologies faster. Enterprises of the "Asian Tigers" countries borrowed to export and sell. That is, in other words, they were engaged in counterfeiting—passing off their products as those of Western enterprises. And their governments covered them up. For example, in 1983, a Taiwanese 'government document entitled 'Intellectual Property Rights Protection, Republic of China Perspective,' said with remarkable candor, 'The R.O.C. government has viewed imitation as a necessary process in the evolution of human civilization and believed that commercial counterfeiting is an inevitable phenomenon in most developing countries.''[352]

However, as these countries rose to a higher level in the global economic pyramid, the situation changed. Many large exporting enterprises realized that Taiwan's ability to export legitimate products was being hurt by the country's reputation as a counterfeiter, especially as they moved to produce higher value-added products. At the same time, after Taiwanese enterprises became wealthy and capable of conducting their research, the government became confident "that better protection of intellectual property rights would stimulate more domestic R&D spending."[353]

State
For the first four decades after World War II, the development of the four "Asian tigers" was led by strong states—in Taiwan, the authoritarian Kuomintang Party was in power, and in South Korea, the government was always "alternating between semi-democratic rule and more overt forms of authoritarianism."[354] In Singapore, there was almost totalitarian power of the ruling party and its chairman personally. Finally, in Hong Kong, the government was subject to control from abroad by officials

who were far from Hong Kong's private enterprise, making the possibility of the decisive influence of enterprises on the state scarce.

Korea

The initial impetus for the Korean rise was Japanese entrepreneurship during the Japanese occupation. Due to the administrative command structure of Imperial Japan, most of Korea's land, labor, and capital were mobilized to produce goods and services to support the Japanese economy. "By the end of World War II, Korea was, after Japan, the second most industrialized nation in Asia . . . the seeds for modernization had been planted."[355] And yet, "In 1945... Korea was still a predominantly agrarian society with large landowners controlling the fortunes of peasant farmers. In the South, powerful landowners used political pressure to resist reform, but the combination of sweeping land reform in the North, fears of South Korean peasant unrest, and American political pressure influenced the Syngman Rhee government to pass land reform legislation in 1949."[356] Former and still existing large landowners were incentivized to invest in business or education—just like their Japanese predecessors, they were encouraged to gradually transform from feudal lords to capitalists.

Until the early 1960s, North Korea's economic growth rate outpaced that of the South. As elsewhere, an economy concentrated in the hands of the state and guided by economic plans was capable of rapid development and comprehensive industrialization. Moreover, North Korea was assisted by the USSR and China. However, South Korea's import-substitution policy emphasized private enterprise-even nationalized Japanese enterprises were privatized. In the future, these enterprises could grow confidently under the protection of duties, in line with the import-substitution policy of the Shinman Rhee government. At that time, the state was supported by the United States (and its assistance was more significant than that of the USSR or China). This assistance allowed Syngman Rhee's government to ignore enterprises (and popular opinion). Government contracts given to certain "favorite" companies helped them grow rapidly. However, the growth of private enterprises often tempted some members of the state apparatus to press these enterprises so that they "share" their success with them. Accusations of collusion and corruption between the state and the "coddled" enterprises caused massive discontent, which eventually culminated in the student riots of 1960. Young and pure hearts wanted 'justice.' Since there were many practical ideas about justice, the result was a helpless government under which South Korea began to slide into chaos. The 13 months of unstable political situation ended with a military coup that brought the junta to power." "On May 16, 1961, General Park Chung-hee led a successful military coup that quelled the unrest and ended the experiment with democracy. The junta initially set out to limit the influence of private businesses (apparently to restore control of the state apparatus). However, the junta's dependence on private investment for its economic renewal program (with a weak public sector), as well as US pressure, forced it to develop more symbiotic ties with private enterprises[357].

Construction of the outer pyramid

The time of the junta in power was a time of rapid development of the South Korean economy and a time when the South Korean economy began to grow faster than the North Korean economy. On the one hand, this was the result of the suppression of the labor movement—trade unions and strikes were banned, the minimum wage was not recognized, periods of free work for the benefit of the country were established, and the working day was twelve hours. On the other hand, this was a consequence of the export orientation of the economy. Private enterprises were encouraged by the state to export by various instruments of influence, the most important of which were loans taken by the state abroad under its responsibility. Through the state banking center, these loans were distributed to the private sector for projects that the state deemed necessary. The South Korean state did not rely much on state-owned enterprises compared to Taiwan, but they were still present and provided about 10% of the country's output[358], primarily in metallurgy and petrochemical synthesis.

General Park was guided by the Japanese model of development. He recreated the Japanese Ministry of International Trade and Industry (MITI) in the form of the Korean Ministry of Trade and Industry (MTI) and the Economic Planning Board (EPB). Park also sought to create huge conglomerates similar to the Japanese keiretsu. Over time, private enterprises entered the global market, grew enormously, and became large conglomerates (chaebols). Private investment skyrocketed from 15.6% in 1971 to 33.1% in 1991. Nevertheless, the state continued to direct the activity of chaebols in areas that the state considered promising—primarily shipbuilding, chemical production, heavy machinery, and the electronics sector.[359]

"President Parkwas the subject of an ever-growing personality cult until his abrupt demise.'[360] which was officially justified by the 'threat from the north.' The lack of protection of workers' rights eventually caused their dissatisfaction, and the constant emphasis on chaebols limited the possibilities of smaller enterprises. The oil crisis of the 1970s exacerbated the discontent. In 1979, at a time of heightened political tensions, Park was assassinated by one of his cronies. After a brief period of democratic reforms, another army officer, General Chun Doo-hwan, seized power.

State-owned banks were the main instrument of influence during this period. Even after privatization in 1980-83, the country's banks remained under state control and continued to be used for industrial policy.[361] State aid to enterprises depended on their success in utilizing previous funds. This tactic contributed to the emergence of chaebols at the beginning of the process.

Korean duties were not generally high. But if we look at them by category and in different periods, the picture looks different. For example, at the beginning of the rise, in the late 1960s and early 1970s, duties reached 67% on consumer goods and machinery and 106% on transportation. Later, in the late 1970s and early 1980s, duties averaged 49%[362]. In 1983, a general reduction of duties was announced and they fell from an average of 23.7% in 1983 to 12.7% in 1989. This is quite understandable because, by the early 1980s, the South Korea had reached a level where it already had its economic pyramid.

It was a time when the willingness of private enterprises to follow state instructions was greatly diminished by the new balance of power between the state on the one hand and private enterprises on the other, leading to natural changes in public policy. This natural process resulted in the transition to a democratic form of government in 1987. "Deregulation occurred in the trade and financial sectors, leading to... less central government involvement in production... growth in high technology industries took off. South Korea emerged as a world leader in the high-tech industry with corporations like Samsung and Hyundai becoming household names. Between 1980 and 1997, real gross domestic product per capita increased by a remarkable 248 percent from 530 to 18,500 USD."[363] Now the state "has been focusing more on basic R&D, leaving commercialization and marketing to the firms and setting its R&D agenda in consultation with them."[364]

Production of cars

In 1962, the state established the first car assembly plant together with Japanese Nissan. Import controls were introduced on finished cars, imports of car parts were exempted from taxes, and taxes on car exporters were reduced. In 1965, the plant was privatized, and an agreement was signed with Toyota. The Japanese were forced to adhere to the agreement on 50% local content of car components. "In 1974, an industry-specific plan for automobiles was published covering the next ten years. The objectives were to achieve a 90 percent domestic content... by the end of the 1970s and to turn the industry into a major exporter by the early 1980s. The government stipulated the three primary producers (Hyundai, Kia, and... Daewoo), each a part of one of the big conglomerates. The government further... had to approve their plans"[365]. The state also encouraged producers to sell their products on foreign markets below cost through substantial subsidies, which helped them conquer foreign markets. Among other things, the state prevented other Korean producers from entering the market to preserve economies of scale[366]. In other words, competition was encouraged, but only abroad. The success of Korean car manufacturers led to the arrival of American companies with proposals for joint production.

Electronics

In the 1960s, despite a general policy of discouraging foreign investment, the South Korean state began to encourage foreign investment in the semiconductor industry. This approach contributed to an increase in Korean exports. However,

293

since American companies established only labor-intensive and peripheral stages of production in the South Korea, the South Korea did not acquire advanced technologies. The 1974 Eight-Year Plan for the Development of the Electronics Industry outlined the establishment of relevant research institutes, both public and private, expansion in the electronics industry, and importation of technology through licensing and hiring of specialists instead of investment. Throughout the 1970s and 1980s, the state provided preferential subsidies, imposed quantitative restrictions on imports of relevant products, and set requirements for local content.

In 1976, a new state research institute, the Korea Institute of Electronic Technology (KIET), was founded. In the best solidarity traditions, this body had representatives of the state and private enterprises in its leadership. Its task was to plan and coordinate research and development activities in the field of semiconductors, purchase technologies abroad, and then help firms master them. KIET also had a branch in the American Silicon Valley, which helped it to be on the cutting edge of the latest scientific and technological trends.[367] This helped the South Korea to have the assistance of American specialists of Korean origin or to facilitate their return to their homeland.

At the same time, the Chaebols bought up existing electronics businesses. The state adopted the Basic Plan for the Rise of the Electronics Industry in 1981. The goal was to imitate the Japanese electronics industry, where semiconductor companies were part of larger electronics companies, which in turn were part of giant conglomerates. Since the telecommunications industry was, until then, closely guarded against foreign capital, foreign multinationals were encouraged to form joint ventures with Korean ones, receiving access to the South Korea as a reward.

Taiwan

Taiwan also had a Japanese occupation government since the late 19th century. The fact that it was foreign made it difficult for the interests of local businesses to influence it. The same Japanese state began the industrialization of Taiwan by building local industrial enterprises and developing infrastructure. Almost all of the industry was just branches of Japanese companies. As a consequence, although local enterprises appeared, they did not influence the state.

After World War II, Taiwan was ruled by a one-party, fairly authoritarian state. The Kuomintang Party (to some extent a socialist, nationalist party of China) had gone through the crucible of the Chinese Civil War and was determined to subordinate the island's economy to the task of a victorious return to the mainland. In addition to the ideological factor of the party's semi-military dictatorship, the fact that state power on the island was in the hands of "exiles" from the mainland, but economic activity was in the hands of local entrepreneurs, also played a role. And, since these two groups of the population kept themselves separate from each other for a long time, this factor also hindered the influence of the enterprises on the state. In addition, the posts of president of the republic, party chairman, and army commander-in-chief belonged to the same person, first to Chiang Kai-shek, and then to his son, Chiang Jing-go. The task of confronting the communist authorities across the Strait justified the suppression of discontent as working in favor of the enemy (meetings and publications that could "confuse popular opinion" were banned). "The ideology specified that the state, under party guidance, should take a tutelary role in the economy... It should minimize commitments to existing social groups so as not to constrain the future options of the vanguard party. In this way, Nationalist ideology was informed by a Leninist orientation to socioeconomic problems, in particular by its vanguard consciousness, and sense of urgency. But it also drew primary reliance on the market and private property, which set constraints on state action."[368] The Kuomintang took over all Japanese enterprises and began industrialization according to four-year plans. Finally, the Kuomintang carried out a land reform in Taiwan (the largest and most decisive in the non-socialist world). By doing so, it eliminated the most widespread and powerful pyramids of socio-economic influence in Taiwan (destroying large landowners as a class). This eliminated large enterprises, whose socio-economic influence could potentially counteract party influence. At the same time, the favor of the people was bought.

"For all its unsavory aspects, Taiwan's authoritarian regime has allowed the country to avoid the political fate of many developing countries, of chronic fluctuations between fragile democratic experiments, incompetent authoritarianism, and demagogues. It has been able to give businesspeople the confidence that it will do what it says it will do. By contrast, contrast businesspeople in Latin America are more hesitant to believe shifts in government policies and make adjustments in their resource allocations; for they are often unsure whether the shift will be sustained or reversed"[369].

Import substitution

As in Korea, industrialization began with import substitution. During this period (the 1950s), the production of plastics, cement, glass, fertilizers, plywood, etc., and most importantly, textiles, was launched. Usually, the state itself established and managed new enterprises or transferred them to selected private entrepreneurs[370]. Their task was to take over the production of those goods that the state considered important for the country, but which were not produced by the private sector. The state redirected capital from state and private enterprises (collected as taxes) to start new industries. Capital investments of the state and state-owned enterprises reached half of all capital investments in the country. They were directed specifically to the introduction of new production, while private investment was mainly used to upgrade existing production.

During the 1950s, state enterprises accounted for more than half of industrial output. In the textile industry, the state, like Dutch merchants in a distributed manufactory, supplied cotton directly to private factories and then bought up their entire output. After this industry was established, the state let it run free, but at the same time limited the possibility of new enterprises entering the market, which allowed the enterprises in this industry to reach a more or less large size and begin an offensive on foreign markets.

Unlike in South Korea, this process did not cause increased dissatisfaction among private enterprises or the people. It is one thing when public procurement, on behalf of the whole nation, go to state-owned enterprises that belong to the whole nation, but it is another thing when they enrich only certain private owners.

The growth of domestic enterprises was protected by rather high duties and quotas, but not only. The state used an over-valued national currency exchange rate against the US dollar. In an environment where exports were predominantly agricul-tural, this policy helped to pump revenues from agriculture to industry by making agriculture receive less in local currency, but industry could purchase technology with less local currency and all foreign currency had to be deposited with the central bank. Moreover, for industrial exporters, the domestic currency exchange rate was set lower!

Finally, American aid was a very important factor—"over the 1950s, economic aid equaled about 6 percent of GNP and nearly 40 percent of gross investment."[371] On the other hand, the United States assisted private enterprises and prevented the Kuomintang from actively attempting to extend state ownership to the projects in which they participated.

As private enterprises, under the influence of government incentives, invested more of their capital in the development of new production, the importance of state enterprises declined. However, with the advent of new technologies in the world (and government projects to introduce them in Taiwan), the need for state-owned enterprises grew again. Initially, light industries were encouraged, i.e. those that were "within the reach" of the existing private sector and could bring in foreign currency—textiles, consumer electronics (radios or record players) etc. But over time, investment in labor-intensive industries began to be discouraged in favor of science—and capital-intensive industries.[372] The role of the public sector in industrial output declined from 56% in 1952 to 44% in 1960 and to 21% in 1970.

Example: electrical and electronics industry

As early as the 1950s, the state began restricting imports of complete radios to help local radio assemblers from spare parts. The First Plan of 1953-56 introduced protectionism for manufacturers of radios, fans, measuring instruments, cables, etc. In 1962, a state-owned company was established to assemble TV sets from Japanese parts. The state also introduced requirements for a minimum percentage of Taiwanese-made parts in the production of refrigerators, TVs, air conditioners, etc.[373]

In 1965, the first free export zone was opened, where foreign and domestic businesses could have unlimited interaction, provided they exported all their products. In the same year, a state-owned company was founded to promote the use of computers in Taiwan. In 1966, a plan was adopted to turn Taiwan into a "center of the electronic industry." The planning body formed an electronics working group to coordinate production and sales, staff training, and quality control. Exports of electronic goods grew by 58% per year between 1966 and 1971.

Construction of the outer pyramid

A new stage came after the crisis of the 1970s and the almost simultaneous withdrawal of recognition of Taiwan's independence by the UN and various countries. Under these conditions, the enterprises whose rise had been fostered by the state for so long began to betray their country (as did the part of the people who could). Emigration and capital flows to the United States increased, university students began to express massive dissatisfaction with authoritarianism, and foreign investment declined.

Under these conditions, the state strengthened its leading role in the economy as well as its political control over the people. The Sixth Four-Year Plan and the subsequent Six-Year Plan again significantly strengthened the role of state-owned enterprises[374]. This was done to make the economy more manageable in the face of the "betrayal" of private enterprises. This was done in those industries where private enterprises, even with government encouragement, were unwilling to take the risk of starting new capital-intensive businesses (e.g., steel, petrochemical, heavy machinery). At this point, state-owned enterprises were initially conceived as helping to establish a more advanced private light industry, which would use the machines, conveyors, fuel, metal, etc. produced for them by the public sector. That is, at this stage, the state, having already created a light industry, began to spend capital not on loans to private enterprises to purchase the necessary machines abroad, but on the production of these machines in the country. It is highly unlikely that private enterprises would have started investing massively in the construction of new heavy industry on their own. They didn't need to, because they were buying what they needed abroad. Moreover, they didn't care whether they bought these machines from foreign corporations or domestic state-owned companies. But the state did care because in the second case, the country was gaining economic independence.

The state has established consortia for research and development activities to help the private sector, for example, in the electronics industry,[375] and has also itself founded companies in knowledge-intensive industries.[376].

At the same time, the Taiwanese state tried to establish cooperation with foreign enterprises, but on its terms. To open their branches, multinational companies (MNCs) had to undertake to export a part (half) of their products. This condition 1. allowed attracting enterprises to Taiwan for which the Taiwanese market was too small; 2. allowed domestic enterprises to survive, as MNCs could "fight them with only one hand" (using only part of their products, the one that was allowed to be sold on the Taiwanese market). Moreover, by competing with such "tied" competitors, domestic enterprises were hardened and prepared to enter foreign markets.

Example: electronics and computer science

In 1972, the state decided to establish itself in the production of semiconductors. In 1974, the state-owned Electronic Research and Service Organization (ERSO) was founded, which opened the first semiconductor wafer production facilities and acquired chip manufacturing technology from an American firm. "Leadership for the industry was vested in public research organizations and public enterprise offshoots from these organizations rather than with existing large private firms. In particular, ERSO was given responsibility for guiding the development of core technologies and new products, and for training microelectronics engineers, some of whom then move to (private) industry."[377] All these measures led to the fact that specialists mostly stopped leaving Taiwan, and private companies became known around the world (first of all, Acer).

Government research organizations continue to be the centerpiece of Taiwan's electronics industry. "ERSO stands between the domestic electronics firms and the rest of the world to facilitate the transfer and assimilation of advanced technologies. It commonly licenses foreign technologies itself and then publishes them to firms, thus eliminating price-raising competition between firms for the same technology"[378]. Another example is biotechnology, where a large state laboratory founded in 1984 to bring together universities and enterprises has formed its branch to put the results of its research directly into production.[379]

Approaching the peak

As Taiwan formed its export empire and moved closer to the peak of the global economic pyramid, private initiative became increasingly important. The role of state-owned enterprises began to naturally decline. The same applies to South Korea. However, Asian countries often hide state ownership behind joint ventures. At the same time, some state-owned enterprises are known as "independent kingdoms." Thus, the line between state and private enterprise is very blurred, as is typical in Japan and now China.[380]. Nevertheless, Taiwan's state-owned banks have begun to reorient their lending to the private sector.[381]

The nurtured private enterprises of Taiwan and South Korea have entered the global market and have grown dramatically. The need for government assistance, especially government guidance, has significantly decreased for them. Accordingly, their willingness to obey government orders has disappeared.

But it was not only the ability of enterprises to disobey government decisions, but also the fact that the expediency of such compliance began to disappear.

On the other hand, strong state power went hand in hand with high levels of corruption.[382] Corruption manifested itself in extortion by low-level bureaucrats in their dealings with small enterprises, as well as in "gratitude" by large corporations to officials and the ruling party as a whole during elections and other situations. Taiwan has long avoided high corruption because of 1. the possibility of funding from state-owned enterprises, and 2. the strong discipline of the ideological party. As long as Taiwan and South Korea were rapidly moving upward (and the standard of living was rising rapidly), the people tolerated both the authoritarianism of the government and its corruption. But as living standards reached levels comparable to those in the West, there was no longer any reason to put up with the shortcomings that seemed (here, near the peak) could have already been eliminated.

As a result of these objective processes of growth and strengthening of private enterprises, on the one hand, and the rise of living standards to a level close to the peak, on the other, both Taiwan and South Korea eventually moved to a democratic form of government. The former ruling parties, instead of pursuing a firm state policy towards enterprises, are now trying to flatter enterprises and are looking for ways to get their support during democratic elections.[383]

General Park, while still in the valley, once said the following: "For such poor people like the Koreans on the verge of near starvation, economics takes precedence over politics in their daily lives, and enforcing democracy is meaningless."[384] Now that South Korea is somewhere high in the mountains, scientists summarize its success: "The single-minded pursuit of growth goals of the Korean leadership has been protected by authoritarian executive dominance, with the legislative and judicial branches or the government being largely irrelevant and the influence of labor unions negligible."[385] Former Vice President of Taiwan Vincent Hsiao said in 1994 (perhaps looking at the developments in the USSR): "Democracy makes the economy more transparent and fair but less efficient. In the days of martial law, we just did what was right for the country. It is much harder now to push through decisions."[386] We should add "less effective" in times of rise. Then transparency and fairness become more important, and the "difficulty" in implementing government decisions becomes appropriate and even beneficial for the economy.

Singapore

Singapore's success is also, to a large extent, a consequence of "administrative guidelines" under a Leninist-style party that manages a profoundly liberalized economy.[387] Like other countries in the region, Singapore started with an import-substitution policy, from which it moved to the development of export industries. However, what distinguished Singapore's economic policy was the early realization of the need for a strong state for the economy to thrive. As the first and long-time leader of the Singapore People's Action Party said, "You can only have a free market if there is a government to manage the rules and enforce them."[388] The correctness of directing efforts to the development of domestic enterprises soon became clear and explicit during the separation of Singapore from Malaysia in 1965. The presence of an industry developed under the import-substitution policy enabled the new country to survive the shock of losing ties. Acting in this context, the Singaporean state adopted a neo-corporatist (solidarist) policy—cooperation between the state, businesses, and workers. In this way, the state managed to coordinate the efforts of enterprises (through their representative organizations). On the other hand, the state resorted to an appropriate social policy, i.e., widespread construction of housing for the people, health care, and support for education. This provided an opportunity for establishing a dialogue with the working class and official trade unions were called upon to cooperate and their representatives were involved in several economic councils (along with the fact that trade union leaders were appointed by the party leadership and free trade unions were banned).[389] This made it possible to virtually guarantee the absence of "class struggles," which in the 1960s and 1970s (during the Marxist offensive) was very important for luring Western corporations. State housing programs, and others, required a lot of land, and it was expropriated from peasants. So, as in most cases, Singapore's industrialization in the 1960s was at the expense of the peasantry. In general, as part of its solidarity policy, the state managed to involve representatives of the new "middle class" working for state-owned companies in political and social activities within state representative organizations. "Direct nominations to political positions also occur within this consultative authoritarianism, which can be compared to a neo-corporatist management of social and political interests."[390]

During the 1980s, when disillusionment with state ownership was spreading in the socialist countries of Eastern Europe and a wave of privatizations was already sweeping across Western Europe, Singapore was strengthening its state-owned enterprises[391]. Among other things, the state purposefully made efforts to establish the Bank of Singapore and develop the port and airport, which are now among the largest in the world and are a further guarantee of Singapore's central position in its region—thanks to them, it locks up large volumes of Asian trade. Whilestill a British colony, Singapore was placed at the center of local trade—the port controlled trade between China and India, and other Asian coastal countries. The party, under the leadership of Lee Kuan Yew, decided to deepen this legacy. The planned conduct of the capitalist economy reached such heights in Singapore that even China, in the 1990s, found it expedient to invite Singaporean experts in planning and development.[392]

Singapore has managed to avoid the "global fashion for privatization". Singapore's (prominent) companies remain wholly state-owned or are owned by state-owned holdings (with other shareholders). The most successful are GIC Private Limited (despite the name, it is fully state-owned) with assets of US$359 billion, and Temasek with assets of US$308 billion (2018). All these companies "not only consolidated their dominance over the commanding heights of the domestic economy but internationalized, becoming pivotal to the integration of state economic and political power."[393] From six hundred to seven hundred of these companies are united under the roof of the four largest holding companies, which looks like a semi-state version of South Korean chaebols. At the same time, even fully state-owned enterprises are separated from the state and formalized as independent corporations, even hospitals, radio and television, and even more so the Singapore port. A special program was also introduced to promote innovations in the public sector.

Anti-corruption

In many cases, the public sector brings with it embezzlement by officials and patronage in the appointment of state-owned enterprises. The Singaporean ruling party has succeeded in maintaining the rule of law to some extent because, unlike the

Soviet Gorbachev, who allowed everything that was not forbidden, it considered permissible only what was permitted. Another secret of Singapore's success was "the secrecy surrounding the high-level decision-making process, which was reinforced by an apparatus ready to apply highly repressive tactics to anyone unwise enough to inquire about the sources of a decision. The fight against corruption took the form of an anticorruption agency (the Corrupt Practices Investigation Bureau (CPIB)) that sought to systematically track traces of misappropriated funds and information within state agencies and state-owned companies."[394] "Legislation obsessed with tracking the slightest leak of information created a paranoid mentality in a bureaucracy that had become sprawling for that very reason. In return, the officials' salaries were raised to the same level as those in the private sector. The results were quickly achieved, and Singapore was soon ranked by Transparency International as the least corrupt Asian state."[395]

The economic leap of the "tigers" was a "miracle." All the 'tiger' states were actively anti-communist. Nevertheless, the miracle was achieved through measures typical of communist countries—suppression of the free market and democracy. Another thing is that, without ideological blinders, these states managed to find and observe optimal doses of both. For the communist countries, the task of economic rise, although important, was still a secondary objective. The main thing was to achieve equality, and the extremes in eliminating the market and democracy corresponded to the extremes of the (unattainable) task*.

* In the last decades of the communist camp, when the task of economic growth (catching up and overtaking) became the leading one, both the market and democracy began to timidly make their way in these countries

STATE ENTERPRISES

State enterprises have existed almost always and everywhere, primarily as monarchical property. The reason for their emergence from the very beginning was the need for the state to have a certain degree of independence from the interests of private enterprises, which was so clearly demonstrated in feudal times. The state desperately needed its sources of income so that it did not depend on the favor of feudal lords, and on the other hand, it did not need to tax them (so all parties had to be satisfied).

But in the 19th century, state-owned enterprises, like the industry itself, became more diverse and more widespread, especially because they were now owned not only by the central government but also by local levels of government, districts, cities, etc. They were now seen as more honest businesses, especially in cases where there were no conditions for competition—it was not practical for different enterprises to run parallel railroads and gas pipes. One of the most common factors was also the fear that foreign companies would gain access to services within the country.

More often than not, the field of activity of enterprises belonging to different levels of the state hierarchy lies in different industries. Germany is a prime example. There, the federal state owns railroads, the post office, and various industrial facilities. Land governments take care of the infrastructure as well as some industrial facilities. And, city and district councils mostly own public utilities and local savings banks[396]. Finally, when there was insufficient private initiative, the state felt obliged to step in, as when the states built roads to the west.

However, the fate of state enterprises and views on them underwent a dramatic change with the spread of Marxism.

Marxism, based on the increasing socialization of the production process, concluded that it was expedient, just, and correct to socialize the means of production, i.e., enterprises. Therefore, pro-Marxist parties saw the nationalization of enterprises, or the creation of new state enterprises, as steps that brought communism closer and made efforts to deepen and accelerate this process (regardless of the practical feasibility in terms of production efficiency). For the same reason, those who did not want communism to come saw nationalizations and the establishment of state enterprises as increasingly restricting private enterprise. Thus, for both sides, the struggle for or against state ownership became a struggle for or against communism. Finally, for both sides, state-owned enterprises were acceptable as a means of providing jobs for the widest possible range of people. Some welcomed this as part of the struggle to improve the living conditions of workers, while others saw it as a way to reduce the intensity of the class struggle and an opportunity to prove that full employment did not require a change in the social order.

Marxist ideology in Western Europe gained strength after the end of World War II. The Communists were one of the most active oppositions to fascism, so after the overthrow of fascism, their authority was high. Western European countries where Marxist parties were in government (socialists or social democrats) were at the forefront of nationalizations—France, Austria, the United Kingdom, the Netherlands, etc. Retention of the state legacy of fascist countries, expansion of nationalization, and establishment of new national enterprises became almost a common feature of European policy after World War II. In Austria, the state took over the property of the German empire, which amounted to 20% of the entire industrial sector. In addition, the state also owned 85% of the electricity sector and the country's three leading banks. In Italy, state-owned enterprises accounted for 20% of the country's industrial output[397]. The Social Democrats who came to power in the Scandinavian countries, Belgium, and the Netherlands pushed forward nationalization primarily in transportation, communications, and natural resources. Most countries nationalized railroads and improved their efficiency. At the same time, in Canada and Australia, a large number of industries, primarily transportation and energy, were also taken over by the states.

In the early 1980s, state-owned production accounted for 10% to 25% of the industrial output of the countries closest to the peak (especially Italy in the West and Taiwan in the East). In developing countries, this percentage was generally much higher. In both the former and latter countries, state-owned enterprises produced, among other things, textiles and clothing, food and beverages, pottery and cement, transportation equipment, machinery, ships, airplanes, and much more[398].

This was accompanied by increased state intervention in the economy—states began to "manage" enterprises through planning bodies. "All governments undertook planning, however, and the impressive economic growth rates suggested that the initiatives were paying off."[399] In France, for example, the Planning Commissariat planned and set targets for state investment in industry.

As the use of state enterprises to reduce unemployment was welcomed by both pro- and anti-communist forces, they became widespread. Their staffing (according to their purpose) was often much higher than necessary, with consequences for the efficiency of these enterprises. In addition, during the oil crises of the 1970s, states deliberately bought up bankrupt private enterprises to save those that were important to the country's economy or employed a large number of workers. Eventually, this led to the overloading of states with debts of state-owned enterprises, which led to the desire to get rid of them through expedient privatization. Thus, privatization processes in the West began in the late 1970s and continued sluggishly until 1992. However, the fall of the USSR increased discontent with state-owned enterprises and privatization started to snowball.[400] And, like before nationalization, they were carried out without regard to practical expediency in terms of production efficiency.

Privatization has dramatically facilitated and intensified the process of globalization, the gates of which were opened by the reforms of Margaret Thatcher and Ronald Reagan, and the beginning of which lies in the desire of American companies to move their branches outside the United States.

THE WORLD NOW

THE RISE OF CHINA

The first stage is the formation of the national economy

China has had a national economy for thousands of years, and its task was to restore independence and modernize this economy. The CCP, having come to power, created and established a strong state after a long period of strife and turmoil in Chinese history. In addition, the resolute isolation from the Western economic world meant that domestic enterprises could develop, and direct financial assistance from the Soviet Union (regarding technology and assets) facilitated their development. These factors finally led to a decisive rise in the Chinese economy. The rise was driven by industrialization at the expense of the countryside, and the rapid introduction of existing world technologies under state leadership, with a special emphasis on American concentration of production to achieve the greatest possible economies of scale.

As in the USSR, this way of development, having given significant rates of development, eventually led to a state in which the lack of private initiative began to slow down development. Therefore, after wandering along the paths of the Great Leaps and Cultural Revolutions, causing horrific casualties, the Chinese state finally came to the need for private enterprises. The first steps in this direction were inspired by the Soviet NEP. China was introducing more and more market elements to build a system that would embrace the best elements of socialism and capitalism. At the same time, the state retained the so-called Leninist "commanding heights". But soon the Soviet Union was already clumsily trying to copy Chinese reforms.

The second stage is the construction own economic pyramid

In the second stage, the Chinese state found its original path, inspired to some extent by the American experience and to an even greater extent enabled by it. The American state, in the second stage, encouraged the inflow of capital, knowledge, and experience from abroad to build industrial enterprises. It also encouraged workers for them, as well as consumers (people and enterprises), to come from abroad. Having developed, these enterprises began the third stage—the construction of their economic pyramids abroad. The Chinese state, luring foreign enterprises with cheap labor and an almost limitless market of consumers, tempted them to transfer their production to China. In this way, China, along with foreign enterprises, immediately received all their business pyramid abroad (i.e., all their previous consumers and suppliers). This immediately made Chinese exports guaranteed. Thus, the second stage became the third.

But to prevent Western corporations from suppressing the development of private Chinese enterprises and bankrupting state-owned ones, these Western corporations were isolated from the Chinese economy within the framework of free economic zones. However, the Chinese economy, isolated from

Western companies, was still able to develop in parallel, observing and adopting their experience.

Two economies

China has thus created two distinct economies. One of them, initially almost entirely state-owned, worked to maintain the Chinese economy at the level it had achieved. Moreover, it was supposed to compensate for the "loss" of parts of the domestic Chinese economy that were now being allocated to free economic zones.* At the same time, having outsourced the organization of exports to foreign companies (and making increasing profits from them), China could focus on improving the efficiency of the inherently Chinese (first) economy. Thus, the two economies helped each other.

But that's not all. As a rule, the arrival of foreign large corporations in a developing country carries the danger of the country's dependence on them (on their investments, jobs, currency brought by their exports, etc.). In addition, the industrialization of the country by foreign companies takes place where they need it, and not in those economic areas that look promising for the country's overall rise. Therefore, the two economies allowed the Chinese state to attract foreign businesses on the one hand, and to continue to organize the economy in the chosen areas on the other.

Economic independence

The consequence of this planned direction of reforms was to preserve economic independence. In addition to the isolation of foreign enterprises in the serpentariums of free economic zones,

---

* which included not only the free zone itself, but also the surrounding territory that was eventually involved in servicing free economic zones as the basis of the economic hierarchy in relation to its top

their ability to form their local pyramids of socio-economic influence was limited by a ban on acquiring Chinese companies. But they were allowed to form joint ventures[401]. This meant that Western corporations had to disclose their technological secrets to their Chinese partners. From these joint ventures, this experience and knowledge were spread to other enterprises. This was done both through employees changing jobs and through the building of pyramids of local suppliers and distributors. Both technological knowledge and production organization skills were first and foremost transferred to these enterprises.

At the same time, a large customs wall continued to surround China, along with several import bans or strict quantity restrictions. This continued to attract foreign corporations—if they penetrated the barrier, they had a hothouse atmosphere without competition. The customs wall also encouraged domestic enterprises to substitute imports.[402]

On the other hand, the Chinese state has been very active and persistent in encouraging Chinese enterprises to enter foreign markets. All businesses in industries designated by the state for growth were allowed to keep most of their earned currency (under controlled exchange rates). In addition, all exporting enterprises were provided with various incentives and rewards. "Part of the industrial strategy of trying to construct large multi-plant corporations was aimed explicitly at building multinational companies that could compete on world markets with the giant corporations of the advanced capitalist world. Export industries were given cheap credit for technical upgrades, and priority access to low-price and raw materials within that part of the material supply system that remained within the state's direct control"[403]. Discounts, refunds, cheap loans, etc. all combined to make the goods worth less to the Chinese company after they were exported abroad than their

314

cost. In this way, the Chinese state helped its enterprises to engage in innocent dumping.

Thus, Chinese enterprises were joining their exports to those of foreign enterprises from the free economic zones. Thus, while fiercely guarding the independence of the domestic economy, the Chinese state was striving to undermine the independence of other economies.

The public sector as a mainland in the sea

The Chinese economy, fenced off from Western influence by barriers around free economic zones, could now slowly and systematically engage in the development of private initiative. The meaning of this development was a very gradual, shrinking state mainland around which a sea of private enterprises grew. "China has purposely encouraged the entry of new private firms rather than undertaking the politically costly and economically uncertain privatization programs that characterized the transition in Russia and other former Soviet republics"[404]. The slowness of the process provided an opportunity for domestic entrepreneurs to form. The fact that the state economy continued to cover most of the economy reduced the risks of private enterprises, providing them with a stable, predictable environment. After all, they mostly continued to buy from the public sector and often sold their products to the same public sector.

At the same time, the state could potentially rely only on the profits of state-owned enterprises, and not on private ones at all. This allowed the latter to rise more easily. On the other hand, by giving free rein to private enterprises, the state was entering unknown territory, and the state economy reduced risks and gave it a stable footing. The profits from state enterprises continued to allow the state to support social programs in the poorest provinces on the one hand and to support the remuneration of the bureaucracy on the other. State enterprises gave and still give it independence from potential oligarchs

The private sea at the edges of the Chinese economy was allowed to grow, and it began to cover more and more of the economy. Private enterprises could already buy and sell from each other, not just from the public sector. Most importantly, the presence of the public sector, which itself was successfully developing, allowed private enterprises to do more complex things than bakeries and hairdressers. They could be formed around capital- and knowledge-intensive enterprises and provide them with research and engineering services. It was such enterprises that, after a period of growth, were ready to participate in the privatization of something more than a brick factory or a garment factory.

At the same time, on the "state island" itself, state enterprises were subject to fewer and fewer planning decisions over time. Moreover, the price reforms that Western advisors had so insisted on, which would have led to the bankruptcy of unprofitable enterprises, were never fully implemented. Instead, the parallel coexistence of two price systems—planned for state enterprises and market for private ones—was steadily spreading.[405]

In this way, the Chinese state allowed foreign enterprises to enter China on the one hand and allowed Chinese private enterprises to be formed on the other. In this way, the state did not fall into dependence on either force and preserved its independence.

As China climbed up the hierarchy of the global economic pyramid, the state began to simplify the Chinese economic system. Since the mid-1990s, the parallel coexistence of the market and the planned system has been eliminated by ending planning and letting state-owned enterprises float free on the waves of the free market. Many of them went bankrupt, but the profitability of the rest increased[406]. In key sectors, such as energy, telecommunications, and electricity, which remained wholly state-owned, competition was introduced by the creation of several state-owned enterprises.

The secret of success is the size of the population

Undoubtedly, China's success was helped by a large and ancient diaspora. As late as the late 1990s, most direct investment came from Taiwan and Hong Kong (Hong Kong provided 60% of all investment)[407]. Another important factor is the large population, which looked like an attractive huge market for Western businesses. The attractiveness of this market, as well as cheap labor and virtually no strikes, pushed Western companies to accept all the conditions of the Chinese state, which locked them into the "serpentariums" of free economic zones and forced them to transfer technology to Chinese joint ventures.

For example, Boeing, to enter the Chinese market, agreed to first help a major Chinese aircraft manufacturer to set up production of spare parts, then whole assembled parts of aircraft, and finally to help set up production of entire aircraft. For its part, Ford Motor Company, to enter the Chinese market, has been helping to technologically re-equip Chinese automotive parts manufacturing companies for several years in a row by establishing several joint ventures[408]. The Chinese state, for its part, has invested heavily in such joint ventures.

The secret of success is the strength and independence of the state

At the same time, India, which has almost as large a population and as large and ancient a diaspora, still has not been as successful as China. India also resorted to state influence on the economy and had numerous state-owned enterprises. What is key to their difference, however, is the power of the state pyramid of socio-economic influence, i.e. the independence of the state and its ability to influence the economy. "India is virtually the only example in the developing world of a long-term commitment to democratic institutions. The need to maintain the political support of vested political groups whose voice could be expressed through the ballot box and whose financial support enables elections to be fought has contributed to the long-term maintenance of policies that have hidden Indian growth. 'It is [the] lack of political insulation from conflicting interests that keeps the Indian state despite its pervasive economic presence avoiding the hard choices and politically unpleasant decisions involved in more active developmental functions.'"[409] The Indian state is too weak and dependent on numerous pyramids of the socio-economic influence —economic, political, class, caste, and national. The Indian state is, to some extent, paralyzed by its democracy. And this does not allow it to move closer to the peak, where this feature would be relevant.

It was only with the establishment of the more authoritarian Modi regime that the Indian economy began to show signs of a more vigorous rise.

The moment of truth
The late 1980s and early 1990s were decisive in the fate of the USSR and China. The collapse of the strong state in the USSR (and the inability of the newly independent countries that emerged to build their own) caused the wealth of these nations to flow abroad in powerful streams, boosting the economies of other countries. This wealth concentrated both in the substantial savings of the population and in the significant assets of large enterprises, instead of boosting their economies, rushed

to buy up the products and services of foreign enterprises. This was the time when the protracted crisis of the 1980s ended in Western countries, Turkey began to feel like a regional power again, and China increased its already high economic growth rates. In addition, neither the USSR during the perestroika period nor the countries that emerged in its place were able to stop the smuggling that was undermining their resources. In the end, the wisdom was that it was necessary to abandon customs duties so that they would not corrupt customs officers. In China, in the 1990s, "a widespread crackdown on smuggling increased China's customs revenues from 31 billion yuan to 224 billion yuan in just two years, between 1998 and 2000."[410] The USSR, by the very fact of the collapse of its industry, which began with liberalization and then privatization and the beginning of large-scale civil conflicts, turned away possible Western investments in its territory. They went, among other things, to China, where the absence of widespread political unrest in society (especially after the brutal suppression of the Tiananmen Square protesters) attracted more investors.

Of course, the states of Western countries whose capital flowed to China (as well as the peoples of these countries) would have liked it better if the capital had gone to those countries that had democratized and voluntarily sought to join the Western economic pyramid. But private businesses have their economic logic and their capital "treacherously" flowed to the place where tanks crushed a naive and honest impulse to democracy in the square; and it did not want to flow to the place where, in the same situation, tanks never moved on the people.

In 1996, at a conference in Taipei, a well-known American economist told the audience that Russia, rather than China, got the reform path about righta view echoed the following year by The Economist's contention that China's economic

319

transformation and its growth could not be sustained if gradual reform was not abandoned in favor of a Chinese variant of shock therapy."[411] However, China seems not to regret that it did not listen to the Economist and did not, like the USSR, confuse the end (a better life for the people) with the means (privatization and liberalization), as Joseph Stiglitz said.

As a result, the Chinese economy has grown more than 10 times in the 30 years of its reforms.[412] The total GDP of the former Soviet Union is still below where it was 30 years ago.

The task of the state in the valley is to pave the way to the peak, not to "jump into the unknown"

The USSR, when it finally embarked on reforms, tried to adopt the Chinese experience. Attempts were made to introduce a dual economy—a planned economy for state-owned enterprises and a market economy for private enterprises with different exchange rates and different pricing. The USSR (and the countries that emerged in its place) also tried to increase industrial exports using cheap energy and raw materials. Various other initiatives were tried. All of them, however, did not work and instead of doing any good, they did the countries enormous harm. The bureaucracy, together with entrepreneurs, exploited all smallest opportunities for self-enrichment: products manufactured at state-owned enterprises from state-owned raw materials and supplied by state energy were sold at market (higher) prices, cheap fuel intended for state-owned enterprises was sold to private ones (at higher prices), and so on. The emerging class of private entrepreneurs corrupted the state apparatus by buying its "not noticing" and the state apparatus corrupted entrepreneurs by deliberately pushing them in this direction.

The main thing was not that the Chinese state remained

totalitarian (money, after all, erode any totalitarianism over time), but that state property was not declared a victim. In other words, in the psychological perception of both the people and the bureaucracy, state property remained an element of the national economy that has always been, is, and will be. This meant that society (and, above all, bureaucrats) did not have the opportunity for huge enrichment and this did not give rise to a grabbing reflex. No one had the feeling that the last train was passing by, that the situation put them in a position to either win and enrich themselves . . . or be a fool.

The absence of mass privatization (and even the absence of the prospect of such privatization) saved China and enabled it to successfully and manageably carry out reforms.

What was important was that the actions of the state, and its ideology, were not questioned in its dialog with the people. The new changes (which to a large extent simply denied the previous ideological attitudes) were presented as flowing smoothly from the previous ones and as their development. In the light of propaganda, everything remained as it was: socialism, the primacy of public property, and the criminality of thoughts aimed at establishing capitalism. The fact that the country was not abandoning (in words) its socialist course, was the psychological deterrent that kept the vast majority of people from a massive shift in behavior—a massive pursuit of profit— right here and right now, as happened in Europe (especially in the former USSR due to the delay in reforms).

Some rebels want freedom, others want to climb to the peak. Those who want freedom seek to destroy the "old world" and then think about where to go from there. Those who want to climb to the peak determine the route and then constantly adjust it depending on the circumstances.

The Fate of the USSR—A Lesson for China

Usually, states were afraid that the country's economy would become dependent on foreign enterprises, which would result in the country being fixed at the base of someone else's economic pyramid. On the opposite the Chinese state (under the influence of events in Europe) was more afraid that the rapid growth of the private sector would lead to the loss of the Chinese state's influence on the economy, which would be anyway followed by the natural integration of the Chinese economy into the foundations of the Western economic world.

Thus, in the mid-1990s, the Chinese state made a U-turn in its economic policy and began to provide more favorable conditions for doing business for foreign enterprises than for domestic ones. "Chinese policy appeared to follow the unusual course of favoring foreign private investors over domestic ones. In the rest of the region, one observes a quite different mix, with the important exception of Singapore."[413]

USA TODAY

Reagan's reforms (at least their intention) were to reduce the bloated bureaucracy and government spending, which, on the one hand, was intended to reduce the need for taxes, and on the other hand, to reduce the influence of the state on the economy. Both of these factors were supposed to unleash the initiative of enterprises, which would lead to rapid economic growth. In addition, the abolition of the weak elements of solidarity that the United States had introduced in the 1950s and 1960s was supposed to free the hands of enterprises both to transfer production abroad and to reduce the labor force at home.

For the country at the peak of the world, all this had to work. For other countries (and especially those close to the peak), to follow the American neoliberal path, it was necessary to crush their trade unions as well. The result would likely be a loss of social peace. But this does not apply to the peak. In the United States, although unions are significantly weakened, labor-management relations are greatly helped by the widely recognized position of the United States at the peak of the world economy. "Even though business and labor increasingly disagree over trade and foreign investment, they continue to share the same vision of America as a global military power fueled by a vigorous and dynamic economy"[414]. In addition, foreign branches are used to provide certain job guarantees to employees in the United States. It is precisely there, abroad, that employment fluctuates depending on demand. As a result, businesses in the United States can maintain a stable level of employment. Thus, the U.S. position at the peak of the global economy gives its large enterprises a unique opportunity to maintain a high level of commitment to their employees. This, in turn, reduces the need for trade unions in the eyes of workers and makes them less militant (no wonder Marxism has never been able to gain a foothold in the United States, unlike in Europe).

The weakening of labor unions and the reduction of government regulation were also supposed to help enterprises free up capital in one industry and quickly transfer it to another to introduce new technologies and simply reduce their production costs. Thus, they could more easily compete with those foreign enterprises that decided to come to the United States. The U.S. government, having opened its customs gates to the products of these foreign companies, demanded that their countries open their gates to American products in return. And there, in their countries, American products were to win again. Neoliberals called for open gates and fair competition. At the same time, the state at the peak (the United States) did not have to fear (as the valley states did) that foreign enterprises (and domestic ones as well) could leave in masse if they were dissatisfied or found better conditions elsewhere. Because the best conditions are always at the peak—the largest and richest consumer market, the largest amount of free capital and various specialists, the broadest scientific and technological knowledge, the experience of past successes, and confidence in future successes.

It's good to be on peak
For the country at the top, even the loss of domestic enterprises in the competition on their own territory is less scary. Unlike any other country in the world, the United States did not have to abandon open borders and impose duties on foreign products or accept the massive bankruptcy of domestic companies. The peak country had other options. When in 1968 American steel mills began to lose competition to Japanese mills, the US government agreed with the Japanese state that it would organize a "voluntary restriction" on steel supplies to the US by Japanese mills.[415] In 1982, a similar agreement was concluded with the European Economic Community.[416] The U.S. government received the same kind of self-imposed restrictions from the Japanese government regarding the export of Japanese cars. Also, in the 1980s, it forced the "Asian Tigers" to look for ways to reduce their trade surplus with the United States. To do this, the "tigers" were forced to buy from the United States what they had previously bought from their former metropolis, Japan. Thus, the interference of the US state in the free market processes not only reduced US losses in trade with the "tigers" but also ricocheted on one of the main economic rivals of the United States.[417]

But the most important thing was that exports of Japanese,

324

German, and other enterprises to the United States were facilitated by the fact that the US dollar was rising, and exports of American products were made more difficult. Since the U.S. economy is at the peak of the world economy, the U.S. dollar is as important to Europe and Japan as it is to the United States. So, in 1985, the United States managed to convince its partners that they needed to raise their currency rates. The result, as expected, was that American exports to Europe grew, while European exports to America fell. The situation with Japan was more complicated. Measures to raise the Japanese yen were supposed to lead to deflation in Japan itself (lower prices), which is considered worse than inflation. So, inflationary measures were introduced—bank rates were lowered, and banks were encouraged to give out loans to customers more easily[418]. As always in such cases, the money that became available was spent on buying real estate and playing the stock market. The result was the great crisis of 1992 and the so-called "Lost Decade" (or rather two).

Thus, the peak did not take the same risks as others when it followed the path of neoliberalism and called on others to follow. The effectiveness of American demands is precisely explained by the position of the United States at the peak of the global economic pyramid. Attempts by other countries to "speak to the United States in its language" would not have worked. The United States is not as interested in its market and its scientific and technological achievements as they are in the United States. The position at the peak of the global economy also explains why Reagan's neoliberal policy in the US yielded significantly more positive results than Thatcher's similar policy in the UK.

The betrayal of enterprises

Taking advantage of the Japanese state's permission to buy shares in Japanese automakers in the 1970s, American automakers became interested in importing Japanese cars to the United States. Therefore, the U.S. government, seeking a compromise, began to avoid imposing duties on these imports and instead demanded that Japan "self-restrict" so that both wolves would be fed and sheep would be safe. However, since General Motors had bought the largest number of shares in Japanese enterprises, it was more interested in importing Japanese cars than anyone else. Thus, the fact that the Reagan administration did not extend the agreement on Japanese self-imposed restrictions on car exports to the United States in 1985 was seen as a victory for General Motors over Chrysler and Ford (and in fact over the state), which were still interested in restricting Japanese exports.[419]

The situation took on a completely different shape with the introduction of free economic zones by the tigers—now imported goods to the United States were the products of branches of American companies in these free economic zones. The weakness of the U.S. state's position on enterprises became even more pronounced with the entry of China into the arena. "At the turn of this century, when China first joined the World Trade Organization and began its mercantilist assault on the American manufacturing base, U.S. corporate executives stood shoulder to shoulder with American workers . . . In the new political calculation, as each additional American job and each new American factory has been offshored to China, so-called "American" organizations like the Business Roundtable, National Association of Manufacturers, and U.S. Chamber of Commerce have been transformed from staunch critics into the meek apologist for a mercantilist China making its way with the American economy and its workers."[420]

The victorious march of American businesses abroad to capture foreign markets has smoothly and imperceptibly turned into a "flight from home." The essence of the third stage of the American ascent to the peak is now becoming an obstacle to the traditional mechanism of raising duties in such a situation. Duties now prevent the importation of products from foreign branches of American companies.

The peak is going down

The purpose of the above-mentioned "forceful" influence of the US state on the economic situation was to force foreign states to make their enterprises buy more from the United States. Then the US trade deficit was supposed to decrease. However, some foreign states began to take the hit and make purchases themselves. They bought American bonds and stocks. The largest economies of their countries began to do the same. This led to the fact that today the United States has become a country with one of the largest foreign debts in the world. Despite this, they happily continue to receive new foreign investment. As IMF Chief Economist Kenneth Rogoff has said, he would be "pretty concerned [about] a developing country that had gaping current-account deficits year after year, as far as the eye can see, of 5 percent or more [of GDP]. with budget ink spinning from black to red." He immediately added that the United States is not a developing country. But 'The United States is no ordinary "developed' country either. The US expects and receives from other governments and international institutions—first and foremost, the IMF—preferential treatment in the handling of its finances that no other state, no matter how 'developed,' could hope to get"[421].

The fact that the ship of the American economy is sailing despite the blows of crises and the weight of foreign debt has given rise to an almost mystical belief that this ship is simply bewitched. But beneath the surface of the financial flow in the United States is another undercurrent in the opposite direction— foreign investors eventually take their profits out of the United States. And this makes it difficult for the United States to balance the books. As the Wall Street Journal noted, the United States has returned to being a borrower of foreign capital. But there is a fundamental difference: "in the nineteenth century, borrowing financed the building of railroads and other infrastructure that strengthened the productivity of the US economy, whereas today it finances private and public consumption."[422] The situation has become more complicated for the United States with the rise of China. American investments in China are increasing, as are Chinese investments in the United States. But these phenomena are not unambiguous. On the one hand, China's rise has made it an attractive place to invest. This meant that part of the flow of third-country capital began to deviate from the United States and flow to China. And this part is increasing. On the other hand, the Chinese state, having concentrated some of these flows in its hands (in the form of taxes or profits from joint ventures), began to invest some of them in the United States. This fact compensated the United States for the loss of financial flows that had gone to China. But now these were capital concentrated in the hands of a single large investor, and that investor was the Chinese state, led by the Communist Party. Together with the investments of Chinese state-owned enterprises (and private ones as well), these investments increasingly make the United States dependent on China's goodwill. The situation becomes even more desperate because virtually all U.S. investments in China are in manufacturing, and most Chinese investments in the United States simply help their state pay off its debt or support high consumption by the people.

The trap of the peak

Thus, American businesses investing in China reduce the cost of their products (due to the lower cost of Chinese labor). At least some of the Chinese investment in the United States increases the purchasing power of the American people. Taken together, this increases the profits of American enterprises. In addition, U.S. enterprises increase their profits because of the increasingly open access to the Chinese market. As a result, American enterprises see no need to change the situation. The people are also satisfied with the possibility of greater consumption.

Bound by the moods of the economy and the people, the US state is forced to watch idly as the United States gradually but inevitably slides from the peak of the global economic pyramid. Any attempts by the US state to openly save the United States will be met with hostility by both the economy and the people. The most traditional tool of influence for the United States—raising duties—will, on the one hand, reduce the profits of American enterprises from importing their products from abroad, and on the other hand, increase the prices that the American people have to pay. All other options for influencing the situation will also reduce in different proportions the profits of most large enterprises reduce the purchasing power of the people and cause their dissatisfaction.

The last line of defense

In such circumstances, the American state resorted to the last means still in its hands, which did not cause general discontent—the Keynesian injection of money into the economy. But according to the free-market ideology adopted and supported by the United States, subsidizing any enterprises is an unacceptable sin, because it distorts the natural operation of market forces and favors some enterprises at the expense of others (who are not subsidized). In addition, in the context of the growing public debt, this injection could not be extensive. Therefore, it was limited only to the last line of defense—scientific and technological development and research.

Since the peak tends to throw out low-paying jobs to the valley and attract high-paying ones, American corporations have been moving all their divisions abroad one by one, except for management and research. So, the US government has taken it upon itself to simply reinforce this trend.

High technology began in the postwar United States in the form of defense projects. Semiconductors were the result of developments in radar technology and were invented at Bell Labs, of course, with government funding. At the same time, the state obliged Bell Labs to license its inventions to other interested American enterprises[423]. By expanding the scope of military research, the range of weapons and equipment needed, and increasing the scale of orders, the American state enabled the private sector involved to achieve economies of scale in the production of various products (e.g., semiconductors). After all, the first developments are very expensive. The first samples of products produced in small batches exclusively for military use are still very expensive. However, increasing the scale of defense procurement makes the products cheaper and finally makes them available for purchase by private enterprises and then citizens.

In 1980, in response to the Soviet Union's success in electronics, the Department of Defense launched a program aimed at developing Very high-speed integrated circuits (VHSIC). This program has brought together the efforts of about twenty electronics companies[424]. Since military requirements often differ from civilian ones, this program also aimed to reconcile the interests of public and private customers. For example, for civilian electronics, such characteristics as service life and cost are more important, but for military orders, the ability to function even after a nuclear attack and increased speed of operations is more important. Therefore, the final characteristics of the orders were often a compromise[425].

The Defense Advanced Research Projects Agency (DARPA) was organized by the US Department of Defense to liaise with industry, with the task of organizing research activities of private companies in the direction required by the Department of Defense.

The main thing remains the state's allocation of funds for research for companies that have managed to get a state contract. In the 1980s, the state's share of U.S. R&D spending was already 40% (more than in any other leading country)[426]. This is mainly done by the Ministry of Defense, but not only. Large expenditures are made on research in space, energy, and even agriculture, as well as in healthcare. The role of the state is also high in the development of supersonic aircraft or nuclear energy applications, ocean exploration, etc. After all, if it were not for government orders for bombers and fighters, there would be no powerful passenger aircraft industry. If it were not for government orders for integrated circuits for ballistic missiles in the 1960s, the electronics industry would not have emerged (which had already achieved economies of scale in military orders themselves, even before entering the civilian market). And it was government orders for computers that helped this industry to emerge, among others[427].

In the end, "all of the technologies that make Jobs' iPhone so 'smart' were government funded (Internet, GPS, touch-screen display and ... SIRI voice-activated personal assistant). Such radical investments—which embedded extreme uncertainty—did not come about due to the presence of venture capitalists, nor of 'garage tinkerers'. It was the visible hand of the State that made these innovations happen. Innovations that would not have come about had we waited for the 'market' and business to do it alone."[428]

The same can be said about the space program of Microsoft co-founder Paul Allen and Blue Origin of Jeffrey Bezos (owner of Amazon) and SpaceX of Tesla owner Elon Musk. If the state hadn't taken the first steps into space and if NASA hadn't been willing to pay for satellite launches, delivery of astronauts to space stations, etc., these entrepreneurs would have looked for other more practical and reliable ideas to invest their money.

The need for a neat rebellion

The United States is not the only country that does this. But the United States has the most capital (its own and foreign, which crowds there and, in particular, buys bonds of the American state). Therefore, the U.S. government has the greatest opportunity to help private businesses.

But there is another side. The US government tries not to interfere in the affairs of private businesses. They love it for that. And it tries to help them. And they love it even more for that. The third stage of the American ascent to the peak of the world economy was the expansion of corporations abroad. This trend eventually turned into what we now call Globalization. Globalization turned large corporations into transnational corporations. The meaning of a transnational corporation is that it is everywhere at home—it has branches in many countries and it is easy for it to move its headquarters to any of them, changing its nationality depending on the circumstances. In such circumstances, the tactics of the US state towards its freedom-loving enterprises are rational: not to bother them with its interference (regulation) and still give them money. This tactic still keeps the "patriotic feelings" of

American large enterprises alive, and despite the threats that are already being made, they remain American, not transnational. The mechanics of the process, in a simplified form, are as follows. American corporations take their subsidiaries abroad and enrich other countries—other countries bring their money to the United States (foreign countries often buy bonds of the American state, in other words, lend it money)—the US government gives this money to American corporations for scientific and technological activities (R&D)—corporations apply the results of R&D in their foreign subsidiaries—and the cycle repeats. Everything is fine in this cycle, except that the American state is constantly increasing its debt. Sooner or later, it will probably have to revolt. However, the rebellion should be very careful because if it is not done well, it could lead to the relocation of corporate headquarters to China or elsewhere.

CHINA NOW

The second step of the third stage of China's ascent to the peak

The second stage of China's rise, the construction of its economic pyramid, was also the beginning of the third stage, the struggle for the peak of the global economic pyramid. And it was done by foreign enterprises that opened their branches in China. But in the end, China has made its own second step of its third stage—exports mainly by state-owned enterprises.

Throughout the period of economic reforms, state-owned enterprises have increasingly focused on the initial and intermediate stages of production (value added), while private enterprises have increasingly taken over the last stage of production—consumer products. It is in response to fashion and changes in market needs that private entrepreneurship is much more effective than state-owned. The state primarily focused on oil refining, metallurgy, chemical industry, and heavy engineering[429]. This is where it could be most effective. Especially because in these industries, capital takes a long time to generate a return. This reduces the enthusiasm of private households. In addition, the longer time for return on investment increases risks due to the unpredictability of markets.

The state-owned enterprises were quickly reorganized on a market basis. After all, they accounted for the largest share of exports, and it was state-owned enterprises that (at the time, and to a large extent even now) were at the forefront of competition with Western enterprises. These exports provided state-owned enterprises with funds to re-equip their production and the state with funds for new projects, many of which are based on imports of advanced foreign equipment.

Large enterprises and exports

Unlike the countries of the former Soviet Union, which have mostly lost their large "industrial associations" (except Belarus), China has placed them at the center of its industrial policy. "The goal is to form competitive and independent industrial giants," the Chinese press wrote at the time[430]. The state singled out more than fifty industrial groups, mostly in heavy industry, and made them a model for other businesses. They were provided with substantial financial assistance, and advisors, and encouraged to establish various alliances with scientific institutions.

A good example is the automotive industry. The state selected eight large enterprises in this industry and formed the core of China's reformed automotive industry, 东风汽车公司 (Dongfeng Motor Corporation), centered on the Second Automobile Plant. This enterprise bought and otherwise organized around up to

300 other enterprises of various sizes. Through it, as a central point of entry, new technologies were distributed to these subordinate companies[431].

But the most important thing is that Dongfeng Motor Corporation has launched an offensive into foreign markets—it exports its products to several countries in Asia and Latin America. It sells them to Russia, which once supplied cars to China as friendly aid, as well as to the United Kingdom, which was at the very beginning of the automotive industry.

The third step of the third stage of China's climb to the peak

The shift from commodity exports to overseas investment was the third step in the construction of the Chinese economic pyramid. It began with the government's "Go Out" policy (also known as "Going Global") in 2000, which encourages domestic enterprises to set up subsidiaries abroad. Foreign subsidiaries are often set up in the valley countries for the same reasons as Western enterprises, such as the use of cheaper labor, proximity to necessary mineral resources, and the desire to tap the local market in case of a customs barrier. By embarking on this path, China could expect the same kind of enterprise betrayal that has befallen Western countries whose enterprises are fleeing to China. But for China, this danger is less, because in most cases, foreign branches are opened by state-owned enterprises. "Chinese companies, many of which are state-owned, have plowed a staggering $2 trillion into foreign businesses and construction projects since 2005, buying up everything from prestigious banks and hotel chains to major energy producers."[432]

Other companies acquired include Irish aircraft leasing company Avolon ($5.2 billion); a stake in a Kazakh oil and gas company ($5.3 billion); General Electric's home appliances division ($5.4 billion); Ingram Micro, a US computer parts distributor ($6 billion); the leasing business of the US company CIT Group ($10.4 billion); Canadian oil and gas company Nexen ($15.1 billion), and many others.

It was the time when the Chinese state finally began to allow foreign businesses to open branches outside the free economic zones, and even to buy up Chinese businesses entirely. It was the time when China decided to join the WTO. China now needed to be able to establish its branches in Western markets, so it agreed to open its markets. This is in sharp contrast to the Eastern European countries, which joined the WTO more to demonstrate their rejection of communist isolation, as they did not yet face the task of conquering Western markets. By opening the gates and surrendering, they hoped that the winners would pull them up closer to their level. But they gave up the chance to rise above the winners. China is heading for this very goal—to rise above everyone else.

The construction of an economic pyramid through foreign branches is only one of the reasons for launching the Going Out program. After all, China has a large foreign trade surplus, and this should lead to an appreciation of the yuan. And China, like Japan in the past, does not want this to happen, because it will make Chinese goods more expensive for foreign buyers and reduce exports. Like Japan in the past, it has also found a way out by buying U.S. government bonds to export its excess currency abroad. But only partially. The Chinese state, through state-owned enterprises, has also begun to buy foreign enterprises. Thus, the task of promoting the export of Chinese enterprises and the task of opening Chinese branches abroad help each other.

The age of knowledge

Until the mid-19th century, valley economies could only compete with the goods of the peak by purchasing the means of production of those goods from the peak. Things became more complicated, however, from the mid-19th century onwards. In the West, the means of production that produced the means of production of final goods (i.e., heavy industry) became widespread. This heavy industry progressed rapidly, producing more and more sophisticated machines for the production of consumer goods. Therefore, the enterprises of the West, with each new generation of machines, produced better (and cheaper) goods and the enterprises of the valley countries could not compete with them again. So, if the countries in the valley of the economic pyramid wanted to continue to compete with the goods of the peak, they had to buy new heavy industry goods (machines) from it or learn to produce them themselves.

When China began its reforms, the arrival of Western businesses in China brought both light and heavy industries. But times have changed. The economic chain of production* is now longer. Now, the chain "heavy industry—machine tools for light industry—consumer goods" has one more link—research and development. These developments are used by the heavy industry to improve machines for the light and heavy industries. And the research and development organizations (R&D) of Western corporations, where these developments take place, have not gone to China. The West still seems to hold the key to further progress. Everyone can buy Western goods, eventually the means of producing these goods, and finally even the means of producing the means of production (heavy industry). But without scientific and technological innovations, all factories and plants become

* a value chain where each link adds its own new value

337

obsolete, and the enterprises of the base countries have to buy new goods and means of production from the peak again, so that after a while everything will happen again.

Science and the Chinese state

This cycle of endless renewal of the means of production has as its side effect the endless reproduction of the dominance of the peak over the bottom of the global economic pyramid. To break out of this "vicious circle," one needs to develop r own scientific and technological base. And this, in turn, requires "unproductive" (at first) expenditures that are beyond the means of the economies of the valley countries.

The large flow of investments that flooded into China allowed the Chinese state to double the country's industrial potential every six to seven years[433] by deliberately directing these investments to the production sector. At the same time, the funds collected as taxes from Western branches and domestic businesses were directed, among other things, to the development of science. "Over the past dozens of years, China's R&D spending has grown at an annual rate of 17 percent, compared to the 4–5 percent reported for the United States, Japan and the European Union."[434]

In addition, from the very beginning of the reforms, the Chinese state encouraged the commercialization of applied science institutions. They were instructed to enter into contractual relations with enterprises and become subcontractors of state basic science institutions. Since they had to start earning their own money, the funds allocated to them by the state were systematically reduced[435]. This left more money for basic science.

China needs scientific and technological developments to catch up with the peak countries, although today China is still able to beat them in the competition due to lower wages.

But China's economic recovery has also brought wage growth (along with a general rise in prosperity). In addition, there are still many countries with low wages around. But China is still beating them, firstly, by steadily improving the skills of Chinese workers, and secondly, by applying innovations in production.

Globalization

The countries of the valley invest in the education of young professionals and the organization of research centers in the hope of catching up with the peak with the help of science and new technologies. However, the processes of globalization are neutralizing these efforts. Specialists from the valley countries are fleeing to the peak. They flee because the peak countries have higher salaries, and the large number of companies that hire specialists in the West makes job searching there guaranteed to be more successful than waiting for a vacancy in a few domestic companies. "Work from home" will further strengthen the ability of peak corporations to "steal" specialists in the valley*.

After all, the West has already formed teams of knowledge-intensive enterprises that know how, when, and what to do. In addition, the presence in the West of many enterprises of the same profile, in a limited area, allows specialists to communicate and share knowledge and experience, which contributes to the spread of knowledge and inventions 'by analogy'. All of this is very difficult to replicate in the valley and takes a long time and large investments that valley enterprises are rarely capable of. It is easier and cheaper for them to buy ready-made scientific developments at the peak (and avoids the risk of unsuccessful inventions that are inevitable). And then there are the costs of

* Moreover, it will become even more difficult for the valley states to collect taxes from such workers

building factories for massproduction of of new inventions, while success is uncertain and profits are rapidly declining with the arrival of competitors. This is why it is difficult for companies in the valley to attract investment for such expenses.

But that is not all. The higher profits of enterprises around the summit are due to high-profit margins, which, among other things, reflect the payments made by enterprises in the valley for the summit's patents and the inability of enterprises in the valley to enter the patent-protected market. Legally enforced ownership of standards, technologies, and trademarks, combined with the benefits arising from the coordination of the information and communications throughout the value chain, tends to increase the value of the non-productive links in the chain[436]. Thus, globalization contributes to the concentration of knowledge-intensive enterprises at the peak and labor-intensive enterprises in the valley. And it is as difficult for enterprises to counteract this trend as to swim against a strong current.

China and the movement against the tide

It was difficult for Chinese enterprises to swim against this current of globalization. They were doomed to find their place wherever this current would take them. But the Chinese state did not want to give up. It organized the actions of enterprises in a certain direction—having accumulated sufficient capital, Chinese enterprises began to come to developed Western countries and buy up knowledge-intensive enterprises, and later, purposefully, research & development organizations (R&D). Thus, the Chinese state is pushing the situation in a given direction—China supplies consumer goods to the West; these goods are produced in China on production enterprises owned by the West; technologies for these production enterprises come from Western R&D owned by China.

For example, the aforementioned Dongfeng company "established" its first R&D office abroad when it acquired 70% of Sweden's T Engineering AB[437]. The activities of other Chinese companies are even more extensive. For example, another automotive private enterprise 吉利控股集团 (Geely Automobile) Jili, which bought a controlling stake in Volvo in 2010, bought the American Terrafugia (a manufacturer of flying cars) and is steadily increasing its ownership in the Volvo Group (a truck company). Finally, in 2018, it started buying shares in Daimler AG (owner of Mersedes-Benz) and now owns 9.7%. The most famous is the purchase by China's 联想集团有限公司 (Lenovo Group Limited) of a controlling stake in the entire IBM personal computer business in 2005. This approach also allows Chinese businesses to use the labor of Chinese specialists who have emigrated to the West.

Several countries in the valley can boast of companies that have managed to get to the peak and establish their branches there. But these are the efforts of individual enterprises that serve the goals of those enterprises. The Chinese state coordinates the organized ascent of Chinese companies to the peak. And it serves the benefit of all Chinese enterprises, the Chinese state, and the Chinese people.

Rebellion and doom
The tactic of the enterprises at the peak is to produce and retain knowledge at home and to produce products in the valley countries on its basis. Those individual enterprises in the valley that managed to acquire sufficient capital and production skills began to show a desire to produce the necessary knowledge themselves. The states, with this in mind, established the necessary universities and research centers. And yet, the further we go, the clearer it becomes that the valley enterprises themselves

prefer to produce knowledge at the peak, and products based on this knowledge in the valley. And even the Chinese, more organized leap to the peak has not changed this essence.

Nevertheless, the Chinese rebellion has led to the formation of another link in the value chain. "The principal role for OEMS' R&D centers in advanced economies is core product development, as building the relevant capabilities is more effective in developed markets because that is where the ...[manufacturers] can hire engineers with the necessary experience... The principal role for R&D centers in ...[valley countries] is to access market-specific knowledge such as customer preferences (e.g. ... color choice, gear shift preferences, engine size preferences ... etc.), and to adapt existing technologies to the peculiarities of local demand (such as emission standards or quality and safety regulations). This seems to reflect the fact that the knowledge necessary for these specific adaptations is best created in the local environment through an embedded R&D center close to the customer and regulatory body"[438]. This leads to the fact that enterprises in the peak countries prefer to keep "[t]he core product development ... while product adaptation, technology scouting, and market knowledge creation are localized in the emerging economies."[439] But the same thing is happening to valley enterprises, which are simply forced to adapt to the reality of globalization. They prefer to keep production and even support R&D for adapting products to the local market in the valley, but they prefer to open R&D for developing new products in the peak countries.

However, there is another reason for the difference in the mountain and valley R&D. Enterprises that compete for the market at the peak (for the top end of the market, e.g., for "prestigious" cars) rely on constant innovation, on continuous product improvement. Enterprises competing in the valley (or in the mountain countries, but in the market for, say, cars for the regular people) rely on lower costs of development and production and faster response to changing consumer preferences. The consequence of this is that the former must constantly deal with less mastered technologies and uncertain consumer demand for their innovations. As a result, they have to experiment by combining new, untested components, while the interdependence of these parts is high and their interaction is uncertain. All this requires the development of the entire complex product as a single whole in all the details of each part and the interaction of these parts (the so-called Integrated Architecture). At the same time, the latter, on the contrary, constantly picks up already known, proven technologies and tries to apply them where it has not been done before or use them in new combinations with each other. Their tactic is to take from suppliers separate, previously used parts (modules) and compose a new product out of them (the so-called Modular Architecture).

Such circumstances quite naturally give integrated architecture to the enterprises of the peak, and modular architecture to the enterprises of the valley. At the same time, it is also clear that it is developments in integrated architecture that drive science and technology forward, developing civilization.

This explains the characterization that was often given to the Japanese economy during its rise: the West invents new things, and the Japanese are good at finding new uses for them. Later, the same was said of the Asian Tigers. The same is now being said about the Chinese economy.

To climb to the peak, you need untied hands

The Czech Republic (an example of a former socialist country) has ended its rebellion and has been integrated into the base

of the EU economic pyramid (actually the German pyramid*[440]).
The fact that the Czech Republic now has no obstacles to supply
its products to the rich market of the European peak countries and, at the same time, its labor force is relatively cheap
and it already has specialists familiar with car production, has
attracted investment. Now, up to 70% of Czech heavy industry
exports come from branches of foreign companies[441]. This has
brought substantial taxes to the Czech state; enabled Czech
businesses to find their profitable place at the base of foreign
business pyramids; and raised the welfare of the people. This
is exactly the "happy ending" that neoliberalism is so eagerly
promoting. From the point of view of the countries at the peak,
this is complete harmony and ideal. But the most important
thing is that both the peak and the valley are happy. And in the
case of the Czech Republic, it seems that this is the case. When

* The predecessor of the EU, the European Economic Community, was already
seen, not officially but quite openly in newspapers and television programs, as
an "enlarged Germany" in the economic sense. With the reunification of West
and East Germany, this truth has become even more apparent. That is why the
EU is torn apart by internal contradictions that are nothing more than economic
rebellions against the top, Germany. From this perspective, Poland's reorientation
toward the United States after joining the EU, the United Kingdom's withdrawal
from the EU, and France's constant dissatisfaction are also understandable.
The recent aggravation in the EU over the signing of an economic agreement
with the Mercosur economic union of South American states is quite typical.
The essence of this conflict can be seen from dry newspaper reports. It was
announced about "the conclusion of the negotiations for a free trade agreement
between the European Union and the Mercosur bloc. Poland, France, and Italy
have expressed opposition to the agreement...For the Germans, that's great
news. Increasingly frantic about industrial decline, the Mercosur agreement
is a prime opportunity to help find new growth markets for Germany's ailing
manufacturing champions" Politico writes. Mercosur will import agricultural
products to Europe that will compete with European farms. Germany is not
afraid of this, just as ancient Athens was not afraid to stop producing its own
bread. This "fearlessness," however, did not extend to other Greek city-states,
just as other European countries do not share Germany's enthusiasm today

all the peasants of a feudal estate were happy with the care of their lord, such an estate was also an ideal entity. The picture is upset only by a few apostates, rebels who do not want to get along in the established order. They don't understand why they are doomed to be peasants. Why can't they be masters themselves?

China has also invited foreign enterprises and increased its exports at their expense. Just like the Czech Republic. But to prevent these giants from crushing local small enterprises, the Chinese state locked them into the serpentariums of of the free economic zones. Their task was to export and bring profit to the state in the form of taxes. The state used the proceeds to help domestic companies open Chinese branches abroad. The goal was profit, but even more important was Western knowledge. In addition, the local market was left to Chinese producers, who watched the serpentariums and tried to copy the actions of the enterprises there.

The Czech state cannot do so, because not only is any special treatment of its state-owned enterprises prohibited in the EU, but even attempts by any private enterprise to increase its capital are now subject to investigation for state subsidies[442]. Therefore, Czech enterprises (as a rule, not an exception) are doomed to remain where the market puts them—at the bottom of Western economic pyramids. The EU has deliberately set itself the goal of "eliminating the anti-market effect of state ownership." China's "Go Out" program guides Chinese businesses and helps them to get to the peak. And in climbing to the peak, they are called upon to pull the whole country to the peak.

The aforementioned Gili is an example of this. By acquiring a controlling stake in Volvo, Gilli could simply enjoy the profits generated by Volvo's design and production divisions. But it could also arrange for Volvo's design departments to design cars for production in Chinese factories. And Gilli did just that. But it went further.

Initially, a joint research and development company, China Euro Vehicle Technology (CEVT), was established with Volvo in Sweden. "The funding to establish CEVT and support R&D development predominantly comes from Geely, which has raised parts of this funding from local governments in China... This also means that Geely China owns the intellectual property rights."[443]. The CEVT is located next to Volvo's R&D division, which helps specialists from both companies to share experiences and also directly attract talent from this division. "For the future, and with further support and funding from the Chinese government, Geely plans to establish an innovation and automotive supplier park near CEVT Sweden. This strategic intention aims to turn CEVT into a pivotal unit in the automotive industry in the West. Talking about this issue, a respondent said: 'CEVT will act as a benchmark for the Chinese government in its future support of Chinese firms establishing themselves in the West[444].

The next step was to establish a CEVT branch in China. The responsibilities between them are currently divided as follows. The first stage, the development of the concept vehicle and detailed design is carried out by CEVT in Sweden (theoretical tasks). The second phase, the launch phase, which includes prototype development, physical testing, and quality assurance before assembly, is increasingly led by CEVT staff in China (practical tasks) as a new test facility is being built there. And more and more theoretical tasks are gradually being transferred to the Chinese part "when the required competence has been deemed to exist in CEVT China."[445] CEVT China regularly sends Chinese engineers to CEVT Sweden for a period of three months to two years to learn from their foreign colleagues. Moreover, one of the key indicators by which the work of employees in Sweden is evaluated is the effectiveness of their training of Chinese colleagues and the achievement of results together with the Chinese team.

So, having lured Western production to China, China is also pulling the R&D function to China. And its companies decide how much, what functions, and when to transfer to China. In the Czech Republic, only Volkswagen and Toyota will decide whether they will transfer any design functions to the Czech Republic and, if so, which ones. In the Chinese case, the transfer of knowledge to China is a final and resolved goal, while in the Czech case, it is a dubious hope. Moreover, by transferring all functions to China, Chinese companies provide work for Chinese suppliers of spare parts. In the Czech Republic, Volkswagen decides who will supply what, and it often decides in favor of its traditional suppliers. Japanese and Korean enterprises are trying to recreate abroad the pyramid of connections that exists at home—they simply come to another country with all their suppliers. Although this approach results in a whole network of branches of various Toyota suppliers opening in the Czech Republic (which provides jobs for Czech workers and taxes for the state), it does not give local entrepreneurship a chance. Because Czech enterprises do not have a chance to stand at the peak of their economic pyramids, they do not even have a chance to stand at the bottom of Toyota's pyramid. (In the Czech Republic, Toyota gave the supply task to Peugeot, but this did not help the Czech Republic much. On the one hand, its state cannot organize domestic enterprises in the EU, and on the other hand, all "domestic" enterprises are actually foreign).[446]

The country's place in global value chains (GVCs)

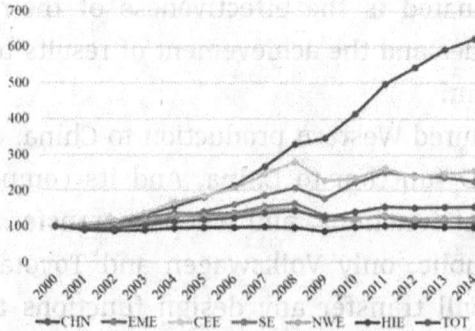

Figure 1: Dynamics of GVC Income in USD2000, country groups, value for 2000 = 100
Source: own elaboration based on WIOD data.

Figure 1. CHN—China, EME—emerging economies,
CEE—Central and Eastern Europe, SE—Southern Europe,
NWE—Northwest Europe, HIE—high-income countries[447]

In the globalized economy of today, the struggle of economies is around increasing the value added by countries in the global value chains. Graph 1. may give the impression that post-socialist countries are quite successful (second after China). But if we look at the data from an earlier period (the table below is from another study[448]), we can see that the time of the end of the rebellion was practically the time of their final exit from the global struggle for shares in the GVCs. Eastern Europe is now behind Latin America West Asia and even Africa.

Another step in the third stage of China's ascent to the peak

China is becoming increasingly well positioned to become a giving peak that acquires clients with carrots, not sticks. And in this, it has entered into a struggle with the United States. However, the US capabilities in this regard are inexorably diminishing, while China's are increasing. "China announced an extraordinary package of $2 billion in loans to the Philippines each year for three years, which made the $200 million offered by the World Bank... look puny; easily outstripped a $1 billion loan under negotiation with Japan; and sheltered the Philippines from Washington's disfavor after President Arroyo pulled the country's troops out of Iraq. This was just one of a large and growing number of similar deals in which China has been out-competing Northern agencies by offering Southern countries more generous terms for access to their natural resources; larger loans with fewer political strings attached...; and large and complicated infrastructure projects in distant areas at as little as half the cost of Northern [Western] competitors."[449]

"China laid out its plans a decade ago when it came to Latin America during the global financial crisis, throwing governments an economic lifeline and promising to 'treat each other as equals'—a clear attack on American dominance... China, which has become South America's main trading partner, has seeded the region with infrastructure and a staggering amount of credit. It has also gained political benefits as Latin American countries have broken off diplomatic relations with Taiwan[450]. "It is a modern-day version of the Marshall Plan... China's strategy is bolder, more expensive and far riskier."[451] China's projects create its pyramid. 41 pipelines and other oil and gas infrastructure help China secure valuable resources. 203 bridges, roads, and railways create new ways to move China's goods around the world. 199 power plants—nuclear, natural gas, coal, and renewable energy = give China new markets for its construction and engineering companies. Seven dams produce almost half of Cambodia's electricity. China built and paid for them all. South Africa has asked China for $1.5 billion for a coal-fired power plant. This is one of at least 63 such facilities financed by China around the world. Zambia has turned to

China for $94 million to build a 50,000-seat football stadium. This is one of more than 600 projects around the world that China has funded to make new friends and develop new markets. Sri Lanka borrowed more than 1 billion from China for a strategic deepwater port but was unable to return the money. Now China has leased it for the next 99 years.

Table 2. Shares in global output, selected country groups, 1970–2016 (percentages)							
	1970	1980	1990	2000	2005	2010	2016
Developed economies	69.7	69.6	78.8	77.2	74.2	63.8	58.9
Transition economies	13.2	8.2	3.8	1.1	2.2	3.2	2.4
Developing economies	17.1	22.2	17.4	21.7	23.6	33.0	38.7
Africa	3.2	4.6	2.4	1.9	2.4	3.0	2.8
Latin America and the Caribbean	5.3	6.3	5.0	6.7	5.8	7.9	6.8
West Asia	1.3	3.2	2.0	2.2	2.7	3.3	3.3
East, South-East and South Asia	7.3	8.1	7.9	10.8	12.6	18.8	25.7
Oceania	0.1	0.1	0.1	0.0	0.1	0.1	0.1

Source: Author's calculations, based on UNCTADstat.
Note: Shares based on market prices and market exchange rates.

The peak of the giving pyramid attracts supporters with carrots. But every giving pyramid also has a stick, which is the withdrawal of assistance, economic and political. China, with its growing economy and large population, is gradually making the Chinese market as rewarding as the US market. The United States, since it reduced its duties and realized how profitable and desirable access to its market is for foreign companies, has begun to use this access as a reward or punishment. "Sanctions" have become a favorite and often effective weapon of the United States. China, too, has now reached the point where it can punish others by banning access to its market. "To protect our national interests, China has decided to take necessary measures and impose sanctions on U.S. companies such as Lockheed Martin, Boeing Defense, and Raytheon, as well as those individuals and companies that have misbehaved in the arms sales process," China said in response to the announced U.S. arms sales to Taiwan[452].

On the other hand, China, at the very approach to the peak, is unwilling to risk its ascent to the very peak. For example, when Ecuadorian President Rafael Correa, elected in 2006 as a result of the left-wing wave in Latin America, decided to turn away from "imperialist" creditors and turn to Communist Party-ruled China, he and his ministers "were staggered by the terms on Chinese loans. Most came from a large state-owned lender, the Chinese Export-Import Bank, which had high interest rates and required Ecuador to use Chinese companies in construction, effectively eliminating competition. China seemed particularly interested in oil from Ecuador, one of OPEC's smallest members. In one deal in 2009, China lent Ecuador $1 billion, to be repaid in oil shipments to the state oil company PetroChina."[453] Nevertheless, Correa's successor, Lenin Moreno, went further and 19 billion Chinese loans were used to build a large hydroelectric power plant, bridges, highways, irrigation, schools, medical clinics, and half a dozen other hydroelectric power plants.

The people who did not rebel

The people of China, in general, did not rebel against their state, as did the people of Eastern Europe, and they did not have democracy. What they do have is a steady increase in their standard of living, which can be seen in the growth of wages. At the same time, the salaries of neighboring countries remain incomparably lower than Chinese ones. "It is estimated that the average factory monthly gross wages in 2016 in China were $828, in Bangladesh $141, India $174, Indonesia $214, and Vietnam $287... In recent years, faced with increasing competition from lower-wage economies, China has been able to reduce labor costs through automation, and has become the world's largest market for robots, with about 20 percent of world sales."[454]

Today, Chinese professionals and entrepreneurs are moving not only from China to the United States but also in the opposite direction. Entrepreneurs are attracted not only by cheaper labor but also by wider opportunities. "Silicon Valley was 'a little bit slow for us,'" said one of them, "If you were to do this in the U.S., you would just be importing the same materials from China anyway."[455]

The wage gap between Silicon Valley and China is narrowing, especially in higher-end science and engineering firms. Engineers there now earn between 70% and 80% of what they could get in America (though the work there lasts from 9:00 to 21:00, six days a week). Because of the salaries that have become larger, more choices of jobs, and more interesting projects, about 80% of Chinese students who get their degrees abroad now return, compared to about 33% in 2007.[456]

THE BETRAYAL OF ENTERPRISES

The lifeblood of the Dutch economy, finance, circulated along trade routes laid out by ships in the seas and oceans of the world and along the rivers and roads of Europe and was also diverted in the form of loans to foreign states and enterprises, to be returned multiplied. Failures and losses were to be a constant companion, but not so frequent and large as to break this successful system. This pyramidal economic system was constantly expanding to include new lands, peoples, states, and economies. There should have been no reason why this constant, uninterrupted cycle should have stopped or dried up. But another system emerged alongside it, growing rapidly and generating great profits. The magnitude of these profits and the speed of their growth made Dutch loans to this other economic pyramid more and more profitable and attracted new surpluses of Dutch capital. The demand was so great that from about 1710 an English credit market was operating in Amsterdam. Dutch enterprises thus contributed their capital to the rise of British enterprises. Alongside this, there were three Anglo-Dutch wars, which also caused terrible holes and cracks in the Dutch pyramid of political and economic influence. The bigger the English pyramid of political and economic influence became, the more it absorbed Dutch finances, and the less finances remained to support their own economic pyramid. The smaller the Dutch pyramid of political and economic influence became, the less it needed capital and the more it was left for the British economic pyramid. "By 1758, Dutch investors were said to hold as much as a third of the Bank of England, English East India Company, and [slave trading company] South Sea stocks. Four years later, a well-informed Rotterdam banker estimated that the Dutch held a quarter of the English debt."[457] The British pyramid grew stronger and finally managed to include India. "The victory of the British at Plassey in 1757 initiated a massive transfer of wealth from India, initially as sheer plunder and after 1774 more and more as plunder disguised in commercial forms."[458] The proceeds of this plunder provided the British with the opportunity to later buy back their debt from the United Provinces. What the Dutch private initiative saw as an innocent opportunity to "make money" eventually put an end to the world economic domination of the United Provinces.

Since the United Provinces were managed by enterprises, there was no state will that could oppose the will of the enterprises. The United Provinces was an absolute oligarchy where the same people who had decisive stakes in the largest enterprises sat in parliament and held the highest government positions. Thus, no one could prevent the Dutch enterprises from contributing to the British rise and the United Kingdom from inexorably rising above the United Provinces.

As in our time, however, the first line of defectors were specialists. As the United Provinces slipped from the peak, working conditions there were no longer the best. The stream of immigration of unskilled laborers into the United Provinces had to be steadily met by an increasingly powerful stream of emigration. On the one hand, the gap in living standards was narrowing, and on the other hand, demand was growing (especially in the UK). Specialists were well paid everywhere, they were welcome and, in most cases, without any hesitation or doubt, they shared their professional secrets with foreign nations. "the great increase of trade and navigation, particularly in many countries, where formerly these pursuits were little attended to, and the consequent great and continual demands for able seamen, both for ships of war and for merchants, have so considerably diminished the supply of them that, in our own country, where there formerly used to be a great abundance of mariners, it is now, with great difficulty and expense, that any vessel can procure a proper number of able hands to navigate her."[459] Not only trade was declining, but also Dutch industry, and most importantly, the base that had previously raised and kept the United Provinces on peak—its advanced shipbuilding.[460]

Subsequently, another economic pyramid began to grow near the British economic pyramid, which grew rapidly and brought in large profits. These two factors were decisive: the amount of profit and the speed of growth. British businesses had almost the whole world at their disposal. However many were attracted to the United States. What attracted them there more than in their British colonies was that the enterprises were protected from direct competition from the UK and the population had

a high purchasing power. For example, in 1870, British enterprises, having crossed the customs barrier and established production in the United States, could sell goods there for $122 in
gold that they would have sold in British Canada for $100 in
gold. Moreover, if a worker in Ontario was paid $100 in gold,
a similar worker in the United States was paid $125 in gold, so
he could buy more goods. The difference was even more striking in the case of the much-maligned Quebec[461]. British enterprises, therefore, also had the opportunity to hire cheap labor
in Canada or even move their production units there. "On the
eve of the Civil War, it has been estimated that 90 percent of
foreign investment in the United States came from Britain."[462]

"As wave after wave of mostly British-financed railroad
construction swept the continent, internal spatial barriers were
overcome; the United States' privileged access to the world's two
largest oceans was established; and a full range of exceptional
productive capabilities not only in industry, but more particularly in agriculture-was brought into existence."[463] British
enterprises contributed to the emergence of a giant that neither
they nor the entire British economic pyramid could tame. The
time had to come for the U.S. to buy back the U.K. debt. And
the time came during the two world wars.

Since the UK was governed by enterprises (see, for example, the description of the British oligarchic state in "The First
Industrial Revolution"[464]), there could be no state will that could
oppose the will of enterprises. Therefore, no one could prevent
British enterprises from contributed to the American rise and
the United States inexorably rose above the UK.

At the same time, the flow of workers from the empire to
the United States was gaining strength in a treacherous trickle.
"Dominion residents were beginning to emigrate to the United
States in sizable numbers (in 1870, almost 500,000 British

North American-born were residing in the Republic)."[465] At the same time, more than half of the emigrants from Great Britain by 1900 chose the United States as their destination instead of its colonies.[466]

Now another economic pyramid is growing near the American one. It attracts American enterprises with its growth rate and potential profits. American businesses have almost the entire world at their disposal, but many are attracted to China, and once they get there, American businesses get a billion-person market of new consumers and cheap labor to supply cheap goods to the United States. And everything is ready to happen again...

"The United States spent the 19th century doing most of the things it now denounces China for doing-stealing intellectual property, protecting its domestic economy at the expense of the global hegemon's, ignoring the environmental consequences of economic development, engaging in exploitative labor practices, and so on"[467]. The United States knows that it defeated the United Kingdom because it did not follow the tenets of the free market. Therefore, they know that their main hope lies in convincing or forcing other countries to follow the rules of the free market. In the case of the Soviet Union, they were lucky. Will they succeed in convincing China, which has seen the experience of its inept "teachers"? If the United States fails, it will face the question: "Will they follow the path of previous leaders or will their state take up the cause more decisively?" This requires dramatic changes. And it seems that Trump's rebellion gives the United States hope for this.

THE AMERICAN CONFRONTATION

The problem is that American corporations have moved their production to China and now Americans are buying their products as imports. This problem is a smooth continuation of American success. The third stage of the American ascent to the peak of the world economy was the relocation of branches of American companies abroad. This was done 1. to continue to grow by bypassing anti-trust legislation, 2. to capture foreign markets (especially those that were closed by the customs wall). However, it was not done to import the products of these subsidiaries back to the United States. After all, the United States was surrounded by perhaps the highest customs wall in the world, and those abroad who wanted to sell in the United States moved their branches there themselves. But over time, to build on its success, the United States (with the help of the Democrats) began to dismantle this customs wall. The goal was to allow buyers of American products to earn dollars by bringing their products to the United States. With these dollars, they could buy even more American products. Thus, the United States had to allow the Smithsonian global division of labor to work in full force, and the United States had to produce the decisive products of the world economy in this division of labor. This plan worked. But it also had another unforeseen consequence. The elimination of the customs wall made it possible for American businesses to import cheap products from their foreign subsidiaries into the United States and make excessive profits. Thus, American products manufactured outside the United States using cheap foreign labor began to displace American products manufactured in the United States. The result was that for other American businesses, going abroad became a matter of survival. And once this process started, it became unstoppable. Therefore, unless efforts are made, it will not stop. The United States must therefore decide whether to relax and swim wherever the waves of the free market take them or to make an effort—to take up the oars and row. What is at stake is the future—whether the United States will remain at the peak of the global economic pyramid, or it will begin to slip to the level of "former" leaders like the Netherlands and the United Kingdom, or whether it will face the unattractive fate of the USSR and its constituent countries.

Is the raw material appendage back at the peak of the global economic pyramid?

If American enterprises did not export their production to China, China would still export agricultural products and textiles to the United States, and the United States would export industrial products to China. If the current processes are left to the free market, the situation will move to the opposite.

As recently as 2013, according to the *China Business Review* (citing the US Census Bureau), the main item of US exports to China was soybeans, followed by cotton, copper and aluminum materials, grain, and coal. Although airplanes, cars, and microchips were also mentioned, they were generally lost in the raw materials.[468] Later, knowledge-intensive exports to China were increased. But this was a consequence of government intervention. The US trade deficit with China, however, reached 378 billion in 2017. This was the moment when the US state decided (once again) to step in and impose a 25 percent duty on Chinese imports worth $34 billion—the first in a series of duties imposed during 2018 and 2019. The reciprocal tariff increases continued until a first-phase trade agreement was reached in principle. The US trade deficit fell to $345.6 billion in 2019 after the first efforts of the government[469]. This agreement did not reduce the current record level of duties and does not require compliance with free market rules. Instead, it forced China to buy specific products worth $200 billion over two years[470].

However, this government intervention has not yielded the

expected results (not least because of the change in American policy itself since 2020). "Once major US manufacturing exports–like automobiles and Boeing jets–have all but disappeared."[471] At the same time, "US farms sales to China in 2022 hit record highs"[472], because under the agreement, China also promised to remove barriers to a long list of US exports, including beef, pork, poultry, seafood, dairy products, rice, infant formula, animal feed, and biotechnology.[473] Thus, U.S. trade with China continues to resemble, to some extent, valley-to-peak trade.

The American think tank (PIIE), which cited the data, sees the reason as "Perhaps out of fear of being dependent, China has become hesitant to buy Boeing products after Western countries imposed sanctions on the export of aircraft parts and services for the fleet of Russian commercial airlines following Russia's invasion of Ukraine in February 2022." But another reason mentioned by the same PIIE seems to be much more important: "When confronted with the costs associated with tariffs in 2018, automakers like Tesla moved their production out of the United States to maintain access to Chinese consumers. US auto exports to China have never recovered."[474]

In other words, the situation in which the United States is increasingly sinking into the role of an economic appendage is largely the result of American corporations moving to China. Not only do they leave their customers in the United States, to whom they bring their products back from China, but they also leave their suppliers of raw materials in the United States, which they now bring to China.

Having come to the edge of a cliff, beyond which it will lose its position at the peak of the world, the United States should already consider the situation from the point of view of a country that is fighting to be a leader, not a leader. Although the United States is still on peak, it has already lost its position as the undisputed leader. This is the same position in which neither the United Provinces nor the United Kingdom have made any decisive changes. Now it's the United States' turn to change or not to change the situation.

The problem of leadership and democracy

Theoretically, to win, the United States would have to bring all its production back to the United States and export its products to China again. American workers and the American state would win. Only the enterprises would lose, because they want to have both Chinese and American markets at the same time (in addition, they would receive lower profits because of the high wages of American workers). Therefore, enterprises are not interested in change. The only one who can change the situation is the American state. But can it?

Once upon a time, the small enterprises that made up the U.S. economy, fearing the excessive power of the state over them, organized it in such a way that it did not threaten them so that democracy could be guaranteed. After passing through the period of the spoils system, American democracy strengthened and became an example for the whole world. But this democracy was guaranteed not so much by the checks and balances of the various branches of government as by the diversity of the American economy. This diversity guaranteed the contradictory interests of the country's various enterprises. On the one hand, the existence of a large number of different industries guaranteed the divergence of interests of different businesses, and the impossibility for them to act as a "united front." On the other hand, this determined the need for these businesses to have an independent state to arbitrate their differences. But in the current situation, an increasing number of American enterprises are beginning to share the same interest. It is still beneficial for them to have their headquarters and research and development offices in the United States, but to take their production abroad. This was unthinkable for the agrarian enterprises that almost exclusively made up the American economy in the 18th century—their fate was entirely tied to the fate of their country and their state. Times have changed, but the structure of the American state and American democracy has not. Therefore, because the patriotic enterprises once designed the state so that it would not be able to oppose their interests, the current state is unable to oppose the selfish interests of the traitorous enterprises.

The interests of globalized businesses are less and less aligned with the interests of the country

Times have been changing gradually over the past decades, and it was only the overtly blatant attack on the interests of multinationals during Trump's first presidency that escalated the situation to the point where the change finally became clear.

Trump's proposed customs wall would make it unprofitable for American businesses to import products made in China to the United States. They will have to reopen their production in the United States. This does not mean that they will move it back, but at least they will open a new one in the United States and work for both the American and Chinese markets. The fact that the Chinese market is less spoiled by high-tech goods and at the same time mostly consists of incomparably poorer consumers will naturally lead to the fact that the technologies used in production there will be less sophisticated, less knowledge-intensive. So to speak, they will belong to modular technologies, not to integral ones. This is what will give the United States a chance to break away from its assertive competitor.

But today's large US enterprises like the current state of

affairs better. They can now 1. work for the huge Chinese market, 2. work for the rich American market, and 3. in many cases, produce for both of these large markets in the same factories (in China), which creates opportunities for huge economies of scale.

Therefore, throughout Trump's presidency, large enterprises were generally not happy, even with Trump's tax cuts for them. Thousands of American companies have sued the government for imposing duties on Chinese goods.[475]

The infamous events of January 6, 2021, unexpectedly gave large enterprises, along with the CEO of the National Association of Manufacturers, which represents 14,000 enterprises, the opportunity to show their attitude to Trump's reforms by joining the accusations of inciting violence. Moreover, the enterprises punished him with "sanctions" whenever they could (closing his account, cutting off his money transfer service, and making life difficult for the companies that remained on his side).[476]

A significant number of large corporations have unanimously issued statements refusing further donations to the Republican Party (see the list in Alex Gangitano, "Here are the companies suspending political contributions following the Capitol riots"[477]), as a consequence of the events in the Capitol. But the years have passed, and in the new election, Trump again has problems with funding from large corporations, see[478][479] and others. And if they gave money to Republicans, they gave it to Trump's rivals.[480]

Big business in the United States is united in solidarity today. In the globalized sea of the free market, which Democrats continue to stand for, the interest of large corporations has begun to diverge from the interest of the country. They are satisfied with the way things are. In the end, the situation is threatening to the country state and the majority of the people it is not a danger to American businesses or to various professionals, all of whom will be able to move to China if its peak rises above the American one. In a globalized world, large enterprises are citizens of the world, as are specialists. Like the cosmopolitans of ancient Greece, their home is wherever there is a haven for them. Globalization is a time when large corporations have nothing to lose but their chains—the chains that tied them to their homelands. But most peoples and their states have something to lose and gain in this world—their countries go up the mountain and down the valley. The state will not move to another country. The whole nation will not move either.

Public choice

Businesses are satisfied with the current situation and are throwing their considerable socioeconomic influence behind maintaining it. So, the situation will get worse for the American leadership if nothing is done. And only the state can do something. But the United States is caught in a contradiction—for a country at the peak, government intervention is harmful because it can prevent private enterprises from effectively reallocating resources to the most promising areas of innovation. In line with this contradiction, the responses to the problem facing the United States are contradictory—both Democrats and Republicans are trying to preserve the free market through increased government intervention. But in different combinations.

The Democrats, are in favor of greater government influence on businesses and economic processes within the country and a completely free market outside. In particular, this translates into increased taxes and government spending in the domestic market and welcoming globalization processes in the foreign market. The Republicans, led by Trump, favor a free market at home and government intervention in the foreign market. In particular, this translates into lower taxes, reduced spending on health care and the environment in the domestic market, and higher duties in foreign trade and a negative attitude towards economic unions.

Since the Democrats do not want to change the existing system, they propose to simply strengthen the existing and effective tool—injecting money into enterprises to organize their scientific and technological research in areas important to the state and use it as a tool to keep enterprises in the United States.

However, Democrats' government procurement is not comprehensive and cannot apply to all companies. Therefore, they can at most suspend the withdrawal of some large companies from the United States. Although Trump's customs wall will not bring the American production that has left back to the United States, it will at least lead to the emergence of new relevant production in the United States. After all, the problem itself ultimately arose because of the lack of such a wall.

Both Democrats and Republicans are trying to preserve the free market through increased government intervention. But it is the approach of the Democrats that contradicts the economic essence of the leading country. Trump wants to intervene in the foreign free market to save the free market at the peak. And the Democrats are saving the global free market at the expense of the free market at the peak.

The reason the economy of the peak is the most successful is that it sensitively turns every moment to where the market demand it most. Government intervention (of whatever kind) weakens this property and thus reduces the efficiency with which the peak market generates and implements innovations. In addition, government intervention, especially increased taxes on enterprises, can also reduce the attractiveness of the peak market for foreign investment. Other countries raise taxes to stimulate faster economic growth, but the peak country has already risen to the peak. Other countries also raise taxes to help reduce the burden on the most vulnerable, but the peak country needs it less—its poor are not as poor as those in other countries.

On the other hand, a customs wall, 1. leaves the domestic market free from government interference (and attractive to domestic and foreign enterprises); 2. creates a barrier around what is still the most attractive market in the world, which will force foreign firms to invest in the United States as a way to sell their goods behind the wall; 3. significantly reduces the attractiveness of the betrayal for American enterprises—that is, taking technology "out of the country". Given a choice, they will mostly choose the United States. For now. If nothing is done at this point, the Chinese market will be more attractive later; 4. If advanced American (and Western) technologies stop flowing like a full-flowing river to China, China will slow down its acceleration and the United States will have a chance to break away fromits nimble rival.

Russia's invasion of Ukraine presented the Democrats with an opportunity to intervene in the foreign free market while maintaining the ideological claim that interference in the market is unacceptable. They certainly saw for themselves that the global free market was increasingly playing in China's favor. But they could not put up outright economic obstacles to it, because that would contradict their ideological statements. Therefore, Democrats used to try to get out of the situation with unofficial instructions within the state apparatus to reduce relations with Chinese companies and to find fault with China's real and imaginary deviations from free-market rules. Now, all free-market laws regarding China can be officially distorted as a result of the official political confrontation. While the Republicans prefer outright interference in the foreign free market (they directly demanded that China buy more American goods), the Democrats prefer a more "delicate" approach, which, because of its insincerity, can be a real threat to American moral leadership in the world.

Shares of World Exports of Manufactures (% Based on Values in US $ at Current Prices)

	UK	US	Germany	Japan
1881–85	43·0	6·0	16·0	0·0
1899	34·5	12·1	16·6	1·6
1913	31·8	13·7	19·9	2·5
1929	23·8	21·7	15·5	4·1
1937	22·3	20·5	16·5	7·4
1950	24·6	26·6	7·0	3·4
1964	14·0	20·1	19·5	8·3
1973	9·1	15·1	22·3	13·1
1979	8·7	14·6	18·7	12·3
1987	7·3	12·6	19·3	16·3

Source: Matthews *et al.* (1982, p. 435); United Nations, *International Trade Statistics Yearbook* (Geneva).

The rise of the United States in the late nineteenth century at the expense of the United Kingdom and the rise of Germany and Japan in the post-1945 period at the expense of the United States and the United Kingdom[481]

Outside of relations with China (and a few other outright enemies), the Democrats intend to continue to hold on to the free market. That is why their approach is not a salvation for the leading economic role of the United States in the world, but rather an even greater deterioration of the situation. After all, since the end of World War II, the United States has been busy creating economic rivals—it has supported West Germany and South Korea, Japan, and Taiwan, etc. in their struggle against political rivals, and then was surprised to see its economic role in the world diminish.

Now, once again, they are going to support other countries as a counterweight to China. And the result will inevitably be the same: a diminishing economic role for the United States in the world. It doesn't matter much if companies move their production not to China, but to India, Indonesia, or any other country in the world. The main thing is that the free global market will continue to give them this opportunity.

<u>And, of course, the most reliable way for liberals (democrats) to preserve the free market and democracy in the United States is to introduce a free market and democracy in China</u>. The unified and unifying will of the State will disappear, and what will be left before the American multinational corporations will be a helpless crowd of Chinese enterprises. It is like destroying the headquarters of an advancing army. It will turn into a helpless crowd of soldiers. This tactic proved to be a very effective weapon in the fight against the USSR, so it is likely to be no less effective in destroying the new rival.

But there is no guarantee of success. The overwhelming majority of the Chinese population, watching the successful rise of their country, sees no point in rebellion. In addition, the collapse of China will not change the globalist nature of multinational corporations. Multinational corporations are increasingly turning into transnational corporations—corporations without a residence permit—where it is better now is where they'll have their headquarters. All of these are consequences of the leftist offensive that is forcing the right to seek change.

Trump's Republicans don't need to say one thing and do another. They consider it necessary to protect the American market and therefore are fighting China and at the same time everyone else. At least, if a leader does not deceive and does not twist, it helps his leadership a lot. And a leader can lead by example. The U.S. government's move to bring domestic industries back to the United States could create a new anti-globalization trend. Even before the start of the Russian-Ukrainian war, European and Japanese states began to take steps in this direction, because they also realized that their "non-interference in the market" policy was also growing the gravedigger of their privileged position in the world. For example, in 2020, the law on foreign trade in Germany was tightened to make it more difficult to acquire German companies. As explained by German Economy Minister Peter Altmaier, it was necessary to ensure "the protection of our German and European companies from unfair competition and illegal technology transfer, as well as from acquisition by state-subsidized competitors, often from countries outside the EU."[482] The events of recent years can only reinforce this trend, and the United States, to the extent that it remains at the peak of the world's economic pyramid, can organize its pyramid of political and economic influence for a common struggle.

The introduction of a high customs wall and various restrictions is only one (albeit very effective) of the steps that could be taken. Among other things, state enterprises could be much more widely used. They do not need to be maintained by public procurement and do not need to be fenced off by duties to keep them in the country. <u>National enterprises will not betray or leave the country. They are part of the blood of the state, they are part of the flesh of the people.</u>

State-private enterprises, the example of the defense industry

In October 2022, the US Department of Defense published a report on the National Defense Industrial Strategy, in which it describes the difficulties preventing the US from mobilizing its industry to compete with Russia and China.

There are many difficulties, but almost all of them boil down to the fact that private industry, to which the state gives its orders for weapons and other necessary products, is silently passive. State funding allows them not only to receive direct profits from government orders but also to use the spin-offs of military developments for civilian use.

However, private companies are not sure that this surge in military activity will last. Thus, they fear that after they expand their production capacities, state arms purchases will stop, as they did after the end of the Cold War. Even dual-use (military/civilian) products, as discussed above, have different requirements when used for peaceful and military purposes. As shown above, most of the innovations made for military purposes eventually found civilian use. But this is unpredictable and not guaranteed. Therefore, private business is not enthusiastic, and the goals of the state are the goals of the state, not private companies.

This current situation with U.S. military orders intended to help Ukraine highlights 1. the flaws in the liberal approach itself, which are evident even at the peak of the economic hierarchy of the world; 2. the difference in the goals and horizons of the state and the private sector; and 3. the advantages that, under certain conditions and circumstances, are entirely on the side of the public sector. In other words, this Report is a particularly vivid illustration of some of the themes raised in this book.

Everyone can read the Report for themselves[483], but below are some translations from the language of the Report into the language of this book.

-Inadequate Domestic Production: Uncertain DoD funding, the prolonged cost-driven offshoring that has been pervasive across the U.S. manufacturing sector, and disincentives to modernize manufacturing processes or maintain excess capacity have resulted in DoD's overreliance on single or adversarial foreign sources for key materials and production capacity.

–Many elements of the traditional DIB [defense industrial base] have yet to adopt advanced manufacturing technologies as they struggle to develop business cases for needed capital investment. This directly impacts DoD's ability to reduce manufacturing lead times and lifecycle costs and to increase readiness.—That is, the private sector is not sure that the expansion of production will pay off.

–Competitive Practices: Unfair trade practices in the post-Cold War era, especially non-competitive policies employed by our adversaries (e.g., unfair subsidies, dominance-driven acquisitions, hidden ownership, transfer of critical technology, flouting trade agreements), have harmed U.S. and Allied defense-related industries.—That is, the world is not fair because many countries follow conservative rather than liberal policies.

And so on, point by point.

The report shows that the interaction between the state and private companies has been a difficult confrontation for a decade.

Dependence on adversarial sourcing poses a mounting national security challenge to the DIB... sole-source dependence on adversary-produced materials and parts presents an obvious vulnerability...Some critical capabilities remain dependent on prohibited adversarial suppliers. Over the past decade, the DoD has struggled to curtail adversarial sourcing and burnish the integrity of defense supply chains. Despite these efforts, dependence on adversarial sources of supply has grown.

The state with its national goals is inexorably losing to private companies and their private goals.

As noted in another interesting analysis of this report[484]

"Despite virtually all the problems the report identifies stemming from private industry's disproportionate influence over the US DIB, the report never identifies private industry *itself* as a problem."

Just as the efforts of the communist ideology in the USSR to rely exclusively on state-owned enterprises led to a lagging behind and eventual defeat, so now the attempt of the liberal ideology in the United States to rely exclusively on private enterprises may ultimately lead to similar results. Let's not forget that during World War II, the United States did not stop at nationalizing all U.S. railroads.

What not to do

The USSR was once one of the world's two superpowers. Many countries looked up to it as the peak of the economic pyramid. Many people in countries that were much more developed than it was, looked at it as a pioneer in the future... This is all in the past. The point is not only that its struggle against private enterprise was self-destructive and it disappeared from the face of the Earth, but even more so that most of the countries that used to be part of it lost the accumulated potential, stopped improving advanced technologies and, in many cases, lost them. Many countries that used to look up on the USSR are now looking down at these countries. The development of other countries has not stopped for all these 30 years, and they have long since bypassed the wreckage of the former second peak of the world.

The people of the USSR, shocked by the truth about Stalin's terror and disappointed in communism, which had failed to produce a "man of the communist tomorrow," decided to end communism. At the same time, however, they decided that they were tired of the leading, organizing role of the state and the isolation of their country from the import of foreign goods.

Ukraine is perhaps the most striking example. At the time of the collapse of the USSR in 1991, Ukraine was one of its richest republics. At its start, this country had the world's third-largest dry cargo fleet (with revenues approaching $1 billion a year), reasonably good healthcare and education, and, most importantly, a developed network of scientific and industrial enterprises that produced seiners, bulk carriers, cruisers and aircraft carriers, military and passenger aircraft, trucks and cars, engines for airplanes and helicopters, ballistic and space missiles, tanks and tractors, and more. As early as 1940, the invention of the atomic bomb was registered in Ukraine and the second nuclear reaction in Europe was carried out. Since the end of 1948, Ukraine has been working on the creation of the first computer in Europe, the Small Electronic Computing Machine (MEOM), which came into operation in 1951. The Kyiv and Dnipro computer projects followed. In 1963, work began on Soviet personal computers. As early as 1962, work was underway to create the Soviet Internet, the National Automated System for Collecting and Processing Information (NASS). The latter project was only partially put into practice for both civilian and, especially, military purposes. In general, in everything that could have military applications, the USSR kept up with the United States and often outperformed it. And Ukraine was involved in almost every project. Accordingly, by the end of its stay in the USSR, Ukraine had 313,079 scientists.

The Soviet Union was the second superpower in the world as long as its state was able to influence economic processes in the country and direct the country's resources to the development of decisive sectors of the economy. This was done by reducing national consumption. The state, the sole owner of all economic enterprises, paid workers reduced wages. In addition, the people were forced to buy imperfect goods from domestic enterprises, whose cost was higher than potential imported goods. Since there were no large private enterprises or other parties in the country, there were no opposing socioeconomic influences that could compete with the socioeconomic influence of the state. Therefore, the state managed to convince the people of the need for additional efforts to raise the whole country and catch up with the first superpower in the world; of the need to limit consumption and postpone it for the indefinite future. It all ended when the state voluntarily handed over the state media to the liberals. National interest-based approach (we are a nation fighting for a better place in the global economic system in an organized way) was replaced by a liberal one, which claimed that if everyone took care of themselves, of how to enrich themselves, then the overall wealth of the country would grow from these numerous riches. The people allowed themselves to be convinced that it was time to stop working hard, relax, and consume.

The media was full of calculations of how much better the people could live if nations stopped wasting money on space programs, cut spending on scientists, and switched missile and tank factories to producing trolleybuses and frying pans. The price of these savings is known. By 2017, the number of scientists had fallen to less than a hundred thousand. A huge number of them went to China, North Korea, Iran, Turkey, Mexico, and all over the world, where they were offered money for all their knowledge. Those who were less fortunate stood on black markets selling Turkish sheepskin coats and Chinese shoes. And today's young people do not go into science, which is not realistically funded.

More and more opportunities were found to save money to improve the lives of the people. Aid to foreign countries was stopped and spending on science, the military, etc. was cut.

Moreover, at the time of its formation, Ukraine had the largest army in Europe and had become one of the largest arms exporters in the world. It was simply selling off its army. But this is not enough. Military technologies, especially in the field of naval equipment and military aviation, were sold to China. But even this is not enough. At the time of its formation, Ukraine had no debts, but by 2018, it had accumulated about $76.3 billion in debts.

Despite all these savings, in the 30 years since gaining independence, Ukraine has not increased its GDP (per capita at purchasing power parity*) and living standards, but has decreased them, and has not been able to rise back to the level of 1991. At that time, the country's fleet was equal to one ship, education almost became a paid service, steel production decreased by 2.5 times, cars and trucks by ten times, tractors by 66 times, and international airlines disappeared. Of the country's 50 formerly active airports, only 20 continued to operate. Production of ships, airplanes, and missiles was practically zero. The last aircraft carrier produced in Ukraine (not completely) was sold as scrap to China, where it was completed and put into operation as the very first Chinese aircraft carrier, the Liaoning (after which China began producing its own aircraft carriers). The country's population decreased from 52 million in 1991 to 42 million before the war with Russia.

The states of the former USSR and the countries that emerged in its place failed to convince their people that they should not exchange the chance of a great tomorrow for a small today. These countries gave away all their advanced technologies, everything that made them the world's second superpower, for better clothes and electronics than they had. Today,

* The per capita measurement is important given that Ukraine's population is declining catastrophically, which is an additional factor in the decline in GDP.

the victorious United States does not notice that it is doing the same thing—it is giving away what makes it the first superpower in the world for cheaper clothes and electronics than it had. Unlike Ukrainian ones, their large industrial enterprises see their salvation in the absence of customs barriers and the transfer of its production abroad. Therefore, their struggle for existence will not save but destroy the United States.

People's choice

In all recent elections, Democrats argued that Trump's policy of stopping (or at least slowing down) globalization was wrong, that his destruction of economic agreements and raising tariffs would make life more expensive for Americans while deepening globalization would accelerate the development of the entire global economy, and thus everyone in the world would be better off.

However, it was the fact that the people of the United States paid much higher prices for goods that was one of the decisive factors in its rise to the peak in the 19th century. The US people are facing a choice—either less effort and more consumption, or they will stay at the peak of the global economic pyramid. <u>The people of the United States must decide whether they need the accelerated development of the global economy at all if they find themselves on the sidelines of development in this economy</u>.

Who are the MNCs afraid of—the American left or the right?

The leftists propose increasing taxes on large enterprises and the rich and using this money to increase government purchases from domestic enterprises and help them with their scientific and technological activities. This will be done on the condition that they produce at least some of their products in the United States and that most of the components of the products they purchase are also produced in the United States. Otherwise, these enterprises operate in a "completely" free market where the most adaptable win. Enterprises do not leave the United States because they receive assistance for research and development and guaranteed sales of some of their products (government procurement). This is the only non-free-market "nail" that is supposed to keep large enterprises in the United States. But the problem is that the state will not buy all the products of all enterprises, so the part that is not purchased can be produced abroad.

At the same time, Democrats, in keeping with leftist tradition, promise to increase social welfare for the poor and to regulate markets and corporations more strictly. Despite this, large enterprises still mostly support the Democrats rather than Trump. This is because they don't believe in revolution of the leftists, but they do believe in Trump's rebellion. They know that under the Democrats they will be able to do without public procurement, but will be able to continue to move their production out of the US and sell their products to private consumers in the US. Under Trump's Republicans, they will have to pay increased duties for this and lose all the benefits of moving production abroad. The revolution of the left is very limited, while the revolt of the right against the globalized world is all-encompassing.

At the time when the United States was just climbing the mountain, people also paid higher prices for goods because of the customs wall. It was only at that time that the industrial enterprises of the north were on the side of the state and, together with the state, convinced the people (and the enterprises of the south) that the customs wall was good for everyone. Now that the US is at the very edge of the descent, the enterprises will not support the state. On the contrary, they will agitate against its actions. The state must go on its rebellion against the impending doom.

AFTERWORD

Regardless of who wins the US election, the objective need for the US to confront an actively and successfully rising rival will dictate that it adopt the policies advocated by the conservatives of the Republican Party. Liberal policies of the current Democrats will increasingly contradict the interests of the United States as the world's economic leader. Just as it will increasingly contradict the interests of the EU. And it's not just China. If it were to somehow withdraw from the arena, other new contenders for world leadership—India, Brazil, Indonesia, etc.—would be waiting behind.

However, liberals in the Democratic Party are looking for a liberal cure for this prospect. The most liberal way would be to persuade China to embrace liberalism at its current stage of development (as was once done with the USSR). As a natural consequence of this, as history teaches, China would begin to lose economic competition, possibly fall apart, and be firmly embedded at the bottom of the American economic pyramid. But there is little hope for this, given that China has closely watched the fall of its former master and has drawn the appropriate conclusions. Therefore, liberals are resorting to another liberal remedy. Since China is a huge market to which US and European companies are fleeing, liberals are trying to make their market no smaller, and maybe even bigger, and are opening the doors of the US and EU to millions of immigrants. Immigration expands the market capacity, increases the GNP, and brings in much-needed specialists. Anyone who increases their population wins. The United States proved this by example throughout the 19th century. But it is also obvious that the titular nations dissolve in the sea of newcomers. It is not the nation that wins, it is the territory on which the nation lives that wins. So liberal political treatments of the problems created by liberal economics are indeed capable of globalizing the world and destroying nations.

But the other way is more likely. Toward the end of Biden's presidency, the Democrats themselves began to take the steps that Trump called for, and against which they fought so hard. For example, the Democratic US Treasury Secretary Janet Yellen told reporters that the US 'does not rule out' tariffs in response to China's subsidized production of clean energy products.[485] And even Biden had started talking about tariffs on Chinese steel products. So perhaps the Democrats, under pressure from reality, will one day lead the United States on a conservative path themselves. The more so will the Republicans do it... The only difference is that for the Republicans, eliminating economic unions and protecting the national market from other countries' products is in line with their philosophy, and therefore their words do not diverge from their deeds. In the case of the Democrats, "the United States says one thing and does another," and the whole world sees this, and it is detrimental to the leadership role of the United States.

PART II

THE IDEOLOGY OF IDEOLOGIES

THE IDEOLOGY OF IDEOLOGIES

The big questions of humanity

World ideologies and political movements are breaking spears over such global issues as what is better for the peoples of the planet—democracy or authoritarianism? Free market or state regulation of the economy? State or private enterprises? And so on. Different answers have been given by different forces at different times. Neither theoretical nor practical evidence has been able to form a single point of view or any form of understanding between them.

Traditionally, ideologies have been widely recognized along a "right–left" spectrum that includes conservatism, liberalism, and Marxism. However, a more challenging approach is based on the vision of society as consisting of three fundamental components: the state, the enterprises, and the people[12].

State   Enterprises

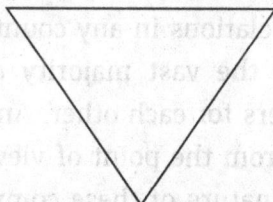

People—Workers

This vision allows us to understand that each of the three dominant ideologies in the world, while building its comprehensive worldview that reflects the whole society, essentially centers around one of the three fundamental social elements. This observation probably explains the existence of three dominant ideologies in the world. The following distinction is obvious: Liberalism is predominantly concerned with enterprises, emphasizing the freedom of entrepreneurship, free markets, and equal opportunities for everyone. Classical conservatism focuses primarily on maintaining order within the country and establishing the country's position in relations with other countries, for which the state is primarily responsible. Marxism is primarily concerned with the fate of workers and sees ways to improve it by eliminating property injustice and spreading public ownership.

Despite the futile and sometimes confrontational debates between these ideologies, this vision opens the way to compromise. The compromise can be found in the realization that neither liberalism, Marxism, nor conservatism is universally applicable. At the same time, they are all suitable for each country, but at different stages of its economic development.

The process of replacing one ideology with another can be understood by modifying the traditional approach of "nascent industries," historically recognized since the days of Alexander Hamilton and Friedrich Liszt, but presented in a new way.

Inter-enterprise relations in any country in the world form a network, in which the vast majority of enterprises act as suppliers and marketers for each other. And this network is not flat. If we look at it from the point of view of the capital—and knowledge-intensive nature of these companies' production, it will look like a hierarchy in which companies producing more capital—and knowledge-intensive products (leading companies)

382

organize their networks of sales and supply units. These net-works around them mainly include less knowledge- and capital-intensive companies, some of which may in turn have their network of suppliers and distributors. Thus, a hierarchy is established between these companies: the leading company at the peak—its contractors—their subcontractors—and so on. Traditionally, such hierarchies have had industrial companies at the peak and agricultural or commodity companies at the bottom. Modern configurations, however, manifest themselves in the form of much taller pyramids, stretching from the most labor-intensive enterprises at the base to the most knowledge- and capital-intensive at the peak. The defining characteristic of these hierarchies is that the higher their position in the hierar-chy, the higher the profits of the companies.[345]

The global economic hierarchy connects such hierarchies of individual countries into a single global economic hierarchy. This hierarchy is formed by foreign economic relations that connect leading companies in one country with contractors in other countries. In this global economic hierarchy, coun-tries with a higher concentration of leading companies occupy higher levels of the hierarchy, rising above countries dominated by contracting companies. While a free global market encour-ages competition, **once established, this hierarchy tends to be self-preserving**. The leading companies bring more profit to their country, and because of this, more capital is concen-trated where there are more of them, and as a result, such a country attracts more specialists from around the world. The inflow of capital and qualified specialists further strengthens the country's scientific and technological potential. This com-bined advantage allows companies in such countries to have an edge in global competition, strengthening their leadership position, and, as a result, the country maintains its advantage as well. Another result is the growth of the population in countries with a high level of development, with a fairly large share of the working-age population achieved through immigration from other countries. Conversely, countries in the lower ranks experience population decline, which reduces the percentage of the working-age labor force and exacerbates economic competitiveness problems, thereby perpetuating the trend of migration to higher-ranked countries.

Each country occupies a position in the global political hierarchy of countries that is determined by the level reached by its companies in the global economic hierarchy of companies. The global hierarchy of companies determines the influence of a country in international relations and the overall relative standard of living of its citizens. Therefore, neither states nor peoples of countries at the bottom of the hierarchy can be satisfied with the current situation. However, the stability of the global economic hierarchy is explained not only by the above processes favorable to the countries at the peak level*[6]. **A more important stabilizing factor is the satisfaction of contractors in lower-tier countries involved in foreign economic relations with their situation.**

After all, the involvement of contractors in a global hierarchical network of economic ties is the source of their profits, which allows them to earn significant profits with minimal risk to capital. The world's leading companies, with their higher demand for semi-finished products and raw materials, offer them a lower-risk environment than domestic companies.

* This was essentially Hamilton's main argument: "The superiority antecedently existing in favor of nations which have possessed the first mover in manufacturing industry, has enabled them to keep possession of foreign markets, in spite of the efforts gradually made by other nations to supplant them; and however unskillfully or oppressively managed, they have not been easily or speedily shaken off."

Participation in the global economic network also allows such contractors to build their economic pyramids in their home countries, which helps to strengthen their socio-economic influence there. These contractors use their considerable influence to preserve this situation, as it is to their advantage.

Thus, the self-sustaining nature of this system ensures that countries dominated by contractors remain at the bottom of the global economic hierarchy. For a country dissatisfied with its position, the logical way out is to use state influence on its companies. **Government intervention should be aimed at increasing the number of domestic leading companies with their economic hierarchy abroad and reducing the number of contractors involved in foreign hierarchies**. This can be achieved by supporting the former at the expense of the latter, which is a pragmatic approach, especially for countries at the lowest levels of the hierarchy. First, such states lack the financial means to create leading companies, and second, these **contractors resist restructuring the country's economy by using their considerable social influence**. Therefore, by withdrawing capital from such companies, the state firstly receives funds for transformation, and secondly weakens resistance to these transformations.

Moreover, the lower the country is in the hierarchy, the more effective the resistance of contractors is, the fewer leading companies there are in the country and the more difficult it is to organize them. Economic planning and state-owned companies may well be effective tools in this case. In such a socialist period, the state should create new high-tech companies that should be aimed at climbing to the peak of the foreign contractors' hierarchies in the future. This should, on the one hand, stimulate active economic growth and, on the other hand, rid the country of the inhibiting influence of powerful local contractors.

As economic growth becomes sustainable, the state starts to help both public and private knowledge- and capital-intensive export companies that have a chance to become leading companies with their hierarchies of foreign contractors. At this stage, the state's actions continue to benefit these leading companies and increasingly limit the interests of contractors. However, as the country's position in the global economic hierarchy rises, the influence of contractors is weakening, and they are getting more and more opportunities to become contractors of leading domestic companies. Thus, their resistance is decreasing. As a result, **as the country rises in the global economic hierarchy, the need for government intervention decreases**.

However, the withdrawal of the state from economic influence at this stage may lead to stagnation of the country at its current level, as free market processes stabilize the hierarchy*[7]. Therefore, the role of the state remains important. This is in line with the classical conservative approach, which emphasizes the central role of the state, its concern for the people, national prestige, and international influence. The dominance of this ideology helps the state to organize the efforts of private companies to continue economic growth.

Once they reach the peak of the global economic hierarchy, enterprises that dominate their hierarchies in other countries become very powerful and influential in their home countries. They no longer need help or guidance from the state. In addition, the influence of contractors associated with foreign leading companies is weakening, and their share in the country's economy is decreasing. Thus, state actions aimed at helping the former and neutralizing the social influence of the latter

* This conclusion is still slightly better than Friedrich Liszt's conclusion: "Industry entirely left to itself would soon fall to ruin, and a nation letting everything alone would commit suicide."

386

and redistributing capital from the latter to the former become unnecessary. This marks the time of liberalism for the country. The primary task of the state of such a country is to promote liberalism abroad on a global scale. After all, the elimination of the idea of state intervention eliminates threats to the free market that may come from new contenders for the peak of the global economy. In this case, market processes themselves will stabilize the existing hierarchy and the leading position of the leading country in it.

The ebb and flow of economic ideologies reflects the dynamic nature of global economic hierarchies. As countries move up or down the hierarchy, their approach to government intervention evolves accordingly.

When nations at the peak of the hierarchy face a challenge from other nations experiencing economic growth, a return to conservatism becomes a necessity until the challenge is suppressed. A country that is losing its position at the peak must increasingly resort to state intervention to slow its decline. If conservatism fails to halt the decline, socialism may come in handy again. Conversely, a challenger that uses state regulation to reach the peak opens a new era of liberalism

The current economic landscape, notable for the rise of China in particular, clearly demonstrates these processes. China's rise initially involved a gradual transition from socialism to conservatism with the emergence of private enterprises while maintaining the prominent position of the state. However, if China reaches the peak of the global economic hierarchy, it will be difficult for the state to maintain control over powerful domestic enterprises that no longer need protection. With the population and enterprises demanding democracy and no longer seeing the need for collective efforts to achieve national goals, China will inevitably become liberalized.

At the same time, the liberal United States faces the risk of losing its leading position. The Trump phenomenon reflects the response to this threat: Republicans are in favor of increasing the state's influence on foreign economic relations, thus trying to change the behavior of both domestic and foreign companies. At the same time, however, they seek to reduce the state's influence on domestic companies. Democrats, on the other hand, use subsidies to influence domestic companies, carefully avoiding interference in their foreign economic relations. At this stage, neither Democrats nor Republicans adhere to a strictly liberal or conservative ideology.

The Trump era is particularly noteworthy given the historical context of pre-Trump Republican neoliberalism. It may seem that Reagan's free-market reforms during the Cold War contradict the claim that a leading country should shift toward conservatism when faced with a powerful rival. However, during the Cold War, the USSR sought to destroy, not capture, the global economic pyramid. Soviet enterprises were not integrated into the global economic hierarchy; they were not contractors or lead companies for American enterprises. In this context, the United States sought to maximize its advantages as a leading country and to do so, in full agreement with the above, it tried to remove the state from interfering in the economy as much as possible. Liberalism in this period was in line with the strategic task of countering the Soviet threat. However, in the current scenario, the United States is confronted by China, a country that is integrated into the global economic hierarchy and seeks to take the peak spot. This prompts a return to state intervention and a new adoption of Hamiltonian conservatism as the guiding ideology for the leading nation.

It is important to note that both parties in the United States recognize the growing role of the state, differing only in their approaches. If China's economic success continues, the role of the state in U.S. economic affairs is likely to grow proportionately, signaling a potential shift toward conservatism in response to the challenges of a rising global economic competitor.

Conclusion.

The stability of the global economic hierarchy is based primarily on the interest of contractor companies in lower-tier countries to be part of this hierarchy. The rise of a country begins only when its government begins to influence domestic companies by facilitating the flow of capital from contractor companies to leading companies.

The interests of the people, enterprises, and the state never fully coincide and therefore require an orderly expression of their point of view—that is, their ideologies. However, despite their differences, they are interconnected elements in the society of each country and around the world. This interconnectedness makes possible an ideology that takes into account the interests of all three components of society and encompasses the three main ideologies. And this ideology should be the ideology of the cycle of economic leadership in the world. Or the ideology of economic growth, which involves the solidarity of all components of society. So, its correct name could be "solidarism". Or better yet, "neosolidarism."

END NOTES

PART I
THE POLITICAL ECONOMY OF REBELLION

1. Mark Cartwright, "Greek Colonization," Ancient History Encyclopedia, https://www.ancient.eu/Greek_Colonization

2. D.Brendan Nagle, Stanley M. Burstein, "The Ancient World, Readings in Social and Cultural History", Prentice Hall, 2010, pg 88

3. Robin W.Winks, Susan P.Mattern-Parkes, "The Ancient Mediterranean World", Oxford, pg 67

4. D.Brendan Nagle, "The Ancient World, A Social and Cultural History", Prentice Hall, 2010, pg 141

5. The Ancient World, A Social and Cultural History, D.Brendan Nagle, pp 139

6. The Ancient Mediterranean World, Robin W.Winks, Susan P.Mattern-Parkes, Oxford, pp 66-67

7. The Ancient World, A Social and Cultural History, D.Brendan Nagle, pg 86

8. В.И.Кузищин (Ed), "История Древнего Рима", Высшая школа, 1981, стр 39

9. В.И.Кузищин (Ed), "История Древнего Рима", Высшая школа, 1981, стр 40

10. В.И.Кузищин (Ed), "История Древнего Рима", Высшая школа, 1981, стр 40

11. Мякин Т. Г. "История Древней Греции и Древнего Рима", гос. ун-т. Новосибирск, 2005, https://classics.nsu.ru/makin/ancient_law.htm (2020-Vus-20).

12. Edward ch. L. van der Vliet, "the Early State, the Polis and State Formation in Early Greece", pg 204-205

13. "The Delian League and the Athenian Empire (478-431 BCE)", http://www.flowofhistory.com/units/birth/3/FC23

14. "The Delian League and the Athenian Empire (478-431 BCE)", http://www.flowofhistory.com/units/birth/3/FC23

15. D. Brendan Nagle, "The Ancient World, A Social and Cultural History", Prentice Hall, 2010, pg 165

16. D. Brendan Nagle, "The Ancient World, A Social and Cultural History", Prentice Hall, 2010, pg 166

17. D. Brendan Nagle, "The Ancient World, A Social and Cultural History", Prentice Hall, 2010, pg 169

18. D. Brendan Nagle, "The Ancient World, A Social and Cultural History", Prentice Hall, 2010, pg 170

19. D. Brendan Nagle, "The Ancient World, A Social and Cultural History", Prentice Hall, 2010, pg 170

20. D. Brendan Nagle, "The Ancient World, A Social and Cultural History", Prentice Hall, 2010, pg 171

21. Britannica, 2019-09-15, "Hellenistic age," https://www.britannica.com/event/Hellenistic-Age/Civic-structures#ref26554

22. Hanson, Victor Davis, "The Other Greeks: The Family Enterprise and the Agrarian Roots of Western Civilization", University of California Press, 1999, pg 390

23. В.И.Кузищин (Ed), "История Древнего Рима", Высшая школа, 1981, стр 49

24. В.И.Кузищин (Ed), "История Древнего Рима", Высшая школа, 1981, стр 49

25. В.И.Кузищин (Ed), "История Древнего Рима", Высшая школа, 1981, стр 50

26. Robin W.Winks, Susan P.Mattern-Parkes, "The Ancient Mediterranean World", Oxford, pg 125

27. D. Brendan Nagle, "The Ancient World, A Social and Cultural History", Prentice Hall, 2010, pg 237

28. D. Brendan Nagle, "The Ancient World, A Social and Cultural History", Prentice Hall, 2010, pg 237

29. Robin W.Winks, Susan P.Mattern-Parkes, "The Ancient Mediterranean World", Oxford, pg 123

30. D. Brendan Nagle, "The Ancient World, A Social and Cultural History", Prentice Hall, 2010, pg 237

31. В.И.Кузищин (Ed), "История Древнего Рима", Высшая школа, 1981, стр 115

32. Robin W.Winks, Susan P.Mattern-Parkes, "The Ancient Mediterranean World", Oxford, pg 143

33. В.И.Кузищин (Ed), "История Древнего Рима", Высшая школа, 1981, стр 172.

34. В.И.Кузищин (Ed), "История Древнего Рима", Высшая школа, 1981, стр 239

35. Robert K. Fleck, "The Origins of Democracy: A Model with Application to Ancient Greece", Montana State University, July 17, 2002, p. 17

36. Jennifer Titus, "The Impact of Necessity: The Athenian Grain Trade: Politics, Economy and Sustenance", 2011, pg 19

37. Ulrike Krotscheck, "Going with the Grain: Athenian State Formation and the Question of Subsistence in the 5th and 4th Centuries BCE", January 2006, Stanford University, pg. 3

38. Ulrike Krotscheck, "Going with the Grain: Athenian State Formation and the Question of Subsistence in the 5th and 4th Centuries BCE", January 2006, Stanford University, pg 5

39. Robert K. Fleck, "The Origins of Democracy: A Model with Application to Ancient Greece", Montana State University, July 17, 2002, pg 25-26

40. Hanson, Victor Davis, "The Other Greeks: The Family Enterprise and the Agrarian Roots of Western Civilization", University of California Press, 1999, pg 386

41. Neil Asher Silberman, Neil Asher Silberman, Alexander A. Bauer, Cornelius Holtorf, Margarita Díaz-Andreu García, Emma Waterton "The Oxford Companion to Archaeology", Oxford University Press, 1996, pg 757

42. В.И.Кузищин (Ed), "История Древнего Рима", Высшая школа, 1981, стр 278

43. В.И.Кузищин (Ed), "История Древнего Рима", Высшая школа, 1981, стр 277, 278.

44. В.И.Кузищин (Ed), "История Древнего Рима", Высшая школа, 1981, стр 278.

45. В.И.Кузищин (Ed), "История Древнего Рима", Высшая школа, 1981, стр 301

46. В.И.Кузищин (Ed), "История Древнего Рима", Высшая школа, 1981, стр 296.

47. В.И.Кузищин (Ed), "История Древнего Рима", Высшая школа, 1981, стр 309

48. D. Brendan Nagle, "The Ancient World, A Social and Cultural History", Prentice Hall, 2010, pg 320

49. Warren T. Treadgold, "A History of the Byzantine State and Society," see chapter "Impoverishment and prosperity"

50. D. Brendan Nagle, "The Ancient World, A Social and Cultural History", Prentice Hall, 2010, pg 319

51. Robin W.Winks, Susan P.Mattern-Parkes, "The Ancient Mediterranean World", Oxford, pg 176

52. D. Brendan Nagle, "The Ancient World, A Social and Cultural History", Prentice Hall, 2010, pg 318

53. Г.Л.Курбатов, "История Византии", Москва, Высшая школа, 1984, стр 106

54. Giovanni Arrighi, "Adam Smith in Beijing. Lineages of the Twenty-First Century", Verso, London-New York, 2007, pg 60, 61

55. Encyclopaedia Britanica, http://www.britannica.com/EBchecked/peakic/548305/slavery

56. Норман Дейвіс, «Європа, Історія», Київ, «Основи», 2008, стр 253

57. Норман Дейвіс, «Європа, Історія», Київ, «Основи», 2008, стр 274

58. Орест Субтельний, «Україна, Історія», Київ, «Либідь», 1991, стр 53

59. Орест Субтельний, «Україна, Історія», Київ, «Либідь», 1991, стр 53

60. Х. Ловмяньский, "Русь и норманы", переклад з польської, Москва, Прогресс, 1985, стр 110

61. Михайло Грушевський, «Ілюстрована Історія України», Київ, 1990, стр 102

62. Норман Дейвіс, «Європа, Історія», Київ, «Основи», 2008, стр 322

63. Melvin M. Knight, "Slavery, Mediaeval", Published in "Encyclopaedia of the Social Sciences", 15 vols. A. Seligman, New York: The Macmillan Company, 1930-1935, Reissued 1937

64. Melvin M. Knight, "Slavery, Mediaeval", Published in "Encyclopaedia of the Social Sciences", 15 vols. A. Seligman, New York: The Macmillan Company, 1930-1935, Reissued 1937

65. Ian Morris, "Why The West Rules—For Now", Picador, 2010, p. 368

66. Immanuel Wallerstein, "The Modern World-system II. Mercantilism and the Consolidation of the European World Economy, 1600-1750", University of California Press, Berkeley, 2011, pg 179

67. Britannica, "Hanseatic League", (copied on 2019-08-28), https://www.britannica.com/peakic/Hanseatic-League/The-League-at-its-outset

68. Immanuel Wallerstein, "The Modern World-system I. Capitalist Agriculture and the Origins of the European World-Economy in the Sixteenth Century", University of California Press, Berkeley, 2011, pg 99

69. Henri Pirenne, "Medieval Cities: Their Origins and the Revival of Trade", Princeton University Press, 1974, p. 85

70. See. Ф.И. Успенский. "История византийской империи", т I, глава 12

71. Г.Л.Курбатов, "История Византии", Высшая школа, 1984, стр 149

72. Г.Л.Курбатов, "История Византии", Высшая школа, 1984, стр 156

73. Г.Л.Курбатов, "История Византии", Высшая школа, 1984, стр 176

74. А. Д. Ролова. «Итальянский купец и его торгово-банковская деятельность в XIII-XV в.в.», Часть 1

75. Г.Л.Курбатов, "История Византии", Высшая школа, 1984, стр 177-178.

76. Г.Л.Курбатов, "История Византии", Высшая школа, 1984, стр 189

77. С. П. Карпов, "История Средних веков", т. 1, Изд-во МГУ, 2000, стр 509

78. Fernand Braudel, "The perspective of the world", vol 3, Harper &Row, 1986, pg 125

79. Fernand Braudel, "The perspective of the world", vol 3, Harper &Row, 1986, pg 125

80. Fernand Braudel, "The perspective of the world", vol 3, Harper &Row, 1986, pg 108

81. Fernand Braudel, "The perspective of the world", vol 3, Harper &Row, 1986, pg 141

82. Fernand Braudel, "The perspective of the world", vol 3, Harper &Row, 1986, pg 142

83. Fernand Braudel, "The perspective of the world", vol 3, Harper &Row, 1986, pg 179-180

84. Fernand Braudel, "The perspective of the world", vol 3, Harper &Row, 1986, pg 209

85. Fernand Braudel, "The perspective of the world", vol 3, Harper &Row, 1986, pg 149

86. Fernand Braudel, "The perspective of the world", vol 3, Harper &Row, 1986, pg 149

87. Immanuel Wallerstein, "The Modern World-system II. Mercantilism and the Consolidation of the European World Economy, 1600-1750", University of California Press, Berkeley, 2011, pg 91

88. С.Д.Сказкин, «Основные проблемы так называемого "Второго издания крепостничества" в Средней и Восточной Европе», «Вопросы истории», 1958, №2, стр 114

89. Czalpinski, XI Congres International des Sciences Historiques, Rapports, IV, p. 37, quoted from Immanuel Wallerstein, "The Modern World-system II. Mercantilism and the Consolidation of the European World Economy, 1600-1750", University of California Press, Berkeley, 2011, pg 324

90. Silvio Zavala, "New Viewpoints on the Spanish Colonization of America", Univ. Of Pensilvania Press, 1943, pg 94

91. Giovanni Arrighi, "The Long Twentieth Century. Money, Power and the Origins of our Times", Verso, London, New York, 2010, pg 100

92. "Эпоха Реформации, Европа", Харвест, 2002, стр 158

93. «County of Flanders», https://en.wikipedia.org/wiki/County_of _Flanders

94. Britannica, "Enclosure", 2019-09-08, https://www.britannica.com /topic/enclosure

95. "Эпоха Реформации, Европа", Харвест, 2002, стр 120-121

96. "Эпоха Реформации, Европа", Харвест, 2002, стр 158

97. Immanuel Wallerstein, "The Modern World-system II. Mercantilism and the Consolidation of the European World Economy, 1600-1750", University of California Press, Berkeley, 2011, pg 43

98. Fernand Braudel, "The perspective of the world", Vol. 3, Harper & Row, 1984, pg 205

99. Fernand Braudel, "The perspective of the world", Vol. 3, Harper & Row, 1984, pg 205

100. Immanuel Wallerstein, "The Modern World-system II. Mercantilism and the Consolidation of the European World Economy, 1600-1750", University of California Press, Berkeley, 2011, pg 66

101. Immanuel Wallerstein, "The Modern World-system I. Capitalist Agriculture and the Origins of the European World-Economy in the Sixteen Century", University of California Press, Berkeley, 2011, pg 304

102. Francis Fukuyama, "The origins of Political Order, from pre-human times to the French revolution", Farrar, Straus and Giroux, 2011, pg 381

103. Peter Mathias, "The first industrial nation. An economic history of Britain 1700-1914", Second Edition, Methuen, London and New York, pp 84

104. Phyllis Deane, "The first industrial revolution", Cambridge University Press, 1979, pp 134

105. Francois Crouzet, "Wars, blockade, and economic change in Europe, 1792-1815", pg 571

106. Francois Crouzet, "Wars, blockade, and economic change in Europe, 1792-1815", pg 575, 576

107. Jeffrey A. Hart, "Rival Capitalists. International Competitiveness in the United States, Japan, and Western Europe", Cornell University Press, Ithaca and London, 1992, pg 101

108. Michael Rowe, "France, Prussia, or Germany? The Napoleonic Wars and Shifting Allegiances in the Rhineland", Central European History 39 (2006), 611-640, pg 630

109. William Milligan Sloane, "The Continental System Of Napoleon", Political Science Quarterly (1886-1905); Jun 1898; XIII, 2; American Periodicals pg 0_002

110. Michael Rowe, "France, Prussia, or Germany? The Napoleonic Wars and Shifting Allegiances in the Rhineland", Central European History 39 (2006), 611-640, pg 630-631

111. Александр Подмазо, "Континентальная блокада как

экономическаяпричина войны 1812 г", http://www.museum.ru /museum/1812/Library/Podmazo2/index.html

112. Трошин Н.Н., "Континентальная блокада и Россия (к вопросу об экономических причинах Отечественной войны 1812 года)", Материалы XVI Международной научной конференции, 6–7 сентября 2010 г., Можайск, 2011, С. 278–297

113. В.Г.Сироткин, "Континентальная блокада и русская экономика (Обзор французской и советской литературы)", http:// www.reenactor.ru/ARH/PDF/Sirotkin.pdf, стр 62

114. И. В. Кузнецов, В. И. Лебедев, "Континентальная блокада и ее влияние на экономику России", Пособие для учитилей "История СССР. XVIII - середина XIX вв", Учпедгиз. Москва, 1958

115. Е. Н. Понасенков, "Континентальная система Наполеона", глава из книги «Правда о войне 1812 года», М., 2004, http://coollib .com/b/348462/read#t11

116. Трошин Н.Н., "Континентальная блокада и Россия (к вопросу об экономических причинах Отечественной войны 1812 года)", Материалы XVI Международной научной конференции, 6–7 сентября 2010 г., Можайск, 2011, стр 278–297

117. Е. Н. Понасенков, "Континентальная система Наполеона", глава из книги «Правда о войне 1812 года», М., 2004, http://coollib .com/b/348462/read#t11

118. Kevin H. O'Rourke, "War and Welfare: Britain, France and the United States 1807-14", Department of Economics and IIIS Trinity College Dublin and CEPR and NBER, February 2006, pg 8

119. Francois Crouzet, "Wars, blockade, and economic change in Europe, 1792-1815", pg 578

120. Francois Crouzet, "Wars, blockade, and economic change in Europe, 1792-1815", pg 579

121. Francois Crouzet, "Wars, blockade, and economic change in Europe, 1792-1815", pg 586

122. Francois Crouzet, "Wars, blockade, and economic change in Europe, 1792–1815", pg 582

123. Peter Mathias, "The first industrial nation. An economic history of Britain 1700–1914", Second Edition, Methuen, London and New York, pg 35

124. Hironori Asakura, "World history of the customs and tariffs", World Customs Organization, 2003, pg 223, 225,226

125. Robert O'Brien &Marc Williams, "Global political economy, evolution &dynamics", 5th edition, Palgrave, 2016, pg 8

126. Kevin H. O'Rourke, "The worldwide economic impact of the Revolutionary and Napoleonic Wars", Department of Economics and IIIS, Trinity College Dublin and CEPR and NBER, 2005, pg 13

127. Kevin H. O'Rourke, "War and Welfare: Britain, France and the United States 1807–14", Department of Economics and IIIS Trinity College Dublin and CEPR and NBER, February 2006, pg 8

128. Kevin H. O'Rourke, "The worldwide economic impact of the Revolutionary and Napoleonic Wars", Department of Economics and IIIS, Trinity College Dublin and CEPR and NBER, 2005, pg 34

129. Britannica, "The United States from 1816 to 1850", https://www.britannica.com/place/United-States/The-United-States-from-1816-to-1850

130. Immanuel Wallerstein, "The Modern World-system III. The Second Era of Great Expansion of the Capitalist World-Economy, 1730–1840s", University of California Press, Berkeley, 2011, pg 250

131. Hironori Asakura, "World history of the customs and tariffs", World Customs Organization, 2003, pg 227

132. "Tariff of 1828", United States History, http://www.u-s-history.com/pages/h268.html

133. Listen to proff Michael F. Holt, University of Virginia, http://www.gilderlehrman.org/history-by-era/national-expansion-and-reform-1815-1860

134. Hironori Asakura, "World history of the customs and tariffs", World Customs Organization, 2003, pg 235

135. Willis Fletcher Johnson, "America's Foreign Relations", Vol. 2, 1916, p. 14

136. Richardson, Heather Cox, "Greatest nation of the earth", Cambridge, Mass: Harvard University Press, 1997, p. 114

137. Hironori Asakura, "World history of the customs and tariffs", World Customs Organization, 2003, pg 236

138. "American History," "Irish and German Immigration," The Independence Hall Association, http://www.ushistory.org/us/25f.asp, accessed 29-02-2020

139. Vera Zamagni, "An Economic History of Europe Since 1700", Agenda publishing, 2017, Table 1.1, pg 2

140. S. N. Broadberry, "Technological Leadership and Productivity Leadership in Manufacturing Since the Industrial Revolution: Implications for the Convergence Debate", The Economic Journal, Vol. 104, No. 423 (Mar., 1994), pp. 298

141. S. N. Broadberry, "Technological Leadership and Productivity Leadership in Manufacturing Since the Industrial Revolution: Implications for the Convergence Debate", The Economic Journal, Vol. 104, No. 423 (Mar., 1994), pp. 299

142. "American History", "Early American Railroads", The Independence Hall Association, http://www.ushistory.org/us/25b.asp

143. "Growth of U.S. Population", http://www.theusaonline.com /people/growth.htm

144. "Growth of U.S. Population", http://www.theusaonline.com /people/growth.htm

145. "Growth of U.S. Population", http://www.theusaonline.com /people/growth.htm

146. Louis, Galambos, "State-Owned Enterprises in Hostile Environment. The U.S. Experience" in "The rise and fall of state-owned enterprise in the Western World" edited by Pier Angelo Toninelli, Cambridge university press, 2008, pg 278

147. Katherine C. Epstein," "Corrupt" Foreign Investment in

the 19th-Century United States", The American Interest, Volume 11, Number 4, January 7, 2016, pg 6, https://www.the-american-interest.com/2016/01/07/corrupt-foreign-investment-in-the-19th-century-united-states

148. Encyclopædia Britannica, https://www.britannica.com/place/United-States/Jim-Crow-legislation#toc77798

149. The Gilder Lehrman Institute of American History, http://www.gilderlehrman.org/history-by-era/essays/rise-industrial-america-1877-1900

150. "The Real Great Depression", Chronicle of Higher Education, October 17, 2008

151. Giovanni Arrighi, "Adam Smith in Beijing. Lineages of the Twenty-First Century", Verso, London-New York, 2007, pg 143

152. S. N. Broadberry, "Technological Leadership and Productivity Leadership in Manufacturing Since the Industrial Revolution: Implications for the Convergence Debate", The Economic Journal, Vol. 104, No. 423 (Mar., 1994), pg. 298

153. S. N. Broadberry, "Technological Leadership and Productivity Leadership in Manufacturing Since the Industrial Revolution: Implications for the Convergence Debate", The Economic Journal, Vol. 104, No. 423 (Mar., 1994), pg. 299

154. S. N. Broadberry, "Technological Leadership and Productivity Leadership in Manufacturing Since the Industrial Revolution: Implications for the Convergence Debate", The Economic Journal, Vol. 104, No. 423 (Mar., 1994), pg. 299

155. N.F.R. Crafts, S.J.Leybourne and T.C.Mills "Britain" in "Patterns of European Industrialization: the nineteenth century", Edited by Richard Sylla and Gianni Toniolo, 2001, Routledge, pg 122

156. N.F.R. Crafts, S.J.Leybourne and T.C.Mills "Britain" in "Patterns of European Industrialization: the nineteenth century", Edited by Richard Sylla and Gianni Toniolo, 2001, Routledge, pg 123

157. Geoffrey Jones, "Great Britain: Big business, management,

and competitiveness in twentieth-century Britain" in "Big business and the wealth of nations" edited by Alfred D. Chandler, Jr. and Tarashi Hikino, Cambridge, 1997, pg 106

158. S. N. Broadberry, "How Did the United States and Germany Overtake Britain? A Sectoral Analysis of Comparative Productivity Levels", 1870-1990, *The Journal of Economic History*, Vol. 58, No. 2 (Jun., 1998), pg 392

159. See Francis Fukuyama, "Political order and political decay: From the Industrial Revolution to the Globalization of Democracy, Farrar, Straus and Giroux, New York, pp 127-132

160. See Stuart M. Blumin, "The emergence of the middle class: social experience in the American city, 1760-1900, Cambridge: Cambridge University Press, 1989, chapters 3, 4"

161. Francis Fukuyama, "Political order and political decay", Farrar, Straus and Girdoux, New York, 2014, pg 146

162. Encyclopædia Britannica, https://www.britannica.com/place /United-States/Jacksonian-democracy

163. Francis Fukuyama, "Political order and political decay", Farrar, Straus and Girdoux, New York, 2014, pg 142

164. Francis Fukuyama, "Political order and political decay", Farrar, Straus and Girdoux, New York, 2014, pg 144

165. Francis Fukuyama, "Political order and political decay", Farrar, Straus and Girdoux, New York, 2014, pg150

166. Francis Fukuyama, Farrar, Straus and Girdoux, "Political order and political decay", New York, 2014, page 150

167. Skowronek, "Building a New American State", p. 123, quoted from Francis Fukuyama, "Political order and political decay", Farrar, Straus and Girdoux, New York, 2014, pg 166

168. The Gilder Lehrman Institute of American History, copied 2021-03-14, http://www.gilderlehrman.org/history-by-era/essays/rise -industrial-america-1877-1900

169. Francis Fukuyama, "Political order and political decay", Farrar, Straus and Girdoux, New York, 2014, pg 155

170. Francis Fukuyama, "Political order and political decay", Farrar, Straus and Girdoux, New York, 2014, pg 154

171. Louis, Galambos, "State-Owned Enterprises in Hostile Environment. The U.S. Experience" in "The rise and fall of state-owned enterprise in the Western World" edited by Pier Angelo Toninelli, Cambridge university press, 2008, pg 282

172. Louis, Galambos, "State-Owned Enterprises in Hostile Environment. The U.S. Experience" in "The rise and fall of state-owned enterprise in the Western World" edited by Pier Angelo Toninelli, Cambridge university press, 2008, pg 282, 283

173. Francis Fukuyama, "Political order and political decay", Farrar, Straus and Girdoux, New York, 2014, pg 152

174. Encyclopædia Britannica, "United States", "The public domain", https://www.britannica.com/place/United-States/The-Haymarket-Riot

175. Francis Fukuyama, "Political order and political decay", Farrar, Straus and Girdoux, New York, 2014, pg 175

176. Francis Fukuyama, "Political order and political decay", Farrar, Straus and Girdoux, New York, 2014, pg 171

177. Erik S. Reinert, "The role of the sate in economic growth" in "The rise and fall of state-owned enterprise in the Western World" edited by Pier Angelo Toninelli, Cambridge university press, 2008, pg 87

178. "Modern tariff history. Germany, United States, France", by Percy Ashley, C.B., John Murray, Albemarle street, London, W. 1, 1920, pg 276

179. John Vincent Nye, "Changing French Trade Conditions, National Welfare, and the 1860 Anglo-French Treaty of Commerce", Department of Economics, Washington University, Explorations in economic history 28, 460-477 (1991), p. 462

180. "Modern tariff history. Germany, United States, France", by Percy Ashley, C.B., John Murray, Albemarle street, London, W. 1, 1920, pg 290

181. Roger D. Price, "Napoleon III and the Second Empire", Routledge, 2002, p. 44

182. Maurice Levy-Leboyer and Michel Lescure, "France", in "Patterns of European Industrialization: the nineteenth century", Edited by Richard Sylla and Gianni Toniolo, 2001, Routledge, pg 156

183. Maurice Levy-Leboyer and Michel Lescure, "France", in "Patterns of European Industrialization: the nineteenth century", Edited by Richard Sylla and Gianni Toniolo, 2001, Routledge, pg 160

184. Percy Ashley, C.B., John Murray, "Modern tariff history. Germany, United States, France", Albemarle street, London, W. 1, 1920, pg 289, 297

185. Percy Ashley, C.B., John Murray, "Modern tariff history. Germany, United States, France", Albemarle street, London, W. 1, 1920, pg 298

186. Percy Ashley, C.B., John Murray, "Modern tariff history. Germany, United States, France", Albemarle street, London, W. 1, 1920, pg 304

187. Percy Ashley, C.B., John Murray, "Modern tariff history. Germany, United States, France", Albemarle street, London, W. 1, 1920, pg 295

188. Olivier Accominotti and Marc Flandreau, "Bilateral treaties and the most-favored-nation clause. The Myth of Trade Liberalization in the Nineteenth Century", World Politics, Vol. 60, Number 2, January 2008, Cambridge University Press, pg 153

189. Percy Ashley, C.B., John Murray, "Modern tariff history. Germany, United States, France", Albemarle street, London, W. 1, 1920, pg 301

190. Maurice Levy-Leboyer and Michel Lescure in "Patterns of European Industrialization: the nineteenth century", Edited by Richard Sylla and Gianni Toniolo, 2001, Routledge, pg 154

191. Allan Mitchell, "The great train race: railroads and the Franco-German rivalry, 1815-1914", Berghahn Books, New York-Oxford, pg 78, 79

192. John Vincent Nye, "Changing French Trade Conditions, National Welfare, and the 1860 Anglo-French Treaty of Commerce", Department of Economics, Washington University, Explorations In Economic History 28, 460-477 (1991), p. 465

193. Allan Mitchell, "The great train race: railways and the Franco-German rivalry, 1815-1914", Berghahn Books, New York-Oxford, pg 166

194. Kevin H. O'Rourke, "Tariffs and growth in the late 19th century", The Economic Journal, 110 (April), pg 474

195. Fernand Braudel, "Civilization and Capitalism, 15th-18th Century: The perspective of the world", Volume III, Harper &Row, 1984, pg 489

196. Fernand Braudel, "Civilization and Capitalism, 15th-18th Century: The perspective of the world", Volume III, Harper &Row, 1984, pg 435

197. Fernand Braudel, "Civilization and Capitalism, 15th-18th Century: The perspective of the world", Volume III, Harper &Row, 1984, pg 489

198. V.I.Pavlov. "Historical Premises for India's Transition to Capitalism", 2nd ed., 1978, p. 243, quoted from Fernand Braudel, "Civilization and Capitalism, 15th-18th Century: The perspective of the world", Volume III, Harper &Row, 1984, pg 496

199. Mariana Mazzucato, "The Entrepreneurial state. Debunking Public vs. Private Sector Myths", Anthem Press, 2014

200. Alfred D. Chandler, Jr., "The United States: Engines of Economic growth in the capital-intensive and knowledge-intensive industries" in "Big business and the wealth of nations" edited by Alfred D. Chandler, Jr. and Tarashi Hikino, Cambridge, 1997, pg 68

201. Alfred D. Chandler, Jr. and Tarashi Hikino, "The large industrial enterprise and the dynamics of modern economic growth" in "Big business and the wealth of nations" edited by Alfred D. Chandler, Jr. Chandler, Jr. and Tarashi Hikino, Cambridge, 1997, pg 26

202. Alfred D. Chandler, Jr. and Tarashi Hikino, "The large

industrial enterprise and the dynamics of modern economic growth" in "Big business and the wealth of nations" edited by Alfred D. Chandler, Jr. Chandler, Jr. and Tarashi Hikino, Cambridge, 1997, pg 36

203. Alfred D. Chandler, Jr., "The United States: Engines of Economic growth in the capital-intensive and knowledge-intensive industries" in "Big business and the wealth of nations" edited by Alfred D. Chandler, Jr. and Tarashi Hikino, Cambridge, 1997, pg 72

204. Alfred D. Chandler, Jr., "The United States: Engines of Economic growth in the capital-intensive and knowledge-intensive industries" in "Big business and the wealth of nations" edited by Alfred D. Chandler, Jr. and Tarashi Hikino, Cambridge, 1997, pg 74

205. Vera Zamagni, "An Economic History of Europe Since 1700", Agenda publishing, 2017, pg 74

206. Vera Zamagni, "An Economic History of Europe Since 1700", Agenda publishing, 2017, pg 76

207. "Внешняя торговля России в XIX в.", джерело: "Краткая история российской экономики. Учебное пособие.2-е доп. изд. под ред. проф. Ю.П. Филякина — М.: Меридиан, 2007" http://21biz.ru /vneshnyaya-torgovlya-rossii-v-xix-v

208. Olga Crisp, "Russia", in "Patterns of European Industrialization: the nineteenth century", Edited by Richard Sylla and Gianni Toniolo, 2001, Routledge, pg 260

209. Внешняя торговля России в XIX в.", джерело: "Краткая история российской экономики. Учебное пособие.2-е доп. изд. под ред. проф. Ю.П. Филякина, М.: Меридиан, 2007" http://21biz.ru /vneshnyaya-torgovlya-rossii-v-xix-v

210. Внешняя торговля России в XIX в.", джерело: "Краткая история российской экономики. Учебное пособие.2-е доп. изд. под ред. проф. Ю.П. Филякина, М.: Меридиан, 2007" http://21biz.ru /vneshnyaya-torgovlya-rossii-v-xix-v

211. Vera Zamagni, "An Economic History of Europe Since 1700", Agenda publishing, 2017, pg 77

212. Richard Sylla and Gianni Toniolo, "Introduction: patterns of European industrialization during the nineteenth century", in "Patterns of European Industrialization: the nineteenth century", Edited by Richard Sylla and Gianni Toniolo, 2001, Routledge, pg 115

213. Olga Crisp, "Russia", in "Patterns of European Industrialization: the nineteenth century", Edited by Richard Sylla and Gianni Toniolo, 2001, Routledge, pg 263

214. Zamagni, "An Economic History of Europe Since 1700", Agenda publishing, 2017, pg 74

215. Paul R. Gregory, "The role of the state in promoting economic development: the Russian case and its general implications", in "Patterns of European Industrialization: the nineteenth century", Edited by Richard Sylla and Gianni Toniolo, 2001, Routledge, pg 73

216. Oscar Sanchez-Sibony, "Red Globalization. The Political Economy of the Soviet Cold War from Stalin to Khrushchev", Cambridge University Press, 2014, pg 30

217. Aleksandr V. Gevorkyan, "Transition Economies. Transformation, Development, and Society in Eastern Europe and the Former Soviet Union", Routledge, London and New York, 2018, pg 40

218. Marcus Ramirez, "The Meiji Secret: The Emergence of Zaibatsu Dominance in Japan", Journal of Student Research, University of Wisconsin, 2019 pg 79

219. Peter N. Stearns, "The industrial revolution in world history", Westview Press, 3rd ed., стр 143

220. Peter N. Stearns, "The industrial revolution in world history", Westview Press, 3rd ed., стр 145

221. Marcus Ramirez, "The Meiji Secret: The Emergence of Zaibatsu Dominance in Japan", Journal of Student Research, University of Wisconsin, 2019 pg 82

222. Peter N. Stearns, "The industrial revolution in world history", Westview Press, 3rd ed., стр 153

223. Marcus Ramirez, "The Meiji Secret: The Emergence of

Zaibatsu Dominance in Japan", Journal of Student Research, University of Wisconsin, 2019 pg 84

224. Peter Mathias, "The first industrial nation, an economic history of Britain 1700-1914", Second Edition, Methuen &Co, 1983, pg 229

225. Peter Mathias, "The first industrial nation, an economic history of Britain 1700-1914", Second Edition, Methuen &Co, 1983, pg 282

226. Peter Hugill, "World Trade since 1431: Geography, Technology and Capitalism, Baltimore, MD: The Johns Hopkins University Press, 1993, pg 305. Quoted in Giovanni Arrighi, "The Long Twentieth Century. Money, Power and the Origins of our Times", Verso, London, New York, 2010, pp. 294

227. Peter Mathias, "The first industrial nation, an economic history of Britain 1700-1914", Second Edition, Methuen &Co, 1983, pg 270

228. Geoffrey Jones, "Great Britain: Big business, management, and competitiveness in twentieth-century Britain" in "Big business and the wealth of nations" edited by Alfred D. Chandler, Jr. and Tarashi Hikino, Cambridge, 1997, pg 105

229. Peter Mathias, "The first industrial nation, an economic history of Britain 1700-1914", Second Edition, Methuen &Co, 1983, pg 373

230. Peter Mathias, "The first industrial nation, an economic history of Britain 1700-1914", Second Edition, Methuen &Co, 1983, pg 229

231. Giovanni Arrighi, "The Long Twentieth Century. Money, Power and the Origins of our Times", Verso, London, New York, 2010, pg. 278

232. Giovanni Arrighi, "The Long Twentieth Century. Money, Power and the Origins of our Times", Verso, London, New York, 2010, pp. 278-279

233. Alfred D. Chandler, Jr. and Tarashi Hikino, "The large industrial enterprise and the dynamics of modern economic growth" in "Big business and the wealth of nations" edited by Alfred D. Chandler, Jr. Chandler, Jr. and Tarashi Hikino, Cambridge, 1997, pg 31

234. Alfred D. Chandler, Jr. and Tarashi Hikino, "The large industrial enterprise and the dynamics of modern economic growth" in "Big

business and the wealth of nations" edited by Alfred D. Chandler, Jr. Chandler, Jr. and Tarashi Hikino, Cambridge, 1997, pg 34

235. Vera Zamagni, "An Economic History of Europe Since 1700", Agenda publishing, 2017, pg 74

236. Andrei Yu. Yudanov, "USSR: Large enterprises in the USSR—the functional disorder" in "Big business and the wealth of nations" edited by Alfred D. Chandler, Jr. and Tarashi Hikino, Cambridge, 1997, pg 397

237. В.И.Ленин, "Полное собрание сочинений", Издание пятое, Издательство политической литературы, Москва, 1970, с 341

238. В.И.Ленин, "Полное собрание сочинений", Издание пятое, Издательство политической литературы, Москва, 1970, с 116

239. Aleksandr V. Gevorkyan, "Transition Economies. Transformation, Development, and Society in Eastern Europe and the Former Soviet Union", Routledge, London and New York, 2018, pg 45

240. Andrei Yu. Yudanov, "USSR: Large enterprises in the USSR—the functional disorder" in "Big business and the wealth of nations" edited by Alfred D. Chandler, Jr. and Tarashi Hikino, Cambridge, 1997, pg 399

241. Andrei Yu. Yudanov, "USSR: Large enterprises in the USSR—the functional disorder" in "Big business and the wealth of nations" edited by Alfred D. Chandler, Jr. and Tarashi Hikino, Cambridge, 1997, pg 397

242. Oscar Sanchez-Sibony, "Red Globalization. The Political Economy of the Soviet Cold War from Stalin to Khrushchev", Cambridge University Press, 2014, chapter "Depression Stalinism"

243. Odd Arne Westad, "The Global Cold War, Third World Interventions and the Making of Our Times", Cambridge University press, 2007, pg 54

244. See Mark Harrison, Soviet Planning in Peace and War, 1938-1945, Cambridge, Cambridge University Press, 1985, pg 163.

245. Aleksandr V. Gevorkyan, "Transition Economies. Transformation, Development, and Society in Eastern Europe and the Former Soviet Union", Routledge, London and New York, 2018, pg 55

246. Paul R. Gregory and Robert C. Stuart, "Soviet Economic Structure and Performance", New York, Harper & Row, 1990, pg 121

247. Aleksandr V. Gevorkyan, "Transition Economies. Transformation, Development, and Society in Eastern Europe and the Former Soviet Union", Routledge, London and New York, 2018, pp 54, 55

248. Andrei Yu. Yudanov, "USSR: Large enterprises in the USSR— the functional disorder" in "Big business and the wealth of nations" edited by Alfred D. Chandler, Jr. and Tarashi Hikino, Cambridge, 1997, pg 403

249. Aleksandr V. Gevorkyan, "Transition Economies. Transformation, Development, and Society in Eastern Europe and the Former Soviet Union", Routledge, London and New York, 2018, pg 49

250. Aleksandr V. Gevorkyan, "Transition Economies. Transformation, Development, and Society in Eastern Europe and the Former Soviet Union", Routledge, London and New York, 2018, pg 56

251. Aleksandr V. Gevorkyan, "Transition Economies. Transformation, Development, and Society in Eastern Europe and the Former Soviet Union", Routledge, London and New York, 2018, pg 58

252. Oscar Sanchez-Sibony, "Red Globalization. The Political Economy of the Soviet Cold War from Stalin to Khrushchev", Cambridge University Press, 2014, pg 60,61

253. Vera Zamagni, "An Economic History of Europe Since 1700", Agenda publishing, 2017, pg 194

254. Oscar Sanchez-Sibony, "Red Globalization. The Political Economy of the Soviet Cold War from Stalin to Khrushchev", Cambridge University Press, 2014, pg 153

255. Peter Mathias, "The first industrial nation, an economic history of Britain 1700-1914", Second Edition, Methuen &Co, 1983, pg 384

256. Robert Millward. "State enterprise in Britain in the twentieth century" in "The rise and fall of state-owned enterprise in the Western World" edited by Pier Angelo Toninelli, Cambridge university press, 2008, pg 159

257. Robert Millward. "State enterprise in Britain in the twentieth century" in "The rise and fall of state-owned enterprise in the Western World" edited by Pier Angelo Toninelli, Cambridge university press, 2008, pg 165

258. Peter Mathias, "The first industrial nation, an economic history of Britain 1700-1914", Second Edition, Methuen &Co, 1983, pg 406

259. Geoffrey Jones, "Great Britain: Big business, management, and competitiveness in twentieth-century Britain" in "Big business and the wealth of nations" edited by Alfred D. Chandler, Jr. and Tarashi Hikino, Cambridge, 1997, pg 104

260. William N. Parker, "Europe in an American mirror: reflections on industrialization and ideology" in "Patterns of European Industrialization: the nineteenth century", Edited by Richard Sylla and Gianni Toniolo, 2001, Routledge, pg 83

261. Robert O'Brien &Marc Williams, "Global Political Economy, Evolution &Dynamics", 5th edition, Palgrave, 2016, pg 23

262. Encyclopædia Britannica, "New Deal", https://www.britannica.com/event/New-Deal/

263. Encyclopædia Britannica, "Works Progress Administration", https://www.britannica.com/topic/Works-Progress-Administration

264. Encyclopædia Britannica, "Civilian Conservation Corps", https://www.britannica.com/topic/Civilian-Conservation-Corps

265. Louis, Galambos, "State-Owned Enterprises in Hostile Environment. The U.S. Experience" in "The rise and fall of state-owned enterprise in the Western World" edited by Pier Angelo Toninelli, Cambridge university press, 2008, pg 285

266. Louis, Galambos, "State-Owned Enterprises in Hostile Environment. The U.S. Experience" in "The rise and fall of state-owned enterprise in the Western World" edited by Pier Angelo Toninelli, Cambridge university press, 2008, pg 296

267. see Robert H. Bates, "Prosperity and violence. The political economy of development", W.W.Norton &Company, 2010

268. see Alfred D. Chandler, Jr, "The United States" in "Big business and the wealth of nations" edited by Alfred D. Chandler, Jr. and Tarashi Hikino, Cambridge, 1997

269. Louis, Galambos, "State-Owned Enterprises in Hostile Environment. The U.S. Experience" in "The rise and fall of state-owned enterprise in the Western World" edited by Pier Angelo Toninelli, Cambridge university press, 2008, pg 286

270. Ann-Marie Burley, "Regulating The World: Multilateralism, International law, and the projection of the New deal regulatory State", in Giovanni Arrighi, "Adam Smith in Beijing. Lineages of the Twenty-First Century", Verso, London-New York, 2007, pg 151,152

271. Alfred D. Chandler, Jr. and Tarashi Hikino, "The large industrial enterprise and the dynamics of modern economic growth" in "Big business and the wealth of nations" edited by Alfred D. Chandler, Jr. Chandler, Jr. and Tarashi Hikino, Cambridge, 1997, pg 29

272. John Kenneth Galbraith, "The New Industrial State", Second Edition, Penguin Books, 1972, pg 49

273. Andrew Hacker, "A Country Called Corporate America", New York Times Magazine, July 3, 1966, quoted from John Kenneth Galbraith, "The New Industrial State", Second Edition, Penguin Books, 1972, pg 210

274. John Kenneth Galbraith, "The New Industrial State", Second Edition, Penguin Books, 1972, pg 18

275. John Kenneth Galbraith, "The New Industrial State", Second Edition, Penguin Books, 1972, pg 22

276. see "Table 4-20: Energy Intensity of Passenger Modes". Bureau of Transportation Statistics. Archived from the original on October 7, 2010. Retrieved October 25, 2010

277. Louis, Galambos, "State-Owned Enterprises in Hostile Environment. The U.S. Experience" in "The rise and fall of state-owned enterprise in the Western World" edited by Pier Angelo Toninelli, Cambridge university press, 2008, pg 289

278. Jeffrey A. Hart, "Rival Capitalists. International Competitiveness in the United States, Japan, and Western Europe", Cornell University Press, Ithaca and London, 1992, see the chapter on the United States

279. Aleksandr V. Gevorkyan, "Transition Economies. Transformation, Development, and Society in Eastern Europe and the Former Soviet Union", Routledge, London and New York, 2018, pg 59

280. Aleksandr V. Gevorkyan, "Transition Economies. Transformation, Development, and Society in Eastern Europe and the Former Soviet Union", Routledge, London and New York, 2018, pg 61

281. Aleksandr V. Gevorkyan, "Transition Economies. Transformation, Development, and Society in Eastern Europe and the Former Soviet Union", Routledge, London and New York, 2018, pg 65

282. Aleksandr V. Gevorkyan, "Transition Economies. Transformation, Development, and Society in Eastern Europe and the Former Soviet Union", Routledge, London and New York, 2018, pg 62

283. Andrei Yu. Yudanov, "USSR: Large enterprises in the USSR—the functional disorder" in "Big business and the wealth of nations" edited by Alfred D. Chandler, Jr. and Tarashi Hikino, Cambridge, 1997, pg 407

284. Andrei Yu. Yudanov, "USSR: Large enterprises in the USSR—the functional disorder" in "Big business and the wealth of nations" edited by Alfred D. Chandler, Jr. and Tarashi Hikino, Cambridge, 1997, pg 411

285. Andrei Yu. Yudanov, "USSR: Large enterprises in the USSR—the functional disorder" in "Big business and the wealth of nations" edited by Alfred D. Chandler, Jr. and Tarashi Hikino, Cambridge, 1997, pg 408

286. Andrei Yu. Yudanov, "USSR: Large enterprises in the USSR—the functional disorder" in "Big business and the wealth of nations" edited by Alfred D. Chandler, Jr. and Tarashi Hikino, Cambridge, 1997, pg 417

287. Oscar Sanchez-Sibony, "Red Globalization. The Political Economy of the Soviet Cold War from Stalin to Khrushchev", Cambridge University Press, 2014, pg 91

288. Oscar Sanchez-Sibony, "Red Globalization. The Political Economy

of the Soviet Cold War from Stalin to Khrushchev", Cambridge University Press, 2014, pg 117

289. Oscar Sanchez-Sibony, "Red Globalization. The Political Economy of the Soviet Cold War from Stalin to Khrushchev", Cambridge University Press, 2014, pg 118

290. Oscar Sanchez-Sibony, "Red Globalization. The Political Economy of the Soviet Cold War from Stalin to Khrushchev", Cambridge University Press, 2014, pp 178, 179

291. Oscar Sanchez-Sibony, "Red Globalization. The Political Economy of the Soviet Cold War from Stalin to Khrushchev", Cambridge University Press, 2014, pp 135, 136

292. Odd Arne Westad, "The Global Cold War, Third World Interventions and the Making of Our Times", Cambridge University press, 2007, pg 51

293. Oscar Sanchez-Sibony, "Red Globalization. The Political Economy of the Soviet Cold War from Stalin to Khrushchev", Cambridge University Press, 2014, pg 242

294. Oscar Sanchez-Sibony, "Red Globalization. The Political Economy of the Soviet Cold War from Stalin to Khrushchev", Cambridge University Press, 2014, pp 130, 131

295. Oscar Sanchez-Sibony, "Red Globalization. The Political Economy of the Soviet Cold War from Stalin to Khrushchev", Cambridge University Press, 2014, pg 149

296. Oscar Sanchez-Sibony, "Red Globalization. The Political Economy of the Soviet Cold War from Stalin to Khrushchev", Cambridge University Press, 2014, pg 181

297. see for example Oscar Sanchez-Sibony, "Red Globalization. The Political Economy of the Soviet Cold War from Stalin to Khrushchev", Cambridge University Press, 2014, pg 166

298. Odd Arne Westad, "The Global Cold War, Third World Interventions and the Making of Our Times", Cambridge University press, 2007, pg 53

299. Odd Arne Westad, "The Global Cold War, Third World Interventions and the Making of Our Times", Cambridge University press, 2007, pg 63

300. Odd Arne Westad, "The Global Cold War, Third World Interventions and the Making of Our Times", Cambridge University press, 2007, pg 53

301. Odd Arne Westad, "The Global Cold War, Third World Interventions and the Making of Our Times", Cambridge University press, 2007, pg 65

302. Sergei Goncharenko, "Sino-Soviet Military Cooperation", in Odd Arne Westad (Editor) "Brothers in Arms: The Rise and Fall of the Sino-Soviet Alliance, 1945-1963", Stanford Univ Pr, 1998, pp 144-147

303. Sergei Goncharenko, "Sino-Soviet Military Cooperation", in Odd Arne Westad (Editor) "Brothers in Arms: The Rise and Fall of the Sino-Soviet Alliance, 1945-1963", Stanford Univ Pr, 1998, pp 147, 148

304. Sergei Goncharenko, "Sino-Soviet Military Cooperation", in Odd Arne Westad (Editor) "Brothers in Arms: The Rise and Fall of the Sino-Soviet Alliance, 1945-1963", Stanford Univ Pr, 1998, pg 157

305. Shu Guang Zhang, "Sino Soviet Economic Cooperation", in Odd Arne Westad (Editor) "Brothers in Arms: The Rise and Fall of the Sino-Soviet Alliance, 1945-1963", Stanford Univ Pr, 1998, pg 202

306. Sergei Goncharenko, "Sino-Soviet Military Cooperation", in Odd Arne Westad (Editor) "Brothers in Arms: The Rise and Fall of the Sino-Soviet Alliance, 1945-1963", Stanford Univ Pr, 1998, pg 160

307. Odd Arne Westad, "The Global Cold War, Third World Interventions and the Making of Our Times", Cambridge University press, 2007, pg 25

308. Franz Schurmann, "The Logic of World Power: An Inquiry into the Origins, Currents, and Contradictions of World Politics", New York, Pantheon, 1974, pg 67 in Giovanni Arrighi, "Adam Smith in Beijing. Lineages of the Twenty-First Century", Verso, London-New York, 2007, pg 252

309. Oscar Sanchez-Sibony, "Red Globalization. The Political Economy of the Soviet Cold War from Stalin to Khrushchev", Cambridge University Press, 2014, pp 64, 65

310. Odd Arne Westad, "The Global Cold War, Third World Interventions and the Making of Our Times", Cambridge University press, 2007, pg 29, 30

311. Odd Arne Westad, "The Global Cold War, Third World Interventions and the Making of Our Times", Cambridge University press, 2007, pp 31, 32

312. Odd Arne Westad, "The Global Cold War, Third World Interventions and the Making of Our Times", Cambridge University press, 2007, pg 27

313. Aleksandr V. Gevorkyan, "Transition Economies. Transformation, Development, and Society in Eastern Europe and the Former Soviet Union", Routledge, London and New York, 2018, pg 83

314. Aleksandr V. Gevorkyan, "Transition Economies. Transformation, Development, and Society in Eastern Europe and the Former Soviet Union", Routledge, London and New York, 2018, pg 86

315. Aleksandr V. Gevorkyan, "Transition Economies. Transformation, Development, and Society in Eastern Europe and the Former Soviet Union", Routledge, London and New York, 2018, pg 87

316. Phyllis Deane, "The first industrial revolution", Cambridge University Press, 1979, pg 235

317. Robert Wase, "Governing the Market, Economic theory and the Role of Government in East Asian Industrialization", Princeton University Press, 1990, pg 231

318. Shu Guang Zhang, "Sino Soviet Economic Cooperation", in Odd Arne Westad (Editor) "Brothers in Arms: The Rise and Fall of the Sino-Soviet Alliance, 1945-1963", Stanford Univ Pr, 1998, pg 205

319. Shu Guang Zhang, "Sino Soviet Economic Cooperation", in Odd Arne Westad (Editor) "Brothers in Arms: The Rise and Fall of the Sino-Soviet Alliance, 1945-1963", Stanford Univ Pr, 1998, pg 206

320. Shu Guang Zhang, "Sino Soviet Economic Cooperation", in Odd Arne Westad (Editor) "Brothers in Arms: The Rise and Fall of the Sino-Soviet Alliance, 1945-1963", Stanford Univ Pr, 1998, pp 196, 197

321. Sergei Goncharenko, "Sino-Soviet Military Cooperation", in Odd Arne Westad (Editor) "Brothers in Arms: The Rise and Fall of the Sino-Soviet Alliance, 1945-1963", Stanford Univ Pr, 1998, pg 157

322. Shu Guang Zhang, "Sino Soviet Economic Cooperation", in Odd Arne Westad (Editor) "Brothers in Arms: The Rise and Fall of the Sino-Soviet Alliance, 1945-1963", Stanford Univ Pr, 1998, pg 212

323. Shu Guang Zhang, "Sino Soviet Economic Cooperation", in Odd Arne Westad (Editor) "Brothers in Arms: The Rise and Fall of the Sino-Soviet Alliance, 1945-1963", Stanford Univ Pr, 1998, pg 213

324. Shu Guang Zhang, "Sino Soviet Economic Cooperation", in Odd Arne Westad (Editor) "Brothers in Arms: The Rise and Fall of the Sino-Soviet Alliance, 1945-1963", Stanford Univ Pr, 1998, pg 214

325. Louis, Galambos, "State-Owned Enterprises in Hostile Environment. The U.S. Experience" in "The rise and fall of state-owned enterprise in the Western World" edited by Pier Angelo Toninelli, Cambridge university press, 2008, pg 295

326. Francois Bafoil, "Emerging capitalism in Central Europe and Southeast Asia", Palgrave Macmillan, 2014, pg 110

327. Francois Bafoil, "Emerging capitalism in Central Europe and Southeast Asia", Palgrave Macmillan, 2014, pg 111

328. Francois Bafoil, "Emerging capitalism in Central Europe and Southeast Asia", Palgrave Macmillan, 2014, pg 119

329. Francois Bafoil, "Emerging capitalism in Central Europe and Southeast Asia", Palgrave Macmillan, 2014, pg 205

330. Aleksandr V. Gevorkyan, "Transition Economies. Transformation, Development, and Society in Eastern Europe and the Former Soviet Union", Routledge, London and New York, 2018, pg 141

331. Shuichi Ikemoto, "Corporate restructuring, foreign direct

investment, and Japanese multinationals in the Czech Republic", in (edited by Bruno Dallage and Ichiro Iwasaki), "Corporate restructuring and governance in transition economies", Palgrave Macmillan, 2007, pp 114, 115

332. Shuichi Ikemoto, "Corporate restructuring, foreign direct investment, and Japanese multinationals in the Czech Republic", in (edited by Bruno Dallage and Ichiro Iwasaki), "Corporate restructuring and governance in transition economies", Palgrave Macmillan, 2007, pp 108,109

333. Oscar Sanchez-Sibony, "Red Globalization. The Political Economy of the Soviet Cold War from Stalin to Khrushchev", Cambridge University Press, 2014, pg69, 70

334. Oscar Sanchez-Sibony, "Red Globalization. The Political Economy of the Soviet Cold War from Stalin to Khrushchev", Cambridge University Press, 2014, pg 95

335. Francois Bafoil, "Emerging capitalism in Central Europe and Southeast Asia", Palgrave Macmillan, 2014, pg 149

336. Francois Bafoil, "Emerging capitalism in Central Europe and Southeast Asia", Palgrave Macmillan, 2014, pg 150

337. AleksandrV. Gevorkyan, "Transition Economies. Transformation, Development, and Society in Eastern Europe and the Former Soviet Union", Routledge, London and New York, 2018, pg 129

338. AleksandrV. Gevorkyan, "Transition Economies. Transformation, Development, and Society in Eastern Europe and the Former Soviet Union", Routledge, London and New York, 2018, pg 232

339. Francois Bafoil, "Emerging capitalism in Central Europe and Southeast Asia", Palgrave Macmillan, 2014, pg 136

340. Francois Bafoil, "Emerging capitalism in Central Europe and Southeast Asia", Palgrave Macmillan, 2014, pg 172

341. Krisztina Than and Jason Hovet, "Auto industry set to put brakes on central Europe's COVID-19 recovery ", Reuters, 2020-07-30, https://www.msn.com/en-ca/money/topstories/auto-industry-set-to

-put-brakes-on-central-europe-s-covid-19-recovery/ar-BB17m5QT?ocid
=msedgdhp, (copied 2020-07-30)

342. Francois Bafoil, "Emerging capitalism in Central Europe and Southeast Asia", Palgrave Macmillan, 2014, pg 137

343. see Jeffrey A. Hart, "Rival Capitalists. International Competitiveness in the United States, Japan, and Western Europe", Cornell University Press, Ithaca, and London, 1992, especially the sections on France

344. see Aleksandr V. Gevorkyan, "Transition Economies. Transfo rmation, Development, and Society in Eastern Europe and the Former Soviet Union", Routledge, London and New York, 2018

345. Robert Wase, "Governing the Market, Economic theory and the Role of Government in East Asian Industrialization", Princeton University Press, 1990, pg 281

346. Stephan Haggard and Yasheng Huang, "The Political Economy of Private-Sector Development in China" in Loren Brandt and Thomas G. Rawski, "China's Great Economic Transformation", Cambridge University Press, 2008, pg 369

347. Stephan Haggard and Yasheng Huang, "The Political Economy of Private-Sector Development in China" in Loren Brandt and Thomas G. Rawski, "China's Great Economic Transformation", Cambridge University Press, 2008, pg 370

348. Stephan Haggard and Yasheng Huang, "The Political Economy of Private-Sector Development in China" in Loren Brandt and Thomas G. Rawski, "China's Great Economic Transformation", Cambridge University Press, 2008, pg 369

349. Robert Wase, "Governing the Market, Economic theory and the Role of Government in East Asian Industrialization", Princeton University Press, 1990, pg 180

350. Robert Wase, "Governing the Market, Economic theory and the Role of Government in East Asian Industrialization", Princeton University Press, 1990, pg 295

351. Robert Wase, "Governing the Market, Economic theory and

the Role of Government in East Asian Industrialization", Princeton University Press, 1990, pg 321

352. Robert Wase, "Governing the Market, Economic theory and the Role of Government in East Asian Industrialization", Princeton University Press, 1990, pg 268, 269

353. Robert Wase, "Governing the Market, Economic theory and the Role of Government in East Asian Industrialization", Princeton University Press, 1990, pg 294

354. Stephan Haggard and Yasheng Huang, "The Political Economy of Private-Sector Development in China" in Loren Brandt and Thomas G. Rawski, "China's Great Economic Transformation", Cambridge University Press, 2008, pg.364

355. Lucien Ellington, Tawni Hunt Ferrarini, "Why Do Some Nations Prosper? The Case of North and South Korea", Foreign Policy Research Institute, 26-04-2017, https://www.fpri.org/article/2017/04/nations-prosper-case-north-south-korea

356. Lucien Ellington, Tawni Hunt Ferrarini, "Why Do Some Nations Prosper? The Case of North and South Korea", Foreign Policy Research Institute, 26-04-2017, https://www.fpri.org/article/2017/04/nations-prosper-case-north-south-korea

357. Stephan Haggard and Yasheng Huang, "The Political Economy of Private-Sector Development in China" in Loren Brandt and Thomas G. Rawski, "China's Great Economic Transformation", Cambridge University Press, 2008, pg 364, 367

358. Stephan Haggard and Yasheng Huang, "The Political Economy of Private-Sector Development in China" in Loren Brandt and Thomas G. Rawski, "China's Great Economic Transformation", Cambridge University Press, 2008, pg 366

359. Stephan Haggard and Yasheng Huang, "The Political Economy of Private-Sector Development in China" in Loren Brandt and Thomas G. Rawski, "China's Great Economic Transformation", Cambridge University Press, 2008, pg 364, 367

360. Robert Wase, "Governing the Market, Economic theory and the Role of Government in East Asian Industrialization", Princeton University Press, 1990, pg 244

361. Robert Wase, "Governing the Market, Economic theory and the Role of Government in East Asian Industrialization", Princeton University Press, 1990, pg 307

362. Robert Wase, "Governing the Market, Economic theory and the Role of Government in East Asian Industrialization", Princeton University Press, 1990, pg 308

363. Lucien Ellington, Tawni Hunt Ferrarini, "Why Do Some Nations Prosper? The Case of North and South Korea", Foreign Policy Research Institute, 26-04-2017, https://www.fpri.org/article/2017/04/nations-prosper-case-north-south-korea

364. Robert Wase, "Governing the Market, Economic theory and the Role of Government in East Asian Industrialization", Princeton University Press, 1990, pg 319

365. Robert Wase, "Governing the Market, Economic theory and the Role of Government in East Asian Industrialization", Princeton University Press, 1990, pg 310

366. Robert Wase, "Governing the Market, Economic theory and the Role of Government in East Asian Industrialization", Princeton University Press, 1990, pg 311

367. Robert Wase, "Governing the Market, Economic theory and the Role of Government in East Asian Industrialization", Princeton University Press, 1990, pg 313

368. Robert Wase, "Governing the Market, Economic theory and the Role of Government in East Asian Industrialization", Princeton University Press, 1990, pg 234

369. Robert Wase, "Governing the Market, Economic theory and the Role of Government in East Asian Industrialization", Princeton University Press, 1990, pg 71

370. Robert Wase, "Governing the Market, Economic theory and

the Role of Government in East Asian Industrialization", Princeton University Press, 1990, pg 78

371. Robert Wase, "Governing the Market, Economic theory and the Role of Government in East Asian Industrialization", Princeton University Press, 1990, pg 82

372. Stephan Haggard and Yasheng Huang, "The Political Economy of Private-Sector Development in China" in Loren Brandt and Thomas G. Rawski, "China's Great Economic Transformation", Cambridge University Press, 2008, pg. 365

373. Robert Wase, "Governing the Market, Economic theory and the Role of Government in East Asian Industrialization", Princeton University Press, 1990, pg 94

374. Robert Wase, "Governing the Market, Economic theory and the Role of Government in East Asian Industrialization", Princeton University Press, 1990, pg 96, 97

375. Stephan Haggard and Yasheng Huang, "The Political Economy of Private-Sector Development in China" in Loren Brandt and Thomas G. Rawski, "China's Great Economic Transformation", Cambridge University Press, 2008, pg. 364, 365

376. Robert Wase, "Governing the Market, Economic theory and the Role of Government in East Asian Industrialization", Princeton University Press, 1990, pg 98

377. Robert Wase, "Governing the Market, Economic theory and the Role of Government in East Asian Industrialization", Princeton University Press, 1990, pg 104

378. Robert Wase, "Governing the Market, Economic theory and the Role of Government in East Asian Industrialization", Princeton University Press, 1990, pg 107

379. Robert Wase, "Governing the Market, Economic theory and the Role of Government in East Asian Industrialization", Princeton University Press, 1990, pg 275, 276

380. Robert Wase, "Governing the Market, Economic theory and

the Role of Government in East Asian Industrialization", Princeton University Press, 1990, pg 178

381. Stephan Haggard and Yasheng Huang, "The Political Economy of Private-Sector Development in China" in Loren Brandt and Thomas G. Rawski, "China's Great Economic Transformation", Cambridge University Press, 2008, pg. 365

382. see Woo, Jung-en. 1991. Race to the Swift: State and Finance in Korean Industrialization. New York: Cornell University Press та Kang, David. 2002. Crony Capitalism: Corruption and Development in South Korea and the Philippines. Cambridge and New York: Cambridge University Press

383. Stephan Haggard and Yasheng Huang, "The Political Economy of Private-Sector Development in China" in Loren Brandt and Thomas G. Rawski, "China's Great Economic Transformation", Cambridge University Press, 2008, pg. 367

384. Lucien Ellington, Tawni Hunt Ferrarini, "Why Do Some Nations Prosper? The Case of North and South Korea", Foreign Policy Research Institute, 26-04-2017, https://www.fpri.org/article/2017/04/nations-prosper-case-north-south-korea

385. Bardhan, P.K. "The political economy of development in India", Oxford: Blackwell, 1984, pg 72, 73 quoted from Peter Nolan, "China's rise, Russia's fall", St. Martin's Press, New York, 1995, pg 65,66

386. PeterNolan, "China's rise, Russia's fall", St. Martin's Press, NewYork, 1995, pg 66

387. Francois Bafoil, "Emerging capitalism in Central Europe and Southeast Asia", Palgrave Macmillan, 2014, pg 65

388. Francois Bafoil, "Emerging capitalism in Central Europe and Southeast Asia", Palgrave Macmillan, 2014, pg 71

389. Francois Bafoil, "Emerging capitalism in Central Europe and Southeast Asia", Palgrave Macmillan, 2014, pg 72, 75

390. Francois Bafoil, "Emerging capitalism in Central Europe and Southeast Asia", Palgrave Macmillan, 2014, pg 75

391. Francois Bafoil, "Emerging capitalism in Central Europe and Southeast Asia", Palgrave Macmillan, 2014, pg 72

392. Francois Bafoil, "Emerging capitalism in Central Europe and Southeast Asia", Palgrave Macmillan, 2014, pg 73

393. Garry Rodan, "Consultative Authoritarianism and Regime Change Analysis. Implication of the Singapore case", 2012, Routledge Handbook of Southeast Asian Politics, New York and London: Routledge, pg 122, quoted in Francois Bafoil, "Emerging capitalism in Central Europe and Southeast Asia", Palgrave Macmillan, 2014, pg 74

394. Francois Bafoil, "Emerging capitalism in Central Europe and Southeast Asia", Palgrave Macmillan, 2014, pg 73

395. Francois Bafoil, "Emerging capitalism in Central Europe and Southeast Asia", Palgrave Macmillan, 2014, pg 73,74

396. Pier Angelo Toninelli, "The rise and fall of public enterprise. The framework" in "The rise and fall of state-owned enterprise in the Western World" edited by Pier Angelo Toninelli, Cambridge university press, 2008, pg 4

397. Pier Angelo Toninelli, "The rise and fall of public enterprise. The framework" in "The rise and fall of state-owned enterprise in the Western World" edited by Pier Angelo Toninelli, Cambridge university press, 2008, pg 19

398. Pier Angelo Toninelli, "The rise and fall of public enterprise. The framework" in "The rise and fall of state-owned enterprise in the Western World" edited by Pier Angelo Toninelli, Cambridge university press, 2008, pg 9

399. Peter N. Stearns, "The Industrial Revolution in World History", Third Edition, 2007, Westview Press 255

400. Pier Angelo Toninelli, "The rise and fall of public enterprise. The framework" in "The rise and fall of state-owned enterprise in the Western World" edited by Pier Angelo Toninelli, Cambridge university press, 2008, pg 21, 22

401. Peter Nolan, "China's rise, Russia's fall", St. Martin's Press, New York, 1995, pg 185

402. Peter Nolan, "China's rise, Russia's fall", St. Martin's Press, New York, 1995, pg 190

403. Peter Nolan, "China's rise, Russia's fall", St. Martin's Press, New York, 1995, pg 189

404. Stephan Haggard and Yasheng Huang, "The Political Economy of Private-Sector Development in China" in Loren Brandt and Thomas G. Rawski, "China's Great Economic Transformation", Cambridge University Press, 2008, pg. 342

405. Barry Naughton, "A Political Economy of China's Economic Transition" in Loren Brandt and Thomas G. Rawski, "China's great economic transformation", Cambridge University Press, 2008, pg 107

406. Barry Naughton, "A Political Economy of China's Economic Transition" in Loren Brandt and Thomas G. Rawski, "China's great economic transformation", Cambridge University Press, 2008, pg 122

407. Paul Hirst and Grahame Thompson, "Globalization in question ", Polity, 2000, 2nd ed, pg 156

408. Peter Nolan, "China's rise, Russia's fall", St. Martin's Press, New York, 1995, pg 187, 188

409. Bardhan, P.K. "The political economy of development in India", Oxford: Blackwell, 1984, pg 38, 74 cited in Peter Nolan, "China's rise, Russia's fall", St. Martin's Press, New York, 1995, pg 66, 67

410. Barry Naughton, "A Political Economy of China's Economic Transition" in Loren Brandt and Thomas G. Rawski, "China's great economic transformation", Cambridge University Press, 2008, pg 117

411. Giovanni Arrighi, "Adam Smith in Beijing. Lineages of the Twenty-First Century", Verso, London-New York, 2007, pg 14

412. Barry Naughton, "A Political Economy of China's Economic Transition" in Loren Brandt and Thomas G. Rawski, "China's great economic transformation", Cambridge University Press, 2008, pg 123

413. Stephan Haggard and Yasheng Huang, "The Political Economy of Private-Sector Development in China" in Loren Brandt and Thomas G. Rawski, "China's Great Economic Transformation", Cambridge University Press, 2008, pg. 363

414. Jeffrey A. Hart, "Rival Capitalists. International Competitiveness in the United States, Japan, and Western Europe", Cornell University Press, Ithaca and London, 1992, pg 225

415. Jeffrey A. Hart, "Rival Capitalists. International Competitiveness in the United States, Japan, and Western Europe", Cornell University Press, Ithaca and London, 1992, pg241

416. Jeffrey A. Hart, "Rival Capitalists. International Competitiveness in the United States, Japan, and Western Europe", Cornell University Press, Ithaca and London, 1992, pg 244

417. Robert Wase, "Governing the Market, Economic theory and the Role of Government in East Asian Industrialization", Princeton University Press, 1990, pg 41

418. Hidemasa Morikawa, "Japan's unstable course during its remarkable economic development" in Nation, State and the Economy in History edited by Alice Teichova, Herbert Matis, Cambridge University Press, 2003, pg 340

419. Jeffrey A. Hart, "Rival Capitalists. International Competitiveness in the United States, Japan, and Western Europe", Cornell University Press, Ithaca and London, 1992, pg 251, 258, 262, 263

420. Peter Navaro and Greg Autry, "Death by China. Confronting the dragon—a global call to action", Pearson Education, 2015, pg 77,78

421. Giovanni Arrighi, "Adam Smith in Beijing. Lineages of the Twenty-First Century", Verso, London-New York, 2007, pg 193

422. M. Whitehouse, "US Foreign Debt Shows its Teeth as Rates Climb", Wall Street Journal, September 7,2005 in Giovanni Arrighi, "Adam Smith in Beijing. Lineages of the Twenty-First Century", Verso, London-New York, 2007, pg 194

423. Jeffrey A. Hart, "Rival Capitalists. International Competitiveness in the United States, Japan, and Western Europe", Cornell University Press, Ithaca and London, 1992, pg 268

424. Jeffrey A. Hart, "Rival Capitalists. International Competitiveness in the United States, Japan, and Western Europe", Cornell University Press, Ithaca and London, 1992, pg 229

425. Jeffrey A. Hart, "Rival Capitalists. International Competitiveness in the United States, Japan, and Western Europe", Cornell University Press, Ithaca and London, 1992, pg 269

426. Jeffrey A. Hart, "Rival Capitalists. International Competitiveness in the United States, Japan, and Western Europe", Cornell University Press, Ithaca and London, 1992, pg 228

427. Jeffrey A. Hart, "Rival Capitalists. International Competitiveness in the United States, Japan, and Western Europe", Cornell University Press, Ithaca and London, 1992, pg 229

428. Mariana Mazzucato, "The entrepreneurial state. Debunking public vs. private sector myths", Anthem Press, 2014, pg 3

429. Peter Nolan, "China's rise, Russia's fall", St. Martin's Press, New York, 1995, pg 205

430. Peter Nolan, "China's rise, Russia's fall", St. Martin's Press, New York, 1995, pg 209

431. Peter Nolan, "China's rise, Russia's fall", St. Martin's Press, NewYork, 1995, pg 210, 211

432. Daniel Coughlin, "How China is buying up the world", 22-08-2019, https://www.msn.com/en-in/money/photos/how-china-is-buying-up-the-world/ss-AAGaCoZ

433. Peter Nolan, "China's rise, Russia's fall", St. Martin's Press, New York, 1995, pg 187, 201

434. G.Naik, "China's Spending for Research Outpaces the U.S.", Wall Street Journal Online, September 29, 2006, in Giovanni Arrighi, "Adam Smith in Beijing. Lineages of the Twenty-First Century", Verso, London-New York, 2007, pg 367

435. Peter Nolan, "China's rise, Russia's fall", St. Martin's Press, New York, 1995, pg 187, 201

436. Jörg Mayer, "Digitalization and industrialization: Friends or foes?", UNCTAD Research Paper No. 25, October 2018, pg 11, https://www.researchgate.net/publication/328232540

437. Dongfeng Motor establishes overseas R&D center". China Daily. 17 October 2012

438. Peter Hertenstein, Peter J. Williamson, "The role of suppliers in enabling differing innovation strategies of competing multinationals from emerging and advanced economies: German and Chinese automotive firms compared", Technovation, Volumes 70–71, February–March 2018, Pages 46-58, University of Cambridge, United Kingdom, pg 53, https://doi.org/10.1016/j.technovation.2018.02.011

439. Peter Hertenstein, Peter J. Williamson, "The role of suppliers in enabling differing innovation strategies of competing multinationals from emerging and advanced economies: German and Chinese automotive firms compared", Technovation, Volumes 70–71, February–March 2018, Pages 46-58, University of Cambridge, United Kingdom, pg 53, https://doi.org/10.1016/j.technovation.2018.02.011

440. Malwina Gadawa, "EU-Mercosur trade deal ignites European tensions", Daily Wrap, 20241207, https://www.msn.com/en-ca/news/world/eu-mercosur-trade-deal-ignites-european-tensions/ar-AA1vrwQ4#:~:text=E%20uropean%20Commission%20President%20Ursula%20von%20der%20Leyen,opposition%20to%20the%20agreement%2C%20while%20Germany%20supports%20it.

441. Shuichi Ikemoto, "Corporate restructuring, foreign direct investment, and Japanese multinationals in the Czech Republic", in (edited by Bruno Dallage and Ichiro Iwasaki), "Corporate restructuring and governance in transition economies", Palgrave Macmillan, 2007, pg 118

442. Nicola Bellini, "The decline of state-owned enterprise and the new foundations of the sate-industry relationship" in "The rise and

fall of state-owned enterprise in the Western World" edited by Pier Angelo Toninelli, Cambridge university press, 2008, pg 26,27

443. Ramsin Yakob, H. Richard Nakamura, Patrik Ström, "Chinese foreign acquisitions aimed for strategic asset-creation and innovation upgrading: The case of Geely and Volvo Cars", Technovation, Volumes 70–71, February–March 2018, Pages 59–72, University of Gothenburg, Sweden, pg 64, https://doi.org/10.1016/j.technovation.2018.02.011

444. Ramsin Yakob, H. Richard Nakamura, Patrik Ström, "Chinese foreign acquisitions aimed for strategic asset-creation and innovation upgrading: The case of Geely and Volvo Cars", Technovation, Volumes 70–71, February–March 2018, Pages 59–72, University of Gothenburg, Sweden, pg 65, 66, https://doi.org/10.1016/j.technovation.2018.02.011

445. Ramsin Yakob, H. Richard Nakamura, Patrik Ström, "Chinese foreign acquisitions aimed for strategic asset-creation and innovation upgrading: The case of Geely and Volvo Cars", Technovation, Volumes 70–71, February–March 2018, Pages 59–72, University of Gothenburg, Sweden, pg 67, https://doi.org/10.1016/j.technovation.2018.02.011

446. Shuichi Ikemoto, "Corporate restructuring, foreign direct investment, and Japanese multinationals in the Czech Republic", in (edited by Bruno Dallage and Ichiro Iwasaki), "Corporate restructuring and governance in transition economies", Palgrave Macmillan, 2007

447. Maciej J. Grodzicki, "Prices of Value Added and Competitiveness in Global Value Chains", SPRU Working Paper Series, Jagiellonian University, August 2018, https://www.researchgate.net/publication/327200801/

448. Jörg Mayer, "Digitalization and industrialization: friends or foes?", UNCTAD Research Paper No. 25, October 2018, https://www.researchgate.net/publication/328232540

449. Giovanni Arrighi, "Adam Smith in Beijing. Lineages of the Twenty-First Century", Verso, London-New York, 2007, pg 383

450. Nicholas Casey and Clifford Krauss, "It Doesn't Matter if Ecuador Can Afford This Dam. China Still Gets Paid", https://www.msn.com/en-ca/news/world/it-doesn't-matter-if-ecuador-can-afford-this-dam-china-still-gets-paid/ar-BBRpmCD?ocid=spartandhp

451. "China Rules. How China became a superpower", The New York Times, 2018-11-18, https://www.nytimes.com/interactive/2018/11/18/world/asia/world-built-by-china.html

452. "China to impose sanctions on U.S. firms over Taiwan arms sales", Reuters, 2020-20-26, https://www.msn.com/en-ca/news/world/china-to-impose-sanctions-on-u-s-firms-over-taiwan-arms-sales/ar-BB1aor34?ocid=msedgdhp

453. Nicholas Casey and Clifford Krauss, "It Doesn't Matter if Ecuador Can Afford This Dam. China Still Gets Paid", https://www.msn.com/en-ca/news/world/it-doesn't-matter-if-ecuador-can-afford-this-dam-china-still-gets-paid/ar-BBRpmCD?ocid=spartandhp

454. Thomas Clarke, Martijn Boersma, "Global Corporations and Global Value Chains: The Disaggregation of Corporations?", Oxford Handbooks Online, March 2019, pg 15, https://www.researchgate.net/publication/331977587

455. Richard Engel and Kennett Werner, "China's rising tech scene threatens U.S. brain drain as 'sea turtles' return home", NBC News, 2019-07-14, https://www.nbcnews.com/tech/tech-news/china-s-rising-tech-scene-threatens-u-s-brain-drain-n1029256

456. Richard Engel and Kennett Werner, "China's rising tech scene threatens U.S. brain drain as 'sea turtles' return home", NBC News, 2019-07-14, https://www.msn.com/en-ca/money/topstories/chinas-rising-tech-scene-threatens-us-brain-drain-as-sea-turtles-return-home/ar-AAEjK40?ocid=spartanntp

457. Giovanni Arrighi and Beverly J. Silver, "Chaos and Governance in the Modern World System", University of Minnesota Press, 1999, pg 33

458. Giovanni Arrighi and Beverly J. Silver, "Chaos and Governance in the Modern World System", University of Minnesota Press, 1999, pg 55

459. Giovanni Arrighi and Beverly J. Silver, "Chaos and Governance in the Modern World System", University of Minnesota Press, 1999, pg 51

460. Giovanni Arrighi and Beverly J. Silver, "Chaos and Governance in the Modern World System", University of Minnesota Press, 1999, pg 164

461. J.G. Snell, "The Cost of Living in Canada in 1870", Social History, Vol 12 No 23 (1979), https://hssh.journals.yorku.ca/index.php/hssh/article/view/38988

462. Katherine C. Epstein," "Corrupt" Foreign Investment in the 19th-Century United States", "The American Interest", Volume 11, Number 4, January 7, 2016, pg 6, https://www.the-american-interest.com/2016/01/07/corrupt-foreign-investment-in-the-19th-century-united-states

463. Giovanni Arrighi and Beverly J. Silver, "Chaos and Governance in the Modern World System", University of Minnesota Press, 1999, pg 78

464. Phyllis Deane," The first industrial revolution", Cambridge University Press, 1979, pp 282-284

465. J.G. Snell, "The Cost of Living in Canada in 1870", Social History, Vol 12 No 23 (1979)), https://hssh.journals.yorku.ca/index.php/hssh/article/view/38988

466. Lloyd, Amy J.: "Emigration, Immigration and Migration in Nineteenth Century Britain." British Library Newspapers. Detroit: Gale, 2007

467. Katherine C. Epstein, " "Corrupt" Foreign Investment in the 19th-Century United States", "The American Interest", Volume 11, Number 4, January 7, 2016, pg 11, https://www.the-american-interest.com/2016/01/07/corrupt-foreign-investment-in-the-19th-century-united-states

468. Ben Baden, "China Business Review", May 15, 2013, https://www.chinabusinessreview.com/what-america-exports-to-china/, copied 2020-05-28

469. SCMP Reporters, "What is the US-China trade war? How it started and what is inside the phase one deal", https://www.scmp.com/economy/china-economy/article/3078745/what-us-china-trade

-war-how-it-started-and-what-inside-phase, 13 Apr, 2020, copied 2020-05-28

470. Ana Swanson and Alan Rappeport, "Trump Signs China Trade Deal, Putting Economic Conflict on Pause", The New York Times, Jan. 15, 2020, https://www.nytimes.com/2020/01/15/business/economy/china -trade-deal.html, copied 2020-05-28

471. Chad P. Bown, Yilin Wang, "Five years into the trade war, China continues its slow decoupling from US exports", March 16, 2023, piie.com/blogs/realtime-economics/five-years-trade-war-china -continues-its-slow-decoupling-us-exports

472. Chad P. Bown, Yilin Wang, "Five years into the trade war, China continues its slow decoupling from US exports", March 16, 2023, piie.com/blogs/realtime-economics/five-years-trade-war-china -continues-its-slow-decoupling-us-exports

473. SCMP Reporters, "What is the US-China trade war? How it started and what is inside the phase one deal", https://www.scmp .com/economy/china-economy/article/3078745/what-us-china-trade -war-how-it-started-and-what-inside-phase, 13 Apr, 2020, copied 2020-05-28

474. SCMP Reporters, "What is the US-China trade war? How it started and what is inside the phase one deal", https://www.scmp .com/economy/china-economy/article/3078745/what-us-china-trade -war-how-it-started-and-what-inside-phase, 13 Apr, 2020, copied 2020-05-28

475. David Shepardson, "Some 3,500 U.S. companies sue over Trump-imposed Chinese tariffs", Reuters, 20200925, https://www .reuters.com/article/usa-china-tariffs-idUSKCN26H03S

476. Julia Horowitz, "Premarket stocks: Corporate America pulls the plug on President Trump", CNN Business, 2021-01-11, https://www .cnn.com/2021/01/11/investing/premarket-stocks-trading/index.html

477. Alex Gangitano, "Here are the companies suspending political contributions following the Capitol riots", THE HILL, 01-12-21

478. Tom Boggioni, "'Their heads explode': Major GOP donors are flipping out as Trump closes in on nomination," Raw Story, 9-Sep-2023, https://www.msn.com/en-ca/news/politics/their-heads-explode-major-gop-donors-are-flipping-out-as-trump-closes-in-on-nomination/ar-AA1gu9mq

479. M.L. Nestel, "Billionaire Republican donor abandons the GOP: 'Trump belongs in jail'", Raw Story, 2023-10-30, https://www.msn.com/en-ca/news/politics/billionaire-republican-donor-abandons-the-gop-trump-belongs-in-jail/ar-AA1j7FXC

480. Alexandra Ulmer and Jason Lange, "Big money fails to stop Trump, prompting a donor reckoning", Reuters, January 26, 2024, https://www.reuters.com/world/us/big-money-fails-stop-trump-again-prompting-donor-reckoning-2024-01-26

481. S. N. Broadberry, "Technological Leadership and Productivity Leadership in Manufacturing Since the Industrial Revolution: Implications for the Convergence Debate", The Economic Journal, Vol. 104, No. 423 (Mar., 1994), Table 3, pg. 294

482. Annette Weisbach, "Germany sees a new tougher line on China and Russia as Merkel leaves the political stage", CNBC, 2021-02-01

483. Defense Industrial Strategy, 2022, https://www.businessdefense.gov/docs/ndis/2023-NDIS.pdf

484. Fatal Flaws Undermine America's Defense Industrial Base, Brian Berletic, New Eastern Outlook, February 15, 2024, https://landdestroyer.blogspot.com/2024/02/fatal-flaws-undermine-americas-defense.html#more

485. Fatima Hussein And Ken Moritsugu, "Yellen calls for level playing field for US workers and firms during China visit", The Canadian Press, https://www.msn.com/en-ca/money/topstories/yellen-calls-for-level-playing-field-for-us-workers-and-firms-during-china-visit/ar-BB1l6psM?ocid=msedgntp&pc=U531&cvid=bd759f0d468849a2a048674f2d11f97d&ei=58

PART II
THE IDEOLOGY OF IDEOLOGIES

1. Jeffrey A. Hart. Rival Capitalists. International Competitiveness in the United States, Japan and Western Europe. New York: Cornell University Press, 1992

2. Paul Hirst, and Grahame Thompson. Globalization in question, Cambridge: Polity, 1999

3. Peter Hertenstein, and Peter J. Williamson. "The role of suppliers in enabling differing innovation strategies of competing multinationals from emerging and advanced economies: German and Chinese automotive firms compared." Technovation, Volumes 70–71 (February–March 2018), pg. 46-58.

4. Thomas Clarke, and Martijn Boersma. "Global Corporations and Global Value Chains: The Disaggregation of Corporations?" In The Oxford Handbook of the Corporation, Oxford University Press, 2019, https://www.researchgate.net/publication/331977587.

5. Ramsin Yakob, H. Richard Nakamura, and Patrik Ström. "Chinese foreign acquisitions aimed for strategic asset-creation and innovation upgrading: The case of Geely and Volvo Cars." Technovation, Volumes 70–71 (February–March 2018), pg. 59-72

6. Alexander Hamilton. Alexander Hamilton's Famous Report on Manufactures Made to Congress, December 5, 1791 : in His Capacity as Secretary of the Treasury. Boston: The Home Market Club, 1892

7. Georg Friedrich List. Outlines of American Political Economy, in a series of letters addressed by Friedrich, LIST. Philadelphia: Samuel Parker, 1827

www.ingramcontent.com/pod-product-compliance
Lightning Source LLC
Chambersburg PA
CBHW010141270326
41927CB00016B/3357